Wings of Fancy

Using Readers Theatre to Study Fantasy Genre

Written and Illustrated by
Joan Garner

Teacher Ideas Press, an imprint of Libraries Unlimited
Westport, Connecticut • London

Library of Congress Cataloging-in-Publication Data

Garner, Joan.
  Wings of fancy : using readers theatre to study fantasy genre / by
Joan Garner.
       p. cm. -- (Readers theatre)
  Includes bibliographical references and index.
  ISBN 1-59158-342-X (pbk : alk. paper)
I. Readers' theatre. 2. Children's literature--Study and teaching
(Elementary) --United States. 3. Fantasy literature, American--History
and criticism. 4. Children's plays, American. I. Title.
  PN2081.R4G37 2006
  372.65--dc22   2006023742

British Library Cataloguing in Publication Data is available.

Library of Congress Catalog Card Number: 2006023742
ISBN: 1-59158-342-X

First published in 2006

Libraries Unlimited/Teacher Ideas Press, 88 Post Road West, Westport, CT 06881
A Member of the Greenwood Publishing Group, Inc.
www.lu.com

Printed in the United States of America

The paper used in this book complies with the
Permanent Paper Standard issued by the National
Information Standards Organization (Z39.48-1984).

10 9 8 7 6 5 4 3 2 1

Table of Contents

Table of Contents

(2006 © Joan Garner) **WINGS OF FANCY:** Using Readers Theatre to Study Fantasy Genre

Preface

On the surface **Fantasy Genre** may seem an easy study. In reality, it's an enormous, complex, and nearly all inclusive literature category. So how is such a complicated subject effectively taught? Two ways:

1. Divide the massive genre into concentrated Subgenres supported with Overviews and clear and simple definitions.

2. Implement Readers Theatre scripts to further illustrate fantasy components and most importantly—to make learning fun!

OVERVIEWS and DEFINITIONS
This book offers three delineation layers:

1. *The Facts About Fantasy*
A brief examination of the origins of fantasy and its development and changes through the centuries. This summary also identifies significant literary works that have defined, redefined, and established **Fantasy Genre** as a major contribution to world culture.

2. *Sections*
Identifying the components comprising each Subgenre including pertinent historical data and applicable references.

3. *Script Background Information*
A more detailed description of the specific fantasy or *Fantastic Elements* used for the script. This may include the evolution and treatment of the particular element.

READERS THEATRE SCRIPTS
The following precedes each script:

A Story Synopsis

Character Descriptions (with optional casting suggestions for some stories)

A Glossary of Terms (possibly unfamiliar to the reader)

Presentation Suggestions

Though well suited for straight reading, these **Fantasy Genre** Readers Theatre scripts have been especially developed to present to an audience (i.e., the rest of the class, other classes, or parents). With a little rehearsal and by incorporating the suggested minimal movement and effects, an otherwise flat reading can magically turn into an enjoyable experience.

(Because **WINGS OF FANCY** *is basically a teaching tool, Overviews and additional materials address the educator while the Readers Theatre scripts and Projects appropriately engage fourth through eighth grade reading levels. As these twenty-eight fantasy scripts progress, vocabulary and story lines advance in sophistication.)*

PROJECTS AND LESSONS
Each **SECTION** has two Projects at the end. The first Project is generally the easier with the second becoming more involved. As with the Scripts, the Projects also advance in sophistication from the first to the last. And a Project may require the reading or viewing of specific material(s) before execution. If this is so, the READING REQUIRED Logo and/or VIEWING REQUIRED Logo will be indicated in the introduction of the Project. All of the reading and viewing materials are popular items of the day and easily acquired.

READING REQUIRED

VIEWING REQUIRED

A Footnote: Although there are many wonderful fantasy stories currently in circulation and worthy of note, this compilation incorporates noted "classics." The reason is twofold: 1. Classics like GULLIVER'S TRAVELS and ALI BABA have greatly influenced subsequent works. 2. Classic stories used for script adaptations here fall within public domain and are free of copyright restrictions.

*In creating clear and simple definitions certain liberties have been taken and a degree of bravado employed in fashioning understandable (albeit not entirely accurate) fantasy terms. Of course articles and essays abound deciphering **Fantasy Genre's** broad scope, but for this compilation the following truncated definitions should suffice.*

Defining Fantasy

SIMPLE DEFINITION: The impossible.

EASY TO GRASP DEFINITION: Any story that couldn't possibly happen in our world as we know it at this time.

TRADITIONAL DEFINITION: An impossible story if set in the real world, yet possible if taking place in another world according to its terms.

For the past sixty years or so **Fantasy Genre** has been the dumping ground for any narrative not clearly falling into another genre. In addition, break-away subgenres (i.e., Science Fiction and Horror) boast loose and indistinctive definitions themselves. With this in mind, perhaps the best approach in describing this category is to identify what it's not. For this compilation, the following is excluded from **Fantasy Genre:**

FABLE: Emphasizes message more than story; a telling of the human condition or social observation; an allegory or parable.

FOLKTALE: Stories originating from oral re-tellings of tradition reflecting local and cultural customs.

MYTH: A false story liked to be believed; a story once thought of as true, but is now known otherwise.

TALL TALE: A personal retelling of events exaggerated to incredible feats and bombastic heroics.

Subgenres Often Placed Under Fantasy Genre

(Not included in this compilation.)

SCIENCE FICTION

EASY TO GRASP DEFINITION: future worlds; beyond Earth; spaceships and aliens; inventions and experiments gone awry.

TRADITIONAL DEFINITION: stories with a scientific or historical base; primarily futuristic worlds and machinery.

HORROR

EASY TO GRASP DEFINITION: stories to frighten and scare; monsters and demons; vampires and werewolves.

TRADITIONAL DEFINITION: stories characteristically monstrous and wrong; stories evoking feelings of terror.

SUPERNATURAL FICTION

EASY TO GRASP DEFINITION: Ghosts and hauntings; zombies, witches and the devil; reaching past our actual world.

TRADITIONAL DEFINITION: other than the physical world; a story contradicting the rules of the real world.

The Issue of the Fairy Tale Versus Fantasy Genre

Fantasy Genre and fairy tales overlap, underlap, phase in, phase out, and share many of the same *Fantastic Elements* like fairies, dragons, giants, talking animals, magic, and so on. Separating the two is about as impossible as pinpointing their definitions. Yet here is such an attempt:

FANTASY GENRE

EASY TO GRASP DEFINITION: Any story that couldn't possible happen in our world as we know it at this time. Stories of novelette and book-length.

FAIRY TALES

EASY TO GRASP DEFINITION: A story relying on the fantastic and involving fairies and magic; always ending happily ever after. Stories usually short in length.

A Word About Legends

Again, it's difficult finding an absolute term for what makes a legend. A practical application for this study follows:

Robin Hood and King Arthur are two of the most famous legends ever told, and substantial research suggests these men lived (admittedly outside their present-day legends). And although both men come from the British Isles, each story reads decidedly differently. The legend of Robin Hood stays within a possible world whereas the legend of King Arthur ventures far beyond conventional boundaries. Where the legend of Robin Hood comfortably fits in Adventure Genre, the legend of King Arthur, with all its *Fantastic Elements*, correctly slides into **Fantasy Genre**.

Fantastic Elements

EASY TO GRASP DEFINITION: Things, beings, and actions not of the actual world.

Fantasy stories must involve *Fantastic Elements*. Several of the more prevalent *Fantastic Elements* are used in this teaching aid with similar elements placed together in the seven Subgenres.

WINGS OF FANCY *doesn't claim to be the end-all in examining* **Fantasy Genre**. *Its purpose is to furnish a better understanding of this fascinating and endearing classification to elementary and middle school students.*

Resources Used
The following has proved especially helpful in writing this book:

John Clute and John Grant **THE ENCYCLOPEDIA OF FANTASY**
St. Martin's Press, 1997, ISBN 0-312-15897-1

Various Contributors **THE ENCHANTED WORLD** *(Series)*
Time Life Books, Inc., 1985, ISBN (multiple).

David Day **THE SEARCH FOR KING ARTHUR**
Facts on File, Inc., 1995, ISBN 0-8160-3370-6

Fantasy Genre
Overview in Brief

All that is unrealistic falls into fantasy. Because "unrealistic" as term changes according to era and culture, literary works continually pass in and out of the category. Subsequently, distinguishing literary pieces as **Fantasy Genre** is much like opinion; it's neither right or wrong, merely personal conjecture based on loose and ever-changing criteria.

However, because this work focuses mostly on high fantasy and sword and sorcery Subgenres (see Fantasy Subgenres Aplenty on page 2), there are *Fantastic Elements* within these stories that automatically place them in **Fantasy Genre**. The following two lists consist of what I affectionately call the **BIG 8 FANTASTIC ELEMENTS**.

BIG 8 FANTASTIC ELEMENTS (Entity)

1. Fairies
2. Dragons
3. Giants
4. Wizards
5. Witches
6. Genies
7. Unicorns
8. Phoenixes

BIG 8 FANTASTIC ELEMENTS (Talents)

1. Flying
2. Magic
3. Appearing and Disappearing
4. Blessings and Curses
5. Animation of Inanimate Objects
6. Time Variances
7. Immortality
8. Prophecy

The Origins of Fantasy

Fantasy stories stem from retellings of primitive fireside tales, evolving from the beginnings of constructed language. More structured fantasy stories draw from ancient mythologies. Where the intent of a mythical story clarifies the why of the unexplained, the intent of a fantasy story enriches and heightens an otherwise ordinary telling.

This author's definition: Man's never-ending search for answers has followed two paths; the spiritual (reasoning of religious ideas and faith), and the spirited (fabrication of specifics to explain the unexplainable). Gods, the devil, cataclysms, and miracles fall along the spiritual path where fairies, magic, and the implausible fall along the spirited path. In other words, the big stuff might be explained by divine intervention (spiritual) and the smaller stuff might be explained by sublime invention (spirited).

The most familiar *Fantastic Elements* ironically originated from the illiterate and ignorant Dark Ages (Eurasia between the fall of the Roman Empire and 1,000 A.D.) when imaginative interpretation replaced scientific theory. Consequently, evident *Fantastic Elements* emerged from this repressive, skittish, and boorish era. Also, as expected, published works and known authors of fantasy runs slight before this time. Still, there are a few pronounced pieces that must have inspired later authors and their works.

Fantasy Genre

Overview in Brief *(continued)*

Fantasy Genre Influential (Antiquity)

To identify the paragons of **Fantasy Genre** before the 1700s, overlapping mythology, fairy tales, and pieces heavily imbued with religious purpose must occur. These authors and works listed below are the forerunners and "influence" of modern fantasy (representing juvenile and mature texts).

1. Author Unknown THE EPIC OF GILGAMESH (3rd Millennium BCE)
2. Homer's THE ODYSSEY *(*8th or 9th Century BCE)
3. Virgil's ANEID (1st Century CE)
4. Dante Alighieri's THE DIVINE COMEDY (1321)
5. Ludovico Arisoto's ORLANDO FURIOSO (1516)
6. Thomas Malory's LE MORTE DARTHUR (1485)
7. Edmund Spenser's THE FAERIE QUEENE (1596)
8. John Milton's PARADISE LOST (1667)

Fantasy Genre Influential (Early Modern and Modern Fantasy)

Although this list omits some prominent fantasy authors, it identifies the true guiding lights of modern **Fantasy Genre**.

1. Madam D'Aulnoy's Fairy Tales *Based on Oral Tradition* (1600s)
2. Charles Perrault's Fairy Tales *Based on Oral Tradition* (1600s)
3. Jonathan Swift's GULLIVER'S TRAVELS (1726)
4. Brothers Grimm's Fairy Tales *Based on Oral Tradition* (1800s)
5. Hans Christian Andersen's *Original* FAIRY TALES (1800s)
6. Lewis Carroll's ALICE IN WONDERLAND (1865)
7. George MacDonald's THE PRINCESS AND THE GOBLIN (1872)

8. L. Frank Baum's THE WONDERFUL WIZARD OF OZ (1900)
9. Eric Rucker Eddison's THE WORM OUROBOROS (1922)
10. J.R.R. Tolkien's THE LORD OF THE RINGS (1954)
11. C.S. Lewis' THE CHRONICLES OF NARNIA *Series* (1950-1956)
12. J. K. Rowling's HARRY POTTER *Series* (1997-)

Fantasy Subgenres Aplenty

To demonstrate the extent of **Fantasy Genre**, this list identifies just some of its Subgenres.

Adult Fantasy	*Heroic Fantasy*
Adventurer Fantasy	*High Fantasy*
Aesopian Fantasy	*History in Fantasy*
Animal Fantasy	*Italian Fantasy*
Arabian Fantasy	*Low Fantasy*
Celtic Fantasy	*Nordic Fantasy*
Children's Fantasy	*Occult Fantasy*
Christian Fantasy	*Oriental Fantasy*
Contemporary Fantasy	*Recursive Fantasy*
Dark Fantasy	*Revisionist Fantasy*
Dynastic Fantasy	*Scholarly Fantasy*
Epic Fantasy	*Science Fantasy*
Gnostic Fantasy	*Slick Fantasy*
Hard Fantasy	*Urban Fantasy*

High Fantasy Subgenre

Often set in invented or parallel worlds high fantasy deals with struggles against supernatural evil forces and where the main hero is usually an orphan or a strange sibling with incredible abilities and skills (particularly magic). Other elements include fantastical races (human or otherwise), magic, wizards, invented languages, coming-of-age themes, and multivolume narratives.

Sword and Sorcery Subgenre

Violent conflict with villains (wizards, witches, evil spirits) those whose powers are supernatural against an *ordinary* hero.

 (2006 © Joan Garner) **WINGS OF FANCY:** Using Readers Theatre to Study Fantasy Genre

Fairies and Other Enchanted Creatures
Overview in Brief

FAIRIES

Fantasy Genre and fairy tales were created for fairies. Or, fairies created **Fantasy Genre** and fairy tales. To the point, *fairy tales*. Ask the greater population of the world if they're familiar with fairies and the answer is "yes." Ask the same population what a fairy is or of their origin and the answer(s) dramatically vary. Fortunately, it's easier finding fairies in literature.

A fairy is a spirit. Humanoid in form and of a higher spiritual nature, fairies often emit an ethereal glow and support wings. They're mostly beautiful and tiny.

Trooping fairies travel in groups and might form settlements. As presumed, solitary fairies are by themselves.

ELVES

Originally elves started as minor gods of nature in Norse mythology. They are creatures of light and caretakers of nature. Known to shapeshift and pass through solid objects, elves possess magical powers and may be immortal (or at least live a very long time). Modern literature portrays elves as wise and superior to all other enchanted beings.

PIXIES

Like fairies yet much more mischievous. Physically, they're wingless with pointed ears and small, narrow eyes.

BROWNIES

Solitary, found mostly around farms and houses in the country. Curiously (and why this would be a point of distinction?), most cannot read. Brown skinned, thus their name.

Fairies and Other Enchanted Creatures
Overview in Brief *(continued)*

GNOMES

Living underground and associated with minerals and ores, gnomes can move through the earth like humans walk on it. Also, tradition has them turning to stone if hit by a ray of sun. In other stories, they turn into toads instead of stone.

DWARVES

A short humanoid creature in Norse mythology, fairy tales, and fantasy fiction and role-playing games. Living underground or in mountains, dwarves resemble humans, but are generally regarded as short and stocky. With magical powers, dwarves can instantly turn pieces of coal into diamonds.

LEPRECHAUNS

Somewhere between an elf and dwarf, leprechauns are shoemakers and treasure hoarders. Once spotting a leprechaun, one must keep an eye on him, or he'll disappear.

MILESTONE, CLASSIC, AND INFLUENTIAL LITERATURE WORKS CONCERNING FAIRIES AND OTHER ENCHANTED CREATURES

William Shakespeare's A MIDSUMMER NIGHT'S DREAM (1590s)
*Classic theatrical play with the fairies playing magical tricks and spells on mortals as well as one another. (See Page 25 of **WINGS OF FANCY** for the Script adapted from this play.)*

William S. Gilbert (and Sullivan)'s IOLANTHE (1882)
Lighthearted operetta where fairies are at odds with the House of Lords, and the consequences when fairies marry humans.

George MacDonald's PHANTASTES (1858)
One of the novelist's most important works tells the story of its narrator's dreamlike adventures in fairyland.

W.B. Yeats' FAIRY AND FOLK TALES OF THE IRISH PEASANTRY (1892)
Yeat's coined the term "trooping fairies" in this collection of stories about fairies and enchanted folk.

Edmund Spenser's THE FAERIE QUEEN (1596)
Epic poem with characters in Faerie symbolic to the real world.

Ludwig Tieck's DIE ELFEN (1811)
One of the earlier Victorian works about magical beings (the Victorians were really into fairies), Ludwig's elves and fairies are one in the same here.

Palmer Cox's THE BROWNIES: THEIR BOOK (1887)
Book of Cox's cartoons about mischievous, but kindhearted Brownies.

Under the Pastel Petals

Original Script by Joan Garner
Inspired by Victorian Fairy Paintings

—BACKGROUND INFORMATION
(genre classification and other data deemed useful)

Fairy tales. Having an entire genre named after fairies attests to their prestige and importance in **Fantasy Genre**. As for fairies, ask the greater world population if they know of fairies and the answer will be yes. Ask the same population to define fairies and the answers become as wide and varied as world cultures themselves. However, to lessen any confusion in identifying fairies as a *Fantastic Element*, a "standard" definition follows.

First, let's address the difference between fairies and faerie:

> FAIRIES—Magical, enchanted folk.
> FAERIE—The land in which fairies live.

"Standard" fairies are small (anywhere from the size of a fly to around the size of a large bird), fly with the use of insect wings, and dispense magic. They are beautiful and delicate, of human form, and mercurial (quick tempered) in disposition.

Tiny and insect like, flower fairies tend and nurture flower blossoms. The ruling spirits of nature, they busy themselves with applying colors and scents to flowers. Functioning beyond human senses, flower fairies represent the "standard" fairy.

A few fairies have broken from the "standard" definition. The three good fairies in SLEEPING BEAUTY possess powers to bless Beauty with special assets and talents. Also, the bad fairy in the same tale places evil curses and spells—much like a witch. In some stories the infamous Morgan Le Fey of King Arthur lore has been called a fairy. But all in all, a fairy is best known as a little incandescent winged being.

— SYNOPSIS OF STORY

(Present Day—U.S.A.) Members of the SSEGF (Society of Special Events in Gardens and Forests) gather in the botanical gardens to observe a fairy sighting under the beautiful flower petals. But their fairy watching plans fall into jeopardy when the security guard finds them at the gardens after hours. Bribing the guard with cookies, he allows the group to stay when—to their delight—they watch not one but three fairy processions: a fairy funeral, a fairy wedding, and a royal procession of the fairy queen.

—GLOSSARY
(terms possibly unfamiliar to reader)

EUCALYPTUS—A tall tree with aromatic leaves.

PROCESSION—Many people or beings moving in an orderly manner.

Under the Pastel Petals
STAGING SUGGESTIONS AND HELPFUL HINTS

— CHARACTER DESCRIPTIONS

SUSAN: (Female) Nice, but perhaps a bit too serious.

GUS: (Male) Concerned about being macho, he tries to pass off his intense interest in fairies as just going along for the sake of the ladies.

CARRIE: (Female) Ready for any adventure. Always prepared for whatever may come up.

STEPHANIE: (Female) Would probably be the leader if **SUSAN** wasn't there first.

OFFICER HANK: (Male) A no-nonsense fellow, but is fair and nonjudgmental.

CARLOTTA: (Female) Very impressed with herself, but knows her business.

— PRESENTATION SUGGESTIONS
(Present Day Clothing and Items)

COSTUMES
THE WOMEN—Dresses, slacks and blouses. Nothing too fancy. Casual shoes.

GUS: Pants and shirt. Sweater over shirt. Shoes.

CARLOTTA—Less casually dressed. Probably wears a shawl she can fan and sweep across her.

OFFICER HANK—Same color pants and shirt with a patch on upper arms suggesting a law officer. A flashlight and walkie-talkie could hang from his belt. Serious shoes (leather).

PROPS
STANDING SIGN—Reading *"Sweet Peas and the Rare Arctic Black Satin Orchid."*

BASKETS—Of the woven variety with napkin covering cookies inside.

COOKIES—Chocolate chip and peppermint.

LIGHTING EFFECTS
Room lights off and on.

SOUND EFFECTS
Can be a recording or the crew behind the PARTITION making trumpeting sounds.

SPECIAL EFFECTS
Small lights (fairies) shining up from behind the lower PARTITION. Penlights waved about by several crew members hiding behind the PARTITION, or strings of Christmas lights rapidly turned on and off (from an extension cord?).

STAGE
WALLS—Sight barriers at stage left and right.

HANDRAILING—A rope hanging upon three or four posts at waist height should do.

PARTITION—Sight blocking structure to hide crew members working lights. Approximately 2½ to 3 feet high.

STAGING
Once on stage, place the **PLAYERS** along the HANDRAILING to stay there until all exit. Since the action takes place in front and below them, a lot of movement isn't necessary.

STAGING
STAGE RIGHT   **STAGE LEFT**

Under the Pastel Petals
SCRIPT

SETTING
United States of America. Present Day. In a GREENHOUSE at Lake City Botanic Gardens. A HANDRAIL stretches across the playing area. Further downstage is a PARTITION following below the RAILING. Plant leaves and such poke up over the PARTITION. A SIGN stands upstage reading *"Sweet Peas and the Rare Arctic Black Satin Orchid."* WALLS or TEASERS stand stage left and stage right.

(The area is dark and empty until a little noise— then SUSAN peeks out from the left WALL.)

SUSAN *(Whispering.)*
I think everyone is gone.

(GUS peeks out from the right wall.)

GUS *(Whispering.)*
If everyone is gone, why are we whispering?

SUSAN *(A little louder.)*
Because the visitors may be gone, but Officer Hank is still here.

(CARRIE peeks out from the right WALL.)

CARRIE *(A little louder.)*
Do you really think Officer Hank will arrest us if he finds us here?

(SUSAN crosses to center stage. She carries a small BASKET on her arm. As she enter, GUS and CARRIE step in from stage right. STEPHANIE follows SUSAN from stage left. She also carries a BASKET.)

SUSAN
That's why we're whispering.

GUS
This is really crazy. Hank is bound to catch us here when he comes through on his rounds.

STEPHANIE
We've talked this over, Gus. We know we're taking our chances of getting caught in the gardens after hours, but if we get to see them, it will be worth it.

CARRIE
Maybe we shouldn't have let Gus come. If he doesn't believe in them, they'll never come out.

GUS
I didn't say I don't believe in them, Carrie. I said it's crazy to risk getting caught.

SUSAN *(Holding her BASKET up.)*
That's why we brought the cookies.

GUS
If Officer Hank takes his security guard job seriously, we won't be able to bribe him out of arresting us with just a few cookies.

CARRIE *(Pointing to STEPHANIE'S BASKET.)*
But these are Stephanie's chocolate-chocolate chip cookies. No one can resist Stephanie's chocolate-chocolate chip cookies.

STEPHANIE
And I know for a fact, the one thing Officer Hank takes as seriously as his job is cookies.

SUSAN
Besides, the cookies are not only for Officer Hank. I made my special peppermint sugar cookies to help bring them out if they're a little shy.

CARRIE
That's right. If Susan's peppermint cookies can't get them to come out, nothing will.

(Suddenly the lights come on scaring the group. OFFICER HANK enters from stage right.)

* LIGHTING EFFECTS
Lights up to full.

OFFICER HANK
What's this? Don't you know we're closed?

CARRIE
Why, hello, Officer Hank. Are you closed? Gosh, we didn't notice, did we?

(The others say "no," acting innocently.)

OFFICER HANK
You know very well we're closed, Miss Carrie. Your group comes to these gardens almost every day. You know our opening and closing times. So what are you doing here this time of night?

STEPHANIE
Well now, that may be a little hard to explain.

GUS
But we're not here to take anything. You have our word on that.

OFFICER HANK
I didn't think you were here to steal anything, but why did you hide away when I locked the doors?

SUSAN
Frankly, we didn't think you would let us stay if we told you why we wanted to stay.

> (*SUSAN* pulls a COOKIE out of her BASKET and holds it out to *OFFICER HANK*.)

SUSAN (Continued.)
Cookie?

OFFICER HANK (Taking the COOKIE.)
What are you people up to?

STEPHANIE
As you know, we are all members of the Society of Special Events in Gardens and Forests.

GUS
Which is why you see us here so much.

OFFICER HANK
Yes, I know—strange society to belong to, but go on.

SUSAN
Well, we've been told that a very special event is to happen here tonight.

OFFICER HANK
And what's supposed to happen here tonight?

SUSAN (Getting a COOKIE from her BASKET.)
Fairies are coming. Cookie?

OFFICER HANK
What?

STEPHANIE (Getting a COOKIE from her BASKET.)
Fairies. Here, have another cookie.

OFFICER HANK
And just who is this nut case telling you fairies are coming here?

> (*CARLOTTA* enters from stage left.)

CARLOTTA
I did, and I resent being called a nut case.

OFFICER HANK
And who are you?

CARLOTTA
You don't know who I am?

OFFICER HANK
Would I be asking if I knew who you were?

CARLOTTA
I am Carlotta Anton, world famous fairy expert. Everyone knows that.

OFFICER HANK
Come on. Who believes in fairies?

CARLOTTA
Hush. If you don't believe, they won't come.

OFFICER HANK
Why *this* flower bed? Don't fairies fly around in enchanted forests and places like that?

CARLOTTA
To be more accurate, fairies flutter.

GUS
And flit.

OFFICER HANK
I beg your pardon.

GUS
Fairies flit. They flit and flutter.

SUSAN
Please let us stay, Officer Hank. What harm would it do?

OFFICER HANK
All right. Let's just say for the sake of argument I do believe in fairies—which I don't—but let's just say I do. What makes this flower bed so special? Why would they fly all the way here?

GUS
Actually, it's flit and flutter.

OFFICER HANK (Annoyed.)
I'll flutter you....

SUSAN (Interrupting.)
The tulips.

OFFICER HANK
What tulips?

CARLOTTA
All the tulips I planted only bloomed yellow. And it rained sideways several times this year.

OFFICER HANK
What does that have to do with anything?

CARLOTTA
You don't know?

OFFICER HANK
Would I be asking if I knew?

CARLOTTA
It's very simple. The fairies paint the flowers and then bring the rain to help the flowers grow.

STEPHANIE
Since the tulips were the wrong color and the rain pattern changed, there must be something terribly wrong in the world of faerie.

SUSAN
It means a fairy must have died.

GUS
And now there's going to be a fairy funeral here tonight in this flower bed.

OFFICER HANK
But again, why *this* flower bed?

CARLOTTA
A fairy funeral can only take place under pastel petals like the ones here—the sweet peas.

SUSAN
It's also important that there's a rare Arctic Black Satin Orchid in the flower bed.

OFFICER HANK
Wait a minute. Even *I* know orchids can't grow in the frozen Arctic.

CARRIE
That's what makes them so rare.

STEPHANIE
And the only Arctic Black Satin Orchid in the whole state is right here in Lake City Botanic Gardens.

* SPECIAL EFFECTS
Suddenly flickering lights shine from the flower bed.

CARLOTTA *(Looking down.)*
Oh, they're here! Someone turn off the lights!

> *(GUS hurries over to stage right and switches off the lights.)*

* LIGHTING EFFECTS
The room lights turn off.

> *(GUS hurries back to the others. Although it isn't completely dark, it's now easier to see the flickering light. Everyone lines up along the HANDRAILING to watch below.)*

EVERYONE
Oo!

OFFICER HANK
I see it, but I don't believe it.

CARLOTTA
An actual fairy funeral. Isn't it wonderful?

OFFICER HANK
Will you look at all those fairies flying around?

CARRIE
Is that first group riding—

SUSAN
—Bumblebees. Amazing.

CARLOTTA
Here comes the close relations. You can tell this because they're wearing buttercup hats—family most likely.

STEPHANIE *(Pointing.)*
There he is. It's the deceased lain out on that eucalyptus leaf hearse. How sad.

SUSAN
How beautiful. Look at the different colored dewdrops all along the edges of the leaves.

OFFICER HANK
How do they get the dewdrops to shine like that?

GUS
Well, they *are* fairies. I guess they can do stuff like that.

CARRIE
Oh no, they're going away.

OFFICER HANK
Look at them going under the Satin Orchid. How can they just disappear like that?

GUS
Well, they *are* fairies after all.

OFFICER HANK
Gus, you're really beginning to bug me.

* SPECIAL EFFECTS
More flickering lights.

SUSAN
Look—something else is happening.

CARRIE
Miss Carlotta, what is it?

CARLOTTA
With these new colors. I couldn't say for sure.

GUS
Dragonflies. At least I think they're dragonflies. Is there such a thing as a white dragonfly?

CARLOTTA
Very rare, but they are—

OFFICER HANK
—Fairies, after all. I get it.

CARLOTTA
Oh, how marvelous. It's a fairy wedding.

EVERYONE BUT CARLOTTA
A wedding!

CARLOTTA
All the fairies are wearing gossamer cobwebs. The ones wearing spun honey hats must be the ushers.

SUSAN
And the bridesmaids adorned with morning mist.

STEPHANIE
Oh, here they come—the bride and groom.

CARRIE
Aren't they adorable?

GUS
I'd say unusual, but not adorable.

OFFICER HANK
Isn't it interesting how they can just disappear under that orchid?

CARLOTTA
They're moving from our time to another.

* SOUND EFFECTS
A small trumpeting.

CARRIE
What's that?

CARLOTTA
Can it be? Oh, she's coming! She must be coming!

GUS
Who's coming? Who's coming?

CARLOTTA
The fairy queen!

EVERYONE BUT CARLOTTA
Oo!

CARLOTTA
See the heralds?

STEPHANIE
What are they playing?

CARLOTTA
Pea pod trumpets and silk spun strings.

CARRIE
And the queen's guard is all riding ladybugs.

* SPECIAL EFFECTS
Many lights now.

SUSAN
There's the queen in her chariot. And see, it's pulled by butterflies.

GUS
Look at all the fireflies.

STEPHANIE
And the rest behind her must be her royal court.

CARRIE
All the colors are almost too much to take in.

* SPECIAL EFFECTS
The flicking lights die down to nothing.

OFFICER HANK
That was really cool.

CARLOTTA
Imagine. To see three fairy processions in one night. It's unheard-of.

SUSAN
And yet we witnessed it all.

CARRIE
How lucky we are. I'm so honored.

GUS
Well, I guess we can all go to dinner now.

CARLOTTA
Yes. Nothing else could possibly happen here again in our lifetime. We've seen it all.

OFFICER HANK
Come on. I'll take everyone to dinner.

(All exit stage right talking with excitement.)

* SPECIAL EFFECTS
More flickering lights than before for a moment and then they abruptly stop.

END OF UNDER THE PASTEL PETALS

Elf, Gnome, Dwarf?

Original Script by Joan Garner

—BACKGROUND INFORMATION
(genre classification and other data deemed useful)

Here is a look at other enchanted folk. Believed to be helpers of fairies, the other folk come in various forms and undertake specific tasks different from fairies. The following is a short description of several enchanted folk.

Elf—Creatures of light and possessed of magical powers. Humanoid in form and often elegant in look, they're majestic in manner. Elves are typically woodland beings, but may dwell in spectacularly large, natural communities.

Gnome—Elemental spirit, the physical appearance of gnomes is more distinct than other enchanted folk. They're small and stout though proportionate in figure. The men wear long beards and longer hair than most males where the women are nearly always rather round. They can be cantankerous. With a subterranean (underground) lifestyle, gnomes move through the Earth just as humans walk on top of it.

Dwarf—Treasure keepers who are often depicted as miners. Dwarves are also short and stout with beards (even dwarf women have beards in some stories). Different from gnomes, dwarfs might have larger heads than the res of their body. Dwarves are excellent smiths shaping armor and swords with special powers.

Brownie—Small and dark skinned (hence their name), brownies inhabit houses and assist in domestic chores. Brownies work at night to avoid detection. Because of this elusiveness, it's easy to accuse brownies of mischief around the house.

Pixie—More mischievous and mean than brownies, pixies enjoy playing tricks on mortals. They may lead travelers astray or steal, but their pranks are customarily minor annoyances. Said to be about three feet high with pointed ears, pixies love money and chocolate.

Leprechaun—Of Irish origin, leprechauns have become a favorite in the real world. Though now distinguished with a green top hat and coat with tails and a shillelagh stick as an accessory, leprechauns are much like the other enchanted folk where their appearance and abilities vary from story to story. Though seldom observed in lengthy conversation, leprechauns speak well, dress well, and can be quite wealthy.

— SYNOPSIS OF STORY

(1900—U.S.A.) An odd looking little man wanders into the precinct house telling he doesn't remember who he is or where he's from. Though the police try to help him remember his past, they appear more interested in figuring out what *he is. Each point out the man's physical attributes claiming he must be a dwarf, or possibly gnome, or elf... The officers then try to get the poor man to perform magical feats. They even bring in an enchanted folk expert, but still can't figure out what he is.*

—GLOSSARY
(terms possibly unfamiliar to reader)

SHORTCOMINGS—A person's flaws and faults.

Elf, Gnome, Dwarf?
STAGING SUGGESTIONS AND HELPFUL HINTS

— CHARACTER DESCRIPTIONS

OFFICER MILO: (Male) A friendly sort ready to help out.

OFFICER SMITH: (Male) A bit brighter than **MILO** with an official air.

MRS. SWEENEY: (Female) Loves doing things for others, she's sweet and good at household activities.

CAPTAIN SWEENEY: (Male) Probably all business when not with **MRS. SWEENEY**. But since she is with him here, the **CAPTAIN** is relaxed and amiable.

STRANGER: (Male) *(Needs to be physically small or short)*. Timid and shy, but charming and polite.

MISS TAWNY: (Female) An average young woman who has an interest in fantasy and so knows more about it than those around her.

— PRESENTATION SUGGESTIONS
(1900's U.S.A. Clothing and Items)

COSTUMES
THE WOMEN—Long skirts, blouses, and shawls. Buttoned boots or simple pumps. Hair pulled up or long.

THE OFFICERS—1900 long, double-breasted dark blue coat with high collar and long sleeves. Ranking badges or pins on upper arm or collar. Dark blue pants with yellow stripe down the outside seam. Smartly polished black shoes. Black belt. Keystone Cop hat.

STRANGER—Long sleeved sweater or sweatshirt. Tights or tight-fitting pants. Felt, long toed shoes. Pointed hat. Long hair and pointy ears.

PROPS
PAPER—Looking like a form to be filled out.

PIE—Placing a napkin over a pie tin should work.

STAGE
WALLS—Sight barriers at stage left and right.

DESK—A high desk for the **OFFICERS** to stand behind sits center left stage.

STAGING
Little movement required here. Placing the **STRANGER** off to the left of the DESK while the others are either behind the DESK or to the right will help distinguish him from the ordinary people.

STAGING

STAGE RIGHT   STAGE LEFT

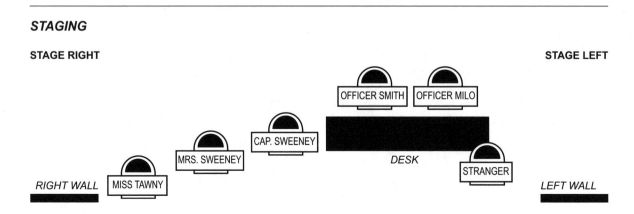

Elf, Gnome, Dwarf?

SCRIPT

SETTING

New York City. 1900. The FRONT DESK at a precinct house.

*(**OFFICER SMITH** stands behind the DESK writing reports when **OFFICER MILO** enters from stage left with a piece of PAPER.)*

OFFICER MILO

Here is my report on the Delancy Street problem, Sergeant.

OFFICER SMITH *(Taking the PAPER.)*

Milo, look at this. How do you expect me to read this report? Your handwriting is terrible.

OFFICER MILO

It's not that bad, Sergeant Smith. I can read it.

*(Enter **CAPTAIN SWEENEY** and **MRS. SWEENEY** from stage right. **MRS. SWEENEY** carries a PIE.)*

OFFICER SMITH *(Looking over.)*

Captain Sweeney—and Mrs. Sweeney. How nice to see you this evening.

MRS. SWEENEY

I was making apple-pies all day and thought you boys would like one.

OFFICER MILO

How nice of you to think of us, Mrs. Sweeney. Your apple-pies are always so good.

CAPTAIN SWEENEY

Tell me about it. It's a wonder I'm not eight hundred pounds with all the delicious pastries, pies, and cakes she's always baking.

MRS. SWEENEY

And just who is forcing you to eat my baked goods, Mr. Sweeney?

CAPTAIN SWEENEY

No one, my love. Why do you think I married you? Of course you were the prettiest girl on the block, but I knew you could cook, too!

*(All chuckle as a **STRANGER** enters from stage left and stands in front of the DESK.)*

STRANGER

Excuse me... Excuse me....

*(**OFFICERS SMITH** and **MILO** look over the DESK while **CAPTAIN SWEENEY** and **MRS. SWEENEY** bend over from the side of the DESK to find where the voice is coming from.)*

OFFICER SMITH

Yes, sir. May we help you?

STRANGER

I hope so. I can't remember who I am.

OFFICER MILO

You don't know who you are?

STRANGER

All I can remember is walking down the street and seeing the precinct sign outside here. I thought I'd come in and see if you could help me.

MRS. SWEENEY

Oh, you poor fellow. Of course we'll help you.

CAPTAIN SWEENEY

So you can't remember anything? Not even your own name?

STRANGER

Afraid not.

OFFICER SMITH

How strange.

OFFICER MILO *(Aside to **OFFICER SMITH**.)*

Speaking of strange. Have you noticed his appearance, Sergeant?

OFFICER SMITH

Of course I have, Milo. But it isn't polite to point out someone's shortcomings.

OFFICER MILO

I don't mean just his size, Sergeant Smith. Look at his clothes. He looks like an elf.

CAPTAIN SWEENEY

An elf? Poppycock, Milo. Elves only live in fairy tales—not on the streets of New York City and certainly not on this street.

MRS. SWEENEY

He does look a bit odd, dear. Maybe not an elf, but... I wonder if he could be a magical being?

CAPTAIN SWEENEY
A normal person doesn't have pointed ears—
that's for sure.
> (To the **STRANGER**.)
Excuse me, sir. Have you had a look at your
clothes and ears? A little peculiar wouldn't you say?

MRS. SWEENEY
Why, he's a dwarf. That's what he is. He's a
magical dwarf.

CAPTAIN SWEENEY
Mamma, he's not a dwarf.

MRS. SWEENEY
How do you know?

OFFICER MILO
He could be a leprechaun.

OFFICER SMITH
Where's his top hat? And he's not wearing green.
How can he be a leprechaun if he isn't wearing
green?

MRS. SWEENEY
We need an expert on little people. Officer Milo,
would you be good enough to step down the block
and fetch Miss Tawny? She knows all about dwarfs
and elves and all kinds of magical folk.

OFFICER MILO
Happy to, Mrs. Sweeney.

> (**OFFICER MILO** exits stage right.)

STRANGER
Still, I'd rather like to know who I am, not what I am.

OFFICER SMITH
Have you anything in your pockets? Have you a
wallet?

STRANGER
No, I already checked.

CAPTAIN SWEENEY
And you remember nothing at all? Where you're
from or someone you might know?

STRANGER
No, sir.

MRS. SWEENEY
He's bewitched. That's what it is. Someone put a
spell on him.

CAPTAIN SWEENEY
Mamma, please.

MRS. SWEENEY
Or maybe one of his magical doings turned on him.

CAPTAIN SWEENEY
Mamma, for Pete-sakes. Such things don't exist.

> (**OFFICER MILO** enters with **MISS TAWNY**
> from stage right.)

OFFICER MILO
Here's Miss Tawny, Captain.

MISS TAWNY
Captain Sweeney, Officer Milo tells me you have a
mystery on your hands.

CAPTAIN SWEENEY
Indeed we do, Miss Tawny. This fellow here doesn't
know who he is and we're kinda' wondering what
he could be.

OFFICER MILO
I think he's a leprechaun.

MRS. SWEENEY
And I think he's a magical dwarf.

> (**MISS TAWNY** stretches her hand out to
> shake the hand of the **STRANGER**.)

MISS TAWNY
Nice to meet you, sir.

STRANGER (Shaking **MISS TAWNY'S** hand.)
Very pleased, miss.

OFFICER SMITH
So what do you think, Miss Tawny? Can you tell
what this fellow is?

MISS TAWNY
He's a charming fellow.

STRANGER
Thank you.

MISS TAWNY
It's hard to tell what he is by looks alone. It would
help to know what kind of magic he can do.

OFFICER MILO
I don't follow.

MISS TAWNY
Well, he could be an elf or dwarf or leprechaun.
He could also be a brownie, pixie, or gnome.

CAPTAIN SWEENEY
Truly? Well, does he look like a dwarf?

MISS TAWNY
A little. He's certainly small enough to be any of the folk I mentioned.

MRS. SWEENEY
But he has pointy ears.

MISS TAWNY
Yes, I see. How special. But dwarfs usually don't have pointed ears. That's more a feature of elves, brownies, and leprechauns. Dwarfs usually have bowed legs.
*(To the **STRANGER**.)*
Sir, do you have bowed legs?

STRANGER *(Looking down at his legs.)*
I don't think so.

MISS TAWNY
The beard is common to gnomes, but the dark skin is like a brownie's. Leprechauns usually wear fancy shoes. He's not wearing fancy shoes.

OFFICER MILO
If he were a leprechaun, he would have a treasure, wouldn't he?

CAPTAIN SWEENEY
It's clear we can't tell what he is by the way he looks. Miss Tawny, would there be other ways to find out about this stranger?

MISS TAWNY
There are other traits. For instance, brownies like farms and country houses. Since we're here in the middle of one of the biggest cities in the world, it's doubtful he's a brownie. Dwarfs are miners. If he was a dwarf, he could be holding a treasure in diamonds like Mrs. Sweeney suggests, but—

MRS. SWEENEY
—We haven't any diamond mines in New York City. I see what you mean, Tawny. I guess he's not a dwarf.

MISS TAWNY
Gnomes can be sort of grumpy. This kindly gentleman certainly isn't grumpy.

STRANGER
Thank you.

MISS TAWNY
Now if he were an elf, he'd be able to pass through solid objects.

OFFICER SMITH
Solid Objects? Like this desk?

OFFICER MILO
Here, fellow. See if you can go through this desk.

MRS. SWEENEY
Oh no, please don't make him do that, papa.

CAPTAIN SWEENEY
Of course not. Sir, you don't have to try to pass through the desk. Although it would help us solve this mystery if you could—pass through the desk, that is.

STRANGER
I suppose I could try.

> *(The **STRANGER** takes a couple of steps back and then walks to the DESK. Clunk. The DESK stops him from going on. The others react—ouch. Again, the **STRANGER** takes a step back holding his bruised nose.)*

OFFICER SMITH
Well, he's not an elf.

OFFICER MILO
I knew it. That must mean he's a leprechaun. That's the only one left.

MISS TAWNY
If he were a leprechaun, he would be able to disappear should we take our eyes off him.

CAPTAIN SWEENEY
Very well, we'll all turn our backs to the stranger and see if he disappears on us.

OFFICER MILO
But Captain, if he disappears we'll lose his treasure. Miss Tawny, doesn't a leprechaun have to take you to his treasure as long as you keep an eye on him?

MISS TAWNY
That's correct, Officer Milo.

OFFICER MILO
Then why should we let him if that's what he wants to do?

STRANGER
Honestly, sir. I don't think I can disappear. I don't know how.

MRS. SWEENEY
Oh, for Heaven-sakes. We're not after any treasure. We need to find out who this gentleman is. Now everyone turn around.

CAPTAIN SWEENEY
You heard Mrs. Sweeney. Everyone turn around.

(All turn their backs to the STRANGER.)

OFFICER MILO
This isn't fair.

CAPTAIN SWEENEY
All right, sir. No one is looking at you. Try to disappear.

STRANGER
I'll do my best.

> *(The STRANGER stands forward, clutches his fists, closes his eyes, and squirms trying to vanish. After a moment of this, he opens his eyes and looks to see he's still there. He tries this maneuver two or three times until he's worn out.)*

STRANGER *(Continued.)*
I'm sorry. I can't do it.

(Everyone turns back to the STRANGER.)

CAPTAIN SWEENEY
Oh, I'm sorry. I thought we had something there.

MRS. SWEENEY
Well, I guess the only thing we can do now is take him down the street and see if anyone recognizes him.

CAPTAIN SWEENEY
Now that's the best idea I've heard tonight. Sir, would you mind coming with us? If we can't find anyone who knows you, we'll take you home and get you some supper. How does that sound?

STRANGER
That's very kind of you, sir. Thank you.

MRS. SWEENEY
Miss Tawny, you come with us, too. I'd like to hear more about magical folk.

MISS TAWNY
Thank you, Mrs. Sweeney. I'd love to.

> *(CAPTAIN SWEENEY escorts the STRANGER out stage right. MRS. SWEENEY and MISS TAWNY also exit stage right.)*

OFFICER MILO
I could have sworn that fellow was a leprechaun.

OFFICER SMITH
It's a strange world, Milo.

OFFICER MILO
It is that, Sergeant Smith.

OFFICER SMITH *(Looking down at the DESK.)*
Huh, will you look at that?

OFFICER MILO
Look at what?

OFFICER SMITH *(Picking up the PIE.)*
I thought Mrs. Sweeney said she baked us an apple-pie.

OFFICER MILO
She did. She said she was baking apple-pies all day.

OFFICER SMITH
Well, this sure looks like a peach pie to me.

OFFICER MILO *(He sniffs the PIE.)*
It smells like a peach pie.

OFFICER SMITH
Mrs. Sweeney must have made a mistake.

OFFICER MILO
No, Mrs. Sweeney seemed pretty sure it was an apple-pie. The Captain said it was an apple-pie, too.

OFFICER SMITH
How could that be? I'm definitely holding a peach pie here.

OFFICER MILO
I don't know. Maybe it was changed by magic or something.

OFFICER SMITH
Magic? Come now, who could magically turn an apple-pie into a peach....

> *(OFFICER SMITH stops his line of thought as the two OFFICERS look at one another for a second, then they both bolt out stage right calling after the CAPTAIN and MRS. SWEENEY.)*

END OF ELF, GNOME, DWARF?

A Glittering Along the Riverbank

Based on a True Event
Original Script by Joan Garner

—BACKGROUND INFORMATION
(genre classification and other data deemed useful)

What makes the Cottingley Fairies story so amazing is it actually happened. For nearly sixty years, two English schoolgirls had people believing in fairies. In 1917 Frances Griffiths and Elsie Wright took a camera down to the nearby riverbank and took pictures of fairies living there. When shown to adults, the debate of the photograph's authenticity began.

The remarkable part of this story is the number of otherwise levelheaded people willing to believe fairies are real. Even the respected author Sir Arthur Conan Doyle (of Sherlock Holmes fame) became enchanted with the photographs to a certain extent. And the American illusionist Harry Houdini became involved to prove the pictures were fraudulent. But in the end, though disbelieving the legitimacy of the photographs, he couldn't refute the charm and good intentions of the girls.

Of the five photographs, the first two were the hardest to discredit (using the knowledge and technology of the day). Also, some factors of the pictures were questionable where other components were not. If the girls (amateur photographers) went about faking a photograph, the entire image would be suspicious.

If the supposed experts had only closely studied the fairies in the photographs, all speculation would have ended. How could these fairies be real wearing styles of 1917?

Still, confirmation the fairies in the photographs came from children's books of the era didn't come until 1978. And although the girls eventually admitted to staging

the later pictures, they continued to claim seeing fairies in the beck, but couldn't photograph them. Thus, the truly fantastic story of the Cottingley Fairy Photographs continues.

—GLOSSARY
(terms possibly unfamiliar to the reader)

BECK—A small brook or creek.

CLAIRVOYANT—The ability to see or sense objects by means other than ones natural senses (hearing, seeing, etc.).

ECTOPLASM—A delicate, substance depicting the presence of a ghost or spirit.

ETHEREAL—A lightness, not of this world.

EXPOSE—To bring forth upon discovery of an otherwise unknown matter.

FORGED—To purposely produce a product not original or genuine.

FRAUDULENT—Not genuine or true.

GROTTO—A cave or cavern typically filled with thick greenery and flowering vegetation.

MEDIUM—A person who can communicate with spirits of another world or dimension—usually the dead.

SUPERIMPOSE—To place something over another or to add items.

THEOSOPHICAL—Philosophy about the nature of souls based on supposed mystical insight.

VIEWFINDER—A part of a camera that shows what will appear in the picture.

A Glittering Along the Riverbank
STAGING SUGGESTIONS AND HELPFUL HINTS

— SYNOPSIS OF STORY

(1917—England) In the English countryside, two schoolgirls take their parents, Sir Arthur Conan Doyle, Harry Houdini, and others down to the beck where they claim they took pictures of fairies. Since their creation, the photographs have generated quite the buzz across Great Britain and around the world leading to speculation about the authenticity of the photographs, and if proven to be genuine, then the existence of fairies.

— CHARACTER DESCRIPTIONS

ELSIE WRIGHT: (Female) Sincere and charismatic, yet cautious and worried about the *snowballing* reaction her photographs have created.

FRANCES GRIFFITHS: (Female) Bubbly and excited to share her experience with the fairies.

EDWARD GARDNER: (Male) A little over-the-top with his enthusiasm. A scatterbrain.

SIR ARTHUR CONAN DOYLE: (Male) Dignified and kindly with a presence everyone respects.

POLLY WRIGHT: (Female) Believing her daughter's photographs, she's supportive and protective.

HARRY HOUDINI: (Male) Reserved and ready to listen to the story, yet never convinced the photos and fairies are real.

ARTHUR WRIGHT: (Male) Hesitant to believe the whole story. A plain and sensible man.

GEOFFREY HODSON: A bona fide medium, he believes in many things that others dismiss as fantasy, but not ready to believe in fairies.

— PRESENTATION SUGGESTIONS
(1917 European Clothing and Items)

COSTUMES
THE GIRLS—Long, puffy sleeved dresses with dusters worn over them. Stockings. Pump-like shoes with straps.

POLLY WRIGHT—Dark, tweed, long sleeved sweater and long wool skirt. High buttoned shoes.

THE MEN—Suits with high collars and ties. A more casual look; long sleeved white shirts with ties and suspenders attached to pants. Color of shoes to match the suit.

ARTHUR WRIGHT— Bulky long sleeved sweater, tattered pants, cap, and work boots.

PROPS
COTTINGLEY PHOTOGRAPHS—Actual photographs are not necessary as long as not directly shown to the audience.

FAIRY DOLLHOUSE—A dollhouse like structure made of twigs and leaves.

SPECIAL EFFECTS
Move the FAIRY DOLLHOUSE offstage by attaching a fish line (invisible—clear plastic) and pulling it offstage.

STAGE
WALLS—Sight barriers at stage left and right.

STAGING
Because there are several people in this script, it's suggested most stay put once entering. It would help to place **POLLY** and **ARTHUR** near the girls.

STAGING

STAGE RIGHT   **STAGE LEFT**

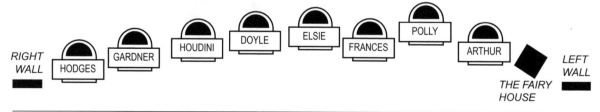

A Glittering Along the Riverbank
SCRIPT

SETTING
England. 1917. Cottingley beck. Stage left stands a small DOLLHOUSE made of leaves, twigs, and other natural materials.

(ELSIE WRIGHT and FRANCES GRIFFITHS hurry in from stage right.)

ELSIE WRIGHT
Here by the riverbank. This is where we took the pictures.

FRANCES GRIFFITHS
The whole area glittered with them. It was so beautiful.

(SIR ARTHUR CONAN DOYLE enters behind EDWARD GARDNER.)

EDWARD GARDNER *(Excited.)*
Imagine being here where they live.

SIR ARTHUR CONAN DOYLE
    (Studying PHOTOGRAPHS.)
Yes, this appears to be it.
    (He looks up and around.)
My, I wasn't aware such a landscape existed in the English countryside. It's almost like a tropical grotto; it's so lush and green.

EDWARD GARDNER
Yes, the very landscape a fairy would settle in, Sir Arthur.

SIR ARTHUR CONAN DOYLE
So you believe these photographs, Mr. Gardner?

EDWARD GARDNER
Oh, yes. I most certainly do.

(ARTHUR and POLLY WRIGHT enter from stage right.)

POLLY WRIGHT
You may think the photographs suspicious, Sir Arthur, but please, I respectfully ask you not question them in front of my girls.

(HARRY HOUDINI and GEOFFREY HODSON enter from stage right.)

HARRY HOUDINI
Come now, Mrs. Wright, isn't the authenticity of the photographs the reason we're down here

to in the first place? I have no doubt in the well-meaning of these two delightful girls. But these photographs are of fairies. And as we know, fairies do not now or have ever existed.

EDWARD GARDNER
Mr. Houdini, how can you say that when the proof is right here? Look—look at this house. Tell me a fairy didn't build this beautiful little house.

ELSIE WRIGHT
Sorry, Mr. Gardner, but fairies didn't build this house.

FRANCES GRIFFITHS
We built it for the fairies.

HARRY HOUDINI
See how easily you're caught up in the illusion, Mr. Gardner?

EDWARD GARDNER
You think me foolish, Mr. Houdini?

HARRY HOUDINI
No, sir. My craft is illusion. Without the willing minds of people like you, no one would come to my shows.

ARTHUR WRIGHT
Because you are the famous illusionist Harry Houdini, perhaps you think everything like these pictures is an illusion or a hoax.

HARRY HOUDINI
Mr. Wright. Again, I'm not saying the pictures are fraudulent, but there are ways of doctoring photographs. For instance, the fairies in this picture with Miss Frances might be superimposed.

ARTHUR WRIGHT
Mr. Houdini, I am an amateur photographer, and not a very good one at that. I don't know how Elsie and Frances could have faked these photographs because I haven't taught them the little I know about it. The girls simply took my camera down here to the beck, saw what they wanted to shoot in the viewfinder, and clicked.

POLLY WRIGHT
To suggest they staged the pictures is rubbish.

SIR ARTHUR CONAN DOYLE
Harry, I was doubtful at first. After all, Edward Gardner here is of the Theosophical Society believing in shining ones—angels and guiding spirits, elves, gnomes, and spirits of the air, *and* fairies. Naturally he would want these photographs to be real.

POLLY WRIGHT
So are you now saying you *don't* think these photographs are real, Sir Arthur?

SIR ARTHUR CONAN DOYLE
We're all friends here looking for the truth. And I must confess I'm charmed by your daughter Elsie and her cousin Frances. They are wonderful young girls. But in all sincerity, I am Sir Arthur Conan Doyle, a respected author. I may personally believe in fairies, but to come out in public and declare these pictures legitimate would be risky. I hope you understand.

ARTHUR WRIGHT
All that I know is that it seems everyone except Mr. Gardner is out to prove the girls are tricksters. Now I'll admit I find what I see in the photographs very hard to believe. But I do believe in these girls.

ELSIE WRIGHT
Thank you, Daddy.

FRANCES WRIGHT
Yes. Thank you, Uncle Arthur.

SIR ARTHUR CONAN DOYLE
Mr. and Mrs. Wright, I think the one thing that isn't in question here is the integrity of your family. If I have offended, I apologize.

HARRY HOUDINI
Of course all questioning would go away if one of these fairies were to show themselves right now. Mr. Hodson, you've been very quiet during this little debate. What do you think?

GEOFFREY HODSON
What do I think? Mr. Houdini, I'm surprised you're even interested in what a medium would think—me being one of the frauds you're so determined to expose.

HARRY HOUDINI
You can fake anything, Mr. Hodson. What we're after here is proof these photographs are real. Can your talents provide us with proof?

GEOFFREY HODSON
I've been very quiet because I'm trying to feel their presence. As a medium I can feel the unseen like angels, air spirits, and the dead.

POLLY WRIGHT
And have you felt anything, Mr. Hodson?

GEOFFREY HODSON
Maybe. I'm not sure.

EDWARD GARDNER
Are you sure there isn't something here, Mr. Hodson? It would back up my theory.

ARTHUR WRIGHT
What theory?

EDWARD GARDNER
Well, I think the girls are clairvoyant and guided the fairies to this spot. Together they created an ethereal field that allows the fairies to metabolize subtle amounts of ectoplasm into their bodies. And that's how the girl's were able to capture the fairies on film.

*(All stand in silence for a moment until **HARRY HOUDINI** bursts into laughter.)*

HARRY HOUDINI *(Still chuckling.)*
So that's how they did it. That clears up everything.

ELSIE WRIGHT
Mamma, I don't understand what Mr. Gardner said.

FRANCES GRIFFITHS
Me neither.

POLLY WRIGHT
Me neither.

GEOFFREY HODSON
Girls, please tell me the names of these fairies.

ELSIE WRIGHT
There's Queen Mab and Prince Malakin.

FRANCES GRIFFITHS
And Nanny Button Cup and Princess Florella.

GEOFFREY HODSON *(Looking about.)*
Queen Mab, we mean you no harm. Prince Malakin, would you please come out for us to see?

FRANCES GRIFFITHS
Oh, they won't come out now.

ELSIE WRIGHT
They only show themselves to people who really

believe in them. And Mr. Houdini and Sir Arthur don't believe.

SIR ARTHUR CONAN DOYLE
Girls, I want to believe so much, I took the pictures to the Kodak Company and had them tested.

EDWARD GARDNER
What did they say?

SIR ARTHUR CONAN DOYLE
They're still testing the pictures, but right now they're saying the pictures could have been forged, but only by a master of photography. And by all accounts, these two lovely girls are not master photographers.

EDWARD GARDNER
Then the photos are real making fairies real.

GEOFFREY HODSON
Still, if they were here in whatever form, you think I could sense them.

HARRY HOUDINI
Obviously I'm sending off some unbelieving vibrations the little things dislike.

POLLY WRIGHT
You don't believe the photographs, do you, Mr. Houdini? You're only here to prove it's all a hoax.

HARRY HOUDINI
Mrs. Wright, I stand against fraud. I am an illusionist, but I go into my shows telling everyone in the audience that it's all a trick of the eye. I'm after the people who make something up and then try to pass if off as the truth. That's wrong and criminal.

ARTHUR WRIGHT
So now you're calling the girls criminals.

HARRY HOUDINI
No, sir. I think these two precious girls photographed something very special. I see nothing in these photographs but joy.

SIR ARTHUR CONAN DOYLE
Yes—to be sure.

POLLY WRIGHT
Sir Arthur, I have baked many sweet cakes for your coming here today. Shall we go back to the house for tea and cake?

SIR ARTHUR CONAN DOYLE
Mrs. Wright, I'd be delighted.

(The adults exit stage right.)

ELSIE WRIGHT
I don't know. This is getting out of hand. I didn't think so many people would show this much interest in our pictures.

FRANCES GRIFFITHS
We just made them to help Aunt Polly feel better.

ELSIE WRIGHT
But now. We knew no one would believe us if we told them about the fairies. That's why we used that book and cutout the pictures to show what they look like.

FRANCES GRIFFITHS
But they're going to find out the photographs are fake sooner or later, Elsie.

ELSIE WRIGHT
Right now I guess we better just go along with it.

FRANCES GRIFFITHS
All right. Whatever you want to do.

ELSIE WRIGHT
I think it's best. I really don't know, Frances.

(FRANCES GRIFFITHS and ELSIE WRIGHT turn stage left and look down to the FAIRY DOLLHOUSE.)

FRANCES GRIFFITHS
I'm afraid it's much too risky for you to stay now.

ELSIE WRIGHT
Frances is right. We'll miss you very much, but it would be best for all of you to find another place to live. We're so sorry to have started all of this.

(The girls wave good-bye.)

FRANCES GRIFFITHS
Good-bye. It was very nice knowing you.

ELSIE WRIGHT
Good-bye. Oh, don't forget your house.

(The girls watch as the FAIRY DOLLHOUSE magically moves out stage left.)

FRANCES GRIFFITHS
Come on, I'm hungry. Let's go get some of Aunt Polly's cake.

ELSIE WRIGHT
All right.

(The girls happily skip out stage right.)

END OF A GLITTERING ALONG THE RIVERBANK

A Midsummer Night's Dream

Adapted from A MIDSUMMER NIGHT'S DREAM by William Shakespeare
Script retelling by Joan Garner

—BACKGROUND INFORMATION
(genre classification and other data deemed useful)

In studying **Fantasy Genre**, fairies, and *Fantastic Elements*, A MIDSUMMER NIGHT'S DREAM is a "must include." Written when fantasy was all but forgotten under a glut of heavy tragedy, leave it to William Shakespeare to present a magical piece of nonsense.

Though widely and wildly popular, admittedly the play isn't Shakespeare's best. If written as a light entertainment to accompany wedding ceremonies as suggested, the lack of or contrived plot is acceptable—more attractive is its production value as spectacle.

A MIDSUMMER NIGHT'S DREAM is one of William Shakespeare's more original offerings. Coming from a playwright who frequently borrowed story ideas from history or previously written material, the plot and characters are imaginative creations. And the story features fairies with the fairy Puck garnering a leading role. Magic also comes into play (or to play) making the theatrical play a true **Fantasy Genre** piece.

WILLIAM SHAKESPEARE (1564–1616). United Kingdom. Arguably the greatest English playwright if not international playwright of all time. Respected for his cavalcade of plays and sonnets, William Shakespeare's most known works lean towards tragedy, yet comedy and fantasy lend their own distinction: THE TEMPEST (1611) is Shakespeare's other fantasy with A WINTER'S TALE (1610) a questionable fantasy work. With a portfolio of other plays such as HAMLET, MACBETH, OTHELLO, ROMEO AND JULIET, KING LEAR, and THE TAMING OF THE SHREW, William Shakespeare's body of work in the envy of every playwright coming after him.

— SYNOPSIS OF STORY

(Present Day) Fairy King Oberon has placed a spell on Queen Titania that makes her fall in love with the next person she encounters. This happens to be Bottom, a mortal amateur actor currently possessed of the head of a donkey. Off to the side is a set of actors diligently rehearsing this scene in the play while, unbeknownst to them, the real fairies Oberon, Titania, and Puck sit on the other side of the stage commenting on the proceedings.

—GLOSSARY
(terms possibly unfamiliar to reader)

CONFOUNDED—Confusing to being exasperating.

A Midsummer Night's Dream
STAGING SUGGESTIONS AND HELPFUL HINTS

— CHARACTER DESCRIPTIONS

PUCK: (Male) A mischievous fellow, agile with a sparkle in the eye.

OBERON: (Male) Stately and commanding.

TITANIA: (Female) Graceful, compassionate, and ready to voice her opinion.

ACTOR PUCK: (Male) Sincere in approach, but not very good in delivery.

ACTOR TITANIA: (Female) Pretty. Better with delivery.

ACTOR BOTTOM: (Male) Silly looking and horrible actor.

ACTOR OBERON: (Male) Overacts. Thinks he's a good actor, but isn't.

— PRESENTATION SUGGESTIONS
(Present Day and Fairy Clothing and Items)

***COSTUMES* OBERON**—Black, tight fitting long sleeved knit shirt and tights. A gold lame hood with crown. Wings optional.

TITANIA—White, tight fitting knit long sleeved shirt and tights. A gold lame hood with crown. Wings optional.

PUCK—Brown, tight fitting long sleeved knit shirt and tights. A leaf laurel crown. Wings optional.

MALE ACTORS—T-shirt and jeans. Cap (optional) and sports shoes.

ACTOR TITANIA—Dress or blouse and jeans. Fashionable shoes. Headband.

PROPS
SCRIPTS—Copies of the Readers Theatre Script.

STAGE
LEDGE— A high partition wide enough to sit on. To have **OBERON** and **TITANIA** above the action shows their royal status.

WALLS—Sight barriers at stage left and right.

STAGING
It's essential the actors do not look at the fairies during the sketch since they're not supposed to know the fairies are there. It isn't necessary for the **PLAYERS** be good at delivering the Shakespearian lines because the actors they're portraying are not good actors.

STAGING

STAGE RIGHT   **STAGE LEFT**

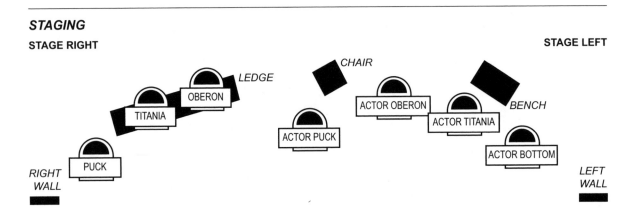

A Midsummer Night's Dream
SCRIPT

SETTING
Anywhere in the world. Present day. A LEDGE stands stage right. A CHAIR or BENCH stands stage left.

> (**OBERON** and **TITANIA** sit on the LEDGE stage right. The actors playing **PUCK**, **OBERON**, **TITANIA**, and **BOTTOM** stand around stage left with SCRIPTS. As the scene begins, the actors mumble and motion possible blocking directions. **OBERON** and **TITANIA** watch as **PUCK** enters from stage right.)

PUCK
What is this here?

OBERON
Yet another rehearsal of Shakespeare's play.

PUCK
Not again.

TITANIA
Oh, yes. They've been performing this silly thing on any given day at any given time since its conception so very long ago.

PUCK
I don't know why.

OBERON
It's the poetry. It's his verse.

TITANIA
Which no one can understand.

OBERON
Just listen....

ACTOR PUCK
And then Puck says:
Then fate o'errules that, one man holding troth,
A million fail confounding oath on oath.

> (The actors resume mumbling as the fairies continue their conversation.)

PUCK
I never said what he just said. What did he just say?

TITANIA
People didn't speak that way in the time of Shakespeare.

ACTOR TITANIA
But back here Titania says:
I pray thee, gentle mortal, sing again.
Mine ear is much enamored of thy note.
So is mine eye enthralled to thy shape.
And that fair virtue's force perforce doth move me
On the first view to say, to swear, I love thee.

ACTOR BOTTOM
Methinks, mistress, you should have little reason for that. And yet, to say the truth, reason and love keep little company together nowadays. The more the pity that some honest neighbors will not make them friends. Nay, I can gleek upon occasion.

> (The actors resume mumbling as the fairies continue their conversation.)

OBERON
"Gleek upon occasion." Brilliant.

PUCK
I don't follow.

OBERON
Of course you wouldn't follow, Robin Goodfellow. You haven't the mind of a mortal. You're a fairy.

TITANIA
We're all fairies, Oberon. What do you know of the mortal mind?

OBERON
The mortal mind is a delicate instrument, my Titania. The mortal mind is more fanciful than us fairies. Shakespeare wrote in verse on purpose. No one understands it, but no one wants to admit they don't understand it, so they speak it and hail it to be exceptional. It doesn't matter if the plot of this play isn't very good; they perform it anyway because of that confounded verse.

TITANIA
It couldn't be.

PUCK
That would explain the oddity. I always knew mortals were fickle. It's why I delight so in pulling pranks and tricks on them.

OBERON
It was your little prank on Shakespeare that started this whole thing, Puck.

TITANIA

You erred in letting yourself be seen. To let a writer see you—and a playwright no less. It's unforgivable and goes against the fairy credo.

OBERON

Shakespeare took the knowledge of you and now there's this.

(*Pointing the actors.*)

How humiliating that people think we're like—that.

ACTOR OBERON

I wonder if Titania be awaked.
Then what it was that next it came in her eye,
Which she must dote on in extremity.

OBERON

Oh, I think I'll disappear forever.

TITANIA

But you can't, dear Oberon. You're king of the fairies. What would the world of Faerie do without you?

OBERON

They would still have you, Titania—the queen of fairies.

TITANIA

How nice of you to think I could rule the Faerie world.

ACTOR BOTTOM

Not so, neither. But if I had wit enough to get out of this wood, I have enough to serve mine own turn.

(*The actors resume mumbling as the fairies continue their conversation.*)

PUCK

Say, I have an idea—a prank to pull on these actors.

OBERON

Robin Goodfellow, you're well-known for your pranks, but may I remind you how often your mischief backfires?

PUCK

Just a little prank, my king. I think you'll like it.

ACTOR OBERON

What thou seest when thou dost wake,
Do it for they true love take.
Love and languish for his sake.
Be it ounce or cat or bear,
Pard or boar with bristled hair,
In thy eye that shall appear,
When thou wakest, it is thy dear.
Wake when some vile thing near.

(*The actors resume mumbling as the fairies continue their conversation.*)

OBERON

Augh! Robin, you have my permission to give that boy a lump on his head.

PUCK

I was thinking of a spell—a spell like you placed on Titania in this play.

OBERON

Don't be absurd. I would never treat my queen like the bard has me do here.

PUCK

Let us put one over on the bard, my king. Let us put a spell of these actors to speak the words everyone can understand.

TITANIA

Have them recite their lines in plain language?

PUCK

How about that as a prank?

OBERON

That would be rich. For once, I like this prank of yours, Puck.

(**PUCK** *smiles and steps out across from the actors.*)

PUCK

People of your time and place,
Actors who this stage you grace,
When I'm done with this rhyme.
No longer shall your verse incline.

ACTOR PUCK

My mistress Titania has fallen in love with a monster. While sleeping in her flower bed, a group of stupid workers from Athens stopped nearby to rehearse a play they wish to perform for Theseus on his wedding day.

OBERON

Now see? *That* I understand.

ACTOR PUCK

When one of the stupidest workers went over and sat by the flower bed, I saw my chance and stuck a donkey's head on his body

(*The actors resume mumbling as the fairies continue their conversation.*)

TITANIA
Oh, dear. He's coming to the part I really don't care for.

ACTOR PUCK
And then Titania woke up and instantly fell in love with the idiot who was now a donkey!

ACTOR OBERON
This is going better than I cold have wished for.

(The actors resume mumbling as the fairies continue their conversation.)

TITANIA
Yes, yes. Everyone knows how the story goes. I'm placed under a spell so when I wake up, I fall madly in love with the first thing I see.

PUCK
Which is an idiot human with the head of a donkey.

TITANIA
Only a man—that Shakespeare *man*—would think of humiliating me in such a way.

OBERON
What does it say of me? According to this play, I'm the one who orders Puck, Robin Goodfellow here to play such a cruel prank on my beloved queen.

TITANIA
I have never blamed you, my darling. Though I should have given Shakespeare a good thrashing when I had the chance.

OBERON
At least he makes it all come out well.

PUCK *(Picking up on the rehearsal.)*
Here. They're skipping ahead.

ACTOR OBERON
They'll only remember all that has happened as a bad dream. But first I'll release the fairy queen from the spell... Be like you were before. Wake up now, my sweet queen.

ACTOR TITANIA
Oberon, what a strange dream I just had. I dreamed I was in love with a donkey!

(The actors resume mumbling as the fairies continue their conversation.)

TITANIA
You see? If you had really placed a spell like that on me, I wouldn't be so forgiving like the play goes on to show later.

OBERON
What would you have done, my sweet?

TITANIA
For one, I would not be speaking to you to this day. And Puck here would still be hanging somewhere between the moon and stars.

PUCK
Then I'm happy none of this actually happened.

OBERON
The poetry *does* have a certain charm.

PUCK
Mm, I best return these actors to their true words.
    (He steps out again.)
Go back to your own place and time,
To acting out this play in rhyme.

ACTOR PUCK
If we shadows have offended,
Think but this, and all is mended—
That you have but slumbered here
While these visions did appear.
And this weak and idle theme,
No more yielding but a dream,
Gentles, do not reprehend.
If you pardon, we will mend.
And as I am an honest Puck,
If we have unearned luck
Now to 'scape the serpent's tongue,
We will make amends ere long.
Else the Puck a liar call.
So good night unto you all.
Give me your hands if we be friends,
And Robin shall restore amends.

(The actors happily pack up and exit stage right talking about the play.)

TITANIA
Yes, it has a nice ending for a mortal play.

OBERON
It's best we put up with this—fiction.

PUCK
Well, we'll have to, won't we? I mean they'll be putting this play on forever.

OBERON
Right you are, Puck.

TITANIA
There are advantages to being mortal. Humans live only so long. They're not hovering in eternity watching this foolish play again and again.

OBERON

And the advantage in that is each new generation of humankind will read and stage the play and learn about myself Oberon, my queen Titania, and our mischief fairy Puck, otherwise known as Robin Goodfellow.

TITANIA

Even if they still don't understand the verse and poetry.

PUCK

Oh, what fools these mortals be.

> *(**OBERON**, **TITANIA**, and **PUCK** exit stage right.)*

END OF A MIDSUMMER NIGHT'S DREAM

Saving Faerie
PAGE 1 (A Lesson Promoting the Imagination)

> This little Project allows students to exercise their imagination.
>
> **PREPARATION AND RESOURCES NEEDED:** Become familiar with the story below. Copy the 2 pages of this Project for each student.

Student Assignment: Read the following short story and help complete it by filling in the blanks with multiple choices (found at the right of the story), or use your own ideas. Let your imagination go wild. The combinations are infinite!

SAVING FAERIE—OR NOT

In the enclave Faerie between the A_____; between the B_____ lived a colony of fairies. The bark of the old cottonwood tree had long lost its sap, and the branches were so brittle they barely swayed in the C_____. Yet this is where the colony chose to live, in the hollowed roots of an ancient tree by a lonesome D_____.

It seemed strange that fanciful folk like fairies who paint the rich colors on flowers and squeeze sweet flavors into fruit would live in such a E_____ thing. But the colony faced a terrible concern—a concern of great danger—a concern of ogres. It's well-known ogres like to eat fairies. Why they like the little beings is a mystery because fairies are not especially tasty. But then, ogres are not especially F_____. So to have ogres invading their way of life and life itself was a very big problem.

For awhile they thought living in the barren oak tree would work believing ogres, who are dumb beasts, would never think of looking for fairies in a G_____ oak tree. And it was purely by accident when one of those big buffoons tripped and fell on them. It took the oaf a good while to figure out he had H_____ onto a fairy colony, but when he got up, he hurried along and the fairies knew he would tell the other ogres of his great find. The fairies had to seek shelter quickly.

Fairy Queen Haden remembered the roots of the cottonwood tree when they decided the oak would be better. They had no choice now but to go there. But Prince Delauter, I_____ fleeing from the ogres, urged everyone to make a stand. The ogres would always be after them, and no matter how stupid they were, would always find their colony—eventually. They needed a way to stop the ogres once and for all. Since they were tiny and the ogres big, it would have to be a brilliant J_____.

Fairies, being far superior to ogres in so many ways, busied themselves with their war tactics and then waited. They huddled down the way—turning down their internal magical light—and watched. It wasn't long until they felt a small tremor in the ground that grew stronger and stronger with each K_____ of the ogres' steps. Soon they saw the beasts with their pinheads, glazed over eyes, and big mouths coming up

MULTIPLE CHOICE
A
1) the morning dew and spider's web
2) flowers and the ferns
3) smog and traffic
B
1) rays of sunlight and a shooting star
2) sunny sky and the deep blue sea
3) burned-out car and the junkyard dog
C
1) breeze
2) wind
3) tornado
D
1) river
2) gully
3) rollerbade park
E
1) dead
2) bleak
3) gnarly
F
1) bright
2) sensible
3) pretty
G
1) lumbering
2) slumbering
3) digitized
H
1) stumbled
2) happened
3) bunny-hopped
I
1) sick and tired of
2) mad and weary of
3) unusually hyped at
J
1) plan
2) scheme
3) brain-burst
K
1) thud
2) pounding
3) tippy-toe

Saving Faerie (Promoting the Imagination) PAGE 2

over the hill. Queen Haden counted six, maybe seven. It was hard to tell since so many fat bellies in a row melted into one big ʟ_____

_____.

"They should be coming to the first line of our defenses," said Prince Delauter as the ogres ᴍ_____ down the hill. And he was right. Suddenly two ogres fell into a gully of quicksand. The others just stood there wondering what was wrong, and another stepped into it because, well, he was just so ɴ_____. Still, no one bothered to help them and the three soon disappeared under the quagmire.

Three! They got three with the quicksand. The fairies wanted to cheer, but kept quiet and watched. The ogres pressed on until one stepped into a ditch filled with thorny branches. He wailed and cried as the thorns dug deep into his skin. And the more he struggled to get out, the more the branches twisted around him. The others left him there as they kept coming towards the cottonwood.

The fairies began to ᴏ_____. There was only one line of defense left to detour the remaining three. Would it work? It was there just in front of the tree. If it failed, the ogres would walk right over the tree roots and destroy their ᴘ_____.

There! They walked right into it, but what was it? The ogres struggled to get free, but couldn't see what from. After a few seconds, they began turning and turning and swinging their arms and legs. They slapped at the air and tried to cover their ǫ_____. One tried to cover his head with his arm and conked himself on the head with the club he carried. Still, they swung and wobbled. Now the fairies could hear the ʀ_____ all around. It became a fearsome drone louder than the screaming ogres. How clever they had been. How clever to drop several beehives down into the trench so the ogres wouldn't see them. But when the big oafs stepped on the hives, thousands of bees came streaming out and immediately began stinging the intruders. The bees wouldn't stop and the ogres reeled dangerously close to the cliff until, one by one, they fell off and down to their s_____.

Success! They got rid of the ogres and not one fairy had to ᴛ_____ _____. How brilliant they were. Of course, it didn't take much to get one over on ogres. Still, the fairies celebrated their victory and decided to stay in the roots of that old cottonwood tree. It brought them good luck, and since good luck is something hard to find, the colony figured they would stick around awhile and see if the tree would bring them any more.

MULTIPLE CHOICE
L
1) glob
2) orb of fat
3) dirt-bike track
M
1) stomped
2) rumbled
3) slid on their heads
N
1) stupid
2) dense
3) clumsy
O
1) worry
2) fret
3) take out life insurance policies
P
1) home
2) domicile
3) beach-front timeshare
Q
1) heads
2) bodies
3) bellybuttons
R
1) buzz
2) hum
3) rock music
S
1) death
2) doom
3) underwear
T
1) die
2) get eaten
3) get their tooth pulled

Peter Pan

PAGE 1 (A Lesson Promoting Observational and Critiquing Skills)

This Project enhances observational skills.

The story of THE ADVENTURES OF PETER PAN by J.M. Barrie has experienced many variations through the years. The Project uses the book, play, movie, and animated feature to illustrate this point. By using two of the four sources mentioned in the Guide below, conduct a classroom discussion by asking what differences the students observed between the tellings. The Guide below helps identify some of these differences and similarities.

PREPARATION AND RESOURCES NEEDED: Read the book and watch one of the three films mentioned in the Guide. Or use two of the three films for the Project. Have your students do the same before conducting a classroom discussion asking what they found to be different and the same in the stories.

The **BOOK** is available through many publications. Downloaded versions are available at certain web sites. However, one easily accessible publication is from the Barnes and Noble Classic Series, PETER PAN, 2005, ISBN 1593082134.

The **PLAY** used is the 2000, A&E, PETER PAN (104 minutes) a musical stage production starring Cathy Rigby—available on Video and DVD.

The **MOVIE** used is the 2003, Columbia Pictures, PETER PAN, Directed by P.J. Hogan (113 minutes)—available on Video and DVD.

READING REQUIRED

The **ANIMATED FEATURE** is Walt Disney's 1953 PETER PAN (76 minutes)—available on Video and DVD. *All four items should be at your larger public libraries and probably in most school libraries as well.*

VIEWING REQUIRED

Use the following Student Assignment instructions in explaining this Project to your students.

Student Assignment: Your instructor will have you read the book and watch a selected film of PETER PAN. While reading and watching, remember the differences in the events of the stories. Afterwards, you will be asked what you found to be different and the same in the two tellings.

EXPLORING THE MANY DIRECTIONS OF PETER PAN

THE BOOK	THE PLAY	THE MOVIE	THE FEATURE
Starts out giving more details about the Darling family. It also talks a lot about the nurse, a dog named Nana, and about taking one's medicine.	Starts out in the nursery with the children preparing for bed while the parents are getting ready to go out to a dinner party.	The movie starts with the quote, "All children grow up, except one." The book starts with the quote, "All children, except one, grow up."	Starts out in the nursery with a narration saying how Peter Pan chose the Darling house because people who live there believe in him.
Wendy is the oldest John is the middle child, and Michael is much younger. All are in their sleeping garments. All three sleep in the nursery.	Wendy is the oldest John is the middle child, and Michael is much younger. All are in their sleeping garments. All three sleep in the nursery.	Wendy is the oldest John is the middle child, and Michael is much younger. All are in their sleeping garments. All three sleep in the nursery. Includes an Aunt Millicent as part of the family.	Wendy is the oldest John is the middle child, and Michael is much younger. All are in their sleeping garments. All three sleep in the nursery.
Mr. Darling gives Nurse Nana (a dog) medicine as a joke. The children feel sorry for Nana. This angers Mr. Darling who ties Nana up in the backyard.	Mr. Darling thinks having a dog as a nurse is ridiculous and the children are old enough not to need one. So he takes Nana out and ties her up in the backyard.	Nana runs into Mr. Darling's place of work and topples his coworkers. Angry, Mr. Darling takes Nana home and ties her up in the backyard.	Mr. Darling trips over Nana. The children make a fuss over poor Nana and not Mr. Darling. This angers Mr. Darling who ties Nana up in the backyard.

Peter Pan (Promoting Observational and Critiquing Skills) PAGE 2

THE BOOK	THE PLAY	THE MOVIE	THE FEATURE
Nana snatches Peter's shadow. Mrs. Darling puts the shadow in a dresser drawer.	Mrs. Darling sees a face in the window (Peter) and puts his shadow in a dresser drawer.	Nana is the one who grabs Peter's shadow and Wendy puts it in the dresser drawer.	Wendy puts Peter's shadow in the dresser drawer.
Peter Pan comes into the nursery looking for his shadow. Tinker Bell (a fairy) comes with him. Wendy sews his shadow back on. Pleased, Peter says, "Oh, the cleverness of me!"	Peter Pan comes into the nursery looking for his shadow. Tinker Bell (a fairy) comes with him. Wendy sews his shadow back on. Pleased, Peter says, "Oh, the cleverness of me!"	Peter Pan comes into the nursery looking for his shadow. Tinker Bell (a fairy) comes with him. Wendy sews his shadow back on. Pleased, Peter says, "Oh, the cleverness of me!"	Peter Pan comes into the nursery looking for his shadow. Tinker Bell (a fairy) comes with him. Wendy sews his shadow back on.
Peter comes to the window at night to listen to stories.	Peter comes to the window at night to listen to stories.	Peter comes to the window at night to listen to stories.	Peter comes to the window at night to listen to stories about him.
Wendy gives Peter a kiss that's really a thimble. Peter gives Wendy a kiss which is an acorn button.	Wendy gives Peter a kiss that's really a thimble. Peter gives Wendy a kiss which is a button.	Wendy gives Peter a kiss that's really a thimble. Peter gives Wendy a kiss which is an acorn button.	Wendy tries to give Peter a kiss, but Tinker Bell stops her from doing so.
Peter's direction to Neverland is, "Second start to the right and straight on till morning."	Peter's direction to Neverland is, "Second start to the right and straight on till morning."	Peter's direction to Neverland is, "Second start to the right and straight on till morning."	Peter's direction to Neverland is, "Second start to the right and straight on till morning."
To fly, you think lovely wonderful thoughts and sprinkle fairy dust on the person.	To fly, you think lovely thoughts and sprinkle fairy dust on the person.	To fly, you think happy thoughts and sprinkle fairy dust on the person.	To fly, you think of a wonderful thought and sprinkle fairy dust on the person.
John takes his Sunday hat (top hat). Michael takes his Teddy Bear.	John takes his Sunday hat (top hat). Michael takes his Teddy Bear.	Michael takes his Teddy Bear. John grabs the hat of Mr. Darling's boss as they fly by.	John takes his top hat while Michael takes his Teddy Bear.
Peter, Tinker Bell, and the Darling children fly to Neverland. Flying to Neverland takes a long time.	Peter, Tinker Bell, and the Darling children fly to Neverland. Flying to Neverland doesn't take too long.	Peter, Tinker Bell, and the Darling children fly to Neverland. Flying to Neverland doesn't take too long. They fly into the universe to get there.	Peter, Tinker Bell, and the Darling children fly to Neverland. Flying to Neverland is quick.
Neverland has a lagoon with mermaids, another area with Indians, and an underground home for the Lost Boys. A pirate's ship is in the lagoon.	Neverland has a lagoon with mermaids, another area with Indians, and an underground home for the Lost Boys. A pirate's ship is in the lagoon.	Neverland has a lagoon with mermaids, another area with Indians, and an underground home for the Lost Boys. A pirate's ship is stuck in the frozen sea.	Neverland has a lagoon with mermaids, another area with Indians, and an underground home for the Lost Boys. A pirate's ship is in the lagoon.
Captain Hook and Mr. Darling are two different people.	Captain Hook and Mr. Darling are the same person.	Captain Hook and Mr. Darling are the same person.	Captain Hook and Mr. Darling are two different people.

PAGE 3 (Promoting Observational and Critiquing Skills) **Peter Pan**

THE BOOK	THE PLAY	THE MOVIE	THE FEATURE
Arriving at Neverland, Captain Hook and the pirates shoot cannon holes in the clouds Peter and the children are standing on.		Arriving at Neverland, Captain Hook and the pirates shoot cannon holes in the clouds Peter and the children are standing on.	Arriving at Neverland, Captain Hook and the pirates shoot cannon holes in the clouds Peter and the children are standing on.
Hook hates Peter because during an earlier fight, Peter had cut off Hook's hand and tossed it to a crocodile. The crocodile (who also swallowed a clock) now follows Hook to get more of him. Hook can hear the crocodile coming because of the clock.	Hook hates Peter because during an earlier fight, Peter had cut off Hook's hand and tossed it to a crocodile. The crocodile (who also swallowed a clock) now follows Hook to get more of him. Hook can hear the crocodile coming because of the clock.	Hook hates Peter because during an earlier fight, Peter had cut off Hook's hand and tossed it to a crocodile. The crocodile (who also swallowed a clock) now follows Hook to get more of him. Hook can hear the crocodile coming because of the clock.	Hook hates Peter because during an earlier fight, Peter had cut off Hook's hand and tossed it to a crocodile. The crocodile (who also swallowed a clock) now follows Hook to get more of him. Hook can hear the crocodile coming because of the clock.
Pirate Mr. Smee is a "yes man" to Captain Hook.	Pirate Mr. Smee is a nicer person in this version.	Pirate Mr. Smee is something of a klutz.	Pirate Mr. Smee is something of a klutz.
A jealous Tinker Bell tells the Lost Boys Peter wants them to shoot down the "Wendy Bird." A boy wounds Wendy and they build a house around her.	A jealous Tinker Bell tells the Lost Boys Peter wants them to shoot down the "Wendy Bird." A boy wounds Wendy and they build a house around her.	A jealous Tinker Bell tells the Lost Boys Peter wants them to shoot down the "Wendy Bird." A boy wounds Wendy and they build a house around her.	A jealous Tinker Bell tells the Lost Boys Peter wants them to shoot down the "Wendy Bird." Peter catches and saves a falling Wendy.
Peter banishes Tinker Bell (from his sight).	Peter banishes Tinker Bell (from his sight).	Peter banishes Tinker Bell (from his sight) saying she is her friend no more.	Peter banishes Tinker Bell (from his sight).
Peter takes Wendy to see the mermaids by Marooner's Rock.	Peter takes Wendy to Marooner's Rock where the mermaids are.	Peter takes Wendy to the mermaid lagoon. (The mermaids are more fish like than human.)	While Peter takes Wendy to the mermaid lagoon, Peter puts John in charge of the Lost Boys.
Wendy and Peter play mother and father to the Lost Boys.	Wendy and Peter play mother and father to the Lost Boys.	While Wendy and Peter play mother and father to the Lost Boys, lost John and Michael are captured by the Indians.	The Indians capture the Lost Boys with John and Michael.
The pirates kidnap Princess Tiger Lily (per Hook's orders) and tie her to Marooner's Rock to drown at high tide.	The pirates kidnap Princess Tiger Lily (per Hook's orders) and tie her to Marooner's Rock to drown at high tide.	Hook and his pirates find and later chain Princess Tiger Lily, John, and Michael to a rock (that's in a cavern) to drown at high tide.	Hook and Smee kidnap Princess Tiger Lily and take her to Skull Rock. They tie her to a rock in the cavern to drown at high tide.
Peter mimics Hook's voice and orders the pirates to let Tiger Lily go.	Peter mimics Hook's voice and orders the pirates to let Tiger Lily go.	Wendy calls out for Peter and Hook overhears it and goes to investigate.	Peter calls out like the Spirit of the Great Seawater. When Hook

Peter Pan (Promoting Observational and Critiquing Skills) PAGE 2

THE BOOK	THE PLAY	THE MOVIE	THE FEATURE
		Peter mimics Hook's voice and orders the pirates to let Tiger Lily, John, and Michael go.	goes to investigate, Peter mimics Hook's voice and orders the pirates to let Tiger Lily go.
Hook and Peter fight. Hook wounds Peter twice, but must swim back to the pirate ship because the crocodile shows up.	Hook and Peter fight. Hook wounds Peter twice, but must swim back to the pirate ship because the crocodile shows up.	Hook and Peter fight. Hook becomes distracted by the crocodile enabling Peter to escape.	Hook and Peter fight until Hook hears the crocodile coming. He flees back to the ship.
The Neverbird pushes her nest to Peter to save him from the rising tide.	Tiger Lily saves Peter from drowning.	Peter and Wendy save Tiger Lily, John, and Michael.	Peter saves Tiger Lily from drowning.
The Indians, Lost Boys, Wendy, and Peter celebrate Tiger Lily's return.	The Indians, Lost Boys, Wendy, and Peter celebrate Tiger Lily's return.	The Indians, Lost Boys, Wendy, and Peter celebrate Tiger Lily's return.	The Indians, Lost Boys, Wendy, and Peter celebrate Tiger Lily's return.
		Wendy and Peter watch fairies dancing in a tree.	
			Hook talks Tinker Bell into showing where the Lost Boys' hideout is.
Wendy wants to go home. John, Michael, and the Lost Boys want to go back with Wendy.	Wendy wants to go home. John, Michael, and the Lost Boys want to go back with Wendy.	Wendy wants to go home. John, Michael, and the Lost Boys want to go back with Wendy.	Wendy wants to go home and talks the Lost Boys into wanting to go with her.
The pirates capture Wendy and the boys taking them to the ship to walk the plank.	The pirates capture Wendy and all the boys taking them to the ship to walk the plank.	The pirates capture Wendy and all the boys taking them to the ship to walk the plank.	The pirates capture Wendy and the boys. They take them to the ship to walk the plank.
Tinker Bell saves Peter by drinking Peter's medicine Hook poisoned.	Tinker Bell saves Peter by drinking Peter's medicine Hook poisoned.	Tinker Bell saves Peter by drinking Peter's medicine Hook poisoned.	Tinker Bell saves Peter from a bomb Hook put in a present to him.
Peter saves Wendy and the Lost Boys. Hook jumps overboard to a waiting crocodile.	Peter saves Wendy and the Lost Boys. A cannonball kills Hook.	Peter saves Wendy and the Lost Boys. Hook falls into the mouth of the crocodile.	Peter saves Wendy and the Lost Boys. Hook falls into the mouth of the crocodile, but gets out and swims away.
The story ends with Peter returning to the house much later. Wendy is grown-up now. She let's Peter take her daughter to Neverland.	The story ends with Peter returning to the house much later. Wendy is grown-up now. She let's Peter take her daughter to Neverland.	The story ends with the children returning home. The Darlings agree to adopt the Lost Boys. Aunt Millicent adopts one of the boys.	The story ends with the children returning home. The Darlings didn't know they were gone. The Lost Boys decide not to come with them, but stay with Peter and never grow up.

Tick Tock Tick Tock

Fantastic Beasts and Talking Animals
Overview in Brief

FANTASTIC BEASTS

It isn't too hard to figure out that fantastic beasts are animals not of this world. Leaving mythological creatures and "gods" out of this Overview makes the category controllable. Of course there are still numerous beasts in folklore and fable, but since this compilation concentrates on fantasy works, I'm addressing the more familiar. *(The more obscure fantastic beasts lurk in Project 1—A Beastly Demand of this **SECTION**.)*

Dragon—Serpent like, scaly, fire-breathing creature predominately found in European Medieval fantasy, Chinese folklore, and Indian tales. Winged dragons are a typical European invention.

Phoenix—A large bird that self-immolates (kills/dies or sacrifices). For a more dramatic telling, the phoenix bursts into flames and then rises from the ashes.

Unicorn—A horned horse possessed of healing abilities. Often immortal, the unicorn's horn composition can have life sustaining properties if crushed to a powder and consumed by a human.

TALKING ANIMALS

Two other categories closely associate with talking animals; beast fables and animal fantasy. Though their definitions seem clear and distinct enough, many titles bounce from one to another.

Animal Fantasy—Features perceptive animals who talk to one another but not to humans. The stories usually take place in the real world.

Beast Fables—Involve animals acting and probably living like humans. They also speak to and interact like humans.

Talking Animals—Falls under Animal Fantasy as a subcategory, but typically refers to animals acting as companions to humans.

Now comes the kicker; Kenneth Grahame's THE WIND IN THE WILLOWS falls under all three categories! To be sure, talking animals always reside in **Fantasy Genre** (especially when counting Science Fiction as a subcategory of **Fantasy Genre**). *(See Page 55 of **WINGS OF FANCY** for the Script adapted from this story.)*

Talking animals populate many fairy tales, but several classic talking animal stories have emerged through the centuries.

MILESTONE, CLASSIC, AND INFLUENTIAL LITERATURE WORKS CONCERNING FANTASTIC BEASTS

Kenneth Grahame's THE RELUCTANT DRAGON (1898)
A young boy comes upon a docile dragon content with reading poetry over acting scary and dragon like. With the aid of an old knight, the boy and dragon stage a joust to prove the dragon's ferocity.

E. Nesbit's THE PHOENIX AND THE CARPET (1904)
Odd story about a magic carpet and a mysterious egg that hatches into a talking phoenix.

Fantastic Beasts and Talking Animals

Overview in Brief *(continued)*

Theodore Sturgeon's THE SILKEN-SWIFT (1953)
Short story about unicorn E. Pluribus Unicorn.

Peter S. Beagle's THE LAST UNICORN (1968)
Obviously about the last unicorn in the world that sets out to find out where the other unicorns have gone.

MILESTONE, CLASSIC, AND INFLUENTIAL LITERATURE WORKS CONCERNING ANIMAL FANTASY

Walter de la Mare's THE THREE MULLA-MULGARS (1910)
Three royal monkeys go on a long journey.

George Orwell's ANIMAL FARM (1945)
Satirical novel about animals ridding the farm of all humans only to slip into a degenerate society they supposedly purged by eliminating the humans.

Richard Adam's WATERSHIP DOWN (1972)
Rabbits go against the decree of the Chief Rabbit and escape from the threatened warren (rabbit burrow) to build their own on the down (hill). The characters here are more rabbit like than human.

MILESTONE, CLASSIC, AND INFLUENTIAL LITERATURE WORKS CONCERNING BEAST FABLES

Joel Chandler Harris' UNCLE REMUS (1881)
African-American folktales placed in a collection of stories and songs highlighting Brer Rabbit, a trickster who's always getting into trouble. (Fun stories, but blatantly prejudice and seldom recognized today.)

Rudyard Kipling's THE JUNGLE BOOK (1894)
Mancub Mowglie encounters many animals in the jungle like friends Baloo the bear and Bagheera the panther, and enemies like Kaa the python and Shere Khan the tiger.

A.A. Milne's WINNIE-THE-POOH (1926)
Young children's stories about a Pooh bear whose love of honey gets him in several predicaments.

MILESTONE, CLASSIC, AND INFLUENTIAL LITERATURE WORKS CONCERNING TALKING ANIMALS

Hugh Lofting's DR. DOLITTLE (Series 1920-1952)
Dr. Dolittle learns to understand and speak with animals. Something of a twist in the Talking Animal category.

E.B. White's CHARLOTTE'S WEB (1952)
Another young children's story, but classic talking animal example about farm and barn animals helping Wilber the pig from becoming someone's dinner.

(2006 © Joan Garner) **WINGS OF FANCY:** Using Readers Theatre to Study Fantasy Genre

The Barking Browkisauds

Original Script by Joan Garner

—BACKGROUND INFORMATION
(genre classification and other data deemed useful)

This sketch addresses chimeras and African religion and mythology. It relies on inventing a new beast by using parts of existing animals. A beast or monster resulting in combining two or more living animals is often referred to as a *chimera*.

The word and application come specifically from Egyptian and Greek mythology. In Greek mythology the beast called chimera is a of lion's head, goat's body, and serpent's tail.

Though probably theorized before, I believe the origins of chimeras started with Egyptian mythology and religion (which is one and the same on many levels) with its gods and deities of human form but with animal or bird heads. For example, the god Seth has the head of a jackal; the god Thoth has the head of an ibis bird; Anubis is seen in hieroglyphics with a dog's head; and a falcon's head dons the god Horus.

Another element used in this sketch is the worship of nature and magic that plays an important role in African mythology. The sketch incorporates a fetish—an object believing to have magical or spiritual powers in shamanism and animism— prominent in most African religions.

— SYNOPSIS OF STORY

(Early Africa) In the African Bush, the Barking Browkisauds have stolen the diamond of the black rhino's horn. Fearing the Sky Spirits would stop the precious rains from coming to the land, young warrior Maub heads out to find the Browkisauds and retrieve the horn. Maub is assisted by the Pigman, an expert on Browkisauds (an apish-lion like beast with sharp teeth, large clawed hands, and a hideous bark). Maub and the Pigman must use their bravery and wits to get the precious fetish back to Maub's tribe.

—GLOSSARY
(terms possibly unfamiliar to the reader)

FETISH—An object worshipped believing to have magical or spiritual powers.

MALICIOUS—Harming others. Spite or ill will.

The Barking Browkisauds
STAGING SUGGESTIONS AND HELPFUL HINTS

— CHARACTER DESCRIPTIONS

PIGMAN: (Male) Older and wiser, the **PIGMAN** has seen a lot and may be a bit weary of it all. Because he appears an intelligent and sensible man, it may seem strange he raises and tends pigs.

MAUB: (Male) A young warrior of determination and endurance. **MAUB** bravely pursues the mysterious beasts though it's dangerous to face them.

SHAYLA: (Female) Like **PIGMAN**, it also seems strange the lovely and graceful **SHAYLA** tends pigs alongside her husband, but there she is.

BROWKISAUDS: (Male and Female—Optional Casting) More ape like, the **BROWKISAUDS** move like an ape, but bark and are more aggressive (deadly).

— PRESENTATION SUGGESTIONS
(Early African and Browkisaud Clothing and Items)

COSTUMES
MAUB and PIGMAN—Animal skin or cloth tunic hanging over one shoulder and tied at the waist with cloth strap. Skin colored, tight fitting "dancer's" shirt and tights. Brightly colored cape attached at the shoulders with cloth strip. Necklace of teeth or stones optional. Bare feet.

SHAYLA—Simple, long shift attached over both shoulders, tied at the waist with strip of cloth. Long, shawl-like, brightly colored piece of cloth over arms. Bare feet.

BROWKISAUDS—Dark brown or black, tight fitting, long sleeved turtleneck knit shirt. Dark brown or black tights. Faces painted brown with blue streaks on cheeks. Large hands with claws (gloves modified with fur and claws pasted on). Large feet with claws (slippers modified with fur and claws pastes on). Bushy fur mane around face. Bushy fur tail. Artificial fanged teeth.

PROPS
SPEARS—Wooden lances sharpened at the end.

BLACK RHINO'S HORN—Horn with diamond inset in its side.

WATER POUCH—Of ragged leather. (Needn't hold water, just look like it does.)

CLAY CUPS—Crudely made cups of clay.

LOAF OF BREAD and FRUIT—Bread wrapped in cloth and fruit.

SOUND EFFECTS
Crew members can oink and grunt offstage left.

STAGING
Because this sketch takes place in two different areas, leave the stage bare.

STAGING
If possible, follow the stage directions in this script. Exiting and entering helps depict **MAUB** and **PIGMAN** traveling distances. It would also help not to have the **BROWKISAUDS** onstage until they come into play.

STAGING

STAGE RIGHT   **STAGE LEFT**

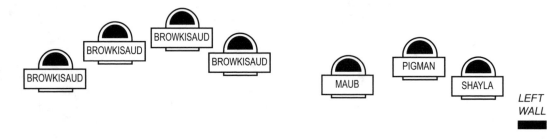

RIGHT WALL   LEFT WALL

The Barking Browkisauds
SCRIPT

SETTING
Early Africa. The base of a mountain.

*(The **PIGMAN** enters from stage left.)*

*SOUND EFFECTS
Perturbed oinking and grunting.

PIGMAN *(Calling back out stage left.)*
Piggy, piggy—stay there, you lazy swine. Since a pigpen bares your name you should like it in there.

*SOUND EFFECTS
More grunting.

PIGMAN *(Continued.)*
Don't you grunt at me, I'll have you for supper.

*(Enter **MAUB** from stage right with SPEAR.)*

MAUB
Pardon me. Are you the one they call Pigman?

PIGMAN
With all of these pigs about, what do you think?

MAUB *(Smiling.)*
Yes, sir.

PIGMAN
And you must be the young warrior we've been hearing about for some time now. Are you Maub from the Serengeti Plain?

MAUB
I am.

PIGMAN *(Calling out stage left.)*
Shayla! Shayla, come here. That youngster from the plain has finally made his way to us.

*(Enter **SHAYLA** from stage left carrying a WATER POUCH, CLAY CUPS, and LOAF OF BREAD.)*

SHAYLA
He has arrived in time for bread and drink.

PIGMAN
This is my wife, the lovely and obviously patient Shayla.

SHAYLA
It's a pleasure finally meeting you, Maub.

MAUB
Thank you. Please. How is it you know of me?

PIGMAN
How could we not? You are the talk before every campfire from your village to here.

*(**SHAYLA** pours a drink for **MAUB**.)*

SHAYLA
You've become a legend, young Maub.

MAUB
I don't feel like a legend. I just feel tired.

PIGMAN
Yet you'll need to gather all your strength for the end of your journey. Up this mountain is the land of the Browkisauds.

MAUB
Yes, the Browkisauds. I think I preferred it when I didn't know their name.

SHAYLA
It's unusual for the animals to travel so far from their mountain here. But you had a most unusual treasure for them to take.

MAUB
You know the story, then.

PIGMAN
We know what others have told us. We've waited to hear from you. There's no telling how much the tale has stretched from the Serengeti Plain to Browkisaud Mountain.

MAUB
There isn't much to the story: Many years ago one of my ancestors, Karim, went down to the river to fetch water. While she was filling her jug, she noticed something shining in the water. Karim reached for it and pulled up a horn from a black rhinoceros.

SHAYLA
A black rhinoceros. I understand they are very rare.

MAUB
They are... While looking at the horn, Karim noticed it continued to shine in the sun; a shine more dazzling than the mere reflection of a wet horn. She saw there was a large diamond embedded in the horn as if it had been growing there for hundreds of years.

SHAYLA
Imagine that. How special.

MAUB
Our ancestors thought as much. They believed the rhino horn came to us from the Sky Spirits to let us know how pleased they were with the way we nurtured and tended the land.

PIGMAN
And you believe the Sky Spirits give us the sun and rain so precious to our existence.

MAUB
To show our appreciation, we built a Temple Ring and placed the black rhino horn within a small altar. The special fetish stayed there for hundreds of years.

PIGMAN
Until the Browkisauds appeared.

MAUB
One night, several months ago, we heard a horrible barking—not like that of a hyena— more like a lion's roar, but short and gruff. We followed the sound to the Temple Ring. They destroyed it.

SHAYLA
And the rhino horn with the diamond was gone.

MAUB
And the thieves who took it.

PIGMAN
The Browkisauds.

MAUB
It's strange how we never heard of them before. I volunteered to track them and get the horn back. The closer I get, the more people know about these creatures. But the last village I stopped at said the Pigman knows more about Browkisauds than anyone else. So here I am. My people fear without the return of the black rhino horn to the Temple Ring, the Sky Spirits will no longer bring the sun and rain when needed, and the land will turn barren. The animals will leave and our people will starve.

PIGMAN
Then you best get your horn back.

MAUB
Yes, sir.

PIGMAN
It could be dangerous.

MAUB
I realize that, but they're counting on me.

SHAYLA
You know that Browkisauds are black and tan apes with the long mane of a lion. They have large hands with claws at the end of their arms and wide paws for feet. From their backside comes a long, bushy tail.

PIGMAN
But the most distinguishing feature is four blue stripes—two on each side of their nose—like a warrior would paint on his face before facing his enemy. Be careful of their razor sharp teeth. They can tear apart a man in seconds.

MAUB
Yes, the people have warned me of this.

SHAYLA
Beyond their physical power, Browkisauds are magical beasts. They can suddenly appear out of the darkness and disappear just as fast. Browkisauds are mysterious creatures—very intelligent yet mischievous and careless. They know many things—many human things, but will not obey mans law and ways of right and wrong.

PIGMAN
They're more curious than considerate and more malicious than curious.

MAUB
It seems strange for an animal to take something that is only valuable to my people. I know a man will take something just because it belongs to another. But an animal doesn't show such pettiness.

PIGMAN
You're wise for being so young, Maub. But Browkisauds are more than animals in many ways. It makes it hard to know what they're thinking or why they do what they do. If you'll let me, I'd like to go with you to get your horn back.

MAUB
Would you? That's very kind. But if these Browkisauds are a dangerous beast, perhaps you shouldn't. I wouldn't want to leave Shayla a widow.

SHAYLA
You have my husband go with you, young man. I'll feel better knowing he's by your side.

MAUB
Thank you. Both of you.

PIGMAN
Come, I'll fetch my spear and we'll be on our way.

> *(MAUB, PIGMAN, and SHAYLA exit stage left. After a moment, four or five BROWKI-SAUDS enter from stage right. They stalk and chortle a low sounds. Once done investigating the place, they sit. One has the BLACK HORN. Another eats a FRUIT. And another attends her young. MAUB and PIGMAN enter stage left. Blood stains drip down PIGMAN'S left arm. The two crawl on their hands and knees and stop on seeing the BROWKISAUDS. They whisper.)*

MAUB
Look, Pigman. Here are some more.

PIGMAN
This bunch seems calm enough. They must not have heard the ruckus the others made when we came up on them.

MAUB
I thought they would never stop barking like that.

PIGMAN *(Amused.)*
A bit upset, weren't they?

MAUB
One of them slashed you pretty good. Are you sure you're all right?

PIGMAN
This? It's my badge of courage. I can show Shayla this later and get an extra serving of supper.

MAUB
Look, Pigman—the big one on the end. Does that look like a horn he's holding?

PIGMAN
It's your horn, Maub. You would know what it looks like more than I.

MAUB
What do we do?

PIGMAN
Well, since pouncing on them hasn't been working, maybe the honest approach is more fitting here. I'll distract them and you sneak in from behind and grab the horn.

MAUB
But what if they attack you?

PIGMAN
Then you better get that horn and scurry down this mountain as fast as you can. Ready, boy?

MAUB
Ready.

> *(PIGMAN stands and steps towards the BROWKISAUDS holding his spear out.)*

PIGMAN
Hello, you wild things, I'm the Pigman.

> *(Immediately the BROWKISAUDS scramble; barking as they hide behind the biggest one. MAUB begins to sneak up on the bunch.)*

PIGMAN *(Continued.)*
Oh, so sorry to startle you like this.

> *(The BROWKISAUDS bark more and wave their arms as if prompting the PIGMAN to go away.)*

PIGMAN *(Continued.)*
I see you have the black rhino's horn. Care to tell how you got it?

> *(More barking from the BROWKISAUDS.)*

PIGMAN *(Continued.)*
I thought not. You want a piece of the Pigman? You, the big one, you want a piece of me?

> *(The big BROWKISAUD drops the HORN and lunges towards the PIGMAN. MAUB leaps for the HORN and tries to get back, but the other BROWKISAUDS are on him, beating him with their claws. Meanwhile, the big BROWKISAUD swipes at the PIGMAN'S SPEAR, trying to bat it away.)*

PIGMAN *(Continued.)*
Maub, get out of there before they start biting.

MAUB
I'm trying!

PIGMAN
Get out of there before they think of using their magic. They can do wondrous things, but fortunately for us, they're not too quick to think about it.

MAUB *(Wrestling.)*
They're not very happy.

> *(The PIGMAN continues to keep the big BROWKISAUD at bay with his SPEAR.)*

PIGMAN

Hurry before the others hear all this noise and come to see what the problem is.

(***MAUB*** *finally manages to crawl out from under the* ***BROWKISAUDS*** *and exits stage right. The* ***PIGMAN*** *makes his way across the stage, keeping all the* ***BROWKISAUDS*** *at bay with his* ***SPEAR***.)

PIGMAN *(Continued.)*

Now if you'll be so kind to stop slapping at me, you big hairy Browkisaud, I have to go.

(*The* ***PIGMAN*** *exits stage right with the* ***BROWKISAUDS*** *chasing after him. After a moment,* ***SHAYLA*** *enters from stage left and looks out stage right.*)

SHAYLA

Such a noise. I hope the men are all right. I wouldn't want to be facing angry Browkisauds like that.

(***MAUB*** *and the* ***PIGMAN*** *enter from stage right. They are a bit out of breath, but happy.*)

SHAYLA *(Continued. She goes to the men.)*

My husband. You're hurt.

PIGMAN

A little—just a little. You should have seen Maub. He's a fine warrior. No fear, just determination.

MAUB

We got it back, Shayla. We found the black rhino horn and got it back.

SHAYLA

Good for you, Maub. Do you think the Browkisauds will come after us now?

PIGMAN

They're upset right now. But when they calm down and figure out what happened, yes, they'll come looking for the horn. Maub, you best get back to your people and have a guard hold vigil at the Temple Ring if you expect to keep this fetish of yours. I don't think you've seen the last of the Browkisauds.

MAUB

But what of you and Shayla?

PIGMAN

The Browkisauds have been here before. They'll leave us alone when they see we have nothing. There are some advantages to being poor. Go now and guard your treasure well.

MAUB

I can't thank you enough. When I tell the story, I'll speak of the Pigman and his beautiful wife Shayla. Thank you.

(***MAUB*** *exits stage right.*)

SHAYLA

You did well this day, my husband. I'm proud of you.

PIGMAN

You praise is *my* treasure, Shayla. Now about these troublesome pigs....

(*The* ***PIGMAN*** *puts an arm over* ***SHAYLA'S*** *shoulders and they exit stage left.*)

END OF THE BARKING BROWKISAUDS

The Blushing Blue Dragon

Original Script by Joan Garner

—BACKGROUND INFORMATION
(genre classification and other data deemed useful)

What makes dragons so fascinating is their universality. With European and Chinese dragons arguably being the most famous, dragons in one form or another roam ancient South American cultures, Southeast Asia stories, and Australian Aboriginal tales.

Whether it's their abilities (flying and breathing fire), or their menacing physical attributes, dragons continue to spring up in fantasy stories from books to film. Originally cited as vicious beasts of destruction, dragons have become a more comic and kinder animal in more recent stories.

Saint George's dragon immediately springs to mind. Beowulf dies fighting a dragon, and of course, J.R.R. Tolkien's *RINGS SAGA* documents an archer at Esgaroth slaying a dragon and establishing a line of kings.

Dungeons and Dragons became one of the most popular games of the 20th Century. Hundreds of today's specialty retail stores exclusively carry dragon merchandise, and many a T-shirt and rock band logo has a dragon incorporated in the artwork. All this confirms the popularity of this awe-inspiring creature.

— SYNOPSIS OF STORY

(5th Century—Ireland) The townsfolk of Durbin are so terrified by a ferocious dragon living nearby, they hire Sir Dwaine, a dragon slayer, to get rid of it. But when they come to the dragon, all discover the beast isn't one to fear but to help. It seems the blue dragon has lost its fire-breathing skills and can only blush red with embarrassment. So Sir Dwaine and the others try to get the fire back into the shy dragon.

—GLOSSARY
(terms possibly unfamiliar to the reader)

DRAGON SLAYER—A person expert in killing dragons. Usually a knight.

LADDIE—An Irish boy.

LAIR—A den or cave for a wild animal.

LASSIE—An Irish girl.

WAIL(S)—To cry loudly in a high-pitched voice.

The Blushing Blue Dragon
STAGING SUGGESTIONS AND HELPFUL HINTS

— CHARACTER DESCRIPTIONS

BLUE DRAGON: (Female) Shy and very distraught. Overly dramatic (for being shy) when crying.

LADDIE TIMMY: (Male) A young man of common sense.

LASSIE COLEEN: (Female) A nice young woman willing to help.

SIR DWAINE: (Male) A good fellow and proper knight.

LASSIE MAUREEN: (Female) Like **COLEEN**, a nice young woman ready to assist when called on.

LASSIE DARLING: (Female) Logical, smart, and kindhearted.

— PRESENTATION SUGGESTIONS
(5th Century Clothing, Armor, and Items)

COSTUMES
BLUE DRAGON—Blue blouse and pants. Blue socks pulled up over pant cuff. Perhaps a little blue ruffled skirt at waist to show the dragon is a girl. Oversized blue robe with the long train rolled and tied to represent a tale. Cardboard wings optional—best small for maneuvering purposes.

LADDIE TIMMY—Brightly colored long sleeved shirt, brown peasant vest and pants. Boots.

LASSIE COLEEN—Blouse with short, puffy sleeves. Jumper with hem below the knee. Flat, pump-like shoes.

SIR DWAINE—Hood. Light shirt and pants.

LASSIE MAUREEN—Blouse with short, puffy sleeves. Jumper with hem below the knee. Flat, pump-like shoes.

LASSIE DARLING—Blouse with short, puffy sleeves. Jumper with hem below the knee. Flat, pump-like shoes.

PROPS
Because props are minimal, it's suggested pantomiming using the COAL, OIL LAMP, and MATCHES. This way the person playing **BLUE DRAGON** doesn't have to eat or drink anything, merely pantomime the action.

If using props, color marshmallows for the coal, make the lamp oil water, and when striking a match against the matchbox, use the wooden end against the friction strip. However, the small blanket-sized HANDKERCHIEF should be real.

SOUND EFFECTS
The person playing **COLEEN** can strike a match against a matchbox, or someone can next to a microphone to amplify the sound making it easier to hear.

STAGE
CARDBOARD CUTOUT of part of a thatched-roof cottage with a stone hedge at stage right.

CARDBOARD CUTOUT of cave wall with stalactites and stalagmites at stage left.

STAGING
Although prompted in the stage directions, it isn't necessary for anyone to enter or exit—just step down in line when their character comes into the scene. **COLEEN**, **TIMMY** and **SIR DWAINE** should cross to the DRAGON'S LAIR on cue and that all should exit when directed. (This will help end the sketch.)

Pantomiming the rest of the action should do nicely for this piece where the silliness of it allows for an unrealistic or "pretend" performance.

STAGING

STAGE RIGHT   **STAGE LEFT**

DURBIN

RIGHT WALL

COLEEN

TIMMY

SIR DWAINE

MAUREEN

BLUE DRAGON

DRAGON'S LAIR

DARLING

LEFT WALL

The Blushing Blue Dragon
SCRIPT

SETTING
Old Ireland, 5th Century. Stage right is the TOWN OF DURBIN. Stage left is the DRAGON'S LAIR.

(COLEEN and TIMMY stand stage right. BLUE DRAGON, MAUREEN, and DARLING stand stage left. BLUE DRAGON wails and cries into a huge HANDKERCHIEF.)

LADDIE TIMMY
There it goes again.

LASSIE COLEEN
It's so awful. Something really needs to be done.

(BLUE DRAGON wails and cries more.)

LADDIE TIMMY
Day and night for weeks now. It's driving me nuts.

LASSIE COLEEN
It's such a horrible roar.

LADDIE TIMMY
He must have captured another one of our lassies. Colleen, have you heard of anyone disappearing this morning?

LASSIE COLEEN
Oh, I hope not. Our little town of Durbin is small enough without losing more folks to that mean 'ol dragon.

LADDIE TIMMY
Well, you'll be happy to know I've taken steps to get rid of the dragon. I've sent for a famous dragon slayer.

LASSIE COLEEN
You have? But Timmy, do you think he'll come?

(Enter SIR DWAINE from stage right.)

SIR DWAINE
Top of the morning to you, good people. Could you tell me where I might find a laddie named Timmy?

LADDIE TIMMY
I'm Timmy. Are you the dragon slayer?

SIR DWAINE
I am, my good man. Sir Dwaine at your service.

LASSIE COLEEN
How wonderful. We're so glad you came.

(SIR DWAINE steps up to COLEEN and takes her hand.)

SIR DWAINE
Why thank you, pretty lassie. You just point me towards that pesky old dragon and I'll take care of him for you.

LADDIE TIMMY
He's right over there in the dragon's lair.

SIR DWAINE
Well now, that's where a dragon would be, wouldn't it?

(SIR DWAINE continues to hold COLLEEN'S hand and flirt with her until BLUE DRAGON begins to wail and cry again.)

SIR DWAINE *(Continued.)*
Good Heavens, what was that?

LASSIE COLEEN
That's the dragon. Isn't his roar the most terrifying sound you've ever heard?

(BLUE DRAGON wails and cries.)

SIR DWAINE
Roar? It sounds more like crying to me. Are you sure it's a dragon?

LADDIE TIMMY
It's a dragon all right.

SIR DWAINE
Well then, let's go see what's what.

(SIR DWAINE, TIMMY, and COLEEN turn stage left, but will not step to the LAIR until after this next sequence. MAUREEN pats BLUE DRAGON on the shoulder.)

LASSIE MAUREEN
There, there. We'll try again later.

BLUE DRAGON *(Sobbing.)*
It's no use. It's simply no use.

(The BLUE DRAGON sneezes into a huge HANDKERCHIEF.)

LASSIE DARLING
You can't give up. If you give up, you're doomed.

BLUE DRAGON
But I'm already doomed. I'm so ashamed.

> *(SIR DWAINE, COLEEN, and TIMMY step to BLUE DRAGON.)*

LASSIE COLEEN
Maureen! Darling! You're alive.

LASSIE DARLING
Of course we're alive. Why wouldn't we be?

LADDIE TIMMY
We thought the dragon ate you.

> *(BLUE DRAGON has coyly stepped behind MAUREEN and DARLING for protection.)*

LASSIE MAUREEN
Oh, she wouldn't do that.

SIR DWAINE
She? The dragon is a girl? How unusual.

LASSIE DARLING *(To SIR DWAINE.)*
Who are you?

SIR DWAINE
Sir Dwaine: Dragon Slayer, Esquire.

BLUE DRAGON *(Alarmed.)*
Dragon slayer! I'm doomed. Its curtains!

> *(BLUE DRAGON cries into her HANDKERCHIEF.)*

SIR DWAINE
Say now, what's all this fuss about? This is no way for a dragon to behave—no way at all.

LADDIE TIMMY
That's right. Dragons are fierce and mean—

LASSIE COLEEN
—And breathe fire.

> *(BLUE DRAGON wails and cries even louder. MAUREEN and DARLING pull BLUE DRAGON between them and put their arms over BLUE DRAGON'S shoulders.)*

LASSIE MAUREEN
Don't fret so, dragon. You need to calm yourself.

SIR DWAINE
This is most curious.

LASSIE DARLING
You see, the Blue Dragon is in such a state because she lost her fire.

LADDIE TIMMY
Are you saying this dragon can't breathe fire?

BLUE DRAGON *(Burying her head.)*
It's so embarrassing.

SIR DWAINE
Can't breathe fire. Whoever heard of a dragon who can't breathe fire? Why, it's downright unnatural.

LADDIE TIMMY
I don't understand. If this dragon can't breathe fire and hasn't eaten the two of you, what are you still doing here?

LASSIE COLEEN
Couldn't you have come back to Durbin?

LASSIE MAUREEN
We couldn't leave this poor creature here alone.

LASSIE DARLING
Not when she's in such pain. We're trying to help her.

SIR DWAINE
How did she lose her fire, anyway?

LASSIE MAUREEN
You see, this dragon is very shy.

LASSIE DARLING
And very meek.

LASSIE MAUREEN
And one day when she blushed—

LASSIE DARLING
—She snorted *in* instead of snorting *out*—

MAUREEN
—And pouf. She blew out her fire.

SIR DWAINE
Well, the solution is obvious.

LASSIE COLEEN
Obvious?

SIR DWAINE
The thing that needs to be done is to put the fire back.

BLUE DRAGON
You mean you're not going to slay me?

SIR DWAINE
No need for that if you're not hurting anyone.

LADDIE TIMMY
But if she gets her fire back, she'll breathe us all to cinders.

BLUE DRAGON
Oh, I would never do that. It's not nice.

SIR DWAINE
A nice and fireless dragon. Doesn't that beat all?

LASSIE COLEEN
How would we even go about putting a fire back into a dragon?

SIR DWAINE
I wouldn't think it too difficult. Let's see... That coal over there. Gather us some of that coal.

(MAUREEN and DARLING bend behind them and pantomime picking up COAL.)

LASSIE DARLING
Now what?

SIR DWAINE
The dragon needs to eat the coal.

LASSIE MAUREEN
Eat the coal?

(MAUREEN and DARLING pantomime shoving pieces of COAL into the BLUE DRAGON'S mouth.)

BLUE DRAGON *(Pantomimes eating.)*
Yuck, how disgusting. Chalky. I could use something to wash it down with.

LASSIE DARLING
Now what?

SIR DWAINE
Has anyone a match?

BLUE DRAGON *(Covering her mouth in horror.)*
You wouldn't!

(COLEEN pulls out a box of matches from her pocket.)

LASSIE COLEEN
Here we go.

(COLEEN steps behind the BLUE DRAGON who turns her back to the audience. You hear the match striking against the matchbox and then the BLUE DRAGON inhaling loudly.)

* SOUND EFFECTS
A match striking against the matchbox.

(The BLUE DRAGON turns back around breathing heavily, swallowing hard and then breathing heavily again. A snort or two to test the result. Everyone watches carefully.)

BLUE DRAGON
Nothing.

(TIMMY steps back and pantomimes grabbing an OIL LAMP. He steps up to the group.)

LADDIE TIMMY
Here, this oil lamp should work better.

(TIMMY crosses to the BLUE DRAGON and pantomimes pouring the oil in the OIL LAMP down the BLUE DRAGON'S throat. The BLUE DRAGON turns around to COLEEN again and they pantomime once more striking and swallowing a match. The BLUE DRAGON turns back around breathing heavily and snorting a bit.)

BLUE DRAGON
Still nothing.

DARLING
This is silly. A dragon's fire doesn't come from the tummy, it comes from the nose. Why try to light it when it's in its tummy?

SIR DWAINE
Quite right. What were we thinking?

(SIR DWAINE steps back and pantomimes picking up a candle. He holds it as if to protect the flame from going out as he approaches BLUE DRAGON.)

SIR DWAINE *(Continued.)*
Here, sniff in the flame of this candle.

BLUE DRAGON *(Holding her nose.)*
But it will burn my nose.

LASSIE MAUREEN
Besides, when she sniffs in, won't it blow the flame out?

SIR DWAINE
Mm, quite right again.

BLUE DRAGON (*Discouraged.*)
I'm afraid there's nothing you can do for me.

LASSIE COLEEN
There must be something else we can do. Sir Dwaine, think.

SIR DWAINE
Perhaps if we went through the other end.

LASSIE DARLING
How would we do that?

SIR DWAINE
If we cut off her tail and shove the fire in—

BLUE DRAGON (*In horror.*)
Augh!

LASSIE MAUREEN
You can't be serious.

SIR DWAINE
My expertise is in slaying dragons, not helping them.

BLUE DRAGON
But why must I breathe fire in the first place? I don't want to burn anything, especially people. I love people.

LADDIE TIMMY
But if you don't scourge the countryside like every other dragon, what will you do?

BLUE DRAGON
Well, I'm a rather good gardener if I say so myself.

LASSIE COLEEN
Gardening? Like growing corn and beans and things like that?

BLUE DRAGON
Why yes. I'm very good with growing potatoes.

LASSIE MAUREEN
Yes, but we've never had much luck growing potatoes around Durbin.

BLUE DRAGON (*Becoming excited.*)
I bet I could. I bet I could grow potatoes all over the place.

SIR DWAINE
Growing potatoes in Ireland. How unusual.

BLUE DRAGON
Oh goodie, goodie, goodie. I'm going to grow potatoes!

(*Happily clapping her hands, **BLUE DRAGON** hurries out stage right.*)

SIR DWAINE
A happy dragon. How unusual.

LASSIE MAUREEN
The Blue Dragon didn't seem so shy just then.

LASSIE DARLING
Maybe that's all shy creatures need. Maybe they wouldn't be so shy if people just believed in them.

SIR DWAINE
Still, growing potatoes in Ireland... It's unheard-of.

LASSIE MAUREEN
If we support and encourage the Blue Dragon, I bet she can do it. Come on.

(***MAUREEN, COLEEN, DARLING** and **TIMMY** exit stage right. **SIR DWAINE** stays back.*)

SIR DWAINE
A blushing blue dragon. How unusual.

(***SIR DWAINE** exits stage right.*)

END OF THE BLUSHING BLUE DRAGON

The Wind in the Willows:
Toad's Day in Court

Adapted from THE WIND IN THE WILLOWS by Kenneth Grahame
Script adaptation by Joan Garner

—BACKGROUND INFORMATION
(genre classification and other data deemed useful)

First published in 1908, THE WIND IN THE WILLOWS has seen many manifestations of itself in picture book and film form.

Easily placed in the *Fantastic Beasts and Talking Animals* **SECTION**, one needn't thoroughly explore its parallels to Homer's ODYSSEY or recognize the plot's heady Edwardian flavor to appreciate this charming story. But what makes THE WIND IN THE WILLOWS special is its illogical assumptions and complete disregard for presupposed boundaries.

For one, the animals own houses, cars, and other items specific to the human community. They wear clothes, drink tea, and conduct themselves within conventional civilian social orders, and speak and walk like humans with their primary concerns being human concerns with few minor exceptions.

Second, WILLOW's animals interact with humans. Many stories involving talking animals establish a distinct division between the two. Although the animals may speak and understand one another, humans involved in the story cannot. Often animals know what the human characters are saying, but again, humans cannot understand an animal's bark, grunt, or roar.

And lastly, what especially separates THE WIND IN THE WILLOWS from most talking animal fantasy stories is the animals are actual size. In other words, Toad is the size of a real toad—Mole the size of a real mole. Yet with keen observation, sizes of objects shrink or grow depending on where the animals are. In Rat's house, everything is proportional to him. At court, all furnishings and accessories fit the human Bench of Magistrates.

Notwithstanding this inconsistency, and though containing a critically denounced, scattered, and complex text for a children's fantasy, THE WIND IN THE WILLOWS makes for a wonderful story.

KENNETH GRAHAME (1859–1932). United Kingdom. Originally a banker and businessman, Kenneth Grahame began writing as a pastime. Unmistakably his most famous piece, THE WIND IN THE WILLOWS (1908) has been defined as classical 20th Century Children's Fantasy. Unlike more prolific writers, Grahame's body of work is remarkably slight. His other works are THE HEADSWOMAN (1898), a nonfantasy set in medieval times, and THE GOLDEN AGE (1895), a compilation of stories with the most familiar being THE RELUCTANT DRAGON.

— SYNOPSIS OF STORY

(This script takes its cue from the animated Disney short feature that concentrates primarily on TOAD'S motor-car mania.)

(1900—England) Ratty, Mole, and Badger try to keep Toad (of Toad Hall, naturally) from his new mania—motor-cars. They even resort to locking Toad in his room. But Toad escapes out the window and goes on a jolly ride. He winds up in jail because of his reckless driving and faces many serious charges. Rat, Mole, and Badger can do little more than quietly watch and listen to Toad's conviction and sentencing.

The Wind in the Willows
STAGING SUGGESTIONS AND HELPFUL HINTS

—GLOSSARY
(terms possibly unfamiliar to reader)

BOUNDER—An impolite person.

FABRICATION—A point or story that is made up.

FARTHING—A British coin. A thing of little value.

GARISH—Showy. Too bright and too much.

IMPERTINENCE—Not showing proper respect and manners. Being a brat.

INHERITANCE—Anything received from another; usually money from one family member to another.

MAGISTRATE—A judge of a police court.

SQUANDERING—To spend recklessly. Wasteful.

TOGS—A coat. Clothes.

— CHARACTER DESCRIPTIONS

MOLE: (Male—Optional Female) A gentle and kindly soul, **MOLE** trusts everyone. He should be a little timid, but an instant friend to everyone.

RAT: (Male—Optional Female) A bit stuffy, **RAT** is the first one to point out rules of decorum and ethics as he knows them well and lives them most earnestly.

BADGER: (Male—Optional Female) Not one to fool around, **BADGER** is stern yet thoughtful and always looking out for his friends' best interests.

TOAD: (Male) Fun-loving and always ready for a party, **TOAD** regrets his disapproving conduct, but also snaps right back into merrymaking once the scolding and punishment lifts.

CHAIRMAN: (Male) Forceful and overbearing. Ready to eat **TOAD** for lunch.

MAGISTRATE: (Male) Stubborn, he's wanting to send **TOAD** to prison before the case is tried.

CLERK: (Male—Optional Female) Efficient, but shy. Speaks well.

— PRESENTATION SUGGESTIONS
(1900's European Clothing and Items)

COSTUMES
Hats, caps, and scarves can help in identifying the characters. *All the characters here are male, but* **RAT**, **MOLE**, **BADGER**, *the* **CHAIRMAN**, *and the* **CLERK** *could easily be female.*

PROPS
PAPER & PEN—for the **CLERK**.

GAVEL—for the **MAGISTRATE**.

LIGHTING EFFECTS
If possible, light only the center where **MOLE**, **RAT**, **BADGER** and **TOAD** stand until the other **PLAYERS** join the scene. (A simple "domed" mechanic's floodlight or a powerful flashlight or search light can substitute.) Use a flashlight for the siren. (Place a red gel or red plastic wrap in front of the bulb. Then take a piece of cardboard and fan it up and down at a moderate speed in front of the light.) When the court scene starts, turn on the classroom lights.

SOUND EFFECTS
Sound effects using the voice will probably work best. But use a recording of the door shutting and siren blaring for a more finished production.

SPECIAL EFFECTS
See *LIGHTING EFFECTS*.

STAGING
Placing the **PLAYERS** in the staging positions below will do, but applying the simple movements used in the script will enhance this presentation.

STAGE

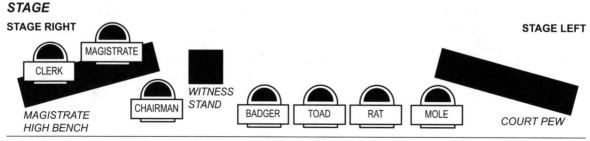

STAGE RIGHT   STAGE LEFT

MAGISTRATE
CLERK
MAGISTRATE HIGH BENCH   CHAIRMAN   WITNESS STAND   BADGER   TOAD   RAT   MOLE   COURT PEW

The Wind in the Willows
SCRIPT

SETTING
England. 1900.

> *(The **CLERK** and **MAGISTRATE** sit behind the HIGH MAGISTRATE BENCH. The **CHAIRMAN** stands in the back (upstage), stage left until the court scene. **TOAD** stands to the back until his cue. The **CLERK**, **MAGISTRATE**, and **CHAIRMAN** stand motionless until they come into play. **BADGER**, **MOLE**, and **RAT** stand up front—downstage, center.)*

MOLE *(Looking nervously.)*
You know, Ratty, Toad isn't going to like this one bit.

RAT
Now you can't lose your nerve, Mole. We must be strong.

MOLE
Yes, but—

BADGER
—No "buts," Moley. This needs to be done for Toad's sake as well as for our own and for all the animals of the countryside.

RAT
Well, we're here at Toad Hall as you asked, Badger. What do we do now? knock on the door, or break it down?

BADGER
Knock, of course. We are reasonable folk here.

MOLE *(Looking outward, excitedly.)*
Badger, look! Is that it?

BADGER *(Looking outward.)*
Mm, I'm afraid so — Toad's new mania.

RAT *(Also looking outward.)*
Ah, yes. A brand-new motor-car.

MOLE
It's very pretty, don't you think?

BADGER
Indeed, it's very pretty, but Toad can't afford it. He couldn't afford the other car he crashed, and he can't afford this one.

RAT
Remember, Moley, if Toad spends one more farthing, he'll lose Toad Hall—this wonderful estate we regard with great pride and affection.

MOLE
Lose Toad Hall? How awful.

TOAD *(Stepping down to the others.)*
Ho, ho, good fellows. How marvelous to see you. You're just in time to go for a ride with me.

RAT *(Whispering to **BADGER**.)*
Look, Badger, Toad is wearing those garish driving togs—and those goggles. Shameful.

BADGER
I was afraid of this. It looks like he has lapsed into a full-fledged mania.

TOAD
Come along, good friends. Everyone in the car. Ah, it's a fine morning for a jolly jaunt.

BADGER
Grab him, lads—before he can get in the car!

RAT
Hurry, Moley!

> *(**RAT** and **MOLE** step to either side of **TOAD** and grab his arms to restrain him.)*

TOAD
Say, now. What is this?

RAT
Come with us, Toad.

TOAD
Unhand me, fellows. I say, this isn't very sporting of you. You're making a crease in my driving coat.

BADGER
Bring him into the house, boys.

TOAD
Badger, my friend, why are you doing this? You're ruining a perfectly splendid day.

* SOUND EFFECTS
A door opening and closing.

(*RAT* and *MOLE* turn *TOAD* around, release him, then turn back to face the audience. *BADGER* steps behind *RAT*. *BADGER* and *TOAD* now hide to a degree behind *RAT* and *MOLE*. Pause.)

MOLE
We've been out here for some time, Ratty. What do you suppose Badger is doing to Toad?

RAT
I hope pounding some sense into Toad's feather-brain. He is always going too far. Toad grabs hold of every fad that comes along. He's squandering away his inheritance with each new craze. Mark my words, Moley, Toad will bring Toad Hall to ruin. And the police are not happy with his madcap driving escapades—disturbing the peace and destroying property. If he should end up before the Magistrate again, they will be rather harsh, I fear.

MOLE
Oh, dear. We wouldn't want that.

* SOUND EFFECTS
The sound of a door opening.

(*BADGER* and *TOAD* step out from behind *RAT* and *MOLE*.)

BADGER
So my friends, I have spoken to Toad and he has promised to return the motor-car and behave himself, haven't you, Toad?

TOAD (*Trying to be sincere.*)
Yes, I am truly sorry. I didn't mean to worry you.

BADGER
And the next time you see a motor-car, you'll turn tail and run away as fast as you can, correct?

TOAD
Well, I haven't a tail to turn, but yes, I ... Yes, yes, I ... Oh, no, no, no. I'm sorry, but I just can't do it. I can't promise what you want of me. My mania is too strong. I simply can't do it.

BADGER
Are you telling us that no matter what we do, you'll continue with this mania?

TOAD
Afraid so.

BADGER
Then you leave us no choice. Ratty, Moley, lock Toad in his room!

(*RAT* and *MOLE* take *TOAD* by the arms again and turn him around. *TOAD* will then cross to upstage left while *BADGER*, *RAT*, and *MOLE* cross to the COURT PEW and sit.)

* SOUND EFFECTS
A siren.

* LIGHTING EFFECTS
The spotlight or floodlight turns off. The Lighting Effects person crosses to center stage and works the siren light. He or she stays there for a moment or two until the other characters are in position. When the siren light turns off, full room lighting comes up.

(*The CLERK and MAGISTRATE now move about. The CLERK writes on PAPERS and gives it to the MAGISTRATE. The MAGISTRATE reviews the PAPERS with a frown. He also shakes his head disapprovingly and clicks his tongue.*)

MOLE (*Looking over to the MAGISTRATE.*)
Dear, dear. This doesn't look good.

RAT
We tried to stop him. Didn't we try to stop him?

BADGER
Of course we did, but I didn't think the rascal would have the nerve to climb out the window and escape down the side of the house using his bed sheet as a rope. Nothing would have stopped Toad shy of tossing him behind bars.

RAT
Well, that may happen now.

MOLE
Poor Toady.

MAGISTRATE (*Pounding his GAVEL.*)
Here, ye. Here ye. The Bench of Magistrates is ready to hear the case of Toad of Toad Hall. Bring in the suspect.

(*The CHAIRMAN escorts a resisting TOAD to the WITNESS STAND.*)

TOAD
But I didn't do it, sir. I tell you, I'm an innocent toad.

CHAIRMAN (*Ignoring TOAD.*)
Here is the felon, Your Magistrate.

(*The CHAIRMAN forces TOAD up onto the WITNESS STAND. TOAD has his hands together as if tied.*)

CHAIRMAN
Get up there and be quiet, you scoundrel.

MAGISTRATE *(To TOAD.)*
Are you or are you not Toad of Toad Hall?

TOAD
Why, yes I am.

MAGISTRATE *(Lifting a PAPER.)*
It says here that you stole a motor-car. How do you plead?

TOAD
Innocent. I am so very innocent, sir.

MAGISTRATE
You may address me as His Honor, or Your Magistrate. Nothing more—nothing less.

TOAD
Then Your Magistrate, I would like to state for the record that these charges are a lie. I'm an innocent victim of someone else's crime.

MAGISTRATE *(Not convinced.)*
Of course you are. Chairman, you may proceed with your case.

CHAIRMAN
Thank you, Your Magistrate... As you may recognize this cad; Toad has already been before His Honor on similar charges of reckless driving and disturbing the peace. But now—now, because His Honor let him off lightly the first time, he is back having committed a much more serious crime. Toad has stolen a motor-car.

MAGISTRATE
Nooooo. Why that's terrible. You bounder, you.

TOAD
But I didn't steel anything, Your Magistrate. I've been trying to tell everyone I—

CHAIRMAN *(Interrupting.)*
—Surely we must teach this crook a lesson by putting him in prison for a very, *very* long time.

MAGISTRATE
Yes, we must—definitely must.

TOAD
But you haven't heard my side of the story.

MAGISTRATE
The convict will not speak unless spoken to.

TOAD
Convict?

CHAIRMAN
Mr. Clerk, what is the stiffest sentence we can give this ruffian?

CLERK *(Surprised, he looks up from his writing.)*
What? Me? Oh. You want me to? Well, let's see...
     (Sorts through his PAPERS, he begins figuring.)
Um, the charges are first, stealing a motor-car, that would be...
     (Figuring.)
Then the second is driving to the public endangerment...
     (Figuring.)
And last but not least would be the charge of gross impertinence to the rural police.
     (Figuring.)
Mm, three — take the one and carry the two... Five, no six. Yes, that would be nineteen years.

TOAD *(Alarmed.)*
CHAIRMAN *(Satisfied.)*   Nineteen years!

MAGISTRATE
Nineteen years it is, then. Take the thief away.
     (Banging his GAVEL.)
This court is adjourned.

     *(The **CHAIRMAN** takes **TOAD'S** arm and leads him offstage left. The **CLERK** gathers his PAPERS and follows the **MAGISTRATE** out, also stage left. **MOLE**, **BADGER**, and **RAT** stand and watch **TOAD** as he's taken away—still yelling he's innocent.)*

MOLE
Poor, poor Toady.

RAT
What bad luck.

BADGER
Luck had nothing to do with it, Rat. If you commit a crime, you must pay the penalty.

MOLE
Yes, Badger. But what if Toad didn't steal that car? He says he didn't do it.

RAT
And what if Toad drove recklessly through the countryside trying to catch the ones who did the wrongdoing?

BADGER
Well, I must admit there are some things that don't make much sense with all of this.

MOLE

I think we should believe Toad. I mean, I know he's a bit excitable, but I have never known him to lie.

RAT

Yes, I agree. Toad isn't one to lie.

MOLE

I feel we should look into this.

RAT

Yes, yes, Moley. Quite right.

BADGER

Yes, maybe we should. We need to know exactly what happened. The most important thing of all is to find out the truth. Whether good or bad for Toad, we must uncover the truth. Let's go, lads. We have a lot of work to do.

(**BADGER**, **RAT**, and **MOLE** *exit stage right.*)

END OF THE WIND IN THE WILLOWS

The Pantheon of the Aztecs

Inspired by an Ancient Aztec Legend
Original Script by Joan Garner

—BACKGROUND INFORMATION
(genre classification and other data deemed useful)

This story comes from the ancient Aztec legend of Popocatépetl and his love Iztaccíhuatl. (The names were modified to Popoca and Izatal to avoid obvious pronunciation problems.) Popoca calls on the god Tezcatlipoca (Tezacan) to wage war against an encroaching enemy. Like many an ancient god, Tezcatlipoca is more animal than human; and in this story, Tezacan is a snake like serpent with no physical human traits other than thought and language.

Gods of the ancients were often bigger than life and symbolically shown in animal form. Like Egyptian religion and mythology, it's difficult to mark where Aztec religion ends and mythology begins. But with a quick glance, the major gods take human form where the lesser entities become more beast-like. However, the well-known Aztec god Quetzacóatl (god of civilization and learning), often reveals itself as a feathered snake with human head. A clawed butterfly symbolizes Izpapalotl (ruler of paradise). Mixocoatl (god of hunting) is a cloud serpent, and Xiuhcoatl (god of drought) blazes in art form as a fire snake.

Aztec supernatural creatures appear more fearsome in their beast-like appearance: Ahuitzotl roams the earth as a dog-monkey, and Tlaltechuhtli is a toad goddess. Another supernatural creature, Nahual, is a shapeshifting sorcerer or witch. As for me, the most fearsome quality of these beasts is properly pronouncing and spelling their names!

— SYNOPSIS OF STORY

(Ancient Mexico) In an ancient Aztec city in the valley of Mexico, Emperor Soom rules with a harsh and greedy hand. Trusting no one, he has forbidden his daughter to marry. But when the city comes under attack by Alakar, Soom's fierce enemy, the emperor must relinquish to jaguar knight Popoca's request to marry Princess Izatal if he can defeat Alakar. To defeat Alakar, Popoca calls on the god of war Tezacan for help. The giant snake-like Tezacan tells Popoca to climb onto its back and the two fly to the edge of the city to defeat Alakar's army. But others are jealous of Popoca and claim he died in battle. Princess Izatal is so upset on hearing this news, she falls dead of a broken heart. When Popoca returns only to find his love gone and that his friends have betrayed him, he seeks the help of Tezacan once more. He asks the god to help him join his beloved Izatal in eternity. Tezacan turns them into the light of the sun.

The Pantheon of the Aztecs
STAGING SUGGESTIONS AND HELPFUL HINTS

— CHARACTER DESCRIPTIONS

PEECANT: (Female) A servant, more sensible and logical than her owner, **PRINCESS IZATAL**, as is often the case.

EMPEROR SOOM: (Male) Greedy and demanding and afraid of losing his power.

COUNCILOR HALICAL: (Male) Benevolent and wise.

PRINCESS IZATAL: (Female) Single-minded, privileged and impetuous, but nice.

WARRIOR MACUUM: (Male) A good warrior, but jealous.

WARRIOR YACTEC: (Male) Another good warrior, but easily led by others.

KNIGHT POPOCA: (Male) A great and confident jaguar knight. Prideful and loyal.

GOD TEZACAN: (Male) More of a pure monster with a powerful and commanding voice.

— PRESENTATION SUGGESTIONS
(Ancient Aztec Clothing and Items)

COSTUMES
PEECANT—White cotton or linen, short sleeved kandys (shirtdress) to floor. Wide, brightly colored (striped) cloth belt. Bare feet. Straight hair with bangs.

EMPEROR SOOM—White cotton or linen, short sleeved kandys (shirtdress) to floor. Wide, brightly colored (striped) cloth belt. Same cloth for long cape attached in front at the belt and flowing over a shoulder and down the back to the ground. Aztec headdress with feathers. Sandals.

COUNCILOR HALICAL—Same as **SOOM**. Different colored cloth and headdress.

PRINCESS IZATAL—Same as PEECANT with cloth for long cape attached in front at the belt and flowing over a shoulder and down the back to the ground. Aztec headdress with feathers. Sandals.

MACUUM, YACTEC, and **POPOCA**—Skin colored tights with shirt. Jaguar fur loincloth. Jaguar headdress. Bare feet.

LIGHTING EFFECTS
If lights can dim when **TEZACAN** appears, it will help strengthen its shadow.

SPECIAL EFFECTS
TEZACAN. Work a floodlight offstage left. Shine it on the blank WALL in the back and then place a small cutout of the beast in front of the light to create its shadow on the back WALL

STAGE
TEMPLES—Place markings of some kind on floor to outline the TEMPLES. Perhaps stone floors to the suggest top the of TEMPLES. Raised platforms would be nice, but not necessary.

STAGING

STAGE RIGHT   EMPEROR SOOM'S TEMPLE   **STAGE LEFT**

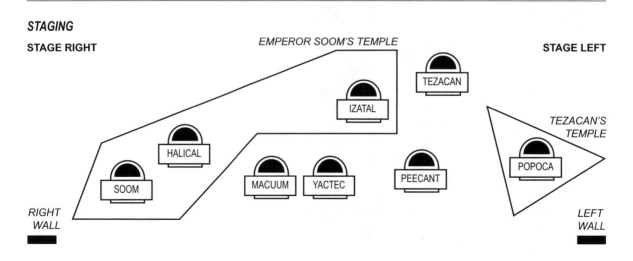

The Pantheon of the Aztecs
SCRIPT

SETTING
Ancient Mexico. At stage left if EMPEROR'S SOOM'S TEMPLE. At stage right is the smaller TEZACAN'S TEMPLE.

> *(**PEECANT** stands center stage. **EMPEROR SOOM** and **COUNCILOR HALICAL** stand on SOOM'S TEMPLE to the right. **PRINCESS IZATAL** stands on the TEMPLE to the left.)*

PEECANT *(Speaks to the audience.)*
Here in the heart of Mexico during a time long ago, Emperor Soom ruled with a severe hand.

EMPEROR SOOM
Halical, the people below my temple are restless and displeased with my rule.

COUNCILOR HALICAL
Your people fear you, my emperor.

EMPEROR SOOM
Yes. As long as I keep fear in their hearts, my rule remains strong. I can trust no one, Councilor Halical.

COUNCILOR HALICAL
It's a sad day, my emperor.

PEECANT *(Speaks to the audience.)*
Emperor Soom had a daughter, the lovely Princess Izatal. My princess. I am Peecant, consort to Princess Izatal.

> *(**PEECANT** turns and crosses to **PRINCESS IZATAL**.)*

PEECANT *(Continued.)*
Princess, I see you are dreaming again. Would it be about a young jaguar knight called Popoca?

PRINCESS IZATAL *(Smiling.)*
We met again last night. He has my heart and I have his. If only we could be together always.

PEECANT
Your father is very protective. It must be a special man to gain his approval.

PRINCESS IZATAL
My father has closed himself off to everyone. He's forbidden me to go beyond these temple walls. He's no longer the father I once knew to be so heartless.

PEECANT
So you must sneak out of the temple to meet with Popoca.

PRINCESS IZATAL
It's becoming so hard to hide our love. If I can't be with Popoca, I might as well be dead.

> *(**WARRIORS MACUUM, YACTEC**, and **POPOCA** enter from stage right and cross to the **EMPEROR** and **HALICAL**.)*

WARRIOR MACUUM
Emperor, there is an urgent matter. Alakar's army marches to the edge of the city.

EMPEROR SOOM
But we have no defenses. There isn't time to gather our army.

WARRIOR YACTEC
All we have to guard the city is the jaguar knights.

EMPEROR SOOM
Yes, my loyal jaguar knights. You must help me.

WARRIOR YACTAC
We'll need more than the knights, my emperor. We are but a few against an entire army.

EMPEROR SOOM
What are we to do?

WARRIOR POPOCA
We must plead to the war god Tezacan for help.

EMPEROR SOOM
Plead to Tezacan? Popoca, if we were in his good graces, the god of war wouldn't have sent our enemy to the city.

WARRIOR POPOCA
I have found favor with Tezacan. He will hear me.

EMPEROR SOOM
Have you? How have you found favor?

> *(**PRINCESS IZATAL** and **PEECANT** cross to the group of men.)*

PRINCESS IZATAL
Popoca is a true jaguar knight of pure heart, father. Only an honest and trusted warrior like Popoca could find favor with Tezacan.

EMPEROR SOOM
Izatal, how have you come to know this warrior?

COUNCILOR HALICAL
Please, my emperor. The urgent matter of saving the city is at hand. If Popoca can help us, we must accept his willingness to try.

EMPEROR SOOM
Popoca, do you really have a connection with Tezacan? Are you on speaking terms with a god? How absurd.

WARRIOR POPOCA
I do speak with the war god, and I will on your behalf. But should he decide to help us, I would expect a reward, my emperor.

EMPEROR SOOM
Ah, hear it is. See, Councilor Halical? It's as I said, I can trust no one. What is it you want? My fortune? My empire?

EMPEROR POPOCA
I don't seek your fortune or empire, my emperor. I seek the hand of your daughter, Princess Izatal.

EMPEROR SOOM
Out of the question.

PRINCESS IZATAL
Why, father? Can there be no worthier husband for me than a jaguar knight who defeat's our enemy? There is nothing I would love more than to be Popoca's wife. Please.

EMPEROR SOOM
Izatal, this man can't talk to the gods. No one can. He's a fraud.

PRINCESS IZATAL
You've already judged this man and he hasn't done anything yet.

WARRIOR POPOCA
I'm going to plead for Tezacan's help. And when we defeat Alakar's army, I'll return for my beloved Izatal.

(POPOCA exits stage left.)

EMPEROR SOOM
I haven't agreed to this!

COUNCILOR HALICAL
Please, my emperor. We're hardly in the position to argue and bargain here. We need to trust that this man can do what he says.

WARRIOR MACUUM
There's no time to wait for Popoca to go talk to his precious god. We have to act now, my emperor.

EMPEROR SOOM
Yes. For once I'm hearing some sensible talk. Macuum, you and Yactec take the rest of the jaguar knights to the edge of the city and stop Alakar at the canals. Select your fastest runner and send him up north to my army. Have the messenger tell my army to march back to the city as quickly as possible.

WARRIORS MACUUM and YACTEC
Yes, my emperor.

(MACUUM and YACTEC exit stage right. PRINCESS IZATAL and PEECANT cross back to the left side of SOOM'S TEMPLE.)

PRINCESS IZATAL
Do you think, Peecant? Do you think Popoca can defeat Alakar? Is it possible my dreams can come true and I'll be with Popoca?

PEECANT
Oh, I do hope so, Princess Izatal.

PRINCESS IZATAL
My heart is racing so. Oh, please let Popoca and Tezacan defeat Alakar.

(PEECANT steps down to center stage and speaks to the audience.)

PEECANT
Now Popoca was as smart as he was brave. And unlike Emperor Soom who trusted no one and no one trusted him, Popoca knew trust must be earned. He earned this trust with Tezacan by praying to the god of war every night. This day Popoca went to Tezacan's temple, climbed the many steps to the top, and looked to the sky.

(POPOCA enters from stage left and stands on TEZACAN'S TEMPLE.)

WARRIOR POPOCA
Oh, great Tezacan, I need your help. Please hear my plea, great Tezacan.

*LIGHTING EFFECTS
Lights dim and a floodlight shines in from the left.

*SPECIAL EFFECTS
The shadow of a snake like image appears on the back wall. This is **TEZACAN**.

TEZACAN *(The voice comes from stage left.)*
Popoca, my most worthy warrior. Why have you come to me?

WARRIOR POPOCA
Tezacan, you know our enemy is at the edge of our city. Please help me repel Alakar's army.

TEZACAN
Popoca, I will be with you to face Alakar. Come climb onto my back and we'll face and fight the enemy together.

(POPOCA exits stage left.)

*SPECIAL EFFECTS
The shadow of **TEZACAN** fades.

PEECANT
The god of war was a giant beast with a lizard's head and serpent's body. He could become very small, or grow to the size of the great temples. Popoca and Tezacan flew through the sky to the canals of the city to face Alakar. When Popoca appeared on the back of Tezacan, the jaguar knights cheered and found new strength to fight the enemy. The battle was swift and victorious. Ravaged by Tezacan's mighty fangs and poisonous tongue, Alakar's army scattered and ran back into the jungle. With the help of Tezacan, Popoca became the hero of the day.

(PEECANT steps back to join PRINCESS IZATAL at the right of SOOM'S TEMPLE while MACUUM and YACTEC enter from stage right—tired from battle.)

WARRIOR MACUUM
Can you believe it? We are victorious. A handful of men against a huge army. Impossible.

WARRIOR YACTEC
And yet here we are. Did you see his strong jaw and long fangs? Who would have believed Popoca could get the god of war to fight for us?

WARRIOR MACUUM
And now Popoca is a hero and will take the beautiful Princess Izatal as his wife.

WARRIOR YACTEC
What nerve to claim the princess like that. We fought just as hard and we didn't have any god to help us.

WARRIOR MACUUM
True. If anything, we're more deserving because we were on our own.

WARRIOR YACTEC
It would serve Popoca right not to get Izatal.

WARRIOR MACUUM
I agree, but how could that happen now?

WARRIOR YACTEC
It would be very simple. Yes, it would be a very simple thing to do. Come with me.

(YACTEC and MACUUM step to EMPEROR SOOM and COUNCILOR HALICAL while PRINCESS IZATAL and PEECANT step over to them.)

WARRIOR YACTEC *(Continued.)*
Emperor Soom, it's your humble servants Yactec and Macuum here to report of the battle.

EMPEROR SOOM
Did it go well? It must have gone well to see the two of you still alive.

PRINCESS IZATAL
Popoca. What of the jaguar knight Popoca?

WARRIOR YACTEC
We fought a fierce fight, Princess Izatal. Popoca was the bravest warrior I ever saw.

PRINCESS IZATAL
Was?

WARRIOR YACTEC
Yes, my princess. I'm afraid a hundred men came down on brave Popoca at once. There was nothing we could do.

PRINCESS IZATAL
No. Oh, no!

WARRIOR MACUUM
Yactec speaks the truth. I saw the fighting with my own eyes. Popoca fought courageously, but there were too many.

EMPEROR SOOM
Then we lost the battle.

WARRIOR YACTEC
No, my emperor. The victory is ours. When we saw Popoca go down, Macuum and I rallied our warriors and we fought off the advancing army.

EMPEROR SOOM
You are the heroes of the day, Macuum and Yactec. To honor such bravery, one of you may take my daughter as your wife.

PRINCESS IZATAL

No! Never. My heart only belongs to Popoca and no one else.

*(**PRINCESS IZATAL** rushes over to the right of SOOM'S TEMPLE and falls to the ground. She remains motionless. **PEECANT** follows and kneels to comfort her. **POPOCA** enters from stage left and crosses to the men.)*

POPOCA

My emperor, we have won the day!

EMPEROR SOOM

Popoca? But these men said you were killed in battle. They saw you go down.

POPOCA

How could they see me go down when I was riding on the back of Tezacan all the while?

COUNCILOR HALICAL

You men lied about Popoca's death? How cruel to lie about such a thing.

*(**PEECANT** rejoins the men.)*

PEECANT

Emperor, horror of horrors. Hearing of Popoca's death, Princess Izatal's heart broke so—she fell and has died, my emperor.

EMPEROR SOOM

No, it can't be. What are we to do now?

POPOCA

My Izatal is dead? And because she thought I was gone. Macuum and Yactec, I thought you were my friends. I thought... My life is over. I must seek guidance from Tezacan.

*(**POPOCA** crosses to stand in the TEZACAN TEMPLE.)*

POPOCA

Great Tezacan, hear me. My beloved Izatal has died of a broken heart. If she must die, take me as well. I do not wish to stay in a world where my emperor rules so selfishly and my friends turn on me with such spite. Please, I must be with Izatal or I am nothing. If she is dead, I wish to be dead.

*LIGHTING EFFECTS

Lights dim and a floodlight shines in from the left.

*SPECIAL EFFECTS

A shadow of a snake-like image once more appears on the back wall.

TEZACAN *(The voice comes from stage left.)*

Good Popoca, I see your enemies are more than those of Alakar's army. These men will be punished for their wrongdoing. People of the city, hear me and turn on these undeserving men! I am the god of war—Tezacan of the Aztecs, and I come to force my will. Too long have you been under the rule of a cold-hearted emperor and I have seen you suffer for it. And so I delegate Emperor Soom to working in the canals of the city to the end of his days. Kind and wise Halical will be your new emperor.

*(**COUNCILOR HALICAL** bows before the shadow of **TEZACAN**.)*

TEZACAN *(Continued.)*

Macuum and Yactec, you shame me with your lies. Once good and strong jaguar knights, your jealousy of Popoca have reduced you to lowly liars and so you shall work as lowly slaves in the fields for the rest of your days. Popoca, go to your precious Izatal and raise her up into the sky.

*(**POPOCA** crosses to **PRINCESS IZATAL** and helps her stand. They stand together holding each other.)*

TEZACAN *(Continued.)*

And may everyone know that when you look into the sunrise of the morning, the bright and joyful light you see will be the love of Izatal and Popoca forever and ever.

* LIGHTING EFFECTS

All lights go off but for the one creating **TEZACAN'S** shadow. After, light fades.

END OF THE PANTHEON OF THE AZTECS

A Beastly Demand

PAGE 1 (A Lesson in Identifying and Applying Discriminating Elements)

This Project concentrates on realizing how the richness of a story is in the detail.

Each student is to think of and create a fantastic beast. Guidelines and a form come with this Project to help with this process. Keep in mind students might then use this creature in the second Project of this **SECTION**.

PREPARATION AND RESOURCES NEEDED: Copy the 4 pages of this Project for each student.

CREATING A FANTASTIC BEAST

Student Assignment: Although there are many enchanting and magical beings in **Fantasy Genre***, this Project asks you to think up a new beast. The list of beasts below should help you imagine your own. The list includes mythological beasts, monsters, creatures made up of several animal parts, and creatures with human parts but also animal parts. The list doesn't include (and your beasts shouldn't be): fairies, water spirits, gnomes and other enchanted beings, giants, goblins, supernatural beings, imps, and races of beings. In other words, not too human—a fantastic beast.*

BEASTS

Amphisbaena (Greek mythology) is an ant-eating serpent with a head at each end.

Bahamut (Arabic mythology) is an enormous fish supporting a huge bull named **Kujuta** that has four thousand eyes, ears, noses, mouths, tongues and feet.

Baku (Chinese and Japanese mythology) "dream eaters" with the head of an elephant and the body of a lion. It may also have the head of a lion, the body of a horse, the tail of a cow, and the legs and feet of a tiger.

Balaur (Romanian lore) is very large with fins, feet, and several serpent heads.

Barghest (European mythology) is a monstrous goblin-dog with huge teeth and claws.

Behemoth (Hebrew lore) is the largest and most powerful animal of the sea. It's a giant hippopotamus with a tail (or trunk) of an elephant.

Bunyip (Australian Aboriginal mythology) has a horse-like tail, flippers, and walrus-like tusks.

Catoblepas (Ethiopia Lore) has the body of a buffalo and the head of a hog.

Centaurs (Greek mythology) part human and part horse, with a horse's body and a human head and torso with arms. The human portion joins at the waist with the horse's shoulders (where the head and neck would be).

Cerberus (Greek mythology) is the hound of Hades—a monstrous three-headed dog (sometimes said to have 50 or 100 heads) with a snake for a tail and thousands of snake heads on its back.

Chimera (Greek mythology) has the body of a goat, the tail of a snake or dragon, and the head of a lion. It's also depicted with heads of both goat and lion, and a snake for a tail.

Chupacabras (The Americas) is a lizard like being with leathery or scaly greenish-gray skin and sharp spines or quills running down its back. It's about the size of a large dog, and stands and hops like a kangaroo.

SOME FANTASTIC BEASTS

A Beastly Demand (Applying Discriminating Elements) PAGE 2

Cockatrice (Hebrew lore) is a legendary creature about the size and shape of a **Dragon** or **Wyvern**, but in appearance resembles a giant rooster, with some lizard-like characteristics.

Dragon (European, Chinese, and Japanese lore) is a large and powerful serpent or reptile, with magical or spiritual qualities. The European dragon usually breathes fire.

Fenghuang (Chinese Lore) has the beak of a rooster, the face of a swallow, and the forehead of a fowl. It also has the neck of a snake, the breast of a goose, the back of a tortoise, the hindquarters of a stag, and the tail of a fish.

Gorgon (Greek mythology) is a vicious female monster with sharp fangs and hair of living, venomous snakes. They're sometimes shown with wings of gold, brazen claws, and the tusks of boars. According to the Myth, seeing the face of a Gorgon turns the viewer to stone. Probably the most popular of these monsters, **Medusa** has brass hands, sharp fangs and hair of living serpents.

Griffin (European legend) is a creature with the body of a lion and the head and wings of an eagle.

Harpies (Greek mythology) is a winged hag with sharp bird-talons.

Hydra (Greek mythology) is a serpent-like water beast with numerous heads.

Kraken (Norse myth) is a sea monster of gargantuan size.

Kumiho (Korean lore) is a nine-tailed fox.

Lammasu (Mesopotamian mythology) is a beast with the face of a man, the body of lion, and the wings of an eagle.

Manticore (Persia lore) is an animal with the head of a man (often with horns, gray eyes, and three rows of iron teeth). It has a lion's body with the tail is of a dragon or scorpion. Sometimes they're shown with wings.

Merrow (Gaelic lLore) is the equivalent of a **mermaid** or **merman**. They are human from the waist up but have the body of a fish from the waist down.

Minotar (Greek mythology) is a creature part man and part bull.

Nue (Japanese lore) has the head of a monkey, the body of a tanuki (raccoon dog), the legs of a tiger, and a snake instead of a tail. A nue can also transform into a black cloud to fly around.

Oni (Japanese lore) is a creature similar to Western ogres. They are hideous, gigantic creatures with sharp claws, wild hair, and two long horns growing from their heads. They are humanoid and sometimes shown with many eyes, fingers, and toes.

Pegasus (Greek mythology) is a winged stallion.

Phoenix (fire bird) is in many cultures, at the end of its life cycle the phoenix builds itself a nest of cinnamon twigs. It will then light itself and the nest on fire. A new, young phoenix arises from the ashes of the fire.

Piasa (Native American lore) is a legendary bird as large as a calf with horns on its head, red eyes, a tiger's beard and a face like a man's. It has a body covered with scales, and a long tail that winds all around the body with a fishtail at the end.

SOME FANTASTIC
BEASTS

PAGE 3 (Applying Discriminating Elements) **A Beastly Demand**

Quazer Beast (Enet mythology) is a creature that originally lived the Arctic Ocean. It's a monstrous serpent, larger than any whale, with six eyes and two horns which protruded from the back of its head.

Raiju (Japanese mythology) "thunder animal" with a body of lightning or fire in the shape of a cat, tanuki (raccoon dog), monkey, or weasel. It may also fly about as a ball of lightning or fire. Its cry sounds like thunder.

Roc (Persian myth) is a white bird of enormous size. It lifts and eats elephants.

Samebito (Japanese lore) "shark men" are monsters of humanoid form with black skin, green, luminescent eyes, and pointed beards. They live in a vast underwater kingdom.

Satyr (Greek mythology) half-man and half-goat. Probably the best known is a satyr named Pan who prances about playing pipes.

Serpopard (Egyptian mythology) has a long neck and head of a serpent and body of a leopard.

Sleipnir (Norse mythology) is the Norse God Odin's magical eight-legged steed—the greatest of all horses.

Sphinx (Egyptian mythology) is a lion with a human head.

Tarasque (French mythology) is a dragon with six short legs like a bear's, an ox like body covered with a turtle shell, and a scaly tail that ends in a scorpion's sting. It has a lion's head, horse's ears, and the face of a bitter old man.

Thunderbird (Native American mythology) by beating its large wings, the thunderbird causes thunder and wind. It creates storms as it flies by pulling together clouds with its beating wing's. The sound of thunder is its wings clapping and sheets of lightning is the light flashing from its eyes when it blinks. A single lightning bolt is a glowing snake that it carries off. Masks show a thunderbird as many-colored, with two curling horns, and sometimes with teeth within its beak.

Unicorn is a legendary creature embodied like a horse, but slender and usually a single, spiral horn growing out of its forehead. The traditional unicorn has a billy goat beard, a lion's tail, and cloven hoofs.

Wolpertinger (European mythology) is an animal living in the alpine forests of Germany. (It's called a **Jackalope** in America.) It has body parts of various animals (usually wings, antlers and fangs, all attached to the body of a small mammal). The most widespread description is that of a horned rabbit or horned squirrel. It is similar to the **Elwedritsche** which resembles a chicken-like creature with antlers, and the Swedish **Skvader**.

Wyvern (European lore) is a winged reptilian creature with two legs and a barbed or snake tail.

Yale (European mythology) is an antelope or goat like four-legged creature with large horns that it can swivel in any direction.

SOME FANTASTIC
BEASTS

A Beastly Demand (Applying Discriminating Elements) PAGE 4

CREATING A NEW FANTASITC BEAST

Below are features of a beast to think about or use in creating a new one. They are suggestions only. You may wish to put in your own ideas. After all, it's YOUR beast!

From Top to Bottom

Its Purpose and Powers

Top of the Head
(Will it have?)
• Horns (curved or
   spiral or both?)
• Hair or feathers
• Scales

**Head, Face, Eyes,
Nose, and Ears**
(Will they be?)
• An animal's
• A human's
• A bird's
• None or several
   heads

Mouth *(Will it have?)*
• Lips
• Teeth (sharp?)
• Tongue (long?)

Hair *(Will there be?)*
• Hair on the head
• Beards
• Hair as something
   else (snakes or
   spike like needles)
• Color

Neck *(Will it be?)*
• An animal's
• A human's
• A bird's
• Long or short

Arms *(Will they be?)*
• An animal's
• A humans
• A bird's wings
• None or many

Hands *(Will they
have?)*
Fingers
Paws
Claws

Body *(Will it be?)*
• An animal's or
   combination of
• A human's
• A bird's
• Something else like
   fire or smoke
• The better part of
   the beast

Legs *(Will they be?)*
• An animal's
• A human's
• A bird's wings
• None or many

Feet *(Will they be?)*
• Hind feet
• Pawed feet
• Webbed feet
• Talons

Tail *(Will it be?)*
• Like an animal's
• Furry and bushy
• Another animal like
   a snake
• Feathers

Skin *(Will it be?)*
• Flesh or leather like
• Fur
• Scales
• Feathers
• Color

Wings *(Will there be?)*
• Large or small
• Usable or not
• With hands or
   claws attached
• Feathers
• Skin or leather like

Stature *(Will it?)*
• Stand on its hind
   legs
• Walk or run on all
   fours (or more
   legs)
• Fly
• Swim

**Where did it come
from?**
• Heavens or sky
• Mountains
• Flatlands
• Water
• Underground

**Where does it live
now?**
• Mountaintop
• Cave
• Trees
• Under water

What does it eat?
• The food humans eat?
• Fire or ice?
• Humans?

**Is it a friend or enemy
to humans?**
• Does it help humans
   by doing something
   for them?
• Does it live with
   humans?
• Does it eat, kill, or bring
   disease to humans?
• Does it destroy where
   humans live or burn
   crops?

**What magical or
special powers does
it have?**
• Can it disappear?
• Can it change humans
   into something else?

Draw Your Beast Below or on Another Piece of Paper

Name of Beast

Dinotopia: A Land Apart from Time
PAGE 1 (A Lesson in Applying Originality While Using the Familiar)

This Project takes the Beast created in the first Project in this **SECTION** and places it in a world of its own.

The world should include humans and their relationship with the Beast (good or bad). Taking its cue from James Gurney's wonderful DINOTOPIA: A LAND APART FROM TIME, students need to first read the book, then imagine and create their own "topia." In doing so, they'll realize how every detail of a world (fantasy or otherwise) depends on who and what populates it.

PREPARATION AND RESOURCES NEEDED: Read the book. Copy the 4 pages of this Project for each student.

READING REQUIRED

PREPARING YOUR OWN SKETCHBOOK JOURNAL

Student Assignment: *James Gurney's DINOTOPIA: A LAND APART FROM TIME is an excellent example of illustrating an idea—specifically, a Lost Word or Other World (See Project 1 of **SECTION** 7 for more on Lost and Other Worlds). Recording a unique concept in sketchbook form, Gurney takes two familiar beings (people and dinosaurs) and creates a world where both live happily. As the main characters (Arthur and Will Denison) make their way across the island, they encounter villages and cities where people and dinosaurs work together. Within these communities, people help dinosaurs and dinosaurs help humans. Also, as expected, the geography of the island is a special mix of tropical and mountainous regions—something where both species can live in harmony. While you read this book and come upon the Egg Hatchery, Treetown, and Waterfall City think of special places like these your "topia" could have. Then create a Journal Sketchbook of your topia like the wonderfully imaginative DINOTOPIA. (Remember, your topia needs to include the Beast you imagined in the previous Project).*

A "Topia" of Your Own—Dinotopia takes its name by combining the words Dinosaur and Utopia. A Utopia is a perfect place or a perfect society for those living in it. Utopia may also mean "a good place." The interesting idea with DINOTOPIA: A LAND APART FROM TIME is how the author James Gurney, takes the word for "perfect," and by attaching it to the word dinosaur, creates a new meaning within **Fantasy Genre**. After which, the suffix "topia" is now also thought of as "another kind of world."

There have been many Utopias created in **Fantasy Genre**. It gives the author their own world where the characters fit in and not around our world. It also allows the author to point out certain problems about the world and society we live in. When creating your Journal Sketchbook, consider putting in an item of two your topia has that would make our world a better one. If your world is fighting your Beast, show how those who might be at war or in disagreement forget their differences and come together to fight the Beast. If in your world people live peacefully with your Beast, emphasize the climate of harmony there.

Keep in Mind—What time or era does your story take place? Will your world be on an island, or on top of a mountain, underground, or somewhere else? Will there be characters coming from our world to your world like in DINOTOPIA? Or maybe your special world won't even know about the rest of our world they're a part of. One thing to note: Do not place your world on another planet. It may be in the sky of Earth, but if it's out in the universe, your story becomes more like science fiction and not fantasy.

*The following pages provide a guideline for your Journal Sketchbook. The following suggestions follow the DINOTOPIA story line with finding the land by accident. Your Sketchbook can have the same story line, or create your own. Make your Sketchbook with regular paper or construction paper. Bind it with staples. **Drawing your ideas is important**. Putting all your creations in logical order will help make your book a special project to share with others.*

Dinotopia (Applying Originality While Using the Familiar) PAGE 2

COVER BACK *You may wish to include another picture on the back.* A good size for your Journal would be 3½" wide by 5" tall. This would let you staple your Journal in the middle with a standard stapler.

COVER FRONT *Title your sketchbook and claim authorship.* These sample pages are in folio form. If you page your Journal the same, it will come out a 6-page booklet with a cover where pages 1 to 6 are in order once it's stapled together.

Introduce Your New World

- Where is it?
- Is it large or small?
- How is it kept from the rest of the world?
- How did you get there by accident, or on purpose?

DRAWINGS:
- A map of the world.
- The place where you come upon it.

Going Home

- How will you get home?
- Do they fix whatever you were in when you got there?
- Do you leave by magic powers?

DRAWING:
- You saying good-bye to the people.

PAGE 1 *Goes on the back of the Cover.* In order to staple your Journal in the middle, your "sheet" should measure 7" wide by 5" tall. You will fold your Journal into book form at the staple.

PAGE 6 *Goes on the back of the Back Cover.* With a 7" wide sheet, you can staple it at 3½" (in the middle) and then fold it in.

PAGE 3 (Applying Originality While Using the Familiar) **Dinotopia**

Resolving the Problem

- Do you help the people with their problem?
- Do you help the people fight the Beast?
- Do the people agree to help you get home?

DRAWINGS:
- You helping solve the problem.
- You helping fight the Beast.

The People There

- Are you found by people?
- Are you found by the Beast?
- Who lives here and where did they come from?
- Are they living in harmony with the Beast?
- Are they afraid of the Beast?

DRAWINGS:
- People greeting you with the Beast(s).
- People showing you a picture of the Beast.

PAGE 5 *Goes on the back of Page 4.* It will be better to write and draw on the front and back of your sheet. Pasting one sheet on the back of the other will work, but it also makes it harder to fold. It might also warp or bunch up.

PAGE 2 *Goes on the back of Page 3.* If you plan to paste one sheet on the back of another—and you don't want it to warp or bunch—fold it first and then paste it with the pieces folded over.

The Beast(s) There

- What does the Beast or many beasts look like?
- Does it help or hinder the people there?
- Where does the Beast live?
- What special powers (if any) does it have?

DRAWINGS:
- The Beast in its home.
- The Beast with people.

Directed to a Special City

- People in the special city can help you get home, but they have a problem to solve first.
- Are the people in the special city preparing to fight the Beast?
- Can you help the people?

DRAWING:
- A view of the special city.

PAGE 3 *Is the left hand page in the middle of your booklet.* Whether a single sheet or two sheets pasted together, your pages might "ride" after folding. Riding means the inside sheets will pop out beyond the outer edge of your cover.

PAGE 4 *Is the right hand page in the middle of your booklet.* Make sure what you put on the edges of your cover and pages won't disappear when cutting the "riding" pages to make the edge of the booklet even.

Dinotopia (Applying Originality While Using the Familiar) PAGE 4

BUILDING YOUR OWN SKETCHBOOK JOURNAL

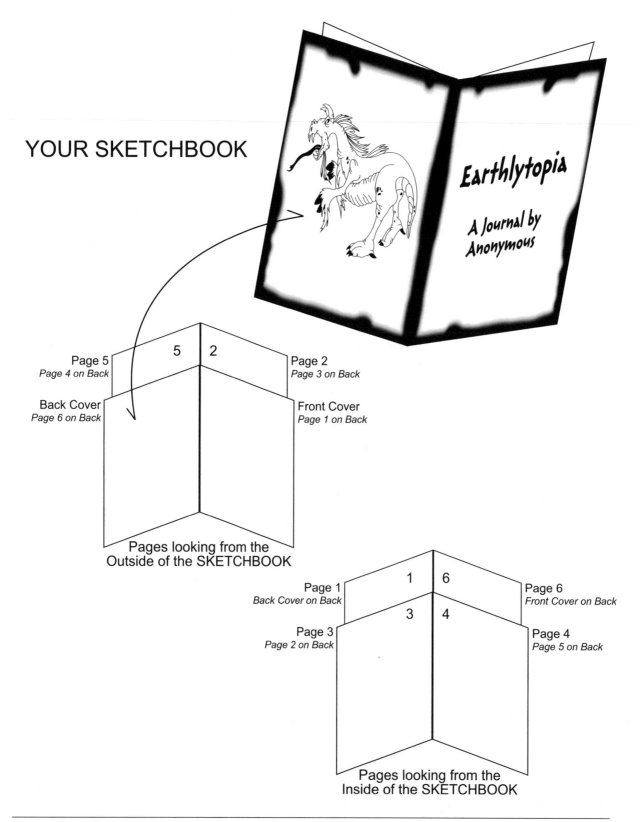

YOUR SKETCHBOOK

Earthlytopia

A Journal by Anonymous

Page 5
Page 4 on Back

5   2

Page 2
Page 3 on Back

Back Cover
Page 6 on Back

Front Cover
Page 1 on Back

Pages looking from the
Outside of the SKETCHBOOK

Page 1
Back Cover on Back

1   6

Page 6
Front Cover on Back

Page 3
Page 2 on Back

3   4

Page 4
Page 5 on Back

Pages looking from the
Inside of the SKETCHBOOK

Quests and Destinies
Overview in Brief

QUESTS

A staple plot device, destiny stories involve a journey towards a specific, predetermined goal. The quest journey usually begins with the hero far from his objective which requires travel through beautiful landscapes and enchantment. More often than not, the hero must traverse through adverse physical barriers like crossing a bottomless chasms or a fire-breathing dragon blocking the only way through the canyon.

Quests also deal with internal enlightenment. It may be a quest for self-purification against temptation or wanting to find a religious meaning or artifact. On the opposite end of the spectrum there are quests for riches and power. Heroic quests have the main character looking for a lost love or saving others from peril. And in most quest stories, the hero may face many a distraction (possibly a love interest) or self-questioning of his reasons for the quest.

DESTINIES

When looking at a dictionary definition for destiny it will say "see fate." When looking at a dictionary definition for fate and it will say "see destiny." Quickly realizing the two are one in the same (and after a big sigh), **Fantasy Genre** identifies destiny and fate as:

The words and their origins help describe the two. Fate comes from the word *fatality* meaning a decree made by fate, or the quality of doom because of disaster or death. Destiny comes from the word *destination* meaning a place one is going to or the intended purpose for someone.

Destiny in literature often associates with religious belief. One must also believe in the concept to act on it. If the hero doesn't believe it's his destiny to become captain of the ship, he won't endure and overcome the many hurdles it may take to be captain. A sense of "my right" accompanies a person's belief in destiny. If the heroine believes it's her right to be queen, she'll work the harder for it. Of course it's this determination and confidence that probably assists in achieving this destiny, but without the "destiny seed" planted in the mind to begin with, the outcome could tell differently.

Fate is a fixed, unchangeable line of events predetermined and enforced by an outside entity or agency. Fate weighs heavily with doom and despair—if it's going to happen, why bother trying to do anything about it?

Destiny promotes a more positive attitude and an unflinching persistence.

Quests and Destinies
Overview in Brief *(continued)*

A Word About THE FATES—The Fates pop up from time to time even in modern literature. They are a Greek mythological creation to explain certain predicaments and outcomes. Taking form of women, the Three Fates are responsible for certain abstractions; Clotho spins threads representing each individual life; Lachesis weaves each thread into a pattern, representing the course of life; and Atropos cuts off the thread with shears. Omniscient and referred to or associated with Oracles at times, the Three Fates—not terribly bright—unwillingly offer information. Traditionally, approaching The Fates is one's last resort. The Nordic Fates (cognates) rule the past, present, and future.

MILESTONE, CLASSIC, AND INFLUENTIAL LITERATURE WORKS CONCERNING QUESTS AND DESTINIES

Homer's THE ODYSSEY (850 B.C.)
Jason seeks the Golden Fleece

THE SEVEN VOYAGES OF SINBAD
(From ONE THOUSAND AND ONE ARABIAN NIGHTS) (1500)
Sinbad the Sailor has numerous fantastic adventures during his voyages throughout the seas east of Africa and south of Asia.

Thomas Malory's LE MORTE DARTHUR (1485)
Includes Arthur's Knights of the Round Table, and the Quest for the Holy Grail.

Algernon Blackwood's BY WATER (1914)
A man told to fear water dies in the desert.

John O'Hara's APPOINTMENT IN SAMARRA (1934)
Sophisticated novel about Julian running away from Death to Samarra only to find Death has a prior appointment with him there.

Dante Alighieri's THE DIVINE COMEDY (Around 1315)
Epic poem about the here-after. Such a classic piece of literature, its been influential in the thoughts of what an afterlife is like in Christian belief.

John Bunyan's THE PILGRIM'S PROGRESS (1678-1679)
More than a historical novel, it also includes an internal quest for truth and enlightenment of the main character.

(2006 © Joan Garner) **WINGS OF FANCY:** Using Readers Theatre to Study Fantasy Genre

Seeking the Green Children

Based on an accounting by William of Newburgh
Original story by Joan Garner

—BACKGROUND INFORMATION
(genre classification and other data deemed useful)

Like the legend of King Arthur, there might be a shred of truth to the story of the GREEN CHILDREN. In investigating this footnote of a tale, two primary versions come to light. What makes the stories themselves equally intriguing is the wide gap of time between the two accounts; one in the 12th and the other in the 19th Century.

The latter rendition takes place in 1887 with the discovery of two strange children in a field near Banjos, Spain. The children speak an unfamiliar language and wear metallic-like clothing. However, the most peculiar feature of the children is their green skin.

With the children terrified and inconsolable, the field hands take them to Banjos where the townsfolk care for them. The boy dies shortly afterwards, but the girl lives for five years. During this time, her skin slowly turns to a more natural Caucasian color.

When the girl learns to speak the native tongue, she tells her caregivers she and her brother came from a land of perpetual twilight where everyone possesses the green skin. When questioned on why they were near the village, she said the two siblings heard a loud noise, felt pushed through—something, and found themselves coming out of the caverns near the village.

The more concrete story comes from William of Newburgh, an English monk of Newburgh, Yorkshire of the late 1100's. As William records it, farmers find a weeping girl and boy in a field near Suffolk, England and take them to Sir Richard de Calne of Woolpit.

In this telling, the children again speak an unknown language and wear unusual

clothing. They refuse to eat at first, but then accept green vegetables and have a liking to green beans once shown how to open the stalks. (Here the two stories merge into a similar telling.)

Subsequent theories offer explanations to this fantastic occurrence:

One presumes the children are from a neighboring village and that malnourishment caused their skin to turn green. Another theory suggests the boy and girl are aliens. Finally, it's reasoned the children were orphaned during civil strife where Flemish immigrants are persecuted (which would explain the unfamiliar language and clothes).

As for the green color of their skin, it might have been the result of "green sickness," a name of old given to describe an anemic condition resulting from dietary deficiencies.

Whatever the case, it makes for an interesting story and entertaining Readers Theatre script.

— SYNOPSIS OF STORY

(18th Century—France) Field hands find two frightened children and take them to the nearby town. Speculation abounds to whom the children are and why they happen to be green. Because of their green color, it's suggested they're enchanted. And once decided the enchanted children would bring good luck, the town people bicker over who will take care of them (believing they will then come into good fortune).

Although this reasoning comes true for two of the families who have cared for the strange children, this enchantment changes once the GREEN CHILDREN start to eat normal foods and their skin begins to turn a more natural color— much to the chagrin of the families who were waiting to care for the kids.

Seeking the Green Children
STAGING SUGGESTIONS AND HELPFUL HINTS

—GLOSSARY
(terms possibly unfamiliar to reader)

COMMOTION—Noise. A racket.

MARQUIS—A nobleman usually from France.

MONSIEUR—"Mr." in the French language.

— CHARACTER DESCRIPTIONS

GREEN CHILDREN: (Female and Male) A young girl and boy. The girl is a year or two older. They should look sickly (besides being green).

BOBBET: (Female) A field worker. Uneducated and a bit crude, but nice.

CLAUDE: (Male) A field worker.

MONSIEUR HUGANO: (Male) Old and grumpy.

MADAME HUGANO: (Female) Old and sweet.

MOMMA DULAC: (Female) I bit weary, but nice.

PAPA DULAC: (Male) Hard worker, but greedy.

PAPA PERALT: (Male) Hard worker, but greedy.

MAMMA PERALT: (Female) Kindly and companionate.

MARQUIS GERARD: Wise, fair, and gentlemanly.

JACQUES: (Male) A regular boy in his teen years.

LOUISA: (Female) A smart girl in her early teens.

— PRESENTATION SUGGESTIONS
(18th Century European Clothing and Items)

COSTUMES *(18th Century Wear)*
TOWN FOLK—Peasant hats, caps and bonnets. Shawls and vests.

MARQUIS GERARD—Dark clothes with a large, floppy bow tie.

GREEN GIRL—Green blouse and long skirt. Gloves and hat.

GREEN BOY—Green shirt and pants. Gloves and cap.

* Having the **GREEN CHILDREN** dress in green clothes will help suggest they are green (without the use of green makeup). To help convey this visual more, it's suggested that no one else in the cast wear green. If wanting a more visual depiction of the green children, it's suggested taking two strips of green cloth and banding one strip around the crown of the head and wrapping the other over the chin and top of the head (a la Marley's Ghost in A CHRISTMAS CAROL). When it's noticed the **CHILDREN** are "not so green anymore," unwrap the second strip of cloth and stick it in a pocket, or hold it behind the back.

LIGHTING EFFECTS
If possible, have your light source dim to low and then back up to normal lighting. Or switch the lights off for a few seconds to show time passing and then back on when the action resumes.

STAGE
Because of the large cast, placing some of the PLAYERS on RAISED PLATFORMS will help to open the area.

STAGING
Again, because of the large cast, little movement is suggested.

STAGING
STAGE RIGHT　　　　　　　　　　　　　　　　　　　**STAGE LEFT**

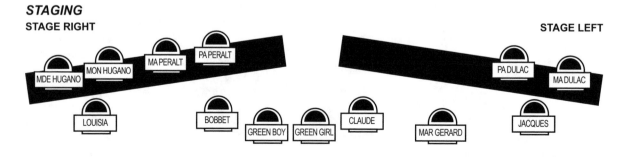

Seeking the Green Children
SCRIPT

SETTING
France. 18th Century. The Town Square of Cree.

*(The **HUGANO, DULAC** and **PERALT FAMILIES** as well as the **MARQUIS** have their backs to the audience. **BOBBET** and **CLAUDE** bring the **GREEN BOY** and **GIRL** from upstage center to downstage center. The **GREEN CHILDREN** are shaking from fright and crying loudly.)*

CLAUDE
I'm telling you, Bobbet, we need to take them to the marquis.

BOBBET
And I'm telling you, Claude, we should have left the creatures near the cave they came out of.

CLAUDE
They are *not* creatures, Bobbet.

BOBBET
Yes, they are. They're howling green creatures and we touched them. Who knows what will happen to us now.

*(The **CHILDREN** cry loudly. **MADAME** and **MONSIEUR HUGANO** turn around to face the audience.)*

MONSIEUR HUGANO
What is going on here?

MADAME HUGANO
We heard such a commotion in the town square here, we came out of the house to see what was the matter.

CLAUDE
We found these children, Madame Hugano.

MONSIEUR HUGANO
My goodness, they're green!

BOBBET
Yes, Monsieur. I think they must be demons.

*(The **DULAC FAMILY** turn to face the audience.)*

MAMMA DULAC *(Blustering.)*
Demons! What are you doing bringing demons to our village, Bobbet?!

BOBBET
It wasn't my idea, it was Claude's.

PAPA DULAC
We should get the marquis. He'll know what to do.

*(The **PERALT FAMILY** turn to face the audience.)*

PAPA PERALT
What is all of this?

MAMMA PERALT
Look, Papa, they're green. Louisa, don't get too close to them, they must be bewitched.

BOBBET
I think so, Madame Peralt.

*(**MARQUIS GERARD** turns around to face the audience.)*

MARQUIS GERARD
Where did they come from?

PAPA HUGANO
Marquis Gerard, we're glad you're here. Bobbet and Claude found these green children near the cave.

MARQUIS GERARD
How extraordinary. The poor little fellows seem quite terrified. Children, are you lost? Where are your parents?

CLAUDE
We have tried to talk to them, my lord. They talk, but it's gibberish to us.

JACQUES
Gibberish? Isn't gibberish the language of the devil, Mamma?

*(All the townsfolk begin to talk among themselves about the possibility of the **CHILDREN** being demons. The **GREEN CHILDREN** huddle together and cry more because of the commotion.)*

MARQUIS GERARD
Hush—hush now, all of you. No wonder these poor children are scared to death. Everyone step back and let me talk to them.

*(**EVERYONE** except **MARQUIS GERARD** and the **CHILDREN** take one step back.)*

MARQUIS GERARD *(Continued.)*
Children, please. No one means you any harm. Children, can you tell me where you're from? We'll try to return you home if you can tell us where you're from.

*(The **GREEN CHILDREN** just cower with fear while listening to **MARQUIS GERARD**.)*

LOUISA
Mamma, I don't believe they are demons at all. If anything, I think they're enchanted.

PAPA DULAC
Enchanted? Do you suppose?

JACQUES
Enchanted? How?

LOUISA
I don't know. But if they are enchanted, it could be good thing. They could bring good luck or great fortune.

PAPA DULAC
Great fortune?

LOUISA
They could.

MARQUIS GERARD
What nonsense.

MAMMA HUGANO
But they *are* green. Explain that.

PAPA PERALT
I think we should take them into our home.

PAPA DULAC
No, they should come be with us.

CLAUDE
I don't think they will go with any of you. We had a most difficult time just getting them here.

BOBBET
And we touched them and now I'm feeling ever so strange.

CLAUDE
Oh, you do not. You're being silly.

MAMMA DULAC
Jacques, offer the boy your apple. They're probably hungry.

JACQUES *(Offering the **GREEN BOY** an **APPLE**.)*
Here, boy. Do you want an apple?

*(The **GREEN BOY** coils behind the **GREEN GIRL**.)*

MADAM HUGANO *(Pulling a **BISCUIT** from her pocket and offering it.)*
Children, I have a yummy cookie. Would you like it?

*(The **GREEN CHILDREN** hold onto each other—more frightened than ever, if that's possible.)*

MAMMA PERALT
Maybe they don't like food. If they are enchanted children, maybe they don't *need* food.

PAPA DULAC
Still, I think we should take them home with us.

PAPA PERALT
Dulac, you only want them with you because you think they'll bring you great fortune.

PAPA DULAC
Well, so do you, Peralt.

MARQUIS GERARD
It *is* a good idea to get them inside. They look cold. Perhaps if we give them a warm place to sleep, they will feel better when awake and can tell us who they are.

MAMMA DULAC
Yes—very wise, Marquis Gerard. *(Motioning.)* Come, children, we'll take you home.

MONSIEUR HUGANO
But you already have a child, Madame Dulac. My wife and I have been childless all these many years. *We* should be the ones to take them in.

MAMMA DULAC
But our Louisa was the one who realized the children are enchanted. They should come with us.

MAMMA PERALT
No! They should come with me!

(2006 © Joan Garner) **WINGS OF FANCY**: Using Readers Theatre to Study Fantasy Genre

(The three sets of families argue with one another about whom should get the GREEN CHILDREN.)

MARQUIS GERARD
Wait! Stop it now! Stop it all of you!

(Everyone settles down.)

MARQUIS GERARD *(Continued.)*
The children will go with the Dulac family. This is my decision.

MAMMA DULAC
Thank you, my lord. We'll take very good care of the children. You have my word on it. Bobbet and Claude, you come with us as well and we'll have supper.

> *(MAMMA and PAPA DULAC, and JACQUES turn back around so they no longer face the audience BOBBET and CLAUDE place a gentle hand on the GREEN CHILDREN and then the four of them turn around to no longer face the audience.)*

MONSIEUR HUGANO
It isn't fair. We should have gotten the children.

PAPA PERALT
One of us, for sure.

LOUISA
Well, we'll find out soon enough if the children are enchanted or not.

* LIGHTING EFFECTS
The lights dim or go out for two or three seconds.

> *(When the lights come back on, BOBBET and CLAUDE turn back around to face the audience.)*

MAMMA PERALT
Bobbet, how are the children doing? Do you know?

BOBBET
The girl is doing better, but the boy is not.

MADAME HUGANO
It's been four days. Are they still not eating?

CLAUDE
Mamma Dulac told me they are eating some vegetables. They especially like the green beans once Jacques showed them how to shuck the stalks.

PAPA PERALT
And the family?

(The DULAC FAMILY turns back around with the GREEN CHILDREN to face the audience.)

MAMMA DULAC *(Excited.)*
Good news! Good news! We just learned Papa's uncle has left him all his wealth.

PAPA DULAC
I didn't even know I had an uncle, little alone a rich one. And now I'm his heir. Isn't it remarkable?

PAPA PERALT
I knew it! I knew those kids would bring good luck. Well, it's our turn. We should get the kids so some of that luck rubs off on us.

MONSIEUR HUGANO
What of us? By all rights, it's our turn.

MAMMA PERALT
What makes you say that?

MADAME HUGANO
We were the first ones in the town to see them.

PAPA PERALT
If that isn't the most ridiculous reason I've ever heard.

BOBBET
Say here, what about us? Claude and I found them in the first place.

CLAUDE
That's right. We should get them.

> *(Everyone except the GREEN CHILDREN begin to argue again. MARQUIS GERARD turns back around to face the audience.)*

MARQUIS GERARD
Friends! Friends, please!

> *(EVERYONE settles down again.)*

MARQUIS GERARD *(Continued.)*
My goodness, what a fuss you're all making. What's the matter this time?

PAPA PERALT
Hugano and I believe it's our turn to take care of the green children.

MONSIEUR HUGANO
That's right. The Dulac's have their fortune now. It's our turn.

CLAUDE
What about us?

MARQUIS GERARD
All right. It's clear the children should go to someone else before there's a riot in the streets. But who should get them?
(Thinking.)
I shall think of a number between one and twenty. The person coming closet to my number shall get the children for three days. Fair enough?

*(Everyone except the **GREEN CHILDREN** nod their heads agreeing.)*

MARQUIS GERARD *(Continued.)*
Peralt, give me a number.

PAPA PERALT
Nineteen.

MARQUIS GERARD
Bobbet?

BOBBET
Twelve.

MARQUIS GERARD
Claude?

CLAUDE
Fifteen.

MARQUIS GERARD
And you, Hugano?

MONSIEUR HUGANO
Last. Why am I always last? All the good numbers are already taken!

MARQUIS GERARD
Play the game or not, Hugano.

MONSIEUR HUGANO *(Grumbling.)*
Oh—three.

MARQUIS GERARD
The number I was thinking of was eighteen. Peralt, your family will have the children for three days.

*(**BOBBET, CLAUDE,** and the **HUGANOS** grunt and huff, disappointed.)*

PAPA PERALT
Excellent.

MAMMA PERALT *(Motioning.)*
Come, children. You come with us now.

*(The **PERALT FAMILY** and the **GREEN CHILDREN** turn around so their backs are to the audience.)*

MONSIEUR HUGANO
That wasn't fair. I was the last one to pick a number. I would have picked Peralt's number.

MARQUIS GERARD
Sure you would have. It was a fair game. Now everyone go home and stop complaining.

* LIGHTING EFFECTS
The lights dim or go out for two or three seconds.

*(When the lights come back on, the **GREEN CHILDREN** and **PERALT FAMILY** turn to face the audience.)*

MAMMA PERALT *(Excited.)*
Isn't it wonderful? Who would have believed we would have a buried treasure right outside our back door?

PAPA PERALT
I started digging up the dirt for this year's spring garden, and hit something hard.

MAMMA PERALT
And what do you think it was? A chest full of jewels and gold coins.

MARQUIS GERARD
It's quite remarkable, all right.

MONSIEUR HUGANO
That's enough! It's our turn with those kids!

MARQUIS GERARD
Very well, Hugano. You get the children now. But remember, only for three days.

MADAME HUGANO
Come with us, children. There's no need to be frightened. We'll take good care of you.

*(The **GREEN CHILDREN** and **HUGANOS** turn their backs to the audience.)*

PAPA DULAC
They have surely been a blessing to this town.

MARQUIS GERARD
Children are a blessing to anyone whether they're enchanted or not. We shouldn't forget that my friends.

MAMMA DULAC
The Marquis is right. Children, in any form, are a blessing.

 (2006 © Joan Garner) **WINGS OF FANCY**: Using Readers Theatre to Study Fantasy Genre

* LIGHTING EFFECTS
The lights dim or go out for two or three seconds.

(When the lights come back on, the GREEN CHILDREN and the HUGANOS turn to face the audience. This time, the CHILDREN are not so green.)

MARQUIS GERARD
Madame Hugano, I see you have the children out on this beautiful spring day. How are they doing?

MADAME HUGANO
Well, Marquis Gerald, the children are doing quite well.

MONSIEUR HUGANO *(Annoyed.)*
Huh, the children are doing very well indeed. For three days they've been eating us out of house and home. But have we gotten anything out of them? Heck, no.

MADAME HUGANO
But you're wrong, my husband. They are sweet and so helpful around the house. It's been a pleasure to have them with us. Children, tell the marquis hello.

GREEN CHILDREN
Hello.

MARQUIS GERARD *(Very pleased.)*
Well, what do you know about that? Hello, precious children. If you are learning to speak our language, perhaps in time you'll be able to tell us who you belong to.

MONSIEUR HUGANO
Then they can have them. Let someone else worry about feeding them.

LOUISA
Monsieur Hugano, have you noticed? Hasn't anyone noticed? The children—they are not so green anymore. This is why you haven't received your fortune, Monsieur.

PAPA DULAC
Louisa, you're right. This must surely be why great luck hasn't come your way, Hugano.

JACQUES
Yes, I see. They're turning to a more normal color. I wonder what's causing it.

LOUISA *(Thinking.)*
I think I may have the answer—possibly....

MAMMA DULAC
Louisa, you have always been such a clever girl. What do you think is the matter?

LOUISA
Madame Hugano, what have you been feeding the children?

MADAME HUGANO
Why just crepes and porridge; some salted crackers, and cauliflower with milk to drink.

LOUISA
Well, there you go—all white foods. That's why they're turning white. They're eating white foods.

MONSIEUR HUGANO
Mamma, you crazy woman. What are you doing feeding them cauliflower?!

MARQUIS GERARD
Surely you're not going to start feeding these children green foods again just so you can come into fortune.

PAPA DULAC
They did like those beans.

PAPA PERALT
And broccoli. They especially liked our broccoli.

(EVERYONE but MARQUIS GERARD and the GREEN CHILDREN begin discussing all kinds of green foods to feed the GREEN CHILDREN.)

MARQUIS GERARD
All right, I've had enough! Enough, I say.

(Everyone becomes quiet.)

MARQUIS GERARD *(Continued.)*
It's obvious I can't trust these children with any of you now. To stop all of this bickering and greed, I'll take the children into my home and raise them properly. And if their skin turns to a flesh color, all the better... Come with me children. I'm taking you home where you can grow up in peace. Come now.

(MARQUIS GERARD holds out his arms and the GREEN CHILDREN go to him. MARQUIS GERARD and the GREEN CHILDREN step out, stage left. The townsfolk look at one another a bit stunned, then MONSIEUR HUGANO calls after MARQUIS GERARD.)

MONSIEUR HUGANO
I know why you're taking those kids. You're going
to start feeding them green food again so you can
have good luck!

*(The townsfolk start to argue and confer
again as they exit out stage left.)*

END OF SEEKING THE GREEN CHILDREN

(2006 © Joan Garner) **WINGS OF FANCY**: Using Readers Theatre to Study Fantasy Genre

Erlic, The Giant Killer

Original Script by Joan Garner

—BACKGROUND INFORMATION
(genre classification and other data deemed useful)

FE-FI-FO-FUM, giants are a lot of fun! Placed in the **BIG 8 FANTASTIC ELEMENTS** (Entity) (see Fantasy Overview, page 1), giants have wandered through many a fantasy story. Although the most familiar giants live in fairy tales (i.e., JACK AND THE BEANSTALK, JACK THE GIANT KILLER, and THE BRAVE LITTLE TAILOR), others sprout up (pun intended) in mythology, tall tales, and the like. Giants also thunder through novels with THE LORD OF THE RINGS Trilogy and its oversized creatures coming to mind.

However, I'll offer a few theories on how giants came to be:

THEORY 1: Imagine an ancient archeologist digging up fossilized bones of a dinosaur. What would be his logical deduction? If such enormous animals once roamed the world, human beings of equal stature must have walked alongside.

THEORY 2: Take another old ancestor coming upon a large rock formation resembling the human form. Perhaps he thinks the poor super-sized person must have fallen into his present petrified predicament by some magical means.

THEORY 3: In explaining our planet's creation, and in recognizing human beings to be the only known entities capable of complex invention, then giant humans must have made the Earth.

Most mythological gods are giants like Ymir the Nordic God. Even the Bible has a giant or two in its stories. Ancient giants, though possessed of malevolence, generally bear a degree of intelligence while medieval giants eventually evolved into brutish, dim-witted man-eaters. There are benevolent giants such as Brân the Blessed who waded across the Irish Sea and Paul Bunyan who provided boomtowns of the Old West (U.S.A.) with lumber by chopping trees down with one swing of his ax. But for the most part, giants are destructive annoyances to the human race.

— SYNOPSIS OF STORY

(5th Century Germany) In their adventures, Sir Rowland and his trusty squire Erlic come upon a town recently flattened by a terrible giant. Hoping to add another item to his Knightly List of Daring Dos, *Rowland sets off to fell the giant. However, with each run at the big guy, Rowland returns with parts of his body broken. Seeing his master's physical abilities rapidly slipping, Erlic takes it upon himself to fell the giant. And he does so in a most unusual way. Add a town crier and two "knight groupies" to the mix and you have a recipe for an amusing tale.*

—GLOSSARY
(terms possibly unfamiliar to the reader)

CAPITAL—A word spoken in exclamation meaning outstanding or excellent.

CORROBORATE—To support a claim with evidence or as a witness.

EXPLOITS—An act or deed, especially a heroic or valorous one.

FRÄULEIN—"Miss" in the German language.

FRAU—"Mrs." in the German language.

Erlic, The Giant Killer
STAGING SUGGESTIONS AND HELPFUL HINTS

— CHARACTER DESCRIPTIONS

GERTRUDE: (Female) A tired individual with a dry and mundane delivery.

SIR ROWLAND: (Male) Impressed with himself. He has a goal to become the most famous knight of all, but it would help if he had more brains than bravery.

ERLIC: (Male) A squire to **ROWLAND**, he must answer his master's demands knowing he's much smarter.

OLGA and **MARTA:** (Females) Rock star groupies in the making. A little flaky.

— PRESENTATION SUGGESTIONS
(5th Century German Clothing and Items)

COSTUMES
GERTRUDE—A blouse with puffy long sleeves. A long skirt. A shawl over the shoulders. A triangle piece of cloth tied over the head and hair.

ROWLAND—A quilted coat/vest of metallic silver or gold metal cloth could serve as the knight's armor. A loose weave (gray) sweater possibly resembling chain mail underneath or a turtleneck shirt. Long pants. He should also wear a belt to hold his sword. If wearing boots such as hiking or weather boots, tuck pant legs into top of boots.

ERLIC—A ragged square piece of cloth for a poncho tied with large leather belt around the middle. Turtleneck, long sleeved shirt underneath. Long pants. If wearing boots such as hiking or weather boots, tuck pant legs into top of boots.

OLGA and **MARTA**—Long sleeved, puffy blouses with long skirt. Bare feet. (If they can dress exactly alike, the better.)

PROPS
BAG—Stuffed old pillow case or cloth sack.

SCROLL—Parchment like paper attached to a paper towel or foil wrap cardboard roll.

SWORD—Made of wood or purchased.

HORSE—**ROWLAND** can sit atop a tall stool (no back) as his HORSE. The STOOL/HORSE should slide easily across the floor.

SOUND EFFECTS
A student can stand behind the LEFT WALL and roar like the giant. Roaring into a microphone would enhance the effect. Make thud noises by banging on items.

STAGE
TOWER—Small stool or desk for **GERTRUDE** to stand on (decorated to look like a castle tower).

WALLS—Sight barriers at stage left and right. By supposedly hiding the giant from sight at stage left, it isn't necessary to try to create/show him in one form or other.

STAGING
ROWLAND and **ERLIC** need to exit and enter when fighting the giant.

Upon entering, **ERLIC** can slide **ROWLAND** in on his HORSE. This will stress his labors.

ROWLAND still needs to move after breaking his arm, leg, and neck. Simply flopping the leg and arm about as if they are limp and useless should do. And as suggested in the script's narrative, a tilted head will demonstrate his broken neck.

GERTRUDE needs to look offstage left when describing the fighting between the giant and the two fellows.

STAGING

STAGE RIGHT   **STAGE LEFT**

TOWER

RIGHT WALL   GERTRUDE   OLGA   MARTA   LEFT WALL
                            ROWLAND   ERLIC

Erlic, The Giant Killer
SCRIPT

SETTING
Germany. 11th Century.

(The main road to a small hamlet and castle.
FRAU GERTRUDE stands atop a tower that
appears likely to fall down any minute. Other
signs of ruin and destruction lay about.)

GERTRUDE
Hear-ye! Hear ye! Ten o'clock and as you can
see, all is not well. This is Frau Gertrude filling
in for my late husband Hintz who was stepped
on and squished last night. In case you haven't
noticed, a terrible giant passed through yesterday
and smashed everything to smithereens… By the
way, I'm fine in case anyone wants to know.

(SIR ROWLAND and SQUIRE ERLIC enter
from upstage center to downstage center.
ERLIC carries a large bundle on his back.)

ROWLAND
I say, Erlic, isn't it a wonderful day?

ERLIC
Wonderful for you, Sir Rowland—you're not the
one walking and carrying all your gear.

ROWLAND
I can't help it if I'm of nobility and you're not. One
must know one's place, Erlic.

ERLIC
Yes, my lord. You're the valorous knight and I'm
just your lowly squire.

ROWLAND
Now you've got it.

ERLIC
Still, it wouldn't be so bad if we didn't have to keep
going over these potholes in the road. First it's
down and then it's up and then it's down again
and then it's up again. It's exhausting.

ROWLAND
You're right about that, squire. I don't believe I've
ever seen a road in such disrepair. It's shameful
on the part of the local civil engineers—simply
shameful.

ERLIC
Yes, my lord.

ROWLAND
Anyway, it's a good day to complete a brave feat
on my list. What have we left to do, Erlic?

ERLIC
Let's see….

(ERLIC pulls out a SCROLL from under his
poncho. When he opens it to read, the end
drops to the ground and rolls out several feet.)

ERLIC *(Continued. Reading.)*
"Sir Rowland's Knightly List of Daring Dos." Um:
save a damsel in distress; joust with an evil
knight and win; slay a three-headed dragon;
single-handedly lay siege to a castle owned by an
ornery warlord; swim the Atlantic Ocean; move a
mountain; and save the whales.

ROWLAND
Capital! I wonder which of those we'll do today.

ERLIC *(Rolling up the SCROLL.)*
Well, since we're in the middle of Germany, I think
swimming the Atlantic Ocean is out.

ROWLAND
Yes, I suppose we need to save that one for
another time. Still, there must be something we
can do here.

(ROWLAND looks about to find something
when he spots GERTRUDE.)

ROWLAND *(Continued.)*
Hark, a fair damsel in yonder tower. Wouldn't it be
keen if she were in distress?

ERLIC *(Looking up at GERTRUDE.)*
She doesn't look in distress to me.

ROWLAND
One can never tell. These things can be tricky,
you know.
     (Calling up to GERTRUDE.)
Say, fair damsel, would you happen to be in
distress?

GERTRUDE
Happen to be? What does it look like?

ROWLAND (*Aside to* **ERLIC**.)
I told you these things were tricky.
    (*To* **GERTRUDE**.)
I am Sir Rowland, knight extraordinaire and this is my squire, Erlic. How may we service you?

ERLIC
We? What's with this *we* business?

GERTRUDE
Well, I guess you could go kill the giant that passed through here.

ERLIC (*Alarmed.*)
Giant!

GERTRUDE
Uh, huh. He took the whole town by surprise last night.

ROWLAND
Capital. Erlic, we shall go kill this giant.

ERLIC
There you go with that *we* stuff again.

ROWLAND
As my squire, it's your duty to come along.

ERLIC
My lord, you haven't even asked how big this giant is. Don't you think that would be a good thing to know how big he is? Because if he's a really big guy, he might be too big for one knight to fell.

ROWLAND
Big or small, I shall cut him down with my trustee sword and save the countryside of this peril.

ERLIC
But a giant, my lord—killing a giant isn't on your list.

GERTRUDE
What list?

ERLIC (*Letting* **GERTRUDE** *see the* SCROLL.)
Sir Rowland's Knightly List of Daring Dos.

GERTRUDE
Nightly list? Can't he do them during the day?

ERLIC
Not bedtime night—knightly as in valorous knight.

GERTRUDE
You're kidding.

ROWLAND
Never fear, dear damsel. I shall do my knightly duty.

GERTRUDE
Nightly duty? Are you going to put out the cat?

ERLIC
You're not getting this, are you?

        (**OLGA** *and* **MARTA** *step in from stage left.*)

MARTA
Look, Olga, a knight.

        (**ROWLAND** *smiles and bows before* **OLGA** *and* **MARTA**.)

ROWLAND
Ladies.

OLGA
Are you a famous knight? Do we know you?

ROWLAND
Sir Rowland at your service.

MARTA
Rowland? Never head of you. Are you sure you're not Sir Galahad or Ivanhoe? We know those knights.

ERLIC
He couldn't very well be either of those knights since both lived a long time ago and are no longer alive.

MARTA
Well, at least he's a knight. He's a rather handsome knight, Olga. Won't he do?

OLGA
Well… I suppose a nobody knight is better than no knight at all. I mean, he could become famous.

ERLIC
What are you two talking about?

MARTA
Olga and I have decided to follow a famous knight around.

ERLIC
Why?

OLGA
We don't know. We just decided to do it.

ROWLAND
I think it's an excellent idea. I'll need witnesses to corroborate my daring dos. Fräuleins, you may join us.

(MARTA and OLGA squeal in delight and jump up and down with excitement.)

ROWLAND
Capital! Then to the giant!

MARTA and **OLGA** *(Alarmed, they abruptly stop.)*
Giant?

ERLIC
Sir Rowland is going to kill a giant.

MARTA
Isn't that a tad difficult to do?

ROWLAND
Tot-tot, nothing to it.

* SOUND EFFECTS
A terrible roar.

GERTRUDE *(Looking out stage left.)*
I see him. The giant is coming back! Everyone head for the hills!

ERLIC *(Heading out stage right.)*
Good idea.

ROWLAND *(Grabbing **ERLIC'S** collar.)*
Steady, man.

ERLIC
But my lord, the Fräuleins are right. This is much too difficult and dangerous.

ROWLAND
Tosh, Erlic.

(ROWLAND gets off his HORSE. MARTA and OLGA step to ROWLAND and make a fuss.)

MARTA
He's so brave.

OLGA
And strong.

ROWLAND
Fräuleins, please. You're keeping me from my knightly duty.

MARTA
Nightly duty?

OLGA
Are you putting out the cat?

ERLIC *(Siding up to **ROWLAND**.)*
Don't grow them terribly bright in these parts, do they?

(ROWLAND steps forward and puffs himself up while drawing his sword.)

ROWLAND
Here I come, you big bad giant.

(ROWLAND exits stage left.)

* SOUND EFFECTS
Several loud roars, banging and bumping.

(Looking out stage left, GERTRUDE begins to tell of the action taking place offstage as if she's a ringside announcer at a boxing match.)

GERTRUDE
I can see them. Here comes the giant and—he's picking Sir Rowland up with one hand. Rowland hacks away at the giant's little finger and—oh, the giant drops him to the ground.

* SOUND EFFECTS
Thud.

GERTRUDE *(Continued.)*
Sir Rowland scrabbles around on the ground while the giant tries to step on him and—oh, Sir Rowland just stabbed the giant's big toe.

* SOUND EFFECTS
Great big roar.

GERTRUDE *(Continued.)*
And now the giant kicks Rowland….

(ROWLAND renters flying through the air and landing in front of ERLIC, OLGA, and MARTA. The three help ROWLAND to his feet.)

MARTA
Oh dear, are you hurt?

ROWLAND *(Standing with a limp arm.)*
Not at all. I believe he just broke my arm… Not at all.

ERLIC
Now will you stop, my lord?

(ROWLAND moves his SWORD from his injured hand to his good one.)

ROWLAND
Nonsense. I still have one good arm… Here I come again, terrible giant. Prepare yourself.

(ROWLAND exits stage left.)

GERTRUDE
And here we are in the second round. Rowland charges in and—oh, the giant picks him up by the seat of his pants and….

* SOUND EFFECTS
Large laughter.

GERTRUDE *(Continued.)*
The giant is laughing at poor Rowland who is just dangling there.

OLGA
How rude.

GERTRUDE
And now—oh, the giant tosses the knight to the ground again.

> *(**ROWLAND** reenter flying in again and landing once more in front of **ERLIC**, **OLGA**, and **MARTA**.)*

ERLIC *(Helping **ROWLAND** to stand.)*
My lord, please stop this. He's too big for you.

ROWLAND *(Standing with a limp arm and leg.)*
No one is too big for a knight of pure heart... I do believe he broke my leg.

MARTA
He's so brave.

ROWLAND
Once more, giant.

> *(**ROWLAND** limps out stage left.)*

GERTRUDE
All right, we're back. Rowland faces the giant and brings his sword down. Now the giant flicks Rowland away with his finger. Now the knight charges back. What valor, what bravery—

ERLIC
—What an idiot!

* SOUND EFFECTS
Another roar.

> *(**ROWLAND** reenters flying in and falling before everyone again. When the Fräuleins help him, **ROWLAND'S** head tilts to one side.)*

OLGA
Are you all right?

ROWLAND
I say, I do believe he broke my neck this time.

ERLIC
Oh, for Pete's sake, enough of this!

> *(**ERLIC** grabs **ROWLAND'S** sword and stomps offstage left.)*

OLGA
What can he do? He's only a squire.

ROWLAND *(Calling out stage left.)*
Erlic, come back here. You're only a squire.

GERTRUDE
Here we are, little Erlic is walking right up to the giant.

MARTA
Wow, that's sorta' brave, isn't it? I mean for a squire?

GERTRUDE
Now Erlic is motioning for the giant to come down to his level like he wants to say something to the big guy.

OLGA
What's happening? What's happening?

GERTRUDE
It looks like the giant is bending down to hear what Erlic has to say.

ROWLAND
Really? How extraordinary.

OLGA
What now, Gertrude? What's going on now?

GERTRUDE
Erlic is talking to the giant and—

* SOUND EFFECTS
A loud and painful roar.

GERTRUDE *(Continued.)*
—Oh my, Erlic just poked the giant in the eye! The giant's rearing up on his heels. My, he's a big lug. Now the giant's holding his eye and stumbling back.

ROWLAND
What of Erlic?

GERTRUDE
I don't see him.

ROWLAND *(Calling out to **ERLIC**.)*
Be careful, Erlic. He's good at stepping on things.

* SOUND EFFECTS
More roaring.

GERTRUDE
The giant is stumbling back to the cliff. He's—whoops, no he—yes, he's—no, he's….

* SOUND EFFECTS
A roar that fades away.

GERTRUDE *(Continued.)*
Whoa, the giant just fell off the thousand foot cliff.

(ERLIC comes running in and past everyone.)

ROWLAND
You did it, man.

ERLIC
No time to talk. I have a very angry giant after me.

GERTRUDE
But you did it, Erlic! You killed the giant. He fell off the cliff.

ERLIC *(Stopping.)*
Are you serious?

GERTRUDE
No one could survive a fall like that—even a giant.

(OLGA and MARTA hover around ERLIC now.)

OLGA
Oh, Erlic, you're so brave.

GERTRUDE
Hurray for Erlic the giant killer! The whole hamlet will celebrate your daring feat. Well, what's left of the hamlet.

ROWLAND *(He offers his limp arm and hand.)*
Yes, well done. I'd shake your hand, but as you can see....

ERLIC
You wish to congratulate me? But I'm just a lowly squire and you're a knightly knight.

ROWLAND
True enough, but you did a courageous thing today and saved many people. Perhaps it's better to realize what is in one's heart than it is to know one's place.

ERLIC
Thank you, my lord. I just used a little common sense.

ROWLAND
Thank *you*, my boy. Now if you'd be good enough to help me onto my horse, I think we need to find a doctor.

ERLIC
Gladly, my lord.

(ERLIC, MARTA, and OLGA help ROWLAND back onto his horse and push him offstage right.)

GERTRUDE
Here ye, here ye. Everyone can go home now and rest easy. Noontime is fast approaching and all is well thanks to Erlic, the giant killer. Good day and all the best to you!

END OF ERLIC, THE GIANT KILLER

Beowulf
A Man Destined to Fight Hideous Beasts

An Accounting of an EPIC POEM
Adaptation by Joan Garner

—BACKGROUND INFORMATION
(genre classification and other data deemed useful)

BEOWULF—the epic poem—required reading for upper education classes—dragons and Grendels—Geats and Swedes. In devoting an entire section of this book to quests and destinies, BEOWULF must be there. The name of a young warrior, Beowulf comes to the aid of King Hrothgar. Gruesome monsters Grendel and Grendel's Mother have attacked Hrothgar and his subjects. Killing both beasts, Beowulf later becomes king of his own people and dies fighting the Firedrake (dragon).

Although a piece of fiction, many historians believe it's based on real people and events taking place between 450 and 600 A.D. Archeologists have used the epic hero poem to unearth data about Scandinavians and later

excavations support the BEOWULF Saga. A burial mound found in 1874 revealed a powerful king placed on a bearskin rug with two dogs. He wore rich clothing and had an elaborately adorned sword at his side. Though doubtful this ancestor *was* Beowulf, it promotes my following *Fantastic Element* supposition: Does man inspire the legend or the legend inspire man?

Examination of the poem's literary merit didn't happen until 1936 when J.R.R. Tolkien wrote the article BEOWULF: THE MONSTER AND THE CRITICS. Before that, the single manuscript passed through several owners, endured a library fire, and underwent questionable translations.

This sketch concentrates on the beasts in the poem and the quest of Beowulf, an unassuming man who used his intelligence and fortitude to defeat the monsters and meet his destiny.

— SYNOPSIS OF STORY

(Medieval Denmark) Historians, heralds, and ministers stand to tell the story of Beowulf and the warrior's battles against three beasts; Grendel, Grendel's Mother, and the Firedrake. They tell how Beowulf downed the beasts and how he feared that some would call him cowardly for using his wits as much as his might to get the job done.

—GLOSSARY
(terms possibly unfamiliar to the reader)

    FEN—A bog or marsh—swampland.

        INADVERTENTLY—By way of another. Unintentional.

            INGENUITY—Cleverness. Using ones skills and imagination.

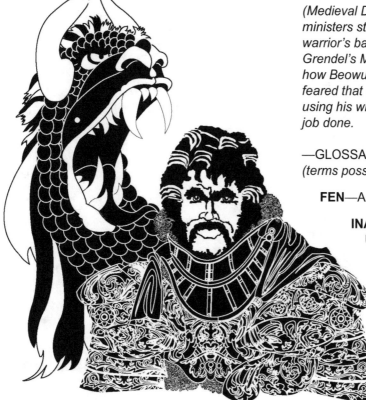

Beowulf
STAGING SUGGESTIONS AND HELPFUL HINTS

— CHARACTER DESCRIPTIONS

HISTORIANS, **MINISTERS**, and **HERALDS:**
(Either Male or Female) Can be either male or female. Should be well-spoken, sharp, and clearly heard.

STANDARDS: (Either Male or Female) Can be either male or female. Will hold the BANNERS. Will not speak.

— PRESENTATION SUGGESTIONS
(Medieval Denmark Clothing and Items)

COSTUMES
HISTORIANS and **DRUMMER**—Blue should be the main color of these outfits. The HISTORIANS should have a more elaborate costume of long coat, tunic, tights, hat and shoes of around 600 A.D. The DRUMMER will not have a hat or coat.

HERALDS and MINISTERS—Also decide a main color for each TRIAD. For instance, GRENDEL'S TRIAD would probably be green. GRENDEL'S MOTHER TRIAD purple, and the FIREDRAKE TRIAD red. The HERALDS and MINISTERS can dress alike. They should wear a long coat, tunic, tights, and shoes of around 600 A.D.

STANDARDS—No hat or coat.

PROPS
DRUM—Like a kettledrum but made of skins and wood to look old.

BANNERS—Each **STANDARD** will hold a BANNER attached to a pole. The BANNER will show a picture of the BEAST the TRIAD represents. The color of the BANNER should coordinate with that of the TRIAD.

LIGHTING EFFECTS
Spotlights shining down on the ODE and TRIADS leaving the rest of the stage dark would help establish the mood of this piece. An optional red light low in the background would help the dramatic effect as well.

SPECIAL EFFECTS
Optional fog rolling along the ground would really enhance this telling.

STAGING
Place **PLAYERS** to suggest funeral or ritual proceedings. There is no need for movement of **PLAYERS**. However, having each TRIAD take a step or two downstage before they begin their portion of the telling would help the audience focus.

* One might notice the cadence and "old flavor" of the dialogue in this sketch. This purposeful poetic telling leaves the grammar and vocabulary not entirely accurate.

STAGING

STAGE RIGHT   **STAGE LEFT**

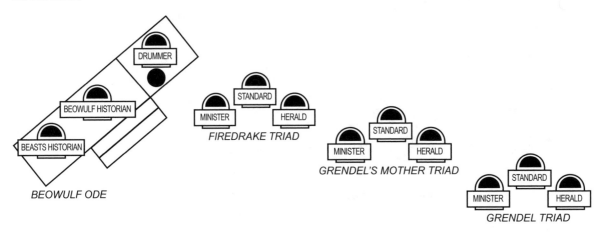

Beowulf
SCRIPT

SETTING
The Land of the Danes. A long time ago. A hillside.

*(Down, far stage right stands the **GRENDEL TRIAD**. Center, stage right stands the **GRENDEL'S MOTHER TRIAD**. Upstage, left stand the **FIREDRAKE TRIAD**. Far stage left stands the **BEOWULF ODE**.)*

DRUMMER
(Pounds his drum in a solemn cadence.)

BEOWULF HISTORIAN
This is a telling of the epic poem *Beowulf*.

BEAST HISTORIAN
It is a heroic poem about a Scandinavian prince and his conquests of hideous monsters.

BEOWULF HISTORIAN
Beowulf, brave prince, used his intelligence as much as his might against the beasts. He used his bravery as much as his calm resolve against the beasts.

BEASTS HISTORIAN
The beasts were the most foul as any before or after his time. The beasts were the most vicious and unrelenting as any before or after his time.

BEOWULF HISTORIAN
Beowulf, himself, was not a giant or god. He possessed no powers beyond mortal man, or carried enchanted weapons against these beasts.

BEASTS HISTORIAN
The beasts, themselves, did not hold special magical abilities other than largeness and strength.

BEOWULF HISTORIAN
It was man versus beast. And because this man used his common sense, and because the beasts were without, he triumphed victorious over them. Beowulf, the man.

BEASTS HISTORIAN
Grendel, Grendel's Mother, and the Firedrake, the beasts.

DRUMMER
(Pounds his drum in a solemn cadence.)

GRENDEL HERALD
King Hrothgar had built a magnificent palace he called Heorot. He hosted a great banquet to celebrate its completion. But when the feasting was over and all fell asleep, an ominous creature crept to the palace doors from the fen.

GRENDEL MINISTER
It was black and slimy with green eyes. It left a trail of mud on the ground where it crawled. Grendel's teeth rotted in crooked swirls, its red claws sprang out quickly slashing anything in its path, and its breath smoked a tremendous stench.

GRENDEL HERALD
When it entered the great hall of Heorot, the beast began to tear apart and eat all who slept there. So large was its presence, so fast was its bite and evil in its devouring ways, there was little time for anyone to react before they, too, fell consumed.

GRENDEL MINISTER
Daylight brought King Hrothgar and his Queen Wealhtheow great sorrow as they looked at the slaughter. Who could have done such an evil deed? Grendel came the name. The horrific beast Grendel from the fen is the only one who could have created such carnage. There were no more banquets—no more merriment at Heorot. They shut the door to keep the terrible monster Grendel out.

GRENDEL HERALD
Now Beowulf heard of the tragedy at Heorot and went to see if could help. Some thought he too small to fight a beast like Grendel. Some thought he very brave. Some thought he was insane.

GRENDEL MINISTER
But Beowulf waited for Grendel one fated night and when the monster came through the doors of Heorot, Beowulf jumped on its back and held on as tightly as he could. It was no easy task as the beast's scales were slimy and Grendel whipped about in powerful spasms trying to dislodge Beowulf from his back.

GRENDEL HERALD

Beowulf would not budge and in the end, he managed to tear an arm off of Grendel. With that, the beast slithered away, wailing and bleeding from having lost an arm. Grendel slithered back to the fen to die.

GRENDEL MINISTER

All hailed Beowulf's bravery and strength in facing Grendel. But now that Grendel was dead, there was another danger. For all to be safe once more, Beowulf knew he faced another ominous matter.

DRUMMER

(Pounds his drum in a solemn cadence.)

GRENDEL'S MOTHER HERALD

Beowulf knew if he killed the beast Grendel, he would also have to kill a beast fiercer than Grendel—Grendel's Mother.

GRENDEL'S MOTHER MINISTER

Beowulf traveled to the edge of a deep pool where blood bubbled on its surface. He figured Grendel had slithered down into the pool to be with his mother at his death. If he were to get to the mother, Beowulf would have to dive down into the deep pool.

GRENDEL'S MOTHER HERALD

Beowulf plunged into the pool and swam down and down until he saw a green light. No sooner had he made his way to the green light, when Beowulf felt large arms with tentacles wrapping around him.

GRENDEL'S MOTHER MINISTER

It was Grendel's Mother who had Beowulf now; a beast so bad she never received a proper name. He began to panic not knowing how much longer he could hold his breath in the murky pool. The deeper the creature took him, the tighter her arms closed about him.

GRENDEL'S MOTHER HERALD

When he could no longer hold his breath, Beowulf burst and began gasping for air. And low, there was air for him to take in. He was in the lair of Grendel's Mother. Regaining his breath, Beowulf pulled his sword and hacked at her arms. But the scales were too tough for a blade to pierce. It would be of no use for him against this beast. He would have to use his wits.

GRENDEL'S MOTHER MINISTER

So Beowulf spoke to Grendel's Mother saying, "I am Beowulf, son of Ecgtheow. I am Beowulf, who am myself. I fear you not." Beowulf's stare was entrancing and Grendel's Mother soon released her hold on him and fell asleep. Beowulf put his strong hands around her neck and strangled her. Her body began to melt. She was dead.

DRUMMER

(Pounds his drum in a solemn cadence.)

BEOWULF HISTORIAN

Now through circumstances not entirely of Beowulf's choosing, he became king of his people. He lived and ruled for forty years until the day he had to face the Firedrake.

BEAST HISTORIAN

The Firedrake, a most vile and evil creature that would haunt the places men bury treasure and the dead. It was a fire-breathing lizard of swift and deadly deed. When angered, its scaly body would swell in size, its golden eyes flash, and its tail flip and snap with damaging accuracy.

FIREDRAKE HERALD

It happened that an escaped slave did anger the Firedrake by taking a piece of treasure from its cave. With vengeance in its eyes, the Firedrake emerged from its mountaintop cave, spread its wings, and swooped down to the countryside below. Fields, houses, shops—the Firedrake's fiery breath spared nothing. When dawn came and the Firedrake withdrew back into its cave, it left the valley in nothing but ash.

FIREDRAKE MINISTER

When word got to King Beowulf, he knew he must take action against this horrible foe. His knights argued with one another about whom should face the Firedrake—not clamoring to volunteer, but suggesting the other should be the slayer. Beowulf, now old and tired, grew weary of the cowardly debate and finally said he would go and kill the Firedrake. After hearing this, twelve knights—ashamed of their complaining—offered Beowulf their swords against the Firedrake. Beowulf accepted their participation, but said swords would not be necessary. However, he could use the knights to carry the hives.

FIREDRAKE HERALD
Beowulf took young Wiglaf up the mountain. He explained his plan which Wiglaf would be a part—Beowulf's plan to kill the Firedrake. Once to the creature's cave, Beowulf had his knights set the twelve beehives down and Wiglaf slipped inside the cave with a tall stake and large glove used by the beekeeper. As Beowulf suspected, Wiglaf found the dragon sleeping after its fire burning rampage of the night before. Wiglaf hid himself and waited for Beowulf.

FIREDRAKE MINISTER
Beowulf now stepped into the Firedrake's liar and blew a horn to awaken the beast. Startled awake, the Firedrake quickly opened its mouth, preparing to spew fire on the intruder. But Wiglaf leaped out of his hiding place and stuck the tall stake upright in the Firedrake's opened mouth and tossed the beekeeper's glove in as well. He then hid himself again to watch what would happen next. Tried as it might, the Firedrake could not dislodge the stake and the glove became caught in its teeth.

FIREDRAKE HERALD
Shortly, the queen bee crawled out of the glove and made a buzzing noise. The Firedrake gasped for air and inadvertently swallowed the queen bee. But it was too late. The alarm already sounded, and thousands of bees flew out of the twelve beehives swarming into the cave. The Firedrake could do nothing but watch the bees fly into its mouth and stomach. Once there, the bees stung and stung the Firedrake until the mighty beast gave up, rolled over onto its back, and died.

FIREDRAKE MINISTER
Wiglaf emerged from his hiding place in wonder. How easy it was to kill such a ferocious beast. But when he looked to praise Beowulf's ingenuity, his heart fell. Beowulf had collapsed at the front of the cave. Wiglaf hurried to his king's side where Beowulf remarked, "If you can't best evil by strength alone, then muster a little cunning. Some may call it cowardly, but a downed beast is a downed beast."

DRUMMER
(Pounds his drum in a solemn cadence.)

BEOWULF HISTORIAN
At his death, Beowulf wondered if history would remember him as the young Beowulf who used his strength against evil or the old Beowulf who used his wits.

BEAST HISTORIAN
It should please Beowulf to know he's remembered as both—as Beowulf who killed the beasts Grendel, Grendel's Mother, and the Firedrake.

DRUMMER
(Pounds his drum in a solemn cadence.)

*LIGHTING EFFECTS
Lights dim to black.

END OF BEOWULF

Morgiana and Ali Baba

Adapted from an ARABIAN TALE
Adaptation by Joan Garner

—BACKGROUND INFORMATION
(genre classification and other data deemed useful)

Perhaps the second most popular story from the ONE THOUSAND AND ONE [ARABIAN] NIGHTS collection after ALADDIN, ALI BABA AND THE FORTY THIEVES enchants to this day. But with a few translations and retellings, it becomes clear that Ali Baba isn't the hero of the story—it's Morgiana the slave who's clever enough to avert the dangers brought on by Ali Baba's actions.

Deservedly so, this sketch features Morgiana as the true heroine of the tale and portrays Ali Baba as the simpleton he clearly is. This sketch also downplays the violence that heavily permeates the fantasy story believing it unnecessary in telling the tale.

THE ONE THOUSAND AND ONE NIGHTS or ARABIAN NIGHTS is a collection of around two-hundred folktales from Arabia, Egypt, India, Persia, and other Middle Eastern countries. In its present form, these stories originated in Arabic in around 1500 with translations by Jean Antoine Galland, John Payne, and Sir Richard Francis Burton in the 17h and 18th Centuries.

The story of the ARABIAN NIGHTS begins with Persian King Shahryar becoming so scared by his wife's infidelity, he has her killed. Then he orders his vizier to get him a new wife every night (in some versions, every third night). To avoid more infidelity, Shahryar has each new bride executed at dawn. Into this unpleasant scene comes Scheherazade (or Shahrazad or Shahrastini) who begins her wedding night by telling the king a story. At dawn she leaves her story in a cliff-hanger. Wanting to hear the end of the story, the king postpones her execution. After three years of telling stories every night (and bearing three sons), Shahryar, believing in Scheherazade's faithfulness, revokes his bride execution order.

— SYNOPSIS OF STORY

(Old Persia) Ali Baba goes into the forest to chop wood when a band of thieves approach and gather around the side of the mountain. Their leader says "Open, Sesame!" and the mountain opens. Ali Baba tries the same trick after the thieves leave and finds treasure inside the mountain. He takes his treasure and story to his brother Kassim who insists on seeing the treasure himself. However, the two brothers come upon the thieves who kill Kassim. The leader of the thieves suspects Ali Baba of stealing from him and enters the house of his brother to kill everyone there. It's left to the slave Morgiana to use her wits and common sense to save all within the household.

—GLOSSARY
(terms possibly unfamiliar to the reader)

FREELOADER—One who lives off another's assets. To take advantage of another's generosity.

Morgiana and Ali Baba
STAGING SUGGESTIONS AND HELPFUL HINTS

— CHARACTER DESCRIPTIONS

ALI BABA: (Male) A nice man with simple thoughts.

KASSIM: (Male) A good merchant, perhaps a bit impressed with his station in life.

FLORINA: (Female) A loving wife—not terribly self-assured.

MORGIANA: (Female) Intelligent and assertive. She takes charge, but may be a little too cautious and suspicious of others.

KALA: (Male) A nice young man with a good and sensible head on his shoulders.

LACCUM: (Male) Swarmy and unconvincing when trying to be sincere and genial.

— PRESENTATION SUGGESTIONS
(Old Persian Clothing and Items)

COSTUMES
THE WOMEN—Pastel blouses with long, large puffy sleeves. Pantaloons. Wide satin sash at the waist. Sandals. Jiggling jewelry for **FLORINA**. Jeweled headbands. Long hair pulled back.

ALI BABA—Kurta (a long white cotton shirt with no collar). Dark pants rolled up to half-calf height. Felt shoes with turned up toes. Turban. Short hair.

KASSIM and **KALA**—Satin blouse with long, large puffy sleeves. Wide satin sash around the waist. Pantaloons. Long sleeved, long coat. Felt shoes with turned up toes. Turban. Short hair. **KASSIM** has a mustache and goatee.

LACCUM—Black clothes like that of **KASSIM**. Full beard.

PROPS
TABLETS—Cardboard and parchments made to look like tablets of medieval times.

SACK—Plain cloth sack large enough for someone to crouch in.

JAR—Dark glass ornately decorated with jewels.

ROPE—To tie up **LACCUM** with.

GOLD COINS—Play money?

LIGHTING EFFECTS
Lights dimming to a dark (nighttime) level and then pulled back up to normal would be ideal. If switching room lights off and on, a floodlight aimed center stage will keep enough light on the action for the night scenes.

SOUND EFFECTS
For the dying men offstage, students can stand behind the RIGHT WALL and scream and moan.

STAGE
COURTYARD WALL—A partition in the back decorated to look like a Persian WALL of a house/courtyard will help the setting. This WALL also gives the **PLAYERS** more exit paths.

WALLS—Sight barriers at stage left and right.

BENCH—A cement or wooden BENCH works nicely. Nothing plastic.

STAGING
The stage directions suggests **PLAYERS** exiting stage right are going out of the main area of the house. Exiting stage left suggests **PLAYERS** are going into the house. Having **MORGIANA** exit behind the COURTYARD WALL could imply she's going into the servant quarters.

* Place a student in the SACK. **LACCUM** and **KALA** need to be strong enough to drag the SACK with the student from stage right to the side of the action.

STAGING

STAGE RIGHT   COURTYARD WALL   STAGE LEFT

RIGHT WALL   LACCUM   ALI BABA   KASSIM   FLORINA   MORGIANA   KALA   LEFT WALL

Morgiana and Ali Baba
SCRIPT

SETTING
Old Persia. A courtyard of **KASSIM'S** house.

*(**KASSIM** sits on a BENCH looking at TABLETS. His wife, **FLORINA** sits next to him and the slave **MORGIANA** stands behind them. Enter **ALI BABA** from stage right.)*

ALI BABA
Good morning to you, Brother Kassim. Florina.

KASSIM
Brother Ali Baba. What brings you to my house?

ALI BABA
I seek the shelter these walls provide.

KASSIM
Relatives... Just because I'm rich and you're poor, you expect me to take you in.

ALI BABA
I'm not a freeloader, Brother. I can pay.

*(**ALI BABA** pulls GOLD COINS from his pockets.)*

FLORINA
Ali Baba, where did you get that gold? With gold like that, you can buy your own room.

ALI BABA
I see. Then I shall seek shelter elsewhere.

KASSIM
Wait, Ali Baba. We'll let you stay for nothing if you tell us how you got that gold.

ALI BABA
I would tell you, Kassim, but I don't think you would believe me.

FLORINA
What I don't believe is how the poorest man in the village has a valuable gold piece like you're holding in your hand.

ALI BABA
I was in the oak forest chopping wood when a band of thieves rode by.

KASSIM
Did they see you?

ALI BABA
No. I hid behind the bushes. The thieves rode up to the side of a mountain and stopped. Then their leader called out, "Open, Sesame!" and the mountain opened for him.

KASSIM *(Laughing.)*
Oh, come now.

ALI BABA
It was so. And when all the thieves rode into the mountain, it closed behind them. I waited a long time until the mountain opened again. When all the thieves rode out of the mountain, the leader said, "Close," and the mountain closed up again.

FLORINA
So this magical mountain is where the thieves hide.

ALI BABA
This is what I thought. When everyone was gone, I stood before the mountainside and said, "Open, Sesame," and it opened for me.

KASSIM
Did you go in?

ALI BABA
There's a fortune in that mountain, Brother. This is where I got the gold.

KASSIM
You stole this gold from thieves?

FLORINA
Is it stealing if you steal from thieves?

KASSIM
You must show me this mountain, Ali Baba. I'll believe this fantastic story if I see it for myself. And if this magical mountain exists, you may live in this house.

ALI BABA
Thank you, Kassim. I'll be happy to show you the magical mountain.

*(**ALI BABA** and **KASSIM** exit stage right.)*

FLORINA
What do you think of Ali Baba's story, Morgiana?

MORGIANA

Mistress Florina, I'm but a humble servant. It isn't my place to say.

FLORINA

You're my most trusted servant, Morgiana. I value your opinion.

MORGIANA

I fear if these claims of Master Ali Baba are true, the men are in great danger. Thieves are also killers. If these men find Ali Baba and Kassim—

FLORINA

—I didn't think of that. *(Calling out.)* Kala! Kala, my son, please come here at once!

*(**KALA** enters from stage left.)*

KALA

What is it, Mother?

FLORINA

Your father and uncle. You must find them....

KALA

What's wrong?

FLORINA

Just bring them back as fast as you can.

*(**FLORINA** exits stage left.)*

KALA

Morgiana, what's this all about?

MORGIANA

You uncle, Ali Baba, found a treasure cave belonging to thieves. He's taking your father there now. They're headed for the oak forest.

KALA

No wonder my mother's upset. Thank you, Morgiana. Your cool head has helped me. I'll try to find them before it's too late.

*(**KALA** exits stage right.)*

MORGIANA

I must prepare the house. It might be a long night.

*(**MORGIANA** exits stage left.)*

*LIGHTING EFFECTS

Lights dim to night.

*(**FLORINA** enters from stage left with **MORGIANA** behind her.)*

FLORINA

Morgiana, I'm so worried. It's been much too long since Kala went to find his father.

*(**ALI BABA** enters from stage right. He's trembling and looks sad.)*

ALI BABA

Florina, my brother's wife.

FLORINA

Ali Baba, are you all right? Where is Kassim?

ALI BABA

It's so terrible, Florina. I'm sorry. When Kassim stood before the mountain and said, "Open, Sesame," the thieves came riding out and chopped Kassim to pieces.

FLORINA

No!

*(**FLORINA** begins to weep. While **MORGIANA** comforts her, **KALA** enters from stage right.)*

KALA

I found them too late, Mother. The dark horsemen were gone when I got there. But I must confess, after putting Father on my horse, my uncle and I went back into the cave and carried out all the treasure we could. My father's death was not to be for nothing.

FLORINA

Poor Kassim. We must prepare for a funeral.

MORGIANA

Mistress, may I speak? We must be careful with my master's death. If Ali Baba and Kala took more treasure, the thieves will be after them. We should set out oil lamps showing sickness in this house and wait to tell of Master Kassim's death for a day or two. It will look like he died of illness. We must also hide the treasure and not spend beyond what we would ordinarily as not to draw suspicion on this house.

FLORINA

Always with the level head, Morgiana. I need you now more than ever. I free you from your bonds of slavery and ask that you become the overseer of this house. Whatever you think best to do, the others will do as you command.

MORGIANA

I don't know what to say, my mistress.

FLORINA
You have more than showed your loyalty to this house. It's only right I reward you. Ali Baba, you'll stay here from now on.

ALI BABA
I'm undeserving of your kindness, sweet Florina. I thank you from the bottom of my heart.

(FLORINA and ALI BABA exit stage left.)

KALA
You're fee, Morgiana. Free to be with me now. You must know how I feel about you.

MORGIANA
I can hardly believe it. I've grown up in this house and watched you become a fine man, Kala. Now it's possible for me to love you.

(KALA tenderly takes her hand.)

KALA
Come. We'll tend to my father together.

(KALA and MORGIANA exit stage right.)

*LIGHTING EFFECTS
Lights come up to full.

(FLORINA and ALI BABA enter from stage left.)

FLORINA
You've been such a comfort to me these past months, Ali Baba. I don't know what I would have done without you.

ALI BABA
Seeing to your needs is the least I can do. I only hope I have carried through on matters of business as well as Kassim did.

FLORINA
You've done well, Ali Baba.

(Enter LACCUM from stage right. He drags a large SACK in and sits it to the side.)

LACCUM
Peace be to this house. I'm Laccum, an oil merchant from the desert. I've come to this village to sell my wares, but cannot find lodgings. An innkeeper suggested I come to the home of Ali Baba, a good and kind patron of this town who might keep me and my goods for a few days.

ALI BABA
You are welcome in this house.

(MORGIANA enters from stage right.)

FLORINA
Morgiana, this is Laccum, a merchant from the desert. He'll be staying with us. Will you see to his room, please?

MORGIANA
Yes, my mistress.

LACCUM
I best get busy unloading. Thank you again.

(LACCUM exits stage right.)

MORGIANA
This man. Do you know him?

ALI BABA
Only that he's a merchant.

MORGIANA
Thieves can be very convincing liars.

ALI BABA
Oh, I see what you mean, Morgiana. But I've seen the leader of the thieves from the magic mountain and this man doesn't look anything like him.

MORGIANA
Maybe not. But if these thieves have enough magic to open a mountain, I think he would be able to change his appearance to fool us.

ALI BABA
There's such a thing as being too cautious, Morgiana. This man is only a merchant.

(ALI BABA and FLORINA exit stage left as KALA enters stage right.)

KALA
Who is the man carrying in all these bags?

MORGIANA
He says he's a merchant, but I have my doubts.

(MORGIANA presses a finger to her lips for KALA to be quiet and then crosses to the SACK left by LACCUM. She jiggles the bag.)

VOICE FROM INSIDE SACK
Is it time?

MORGIANA
Yes, it is. Come on out.

(The SACK moves.)

VOICE FROM INSIDE SACK
I can't come out until you say the magic words.

*(Alarmed, **MORGIANA** and **KALA** step away from the SACK.)*

KALA
All of these sacks must have men in them.

MORGIANA
And if they cannot come out of the sacks without the magic words, the merchant must be the leader of the thieves who said "Open, Sesame" at the side of the mountain.

KALA
The plan must be to wait until dark and then have his men emerge from the sacks to kill us all.

MORGIANA
We'll boil caldrons of oil and I'll say a charm over them. Then I'll take the house staff and we'll pour the hot oil into each sack. That should be the end of them. But we must keep an eye on the merchant so he can't spring his plan before we have time to carry out ours.

KALA
I can do that. And once we quell this evil plot, I can subdue and take him to the authorities.

MORGIANA
Please be careful, Kala.

KALA *(Pleased.)*
We make a good team, don't we?

*(**KALA** kisses **MORGIANA** on the cheek before exiting stage right with the SACK. **MORGIANA** smiles and exits stage left.)*

***LIGHTING EFFECTS**
The lights dim to night.

*(Pause. **ALI BABA** and **FLORINA** enter from stage left as **LACCUM** and **KALA** enter from stage right.)*

LACCUM
Lady Florina, your son has been showing me around your estate. I'm very impressed. I can't thank you enough for your hospitality, but I believe I'll go to bed now.

FLORINA
But it's early. We were going to listen to the house musicians.

LACCUM
It sounds tempting, but I'm quite tired.

KALA *(Suspicious.)*
Of course you are.

LACCUM
Sir?

***SOUND EFFECTS**
Screams of agony offstage.

FLORINA
What is that?

*(**MORGIANA** enters with a JAR.)*

MORGIANA
That would be your men, Laccum. They died in agony just like my master died at your hand.

*(**KALA** slips behind **LACCUM** and quickly ties **LACCUM'S** hands behind his back.)*

KALA
You killed my father, and now you're here to kill the rest of us. But Morgiana was too clever for you. She saw who you were, and had the servants pour boiling oil over your men killing them instantly.

MORGIANA
They couldn't get out of the sacks because you needed to say the magic words "Open, Sesame."

LACCUM
Who is this mere servant to have ruined everything?

KALA
Not a servant, Laccum. This is Morgiana, the smartest woman I have ever known and soon to be my wife.

FLORINA
You've saved us once again, Morgiana. I'll cherish you as a daughter-in-law. Kala, you have proven yourself to be a good and intelligent man. I give this house to you and Morgiana. I only ask that you let your uncle and I stay.

KALA
Thank you, Mother. You and Ali Baba may stay as our as long as you wish. Now we need to take this evil man to the authorities to face his dues.

ALI BABA
What a wonder you are, Morgiana. How fortunate we are to know you and have you as our friend and protector.

(All exit stage right.)

END OF MORGIANA AND ALI BABA

The Brave Little Tailor
PAGE 1 (A Lesson in Story Structure and Plot Building)

This is a quick Project identifying story structure and plot building.

It tells of the "loosely" agreed difference between story and plot, and explains progression and plot point objectives. This Project also provides a basic Outline for the student to write their own short-short story using the "David and Goliath" theme like THE BRAVE LITTLE TAILOR.

PREPARATION AND RESOURCES NEEDED: Read the short story below. Copy the 4 pages of this Project for each student.

Student Assignment: Read the review of Story and Plot line structure provided. Then read the shortened Brothers Grimm story of THE BRAVE LITTLE TAILOR on the following pages. Afterwards, write your own story using the Outline set forth on the last page.

Plotting a Story

Writing stories can be fun. Writing stories properly may sound boring and complicated, but it isn't. It's really quite simple. By following just a few basic rules, a good story idea can turn into a great read. And although you may already know all about story building, the following should give you a few more "tips" and things to remember when beginning your story.

Is it a Story or a Plot line?

Good question. It's also hard or easy to understand depending on how it's answered.

A story is just a series of events. *He went swimming. She sat on the shore.* Believe it or not, this is a story because it tells of two events.

Now if you add just one word, it turns into a plot line. He went swimming *while* she sat by the shore. The word "while" connects the one event (he went swimming) to the other event (she sat by the shore). *By adding a reason, you then begin to build a plot. He went swimming while she sat on the shore, afraid to go in the water again.*

This should lead the reader to ask, "Why is she afraid to go into the water?" Here is your base for a plot. Is the reader interested enough in the story (events) to ask why?

A story is a series of events: this happened and then this happened and this happened. Hopefully your events will prompt the reader to want to know what happens next.

A plot connects the series of events by answering the "whys" like *this event happened because of this*

other event or *this was the result of an event that occurred earlier*.

Granted the two are very similar, but there is a difference. All the writer should remember is: A story is really just an idea of events to take place. The plot will string all the events together.

Onward to Structure

Structure—sounds like something complicated. Well, it can be—or not. Structure in a story (or plot) is simply moving your idea from point A to point B. How does your main character start out and where does he or she end (with many things going on between)? To build the most basic story structure, you only need three things:

A Beginning • A Middle • An End

That's it. Can't be, you say? How can the billions of stories told and written since the beginning of time have this simple structure? Think about it. A story is two or more events. The first event would be your beginning. The second event could be your end. But to make the beginning and end come together there needs to be a middle. Any story you read whether it's one page or a thousand pages has this simple story structure. Stringing these elements together to make the events interesting enough to read is plot.

The beginning of the story is the *setup*. It explains a situation and usually has a problem that needs solving or resolving. The beginning also introduces the main character and tells of his or her situation at the moment. And what does your character want or what is he or she after? You now have a beginning of a plot line.

The middle of your story has your main character working towards their goal or want. Obviously if your main character gets what they want right away, there won't be much of a story. So obstacles and barriers must come up. When the main character faces a barrier they'd rather not, it's a problem. This is commonly called conflict. If there isn't conflict, it won't be much of a story.

The Brave Little Tailor (Story Structure and Plot Building) PAGE 2

The end resolves the problem. The main character may have to overcome many obstacles, but will face the final one at the end of the story. Often the final obstacle is the biggest and hardest one to overcome. This last event is called a climax. Afterwards, the action of the story falls away followed by a "wrap-up" sequence. In most stories the wrap-up tells what the main character achieved, learned, or defeated; what kind of reward they receive (whether personal or publicly); and how the main character, now a better person or being for going through what they did, is ready to face the next day or challenge. (There is more about story development in Projects 1 and 2 in **SECTION** 4.)

THE BRAVE LITTLE TAILOR
by the Brothers Grimm

One summer's morning a little tailor was sitting on his table by the window. He was in good spirits and sewed with all his might. A peasant woman came down the street calling, "Good jams, cheap. Good jams, cheap."

This rang pleasantly in the tailor's ears, so he stretched his delicate head out of the window, and called, "Come up here, dear woman. You can sell your goods here."

The woman came up with her heavy basket. He inspected each pot of jam and said, "This blackberry jam seems to me to be good." So the woman sold him the jam and went on her way.

"Please bless this jam to give me health and strength." He brought the bread out of the cupboard, cut a piece right across the loaf and spread the jam over it. But just as we was to take a bite out of his sweet treat, he thought, "I should finish this jacket before I eat this. It will taste sweeter when I'm done with my work."

He laid the bread near him and sewed on. In the meantime the smell of the sweet jam rose to where the flies were sitting in great numbers. Attracted to the smell, the flies swooped down onto the bread.

"Ha! Who invited you?" said the little tailor driving the annoying guests away. But the flies only came back again in ever-increasing companies. The little tailor at last lost all patience and drew a piece of cloth from the hole under his table saying, "Wait, and I will give it to you!" He struck the cloth mercilessly on them. When he drew it away and counted, there lay before him no fewer than seven dead flies.

"Ha, look what I have done!" he said admiring his own bravery. "The whole town shall know of this." And the little tailor hastened to cut himself a wide belt embroidering on it in large letters,

"SEVEN AT ONE STROKE!"

"Just, the town?!" he continued, "the whole world shall hear of it." And his heart wagged with joy like a lamb's tail. The tailor put on the belt and resolved to go forth into the world because he thought his workshop was too small for his valor. And he took to the road to show the world his bravery.

After the little tailor had walked for a long time, he came to the courtyard of a royal palace. Feeling weary, the fellow rested on the grass and fell asleep. While there, people came and read his belt, "Seven at one stroke."

Assuming the claim involved the killing of men, the people said, "And what is a great warrior doing here in the midst of peace? He must be a mighty lord."

They hurried to the king and told him of his discovery. They also suggested such a mighty warrior could be a useful man to have around. The counsel pleased the king, and he sent one of his courtiers to the little tailor to offer him a military rank. The ambassador conveyed to the little tailor this proposal.

"This is why I'm here," the tailor replied, "I'm ready to enter the king's service." He was therefore honorably received and a special dwelling was assigned him.

However, the soldiers were set against the little tailor wishing him a thousand miles away. "What is to be the end of this?" they said among themselves. "If we quarrel with him, and he strikes about him, seven of us will fall at every blow, not one of us can stand against him." So they came to a decision and begged for their dismissal. "We are not prepared," said they, "to stay with a man who kills seven at one stroke."

The king was sorry that for the sake of one he should lose all his faithful servants. He wished that he had never set eyes on the tailor and would willingly have been rid of him again. But he did not venture to give him his dismissal, for he dreaded lest he should strike him and all his

The Brave Little Tailor (Story Structure and Plot Building) PAGE 3

people dead, and place himself on the royal throne. He thought about it for a long time, and at last found good counsel. He sent to the little tailor and caused him to be informed that as he was such a great warrior, he had one request to make of him. In a forest of his country lived two giants who caused great mischief with their robbing, murdering, ravaging, and burning. And no one could approach them without putting himself in danger of death. If the tailor conquered and killed these two giants, he would give him his only daughter to wife, and half of his kingdom as a dowry, likewise one hundred horsemen should go with him to assist him.

"That would indeed be a fine thing for a man like me," thought the little tailor. "One is not offered a beautiful princess and half a kingdom every day of one's life."

"Oh, yes," he replied, "I will soon subdue the giants, and do not require the help of the hundred horsemen to do it; he who can hit seven with one blow has no need to be afraid of two."

The little tailor went forth, and the hundred horse-men followed him. When he came to the outskirts of the forest, he said to his followers, "Just stay waiting here, I alone will soon finish off the giants."

Then he bounded into the forest and looked about right and left. After a while he saw both giants. They lay sleeping under a tree, and snored so that the branches waved up and down. The little tailor, not idle, gathered two pockets of stones and with these climbed up the tree. When he was half-way up, he slipped down by a branch, until he sat just above the sleepers, and then let one stone after another fall on the breast of one of the giants.

For a long time the giant felt nothing, but at last he awoke, pushed his comrade, and said, "Why are you knocking me?"

"You must be dreaming," said the other, "I am not knocking you."

They laid themselves down to sleep again, and then the tailor threw a stone down on the second.

"What is the meaning of this?" cried the other. "Why are you pelting me?"

"I am not pelting you," answered the first, growling.

They disputed about it for a time, but as they were weary they let the matter rest, and their eyes closed once more. The little tailor began his game again, picked out the biggest stone, and threw it with all his might on the breast of the first giant.

"That is too bad!" he cried and sprang up like a madman, and pushed his companion against the tree until it shook. The other paid him back in the same coin, and they got into such a rage they tore up trees and belabored each other so long, that at last they both fell down dead on the ground at the same time. Then the little tailor leapt down.

"It is a lucky thing," said he, "that they did not tear up the tree on which I was sitting, or I should have had to spring on to another like a squirrel, but we tailors are nimble." He drew out his sword and gave each of them a couple of thrusts in the breast, and then went out to the horsemen and said, "The work is done, I have finished both of them off, but it was hard work. They tore up trees in their sore need, and defended themselves with them, but all that is to no purpose when a man like me comes, who can kill seven at one blow."

"But you are not wounded?" asked the horsemen.

"You need not concern yourself about that," answered the tailor, "they have not bent one hair of mine."

The horsemen would not believe him, and rode into the forest, there they found the giants swimming in their blood, and all round about lay the torn-up trees.

The hero however went to the king, who was now, whether he liked it or not, obliged to keep his promise, and gave him his daughter and half of his kingdom. Had he known that it was no warlike hero, but a little tailor who was standing before him it would have gone to his heart still more than it did. The wedding was held with great magnificence and small joy, and out of a tailor a king was made.

So the little tailor was made and remained a king to the end of his life.

The Brave Little Tailor (Story Structure and Plot Building) PAGE 4

THE BRAVE LITTLE TAILOR is referred to as a "David and Goliath" story. This means it's a story about a little guy overpowering the big one. Although the situation seems impossible for the little guy to be victorious over the bigger, he or she somehow figures out how to do it. Writing a story with this theme should be easy. It doesn't have to be about a little person and giants. It can be about some lowly worker in the mail room who reveals wrongdoing by the presidents and CEOs of a big company bringing them down. Or, a young man wants to save his village and alone, faces an army of one hundred men. Yet he defeats the army by using his wits and forces of nature. But for this Exercise, the Guideline uses a little peasant going up against a monstrous beast to save the village. Follow the Guideline below to create your own "David and Goliath" story.

(This Outline refers to the main character as "she," but could easily be a "he." It depends on what you want the main character to be.)

THE BEGINNING

The main character lives a simple life working in the fields, but spends all day dreaming of how she would run the kingdom if only given the opportunity knowing she could do a better job of it.

People down the road are seen fleeing past the village. One stops just long enough to tell the others of the village a huge monster is destroying the countryside.

The people of the village think they must get out of the way and start to leave. But the main character thinks all should spend their time thinking of how they can defend their village from the monster. After all, if they lose their village, where will they go?

THE MIDDLE

Some friends stay with the main character and they figure out what can be done to stop the monster from destroying their homes.

Another subject of the kingdom hurries by. They say the kingdom has been nearly destroyed by the monster and the king and queen is offering the whole kingdom to whoever can stop the fierce beast.

Now the main character sees how there is a way to rule the kingdom "properly" if it's hers to rule. The main character is determined more than ever to destroy the monster and places her plan into action.

THE END

The monster comes into the village and the main character with her friends sets the plan into action. The monster fights back, but is eventually defeated.

The main character along with the ones that stayed behind to help defeat the monster go to the king and queen to claim the kingdom as promised. The king gives the kingdom to the main character. As the main character sets up a new kingdom, she remembers the friends that helped her and rewards them with important positions of the royal court.

Happy with having the opportunity to do something good for the kingdom, the main character realizes her greatest blessing over ruling a whole kingdom is the relationships and loyalty formed with her friends.

Beowulf Versus King Arthur

PAGE 1 (A Lesson in Research and Identification of Similar Elements)

This Project looks at the similarities of two characters in **Fantasy Genre**.

Still proving popular, Beowulf and King Arthur continue to appear in new publications and motion picture productions. Because of this, these kings deserve a more in-depth look and consideration as men in history, literature, and characters facing human challenges and showing heroics and valor. A Review Sheet of questions follows to assist in conducting a classroom discussion of the two famous kings. Recommended for more information and easy reads are Robert Nye's BEOWULF: A NEW TELLING and David Day's THE SEARCH FOR KING ARTHUR. But there are many books on both men to choose from.

PREPARATION AND RESOURCES NEEDED: Have students read out-loud the summary of the two kings (below). Then ask students for their answers and thoughts about the questions on the following page. Copy the 2 pages of this Project for each student.

READING DESIRED BUT NOT REQUIRED

A TALE OF TWO KINGS

Beowulf is an epic poem about a warrior who became king of his people, the Geats of Scandinavia. His story begins around 450 to 600 A.D. To repay a debt, Beowulf journey's to King Hrothgar's palace and offers to rid it of the monster Grendel that has brought death to it. Beowulf kills Grendel and Grendel's Mother, and later as king to his people, faces and kills the Firedrake (dragon).

Physical Characteristics—Beowulf is a small and stocky man. His hands are powerful, but his overall strength is just a bit more than an average man's.

His Strengths—Because he's but a man and knows his limits in strength and force, Beowulf uses his ability to stay calm and think things through during harrowing situations.

His Weaknesses—Beowulf does not possess any special magical pieces to help him fight.

As a Battle Leader—Beowulf holds great respect and love by his men as he is usually the one in front leading the charge. He wouldn't ask any to do more than he.

As a Warrior—He's brave and strong—fearless to a point of being a bit reckless.

As a King—He is fair and compassionate. He feels for his people and does his best to serve and take care of their needs.

As a Real Figure in History—In trying to prove Beowulf an actual person, many scholars and archeologist have stretched to find him. They have tried to prove various regions of northern Europe to be his, and burial chambers and mounds as Beowulf's resting place. In truth, it's all a wild guess because no one has been able to prove Beowulf is nothing more than a story.

Arthur is the ultimate British Legend. It's difficult to think of Great Britain today without thinking of Arthur of long ago (5th or 6th Century). There are many stories about Arthur's kingdom of Camelot and his reign as King of England. The most familiar deals with Arthur becoming king by pulling the sword from the stone, marrying Guinevere, forming the Knights of the Round Table, and sending his knights out to look for the Holy Grail.

Physical Characteristics—Arthur's appearance as well as his story is up for grabs. Even Geoffrey of Monmouth's accounting in THE HISTORY OF THE KINGS OF BRITAIN recognizes Arthur as Legend. But Geoffrey's history is uncertain leaving future authors (like Sir Thomas Malory) to create an Arthur however they wish.

His Strengths—Arthur's humility comes through most stories. He struggles with his power and command which endears others to him.

As a Battle Leader—Arthur is a commanding leader, brave and concerned for his men in battle.

His Weaknesses—The very thing that makes him strong also becomes his failings. Arthur is reluctant to take a stand or decision when he needs to most.

As a King—Becoming so wrapped-up in his own drama, Arthur forgets his subjects and when his kingdom struggles with famine and disease, he does little to correct it.

As a Real Figure in History—It's thought Arthur was an actual figure in British history, but there seems two camps of thought on the subject. Some believe him a great warrior (either Roman or Celtic), and others refer to historical documents and places in declaring him a real king.

Beowulf Versus King Arthur (Research and Identification) PAGE 2

Student Assignment: *Read the brief summary of Beowulf and King Arthur on the first page, then offer your thoughts to the questions posed below this introduction.*

THE SIMILARITIES AND DIFFERENCE BETWEEN
TWO GREAT KINGS OF FANTASY

Beowulf and King Arthur are two of the most famous figures in modern **Fantasy Genre***. Interestingly enough, Beowulf's notoriety didn't take off until J.R.R. Tolkien of HOBBIT and THE LORD OF THE RINGS fame wrote a 1930's article about the merit of Beowulf as a story. Until that time, educators used Beowulf as a primary study of the English language. Although Beowulf and King Arthur take their own path in fiction and questionable history, at times it seems they may be one in the same. Did the story of King Arthur take elements from the Beowulf story or did Beowulf take elements from the King Arthur story? No matter each began at a different point in time, through the years each has grown with reinterpretations and revisions until one could be a continuation of the other. But which should be the first? Perhaps each garners enough merit to remain independent of the other.*

1.) What makes Beowulf different from Arthur as a man and a king?

2.) What makes the story of Beowulf different from Arthur's?

3.) Do you think Beowulf would have become a greater king (of more land and subjects) if he had Arthur's magical sword Excalibur?

4.) If Arthur had to fight Grendel and Grendel's Mother, do you think he would have won?

5.) Beowulf fought the Grendel monsters and the Firedrake dragon. Did Arthur have to fight any monsters?

6.) Why didn't Beowulf marry?

7.) Do you think Arthur's reign as king would have been perfect if he hadn't married Guinevere?

8.) Who made the better king, Beowulf or Arthur? Why?

9.) Did Beowulf readily accept the crown, or was he reluctant to do so? Was Arthur also reluctant to become king?

10.) In accepting the crown, Beowulf didn't have to fight many nobles claiming their right to be king like Arthur. Why not?

11.) In battle, did both men fight well? Were they always victorious?

12.) Do you think Beowulf would be able to kill his son and heir if he were evil like Arthur's son Mordred? Did Arthur have any other recourse than to battle and kill Mordred?

13.) What differences and similarities are there with each king's death and burial?

14.) Are Beowulf and Arthur remembered in death? How?

15.) In fantasy as well as history, it seems the destiny for all kings (and queens) is to wage war and keep fighting to hold onto their kingdoms. Why do you suppose this is?

16.) In bestowing power to a person as a king or queen, would you say the better person for the job is the one who doesn't want it?

17.) Would you like to be a king or queen? If so, what would you do for your kingdom and subjects?

Magic, Conjuring, and Shapeshifters
Overview in Brief

MAGIC

Though associated with paganism and Satanism in the real world, Magic—though possibly sinister in fantasy—is generally individual in practice (not being a part of a cult or belief), and administered for self-purposes like the wizard turning the land barren to gain control over its people. Magic in fantasy usually takes on a "marvel" quality to seek out and not to avoid for fear of ominous consequences. In the same league as the impossible, magic clearly defines **Fantasy Genre** as it can do anything and take the characters anywhere they wish.

CONJURING

Correlating with magic, conjuring in fantasy usually means "bringing forth" magic through potions, incantation, or other methods and acts. The witches' caldron full of bat wings and eye of newt is a perfect example of a conjuring device. Mickey Mouse as the Sorcerer's Apprentice on top of a rocky apex gesturing with arms and hands to pull up magical sparks and lightning flares is conjuring. Using a cat to carry a spell to an unsuspecting victim is also conjuring. *Magic* is the result.

SHAPESHIFTERS

Those who can change shape and change the shape of others are shapeshifters. Again, a broad definition, shapeshifting may involve voluntary transformation or unwanted changing. In other words, those with such powers can turn themselves into iother creatures or things and back, or can turn others into whatever (with or against someone's will). Because of my ever-present need to keep all things in neat little cubbyholes, I think of shapeshifters and shapeshifting as such: Voluntary transformation is shapeshifting. Magic creates involuntary transformation.

MILESTONE, CLASSIC, AND INFLUENTIAL LITERATURE WORKS CONCERNING MAGIC

E. Nesbit's FIVE CHILDREN AND IT (1902)
Children discover a sand-fairy who now must grant one wish each day. Because the children are not specific with their wishes, the results are not always what they expect.

L . Frank Baum's THE MAGIC OF OZ (1919)
The thirteenth and final LAND OF OZ book tells of the failed attempt of the Munchkin boy Kiki Aru and King Ruggedo to take over and rule Oz.

Magic, Conjuring, and Shapeshifters
Overview in Brief *(continued)*

Lord Dunsany's THE KING OF ELFLAND'S DAUGHTER (1924)
A human nobleman falls in love with an elf princess. (It's suggested this story inspired J.R.R. Tolkien's LORD OF THE RINGS Aragom and Arwen characters.)

C.S. Lewis' THAT HIDEOUS STRENGTH (1945) or THE MAGICIAN'S NEPHEW (1955)
Two children stumble on a magician who talks the girl into putting on a magic ring. When she disappears, he talks the boy into putting on another magic ring. Originally transported to a wooded area, they also travel to different worlds via the magic rings.

J.K. Rowling's HARRY POTTER (Series) (1997-)
An orphaned boy receives admittance papers into a school for witchcraft and wizardry where he learns his craft and embarks on numerous adventures within the enchanted environment.

MILESTONE, CLASSIC, AND INFLUENTIAL LITERATURE WORKS CONCERNING SHAPESHIFTING

C.S. Lewis' THE SILVER CHAIR (1953)
Eustace and Jill find each other at school while running from bullies. They magically travel from the garden shed to the world of Narnia and start a journey to rescue Prince Rillian from the Green Lady. They encounter geographical challenges as well as dragons and giants.

Piers Anthony's A SPELL FOR CHAMELEON (1977)
The first (and what most consider the best) book in the Xanth Series. Xanth is a fantasy world where Bink finds himself. Xanth is a world ruled by magic. Having no magical ability, Bink must discover his own talents. Populated by centaurs, harpies, gargoyles, and a slew of other magical beasts, Bink faces many a magical assistance and hindrance in his pursuit of self-discovery.

Patricia McKillip's RIDDLE MASTER OF HEAD (1976)
The Prince of Hed Morgon wins a riddle match against the ghost Peven and goes to An to claim his prize—marriage to the second most beautiful woman of An. His trip disrupted by a shipwreck and now voiceless and nameless, Morgon must embark on a perilous venture facing mysterious shapeshifters.

Sallas, the Enchantress of Granada

Original Script by Joan Garner

—BACKGROUND INFORMATION
(genre classification and other data deemed useful)

Look up enchantress and it notes sorceress or witch. Look up sorceress and it notes enchantress or witch. Look up witch and it notes enchantress or sorceress. Definitions suggest these three magic users are one and the same. But there are a few subtle distinctions.

For one, an enchantress is typically thought of as beautiful, charming and alluring. Her magical powers come from chanting and incantations. And while an enchantress may be good or bad, the consensus is most practice magic for the good.

With this in mind, arguably the most famous enchantress is Morgan Le Fey (who, if not altogether bad, was certainly a pain in King Arthur's side). Circe of Greek Mythology is also a well-known enchantress.

Usually associated with the world of faerie, an enchantress has gradually transformed into a human. They are more powerful, better dressed, and of a higher class than a witch. In specifics, an enchantress' magical totem is a swan, magical herb cocoa, and magical tool perfume. These properties have helped perpetuate the elegant appeal of an enchantress.

— SYNOPSIS OF STORY

(Late 16th Century Spain) Four travelers on their way to historic Granada, Spain stop to make camp for the night. While settling in, a young woman named Sallas rushes in begging for protection. An angry mob believing Sallas an evil enchantress is after her. Sallas explains she isn't an enchantress but a physician possessed of certain healing powers. Though a bit skeptical of Sallas, the travelers are sympathetic to her plight and unwilling to condemn her. Later, Sallas awards them for their kindness.

—GLOSSARY
(terms possibly unfamiliar to the reader)

AFFLICTION—An ailment causing distress.

CRUX—The heart or focal point of a matter.

CUTTHROAT—A murderer. A ruthless person.

ENCHANTRESS—A woman practicing magic.

HIGHWAYMAN—A hold up man who robs travelers on a road.

INCANTATION(S)—Ritual reciting of charms or spell to create magic.

MALADIES (MALADY)—A disease. An ailment.

PASSIVELY—To submit. Not to argue or show resistance. To stand by and not act.

Sallas, the Enchantress of Granada
STAGING SUGGESTIONS AND HELPFUL HINTS

— CHARACTER DESCRIPTIONS

ISABELLE: (Female) Sweet and curious.

FREDRICO: (Male) A leader and good friend.

MIRANDA: (Female) A lovely woman of grace and spirit.

MANUEL: (Male) A good man, but leery and cautious.

SALLAS: (Female) Mysterious, but kind.

— PRESENTATION SUGGESTIONS
(Late 16th Century Spanish Clothing and Items)

COSTUMES
ISABELLE and **MIRANDA**—Long sleeved blouse and long skirt. A large traveling cloak with hood should cover everything so the clothes underneath needn't be terribly accurate. Flat shoes/slippers. Long hair pulled back in plaited hairstyle.

MANUAL and **FREDRICO**—Long sleeved shirt and vest. Pants and shoes. A large traveling cloak trimmed with fur should cover everything so the clothes underneath needn't be terribly accurate. Brimless squared cap trimmed with feather or tall velvet cap with six sides.

SALLAS—Elegant, low cut embroidered dress with attached and slashed sleeves. Rich, beautiful shawl. AMULET (hidden in dress). Slippers. Long flowing hair.

PROPS
CLOTH SACKS—Cloth sacks like pillow cases of one color stuffed with presumably traveling clothes and gear.

AMULET—A large, round disk of ornate silver and/or gold decoration. Should look very old.

STAGING
With only five **PLAYERS** and little movement needed, this is a simple sketch to stage. Keep **SALLAS** a fair distance from the others until she tends **FREDRICO**. This separation distinguishes her as *different* from ordinary people.

STAGING

STAGE RIGHT　　　　　　　　　　　　　　　　　　　　　　　　　　**STAGE LEFT**

*RIGHT
WALL*　■　　MANUEL　MIRANDA　ISABELLE　FREDRICO　　SALLAS　　*LEFT
WALL*　■

Sallas, the Enchantress of Granada
SCRIPT

SETTING
Late 16th Century. A clearing in the mountains above the city of Granada, Spain.

> *(MANUEL, MIRANDA, FREDRICO, and ISABELLE enter from stage right. They carry their CLOTH SACKS.)*

ISABELLE
It's getting late. We should stop for the night.

FREDRICO
You're right. Isabelle. This looks like as a good a place as any.

MIRANDA
I'm so tired. I feel like we've been walking for a hundred years.

MANUEL *(He sneezes.)*
You're the one who wanted to see Granada.

MIRANDA
I wanted to see Granada, not the whole of Spain.

ISABELLE
If we don't come out of these mountains soon, we won't see anymore of Spain including Granada.

FREDRICO
Everyone stop your complaining. You'll feel better once you've had a good night's sleep.

ISABELLE
I'd feel better if we had engaged a coach.

MANUEL *(Sneezing again.)*
If we had hired a coach, we wouldn't have enough money for lodging once we arrive in Granada.

MIRANDA
We could very well lose that money should we happen on a highwayman.

ISABELLE
What a dreadful thought.

MIRANDA
I hear tell these back roads are teaming with thieves and cutthroats. I think we're most fortunate not to have met one or two so far on our journey.

FREDRICO
It's unlikely any of us will sleep well tonight if you keep on with such stories, Miranda. Let's just get a fire started and have our evening meal.

MANUEL
I know I'll feel better after drinking a tankard.
    (He sneezes and coughs and wipes his nose.)
Augh, blast this cold.

ISABELLE
It's getting worse, Manuel.

MANUEL
I can't shake it.

> *(Suddenly SALLAS rushes in from stage left.)*

SALLAS
People, good people, please help me.

FREDRICO
What's this?

SALLAS
Please, don't turn me away. I beg you.

MANUEL
Why would we turn you away, señorita?

SALLAS
They're following me.

MIRANDA
Is it a bear or wolf?

SALLAS
A mob is chasing me.

FREDRICO
A mob?

SALLAS
To be specific, an angry mob from the nearby town.

MANUEL
Why are they after you?

SALLAS
On second thought, I think it best to continue on and leave you good people alone. I apologize for disrupting your peaceful camp. Forgive me.

> *(SALLAS starts out stage right, but FREDRICO stops her.)*

FREDRICO
Wait, lovely lady. We're not callas people or quick to judge. Tell us of your troubles and we'll decide whether to turn you out or not.

SALLAS
Señor, you're too kind. It's been so long since anyone has treated me decency, I hardly know how to respond.

ISABELLE
For goodness sakes, señorita, what has you in such a state?

(SALLAS warily looks at the four.)

FREDRICO
Will you not trust us, señorita?

SALLAS
Yes, I believe I can trust perfect strangers more than the people I know.

MIRANDA
Then please tell us of your problems. Perhaps we can help.

SALLAS
I come from Granada, but have been living in these hills above the great city for some time now. My name is Sallas.

FREDRICO
Oh, yes—introductions... I'm Fredrico. Manuel, Isabelle, and Miranda.

ISABELLE
Pleased to meet you.

SALLAS
You won't be.

MANUEL
Enough of this mystery. Just tell us what's wrong.

SALLAS
I'm known as a physician.

FREDRICO
A woman physician are you? It's an unusual profession for a woman, but not one to incite an angry mob.

SALLAS
I'm a physician, or call myself one to disguise my true talents.

MIRANDA
Which are?

SALLAS
The others call me an enchantress.

ISABELLE
Why?

SALLAS
Since my youth I've had this ability to detect and heal people of their maladies. I don't know how or where it comes from, I only know I can. It would be safer to ignore this talent, but how can you stand passively by and watch someone suffer when you know you can help them?

FREDRICO
Do you practice folk medicine, then? What's the harm in that?

SALLAS
No, you don't understand. These abilities are more like powers.

MANUEL
I see why they call you an enchantress and not a witch. You're much too beautiful and dignified to be a witch.

MIRANDA
Supposedly an enchantress is more powerful than a witch.

SALLAS
Again, I appreciate your patience with me, but simply, I have the power to heal people.

ISABELLE
Yes, but some would consider that a gift—a miracle even. Why would they call you an enchantress?

SALLAS
Because I can't heal everyone of everything.

FREDRICO
Yes, I daresay we would have heard of you if you could do that.

MANUEL
Nonsense. This is all nonsense. It makes for a nice story, but nothing more.

MIRANDA
But why would she make something like this up, Manuel?

MANUEL
Why to fool us, that's all. This story gets her into our camp and into our confidence. Like Miranda said, there are highwaymen and cutthroats about. She may be here to take our money.

ISABELLE
Manuel, she isn't a cutthroat. For goodness sakes.

SALLAS
I can see where you would suspect me of foul play. I almost wish this was my intent.

FREDRICO
Well, there's a way to find out if you are who you say you are, Sallas, enchantress of Granada. My friend Manuel here has a cold. Make it go away.

SALLAS
You see? This is the crux of my problem. I don't know if I can make it go away.

ISABELLE
This power is more at its will, not yours.

SALLAS
Yes, señora. This is precisely the predicament I find myself in.

MANUEL
How convenient for you. Sometimes it works and sometimes it doesn't.

SALLAS
And this is why I'm called an enchantress and why a mob is after me.

MIRANDA
What happened?

SALLAS
The mayor of the town has the gout. He wanted me to rid him of this affliction.

ISABELLE
I can only guess. The mayor still has the gout.

SALLAS
Of all the times for this power to misfire.

FREDRICO
And with the mayor naturally being upset—

SALLAS
—He accused me of being an evil enchantress.

MANUEL
It's still just a story.

MIRANDA
Manuel, have you noticed you haven't sneezed since this young woman has been here?

MANUEL
That means nothing, Miranda, dear.

FREDRICO
Señorita Sallas, when you heal these people, do you use potions, spells, and incantations?

SALLAS
I use some herbal mixtures to calm a restless stomach and ease a painful head. But no, I don't know any spell, or incantations.

FREDRICO
Then how can they can call you an enchantress?

ISABELLE
Fredrico, what is an incantation? I've heard of it, but what is it exactly?

FREDRICO
Incantations are words or verses repeated over and over to activate a spell or hex—maybe a curse on someone. Sometimes a familiar like an animal or object is used—an amulet for example.

ISABELLE
Sallas says she doesn't know any incantations.

MIRANDA
Fredrico is right. It doesn't make sense that a mob would be after you.

SALLAS
Nonetheless, here I am and here they soon will be.

MANUEL
Forget about my cold. Fredrico has difficulty seeing anymore. Heal him of this infirmity and I'll believe you are as you say.

MIRANDA
Manuel, how cruel to put her on the spot like that.

FREDRICO
No one can restore my eyesight but the gods and prophets.

SALLAS
Of which I am neither. Still, I can try if you would like. I need to see your eyes, señor.

ISABELLE
Show her you eyes, Fredrico. What would it hurt?

*(**FREDRICO** steps to **SALLAS**.)*

FREDRICO
Here are my eyes, señorita.

SALLAS *(Looking into **FREDRICO'S** eyes.)*
There is cloudiness about them as if the sea's mist has settled over the windows of your soul.

MANUEL
Poetic, but far from healing.

SALLAS
Do you really want everyone to see into your soul, señor Fredrico?

FREDRICO
To see faces more clearly, yes I believe I would.

SALLAS
If you so desire it, it will be so. Close your eyes, please.

FREDRICO
Then I won't see anything at all.

ISABELLE
Fredrico, stop your teasing and do as she says.

> (*FREDRICO chuckles and closes his eyes.*)

SALLAS
If you wish to see clearly, then you will.

FREDRICO
And if I open my eyes now, I will see?

SALLAS
If you wish it so.

MANUEL
How clever she is, Fredrico. Notice how she lays the burden of this miracle at your feet. If *you* wish it. If you open your eyes and can see no better, then it was your fault for not wanting it enough.

ISABELLE
Don't listen to Manuel, Fredrico. Open your eyes and tell us what you see.

FREDRICO
I'm almost frightened to now.

MIRANDA
You'll have to sooner or later.

> (*FREDRICO opens his eyes and looks around.*)

ISABELLE
Can you see?

> (*FREDRICO steps to ISABELLE and places a gentle hand on her face.*)

FREDRICO
Yours has always been such a lovely face, my dear.

> (*FREDRICO and ISABELLE hug with joy.*)

MIRANDA
How marvelous!

MANUEL
Yet I still have my cold. You would think a thing as simple as a cold would be easy to cure.

MIRANDA
Do you expect the enchantress to favor you when you're continually challenging her?

SALLAS
Please, I don't want to be the cause of strife within this pleasant group. Down this path is a meadow with soft grass and a clear water brook. It should make for a comfortable night's sleep. Please go before the others get here.

FREDRICO
We're going to stay here and help you. It's only fair after what you've done for me.

ISABELLE
Or come with us. We'll hide you if the townspeople come on us.

SALLAS
You're too kind, but please leave me. I will be all right. I'm most adept in confronting many displeased clients.

MIRANDA
If she insists, Fredrico, she insists. The one thing you don't want to do is anger an enchantress. That much I do know.

> (*FREDRICO steps to SALLAS and kisses her on the cheek.*)

FREDRICO
If you change your mind, please come find us. I can't thank you enough.

SALLAS
Thank you for your compassion, señor. I'll remember you always.

> (*The four say good-bye and exit stage right. SALLAS watches them leave and then pulls out an AMULET from under her clothing, holds it tightly and recites.*)

SALLAS
Amadu, arillious, immus, adreev.
Amadu, arillious, immus, adreev.
Good fortune to you and yours.
Best to all and best to you.

> (*SALLAS smiles and exits stage right.*)

END OF SALLAS, THE ENCHANTRESS OF GRANADA

Are You a Good Witch or a Bad Witch?

Inspired by the Memorable Line from the Motion Picture THE WIZARD OF OZ
Original Script by Joan Garner

—BACKGROUND INFORMATION
(genre classification and other data deemed useful)

Back in the good old days nearly all witches were bad. Then a fellow named L. Frank Baum put a good witch in a quaint little story titled THE WONDERFUL WIZARD OF OZ and the idea of good witches took off. In fantasy and fairy tales of old, witches were infamous for their bad deeds. Baba Yaga eats the souls who visit her unprepared and unclean of spirit, or enslaves them. The Three Witches in MACBETH steer Macbeth to do evil and murder. And the witch in HANSEL AND GRETEL either turns children into animals or bakes them in her oven.

But with the issuing in of the 20th Century, Baum's THE WONDERFUL WIZARD OF OZ (1900) inspired subsequent "good" or at least "marginal" witch stories. This change is most noticeable in the performing arts. Gillian Holroyd (stage play BELL, BOOK, and CANDLE, 1956) uses magic to cast love spells. Jennifer, a witch of 17th Century Salem returns to life in the 20th Century and messes with love potions to right the path of those obviously going down the wrong one in the movie I MARRIED A WITCH (1942). Of course television has made its own contribution to the good witch "vogue" with TABITHA (1977—1978), the more recent CHARMED (1998—2005), and the hallowed classic BEWITCHED (1964—1972).

This sketch applies the premise of the bad witches of literature and screen meeting the good ones. Naturally the bad witches feel witches should be bad and the good witches believe their craft can be used for good. Whatever the agreement or discord, it makes for a humorous confrontation.

The Subject of Witchcraft—Otherwise known as illicit magic, the practice of witchcraft has carried on from ancient times to present. Whether as a pastime or religion, witchcraft intrigues and

scares the common person. Usually avoided, at times witchcraft comes front and center in certain societies and eras (e.g., the Inquisition). Generally dealing with potions and spells, witchcraft also includes conjuring the dead, reading tarot, manipulation of energy or aura, healing, runes and incantations, and fortune-telling. But mostly, witchcraft influences another person's body or possessions against their will, or unknown to them. To do so with malevolence in mind makes the practice or witchcraft bad. And a bad witch is always good for a fantasy adversary.

— SYNOPSIS OF STORY

(Present Day—Maybe. Location Undetermined)
Witches from popular fantasy stories and fairy tales meet to discuss their image. Glinda, the Good Witch of the North proposes all the witches perform only good magic, but this doesn't set well with the bad witches from literature like Baba Yaga and Mowimm, Hansel and Gretel's witch. Other witches from page, stage, and screen clock in and some comments create a near fight. But in the end, Samantha Stephens steps in to pacify the debate and most go away happy and content with their contribution to fantasy literature.

Are You a Good Witch or a Bad Witch?
STAGING SUGGESTIONS AND HELPFUL HINTS

— CHARACTER DESCRIPTIONS
(All Characters in this Script are Female)

MARY SANDERSON: Not all evil, but not all good.

WINIFRED SANDERSON: More of a true witch than her sister, **WINIFRED** is not the patient sort.

SARAH SANDERSON: Like a middle-child, highly capable yet seldom recognized.

BABA YAGA: Old, ugly, and crabby.

WICKED WITCH OF THE WEST: A truly wicked witch beloved for her wickedness.

ENDORA: Powerful and intolerant of incompetent witchery.

AUNT CLARA: Fumbling, flustered, yet adorable and loved.

EVA ERNST: Possibly the second most powerful and revered witch after **SAMANTHA STEPHENS**.

GLINDA: Her typical, near irritatingly spunky self.

MOWIMM: Old, ugly, and cantankerous.

THE THREE WITCHES OF MACBETH: Old, ugly, and dumb.

MALEFICENT: Stately but relishes in being bad.

SAMANTHA STEPHENS: The best witch of them all. Good, powerful, and sensible.

— PRESENTATION SUGGESTIONS
(Witch like Clothing and Items)

COSTUMES
ALL WITCHES EXCEPT GLINDA—Black, long flowing dress. Long black cloak. Black hose and slippers. Black pointed hat.

GLINDA—Fancy, glittering gown like in the movie.

PROPS
WANDS—For those who want one.

SOUND EFFECTS
MICROPHONE—On the PODIUM (optional).

STAGE
CHAIRS and BENCHES—As needed.

STOOLS—As needed.

PODIUM—For standing behind.

STAGING
Sit the **WITCHES** in the back on STOOLS, or have them stand. Hide **SAMANTHA STEPHENS** a little until her time to come to the PODIUM. Though not speaking parts, additional witches mentioned in the sketch can also sit and stand about if desired.

STAGING

STAGE RIGHT   **STAGE LEFT**

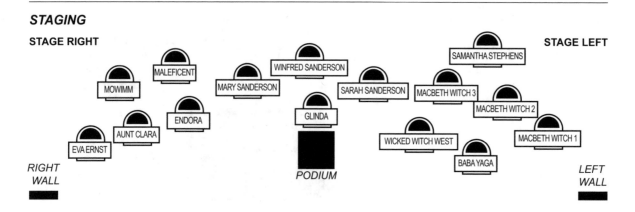

Are You a Good Witch or a Bad Witch?
SCRIPT

SETTING
CHAIRS, BENCHES, and STOOLS sit about. A PODIUM with MICROPHONE rests in the center.

*(Witches walk about and talk among themselves. **WINIFRED, MARY**, and **SARAH SANDERSON** from HOCUS POCUS hover around the PODIUM. **WINIFRED** searches for something.)*

MARY SANDERSON *(To **WINIFRED**.)*
What are you looking for?

WINIFRED SANDERSON
The minutes to last month's meeting. I just found out Glinda is running late—something about having bubble trouble.

SARAH SANDERSON
We're already late getting started. The others are becoming restless. The one thing I know is you don't want a bunch of restless witches meandering about.

MARY SANDERSON
Oh, you're so right, Sarah. Nothing good can come from dawdling witches.

WINIFRED SANDERSON
That's why I thought I'd start this meeting myself.

MARY SANDERSON
Can we do that?

SARAH SANDERSON
Of course we can do that. We're witches, aren't we?

MARY SANDERSON
Oh, right.

WINIFRED SANDERSON
(Into the MICROPHONE.)
Attention... Attention, please. Everyone settle down, please.

(The witches become quiet.)

WINIFRED SANDERSON *(Continued.)*
Thank you... Um, I know you were expecting Glinda, the good witch of the North. But apparently the Munchkins got hold of her bubble and now there's this gyro problem with it. Anyway, most of you know me.

(The witches look at one another, shrug their shoulders, and nod "no.")

WINIFRED SANDERSON *(Continued.)*
I'm Winifred Sanderson and these are my sisters Mary and Sarah.

*(**MARY** and **SARAH** wave. Still no recognition from the witches.)*

WINIFRED SANDERSON *(Continued.)*
From the movie HOCUS POCUS. All right, I admit it wasn't a really successful movie, but here we are... Now I think they called this emergency meeting tonight to address public relations.

MARY SANDERSON
Glinda feels us witches have gotten a bad rap long enough.

SARAH SANDERSON
And she thinks it's about time we do something about it.

(Murmurs among the witches.)

MARY SANDERSON
So if anyone has any ideas, speak right up.

BABA YAGA
About what?

SARAH SANDERSON
Uh, about how we witches can improve our image.

BABA YAGA
Why?

SARAH SANDERSON
Why?

BABA YAGA
We're witches. Duh. Why should we worry about our image?

MARY SANDERSON
Well, I guess Glinda feels if we had a better image, people would stop killing us off at the end of most stories.

WICKED WITCH OF THE WEST
It would be just like goodie, goodie Glinda to present such a ridiculous notion.

MARY SANDERSON
Well, I think it's fair to say that you, Wicked Witch of the West, have some unresolved issues with Glinda and therefore bring a slightly slanted opinion to the table.

(More murmurs from the witches.)

ENDORA
Well, I think—

WINIFRED
—The chair recognizes Endora from BEWITCHED. Endora, would you like to take the podium?

(ENDORA crosses to the PODIUM.)

ENDORA
Thank you, uh....

WINIFRED SANDERSON
Winifred. Winifred Sanderson from HOCUS POCUS.

ENDORA
Thank you... I, for one, am willing to look at anything helping dispel the misconception that all witches are ugly old hags.

(The witches cautiously "Oo.")

ENDORA *(Continued.)*
No offense, Baba Yaga.

AUNT CLARA
Well... Well, I think... I... I... Well, I'm wondering—

ENDORA
Oh, for Pete's sakes, Clara. Spit it out.

AUNT CLARA
Well, oh dear. I thought... Eva?

(EVA ERNST, sitting next to AUNT CLARA, stands to speak.)

EVA ERNST
Aunt Clara wants to know if Glinda's problem with us witches and our image has to do with our appearance or what we do?

(EVA ERNST sits.)

AUNT CLARA
Uh, yes, yes. And to whom—or is it who? I never get that rule right.

ENDORA
Eva, I don't know what Glinda has in mind here. I'm as much in the dark with this as you are.

(Enter GLINDA from stage left.)

GLINDA, THE GOOD WITCH OF THE NORTH
So sorry everyone. Of course if you're in the dark, it's difficult to talk about it. Thank you, Endora. I'm here now. You may go back and sit with Aunt Clara.

ENDORA
Must I?

(Reluctantly, ENDORA returns to her seat.)

GLINDA, THE WITCH OF THE NORTH
Thank you for coming. The subject is; are you a good witch or a bad witch?

WICKED WITCH OF THE WEST
(Aside to BABA YAGA.)
It's the best line she has in the whole story and she milks it for all it's worth.

GLINDA, THE WITCH OF THE NORTH
Now I know some of you are hovering somewhere in between—take the Witches of Eastwick for example.

WINIFRED SANDERSON
And Sally and Gillian Owens and their aunts from PRACTICAL MAGIC.

EVA ERNST
No, Sally and Gillian are more good than bad.

ENDORA
Eva Ernst, the Grand High Witch in WITCHES should know.

(The witches applaud as EVA ERNST stands, bows, and then sits back down.)

AUNT CLARA
Is it still how? I mean, how someone looks?

GLINDA, THE WITCH OF THE NORTH
It's about everything, Aunt Clara. Now I admit we witches have been portrayed more kindly in recent years like Gillian Holroyd of BELL, BOOK, AND CANDLE, and of course—me. But the earlier witches... Well, Mowimm would know better than anyone here.

WITCHES
Who?

(MOWIMM steps out from the crowd.)

MOWIMM
I'm Mowimm. Does anyone know who I am? No. But say, "Hansel and Gretel's evil witch" and everyone—

WITCHES (*Now recognizing* **MOWIMM**.)
Ohhh!

MOWIMM
Ah, ha. Exactly. I'm not an individual. I'm not thought of as another human being. I'm that nasty old witch that lives in a gingerbread house. Everyone hates me.

AUNT CLARA (*Aside to* **EVA ERNST**.)
Well, her baking children—um—might have something to do with it.

BABA YAGA
But again, we're *witches*. What do you expect?

EVA ERST (*Standing.*)
Baba Yaga has a point. If it wasn't for us witches, there would be no story at all. Every story needs a villain. Who is a more perfect villain than a witch?

(*The witches murmur in agreement.*)

ENDORA
Yes, Eva. I agree.

WINIFRED SANDERSON
The Three Witches from MACBETH are ugly hags. What do they think of all this?

THREE WITCHES FROM MACBETH
Double, double toil and trouble;
Fire burn, and cauldron bubble.

WINIFRED SANDERSON (*Pause.*)
Uh, huh. Does anyone else have an opinion on improving our image?

MALEFICENT (*Stepping up.*)
I do.

BABA YAGA
Maleficent, what are you doing here? You're not a witch. You're a fairy.

MALEFICENT
Yes, but I'm a *bad* fairy.

BABA YAGA
How did you get in here? Who let her in here?

GLINDA, WITCH OF THE NORTH
Sorry, Maleficent. As wonderfully bad as you are in SLEEPING BEAUTY, technically you're a fairy. This meeting is for witches only.

MALEFICENT
Well, I never.

(**MALEFICENT** *storms offstage right huff.*)

MARY SANDERSON
Boy, she was pretty mad.

WINIFRED SANDERSON
Mm, witch envy.

SARAH SANDERSON
Maybe everyone should stay clear of spinning wheels for awhile.

GLINDA, WITCH OF THE NORTH
Back to my proposal of improving our image—

ENDORA
—Maybe we should vote on whether we want to improve our image or not.

EVA ERNST
That's an excellent idea, Endora.

GLINDA, WITCH OF THE NORTH
Certainly. We can do that. We'll start with me. I vote yes, that we improve our image.

WICKED WITCH OF THE WEST
And I vote no.

MARY SANDERSON
Well, you would vote no, wouldn't you?

GLINDA, WITCH OF THE NORTH
Mary Sanderson, how do you vote?

MARY SANDERSON
I think we need to form a committee to look into the pros and cons.

WICKED WITCH OF THE WEST
She didn't ask for your suggestion. She asked for your vote, nitwit.

SARAH SANDERSON
Don't you talk to my sister like that.

WICKED WITCH OF THE WEST
Yeah, and what are you going to do about it, huh? You're all wimpy witches. I could take all three of you in one spell.

WINIFRED SANDERSON
Oh, yeah? Well, just try it!

(*The three* **SANDERSON WITCHES** *roll up their sleeve and start to approach the* **WICKED WITCH OF THE WEST**. **ENDORA** *and* **EVA ERNST** *step between them to stop any fighting.*)

EVA ERNST
Now ladies, you know the rules. We leave our witchcraft at the door.

ENDORA
Come to think of it, that's another thing. Why are we forced to resist what comes naturally? Why can't we use witchcraft at these meeting?

*(The **WICKED WITCH OF THE WEST** waves her hands over the **SANDERSON WITCHES**. They try to talk, but nothing comes out. This creates a general commotion that continues as the dialogue goes on.)*

AUNT CLARA
Um, I think that's why.

GLINDA, THE WITCH OF THE NORTH
To get back to the matter at hand. The Three Witches from MACBETH, how to you vote?

THREE WITCHES FROM MACBETH
Double, double toil and trouble;
Fire burn, and cauldron bubble.

GLINDA, THE WITCH OF THE NORTH
Would that be a yes or no?

THREE WITCHES FROM MACBETH
Double, double toil and trouble;
Fire burn, and cauldron bubble.

ENDORA
We're getting nowhere with this.

(A voice comes from the back of the crowd.)

SAMANTHA STEPHENS
I'd like to say something.

*(The witches calm down as the crowd parts allowing **SAMANTHA STEPHENS** to step to the PODIUM. All bow as she passes.)*

GLINDA, THE WITCH OF THE NORTH
I'm honored to turn the podium over to the most powerful and respected witch of us all, Samantha Stephens.

SAMANTHA STEPHENS
Thank you, Glinda... I know we all have faced prejudice and misunderstanding at one time or another in our lives. It's expected when you're different from the rest. Personally, I have tried very hard to fit into the human world by denying what I am. But the fact is I'm a witch. And to be honest, I'm very proud to be a part of the sisterhood. I also think each and everyone of us should be proud of

the contribution we've made to storytelling. I don't think anyone should be ashamed of what we are and feel we need to change. I think we should stay just the way we are.

*(The room erupts in applause as all stand and cheer. All but the **WICKED WITCH OF THE WEST** and **GLINDA** huddle around **SAMANTHA STEPHENS** and exit stage right, patting her on the back and so forth.)*

WICKED WITCH OF THE WEST
Well, well, well. Look what just happened here. You're little goodie, goodie plan just blew up in your face.

GLINDA, THE WITCH OF THE NORTH
Rubbish. In general, people don't like change, that's all. It's unsettling. But without change, we can't move forward. All they need is a little time to think about it.

WICKED WITCH OF THE WEST
Oh sure—sure. What's the matter, Glinda? Didn't the witches fall all over your suggestion? It's not so easy being the heavy, is it?

(The two start to exit stage right.)

GLINDA, THE WITCH OF THE NORTH
Nonsense.

WICKED WITCH OF THE WEST *(Mocking.)*
Nonsense.

GLINDA, THE WITCH OF THE NORTH
Gloating is very unbecoming, you know.

WICKED WITCH OF THE WEST
You're just bent of joint because the witches are on my side for once.

GLINDA, THE WITCH OF THE NORTH
Oh, be gone before someone drops a house on you.

*(**GLINDA** exits stage right. The **WICKED WITCH OF THE WEST** crouches and looks to the sky to see if there is a house coming at her before she exits stage right.)*

END OF ARE YOU A GOOD WITCH OR A BAD WITCH?

After Midnight

Adapted from an Old German Tale by E.T.A. Hoffmann, Later Becoming the Popular Nutcracker Ballet
Original Script by Joan Garner

—BACKGROUND INFORMATION
*(genre classification and other data
deemed useful)*

An interesting development occurred in researching background information for this sketch. Data on the original 19th Century story THE NUTCRACKER AND THE MOUSE KING nary exists. Connect the story with the ballet THE NUTCRACKER and an avalanche of material tumbles forth. Consequently, background information offered here combines the two.

The story of a soldier (prince in some versions) magically turned into an ugly nutcracker begins at the pen of author E.T.A. Hoffmann (see Hoffman's biography below). In 1891, famous choreographer Marius Petipa commissioned Pyotr Ilyich Tchaikovsky to compose the music for the ballet THE NUTCRACKER. And in 1892, the ballet's first performance took place at the Mariinsky Theatre of Russia. Making its way through Western Europe and over to America by the 1940s, the ballet has since become a standard holiday fair. However, it might be prudent to note Hoffmann's story makes up only Act I of the ballet. Act II with the sugarplum fairies and other fanciful groups dancing about seem nothing more than filler to expand the piece for full performance purposes.

THE NUTCRACKER AND THE MOUSE KING, like many of Hoffmann's stories (and like many a fantasy story later labeled "children's literature") begins as political commentary. And like many a social criticism, it combines the macabre with the darker side of the human spirit. War, battles, hacking and dismemberment, and blood appear consistently in fantasy stories and fairy tales. Deprivation (of the poor) and affluence (of the rich and royal) also crop up symbolically in character and situation within these romantic tomes.

Romanticism—An artistic and intellectual movement of ideas beginning in the late 18th Century and continuing through the 19th Century that focuses on emotion, often imposing awe and horror conventions. Its primary purpose is to comment or revolt against aristocratic social and political status quo of the day. German romanticism of which E.T.A. Hoffmann participated

varies from the European concept by valuing humor and wit and favoring imperfection; therefore, the ugly Nutcracker.

E.T.A. (Ernst Theodor Amadeus) HOFFMANN (1779–1822). Prussia. A romantic and fantasy author and composer, Hoffmann's THE NUTCRACKER AND THE MOUSE KING later turned into Tchaikovsky's ballet THE NUTCRACKER as was THE SANDMAN into the ballet COPPELIA by Léo Delibes. Yet his greatest work KATER MURR, a study of artistry and the journey of creating is relatively unknown. Influencing later authors like Poe, Kafka, and Dickens, Hoffmann died in Berlin ostracized from Poland accused of spying for the Prussian king.

— SYNOPSIS OF STORY

(18th Century Germany) Marie Lutter wakes from supposed brain fever. She tells her parents and doctor the family friend Mr. Dollsimere, a clock maker, magically turned her into a tiny person. He did so for her to join her beloved nutcracker, a toy Dollsimere gave her for Christmas earlier that evening. When the toys strewn about come to life, mice crawl out of the shadows with the Mouse King and a battle between the toys (soldiers), nutcracker, and mice follows. Of course Marie's parents and the doctor don't believe such a fantastic tale, but clock maker Dollsimere does.

After Midnight
STAGING SUGGESTIONS AND HELPFUL HINTS

— CHARACTER DESCRIPTIONS

MAMMA LUTTER: (Female) Lovely and concerned mother.

PAPA LUTTER: (Male) Loving father, but not of great patience.

DOCTOR HURST: (Male) A man of science, he's not about to believe **MARIE'S** story.

MARIE LUTTER: (Female) A beautiful and sensitive young woman.

MR. DOLLSIMERE: (Male) Mysterious with an air about him: approach with caution.

— PRESENTATION SUGGESTIONS
18th Century German Clothing and Items)

COSTUMES
MAMMA LUTTER—Fancy laced robe and gown. Or, a chemise gown with long train falling from a sleeveless waistcoat. Hairstyle of ringlets with chignon (Headband).

PAPA LUTTER—High collar shirt with cravat. Spencer jacket over tailcoat, long, tight-fitting pantaloons with straps passing under the shoes. Short hair.

DOCTOR HURST—High collar shirt with cravat. Long coat. Striped waistcoat. Shoes. Short, curly hair. Bushy sideburns.

MARIE LUTTER—Nightgown. Bare feet. Long, loose hair.

MR. DOLLSIMERE—High collar shirt with cravat. Long coat. Striped waistcoat. Shoes. Semi-long hair with long sideburns. Eye patch.

PROPS
NUTCRACKER TOY—an ugly nutcracker carved from wood (easily found in Christmas decorating shops).

STAGE
MARIE'S BED—Place a few blankets over a long folding table, wrap a sheet over them, place pillows on top, and a quilt on top of all—voilà— a bed!

STAGING
This is a simple sketch. Exiting in and out stage right suggests going into the rest of the house and a normal world. When MARIE and MR. DOLLSIMERE exit stage left, they're leaving into magic and enchantment.

STAGING

STAGE RIGHT   **STAGE LEFT**

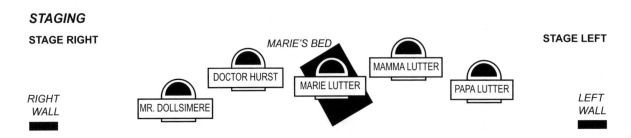

RIGHT
WALL

LEFT
WALL

After Midnight
SCRIPT

SETTING
18th Century Germany. **MARIE'S** Bedroom. A BED sits center stage.

(A sleeping MARIE lies in her BED. MAMMA LUTTER sits on the edge of the BED patting MARIE'S hand. PAPA LUTTER and DOCTOR HURST stand to the side.)

MAMMA LUTTER
Marie. Marie, wake up, dear. Come on, sweet daughter, wake up now.

(MARIE LUTTER opens her eyes.)

PAPA LUTTER
There she is. Our sweet girl is going to be just fine.

MARIE LUTTER
Papa, what am I doing in bed? How long have I been here?

PAPA LUTTER
We found you this morning in the parlor, Marie. You were on the floor.

MAMMA LUTTER
When we couldn't wake you, we sent for the doctor.

DOCTOR HURST
How are you feeling, Marie? Can you see me all right? Sometimes a bump on the head like that can make your vision a little fuzzy for a spell.

MARIE LUTTER
I see everyone fine, Dr. Hurst.

DOCTOR HURST
Oh, that's good. That's very good. We'll need to keep an eye on you for a day or two. I'm afraid brain fever can cause other delayed ailments.

MARIE LUTTER *(Alarmed.)*
Brain fever?

MAMMA LUTTER
You fell and hit your head on the glass cabinet. The glass must have broken and cut your head because there was blood on the rug where we found you.

MARIE LUTTER
That wouldn't be my blood. That blood belongs to the Mouse King.

PAPA LUTTER
The what?

MARIE LUTTER
The Mouse King. There was a horrible battle and the nutcracker chopped off the Mouse King's seven heads.

MAMMA LUTTER
Oh, dear. I'm afraid the fever is still with her.

MARIE LUTTER
No, Mamma. Last night after midnight there was a great battle between the mice and the toy soldiers.

PAPA LUTTER
What a nightmare you had, Marie.

MARIE LUTTER
No, Papa. It really happened.

MAMMA LUTTER
Marie, are you telling tales so we won't punish your for leaving the parlor in such a mess? It's all right, dear. Whatever went on last night— whatever you did, we're just glad you're not hurt.

MARIE LUTTER
I didn't do anything, Mamma. It wasn't me, honestly. It was the mice. They sprang up from the shadows and began running all over the place. It was as if the whole room was moving.

PAPA LUTTER
Such dreams. You ate too many sweets, Marie Lutter. That's what you did. All that sugar made you dream crazy things.

MARIE LUTTER
But I didn't eat any sweets, Papa. It really happened. The clock maker wanted me and Fritz to meet to him in the parlor after midnight.

MAMMA LUTTER
Mr. Dollsimere? Why would he want that?

MARIE LUTTER
It had to do with our toys and the nutcracker he made for me. *(Looking around.)* Where is it?

MAMMA LUTTER
If you and your little brother met Mr. Dollsimere in the parlor last night, why haven't they said something about it?

MARIE LUTTER
Fritz was sleepy and went to bed before the battle started. Have you asked Mr. Dollsimere what happened last night?

PAPA LUTTER
Mr. Dollsimere is out in the hall. He's been waiting to see how you're doing. He's very concerned.

(PAPA LUTTER exits stage right.)

MARIE LUTTER
He should be concerned. He's the one who made everything happen.

MAMMA LUTTER
Made what happen, dear?

MARIE LUTTER
He used his magic to make the toys come alive so they could fight the mice.

MARIE LUTTER *(Patting MARIE'S hand again.)*
Oh, honey.

(PAPA LUTTER enters from stage right with MR. DOLLSIMERE.)

PAPA LUTTER
See, Mr. Dollsimere? She's fine.

MR. DOLLSIMERE
I'm so glad to see you awake, Miss Marie. I believe this belongs to you.

(MR. DOLLSIMERE pulls a NUTCRACKER TOY from his coat. MARIE gladly takes the NUTCRACKER and cradles it in her arms.)

MARIE LUTTER
My nutcracker. My dear nutcracker.

MR. DOLLSIMERE
Your father tells me you had a fantastic dream.

MARIE LUTTER
It wasn't a dream, Mr. Dollsimere. You of all people should know that.

MR. DOLLSIMERE
Why don't you tell us about you dream?

PAPA LUTTER
Why encourage such nonsense, Mr. Dollsimere? Our daughter is well now. We need to let it rest.

DR. HURST
Well now, Mr. Lutter, it may help Marie to talk about her dream. It might help to lessen the brain fever.

MARIE LUTTER
I wish all of you would stop calling it a dream. I'm not a child anymore. I should know what a dream is and what isn't.

MAMMA LUTTER
What happened, dear?

MARIE LUTTER
Mr. Dollsimere said Fritz and I should come to the parlor after midnight. He said he had something magical for us to see. Fritz grew weary and went back to bed, but I stayed awake and met Mr. Dollsimere in the parlor.

DR. HURST
Is this true, Mr. Dollsimere? Did you meet Marie in the parlor?

MARIE LUTTER
Mr. Dollsimere wasn't there at first. When I got there, the room was empty—at least I thought it was. But I saw a miniature palace in the corner. The enchantment started when I looked into the small palace. There were hundreds of candles lighting the rooms inside—tiny little candles with a flame no bigger than a grain of wheat. And in one of the rooms were two tiny people dancing about. The two people looked just like me and Fritz.

DR. HURST
These toys were moving?

PAPA LUTTER
Did you make this little palace, Mr. Dollsimere? You have made many wonderful toys for my children through the years. Yes, wonders to behold. It wouldn't surprise me if you made little dolls that could dance about.

MARIE LUTTER
It was Mr. Dollsimere, Papa. When I looked into another room, there was a little Mr. Dollsimere looking back at me.

MAMMA LUTTER
Marie, that would make Mr. Dollsimere something of a magician—like a wizard or enchanter. And we know magic only exists in stories. If you claim to be all grown up, you know this couldn't possibly be.

MARIE LUTTER
I couldn't believe what I was seeing myself, Mamma. But when the little Mr. Dollsimere vanished from the miniature palace, that's when the mice came out of the walls. There were so many of them, I thought they would quickly swarm all over me. And then the Mouse King appeared

with his seven crowns on his seven heads. I panicked when the mice began to swarm all over me. But then I saw Mr. Dollsimere again.

MAMMA LUTTER
Where did you see him?

MARIE LUTTER
On the clock that sits on the fireplace mantel. When I cried out because the mice were smothering me, Mr. Dollsimere raised his cloak and all the toys in the room came to life—the dolls, the toy soldiers, and my precious nutcracker.

PAPA LUTTER (Pointing.)
This nutcracker?

MARIE LUTTER
Yes. He turned into a handsome soldier and led the toy soldiers against the Mouse King and mice. It was such a fierce battle with legs and limbs flying everywhere. All the blood was terrible. Then my nutcracker faced the horrid Mouse King. They fought and fought, but in the end, my nutcracker lopped off all the heads of the Mouse King. He saved me. When this happened, all the mice suddenly disappeared and all the toys turned back to their lifeless selves. That's when I looked for Mr. Dollsimere on the clock, but he wasn't there. The next thing I remember is waking a few minutes ago.

(All are silent for a moment.)

DR. HURST
Well, that's certainly a magnificent story.

MARIE LUTTER (Becoming perturbed.)
It isn't a story.

MR. DOLLSIMERE
I'm afraid all of this is my fault. I'm so sorry to have troubled everyone so. I wonder if you would mind if I spoke to Marie alone?

DR. HURST
To what purpose?

MR. DOLLSIMERE
Please. The Lutters and I have been friends for many years. They know I wouldn't dream of causing any harm to our Marie.

PAPA LUTTER
If you think it would help.

MR. DOLLSIMERE
Thank you. I honor your trust.

(*PAPA* and *MAMMA LUTTER* exit stage right with a hesitant *DR. HURST.*)

MARIE LUTTER
Please, Mr. Dollsimere, you're not going to say I was dreaming all this.

MR. DOLLSIMERE
No, my dear. I'm not going to say anything of the kind.

MARIE LUTTER
It *did* happen.

MR. DOLLSIMERE
It did.

MARIE LUTTER
Well, why didn't you tell Mamma and Papa it was real? They surely think I'm crazy. Dr. Hurst is calling it brain fever.

MR. DOLLSIMERE
Yes, yes. But my admitting it all happened would only lead the adults to think I'm crazy, too. Then I couldn't continue with my magic or be able to offer you a very special chance of a happy future.

MARIE LUTTER
I don't understand.

MR. DOLLSIMERE
Marie, you have always been my most favorite child because you believe in enchantment. I've watched you grow up to become a lovely young lady and want to give you a magical life.

MARIE LUTTER
What kind of life?

MR. DOLLSIMERE
No one else could see how special the nutcracker was. That's why I gave him to you.

MARIE LUTTER (Cradling the *NUTCRACKER*.)
May I tell you a secret? When I fainted and hit my head, it wasn't because of the mice or seeing the Mouse King killed. It was because my beautiful soldier turned back into this nutcracker. It broke my heart.

MR. DOLLSIMERE
Yes, I could see that. But what you don't know is the nutcracker didn't turn into a handsome soldier. I turned the handsome soldier into an ugly nutcracker.

MARIE LUTTER
You turned my soldier into this nutcracker? Why?

MR. DOLLSIMERE
Because a young lady as special as yourself deserves more than a normal human life. Marie, would you like to be with your soldier?

MARIE LUTTER
Oh, more than anything I have ever wanted before. I know it sounds irrational, but I love him so much my heart aches.

MR. DOLLSIMERE
You see, Marie. I can give you that life. I can use my magic and turn you into the little doll you saw in the miniature palace. And I can turn the nutcracker back into the small soldier you fell in love with. I can place both of you in the palace and there you can live happily for the rest of your days.

MARIE LUTTER
You can do that?

MR. DOLLSIMERE
I can. But you wouldn't be able to come back and visit your parents. The ordinary world would no longer exist for you. You need to know this and choose very carefully.

MARIE LUTTER (*Thinking hard.*)
I know how lucky I am to have the love of my parents. But it won't be long now until I leave them to marry in a real world or enchanted one. To find your true love—I know this is the greatest gift of all. Yes, Mr. Dollsimere. Would you do that for me? Will you work your magic and join me with my soldier? I would be eternally grateful.

MR. DOLLSIMERE
Nothing would please me more, Marie. Come with me and we'll return you to your soldier.

> (**MARIE LUTTER** and **MR. DOLLSIMERE** exit stage left. After a moment, **PAPA** and **MAMMA LUTTER** and **DR. HURST** enter from stage right.)

PAPA LUTTER
Where did they go?

MAMMA LUTTER
Should Marie be out of bed yet?

DR. HURST
I didn't want to tell you what to do, but I don't trust that Dollsimere. It's something about his eyes.

PAPA LUTTER
I know. I bet they went back to the parlor to have a look around. That's what it is.

MAMMA LUTTER
Maybe they went back to clean it up.

PAPA LUTTER
I wouldn't think that. But we'll go to the parlor and find Marie. This I'm confident of.

DR. HURST
Yes, we'll find her, but in what condition? Will she be Marie or changed into a little doll?

MAMMA LUTTER
Oh, Dr. Hurst. What a funny notion—our Marie as a little doll. As if that could happen.

> (**PAPA** and **MAMMA LUTTER** and **DR. HURST** exit stage right.)

END OF AFTER MIDNIGHT

Gilded Horns Against the Fray

Original Script by Joan Garner

—BACKGROUND INFORMATION
(genre classification and other data deemed useful)

A key talent of fantasy characters is shapeshifting. Usually turning into an animal and back, shapeshifting as a *Fantastic Element* was often employed in mythology and fantasy. (In Science Fiction, shapeshifting typically involves an alien turning human to commit dastardly deeds.)

In terminology, confusion often emerges between shapeshifting and transformation because a definitive definition of the two isn't available. For this author, shapeshifting sounds like an old word while transformation springs from technological lingo. Hence, I use the word shapeshifting when talking about fantasy and mythology and reserve the word transformation for science fiction discussions. Although this distinction doesn't correlate with the words' true definitions, it works for me.

Also, shapeshifting rings throughout horror or monster stories with the Wolfman (man turning to wolf), Dracula turning into a wolf or bat, and Cat People (people to cats) being the most familiar. But in fantasy, shapeshifting belongs to sorcerers and sorceresses (or wizards as is the case for this sketch).

Were-creatures commonly involve those who can only shapeshift to one other form. But were-creatures show the diversity shapeshifting commands in cultures around the globe. For example, Bouda are hyena-men in African lore, and Encantados from Brazil are dolphins who turn into humans. Thunderbirds are large birds who can turn into human beings in Native American lore, and Nagas of India and Nepal are snake-people—snakes that either turn human or show physical characteristics of both.

Fortunately, fairies, wizards, and witches haven't this one form restriction. Merlin, the most famous wizard of all, shapeshifts in some stories, but most often preserves his humanness. Witches and fairies also shapeshift, but here they usually exact shapeshifting on someone else for vengeance or spiteful purposes (princess into a swan, prince into a toad).

— SYNOPSIS OF STORY

(Old Russia) In the days after Genghis Khan, all of Russia turns to Volga, the Wizard of Kiev, for protection against the advancing Tartars. A revered shapeshifter, Volga turns into several animals to get into the Tartar encampment. As a bird perched on the windowsill, Volga overhears the Tartar leader Khan tell his wife of his murderous intentions against the Russians. Volga then turns his troops into ants that they might enter the Tartar stronghold undetected. Once inside, Volga turns his soldiers back to human form and his army quickly defeats the surprised Tartar defenses.

—GLOSSARY
(terms possibly unfamiliar to the reader)

ARMORY—A building to store arms and equipment.

KIEV—A large city and capital of present-day Ukraine. It was the center of the first Russian state.

RUSSIAN STEPPE—Basically a flat plain with short grasses and no trees except near rivers and streams. The Russian Steppe covers a vast portion of Russia and adjoining countries like Mongolia and China.

Gilded Horns Against the Fray
STAGING SUGGESTIONS AND HELPFUL HINTS

—GLOSSARY *(continued)*

SHAPESHIFTER—One with the power to change its shape—usually from human form to that of an animal or inanimate objects.

— PRESENTATION SUGGESTIONS
(Russia of the Medieval Ages Clothing and Items)

This sketch relies on reciting and pantomime. To present as intended, divide **PLAYERS** *into* HUMANS *and* PUPPETS. **COSTUME** *suggestions show where* **PLAYERS** *can double up on parts.*

COSTUMES
—HUMANS

RUSSIAN SINGERS: (Male or Female) Old Russian folk costumes would serve best. If not that, then wearing black shirts or blouses with long, puffy sleeves and black pants will do. Black boots. A red sash around the waist and/or fur fez-like cap would add a nice flare to the outfit. The three **SINGERS** should dress alike.

PRINCESS and **WIFE:** (Female) A long, flowing, lightweight cloak covers from head to foot with only eyes and face seen for the **PRINCESS**. Under the cloak can be the **WIFE'S** costume consisting of a Chinese damask and cloth shoes. Hair pinned up.

LION, **RAM**, and **KHAN:** (Male or Female) Tan shirt, pants, and socks. Lion's mask or bushy mane made of yarn around the head. Replace Lion's mask with **RAM'S** when playing the **RAM**. Caftan-like satin robes of elaborate pattern for **KHAN**. Belt or sash cinches robes at waist. Cloth shoes. Squared, brimless cap. Fu Manchu mustache.

FISHERMEN and **SOLDIERS:** (Three Males) Long pants with cuff rolled up to half-calf height. Bare chest and no shoes for **FISHERMEN**. For the **SOLDIERS**, a bascinet (coned helmet) with aventail (flexible chain mail fabric that flows down to cover neck and shoulders). Or replace helmet with metal headband. Long, puffy sleeved shirt. Quilted tunic with half shoulder sleeves or no sleeves and cinched at waist with belt. Tight-fitting pants tucked into the top of calf-high boots.

VOLGA: (Male) Same as SOLDIERS, but more elaborate in decoration.

—PUPPETS

SERPENT, **BIRD**, **FERRET**, and **FALCON**—Cut-out, two-dimensional figures attached to sticks for manipulation over the BLACK CURTAIN.

PROPS
FISHNET—Optional for the **FISHERMEN** or pantomime tossing a fishnet.

SWORDS—Either wood or purchased plastic.

LIGHTING EFFECTS
At end of sketch, dim to black or switch lights off.

STAGE
BLACK CURTAIN— Strung across the stage, rising to about four or five feet high.

STAGING
The nice part about this sketch is the **PLAYERS** involved with pantomime haven't any lines to speak and the **SINGERS** have little movement needing to only step up and back.

* A SPECIAL NOTE
The verse recited by the THREE SINGERS carries a cadence and rhythm similar to the most known segment of the RUSSIAN SAILOR'S DANCE by Reinhold Gliere. The verse easily adapts to the distinct "thump, thump, thump-thump" music at the beginning of the piece.

STAGING

STAGE RIGHT	LOW BLACK CURTAIN	STAGE LEFT

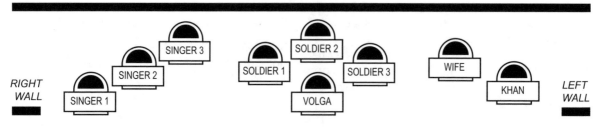

Gilded Horns Against the Fray
SCRIPT

SETTING
The Russian Steppe. Old Russia. A BLACK CURTAIN extends head high across the stage, upstage.

DIALOGUE	NARRATIVE

DIALOGUE

THREE RUSSIAN SIGNERS
There's a story of a boy soldier
With an army against the Golden Horde.
Volga warrior, Volga wizard,
The boy from Kiev who beat the Golden Horde.

RUSSIAN SINGER 1
This is a story of Volga, the wizard warrior of Old Russia. Volga's mother was a beautiful princess from Kiev, and his father was an enchanted serpent from the depths of the great Volga River. From his mother, he received courage and wisdom, and from his father, he received magical powers.

RUSSIAN SINGER 2
As Volga grew, he found himself able to shape-shift into many animals. He used this ability to help provide food for his village. At night, Volga turned himself into a lion to hunt forest animals. When the men of the village went fishing, Volga turned himself into a pike, dove into the river, and guided the other fish into the men's nets.

RUSSIAN SINGER 3
And when he was a young man, Volga became a warrior leader. Volga cut a handsome figure. In full armor and with sword and shield, Volga stood proudly—an imposing soldier before his army of 7,000 men, though he was only 15 years old. And his men would shout, "Volga, the great warrior wizard" so loudly, one could hear the thunderous roar across the entire Russian Steppe.

THREE RUSSIAN SINGERS
When the Tartars marched up from China,
Volga went out to save his Russian home.
Facing Tartars, Volga was cunning.
He used his magic against the Golden Horde.

NARRATIVE

(THREE RUSSIAN SINGERS stand downstage, right.)

(The THREE RUSSIAN SINGERS take one step forward before singing.)

(RUSSIAN SINGERS 2 and 3 step back.)

(A pretty veiled PRINCESS gracefully crosses the stage from left to right. When the SERPENT is mentioned, a SERPENT rises up and down from behind the BLACK CURTAIN as if swimming from right to left.)

(RUSSIAN SINGER 1 steps back and RUSSIAN SINGER 2 steps forward.)

(A LION enters from stage left, stalks for prey, and then quickly leaps off stage right. Three FISHERMEN enter from stage right, pull out a FISHING NET, and swoop it in the air as if scooping up fish. They exit stage left.)

(RUSSIAN SINGER 2 steps back and RUSSIAN SINGER 3 steps forward.)

(VOLGA enters from stage left. He poses center stage. Three SOLDIERS enter from stage left and stand behind VOLGA.)

(The SOLDIERS raise their SWORDS in the air, hailing VOLGA.)

(RUSSIAN SINGERS 1 and 2 step up to join RUSSIAN SINGER 3. They sing another verse.)

DIALOGUE

RUSSIAN SINGER 1

One day word came to Kiev the Tartar heirs of the infamous Genghis Khan were forming an army to invade Russia—the army known as the Golden Horde. Volga needed to know how many soldiers were in the Golden Horde and what weapons they had. When he asked for a volunteer to cross the Russian Steppe and spy on the Tartar stronghold, the men turned away, too scared and unwilling to accept the mission.

RUSSIAN SINGER 2

Volga sneered at his cowardly crew. Then in an instant, Volga turned himself into a ram. The ram ran for days across the Steppes of Russia with his gilded horns shining in the evening sunset. The ram continued towards the Golden Horde until he came to a high mountain crag and found sentries marching along the ramparts of the Tartar fortress. As a ram, Volga studied the stronghold and figured no army could get inside such a heavily fortified encampment. He would have to think of another way.

RUSSIAN SINGER 3

That evening, high up in the fortress, the mighty Khan and his wife came into a room discussing a mystery. They were so involved with their talk, they failed to notice a scarlet-crested bird that had flown onto the windowsill. The bird was ever so interested in what the Khan had to say and listened as he told his wife how he planned to divide the rich lands of Russia among his many sons. But this worried the Khan's wife. She told her husband of a dream she had. She said in her dream, there were two birds fighting. The smaller scarlet bird from the north killed the larger raven from the south. Khan's wife said the smaller bird was the enchanter Volga and if Khan's army goes up against Volga's army, they will lose. But the Tartar Khan dismissed his wife's dream believing it to be so much silliness.

THE THREE RUSSIAN SINGERS

Volga wizard turned into a wild bird,
And listened in on the dream the wife retold.
He used his magic and turned into a ferret.
And went to work on the Tartar's large stronghold.

NARRATIVE

*(**RUSSIAN SINGERS 2** and **3** step back.)*

*(**VOLGA'S SOLDIERS** gather around him. He gestures his request for a spy.)*

*(**RUSSIAN SINGER 1** steps back and **RUSSIAN SINGER 2** steps forward.)*

*(**VOLGA** slips under the BLACK CURTAIN. Quickly, a **RAM** rolls out from under the BLACK CURTAIN. The **RAM** slowly moves from stage left to stage right with its shining horns rolling up and down with movement.)*

*(The **RAM** turns to look out into the audience and then exits stage right.)*

*(**RUSSIAN SINGER 2** steps back and **RUSSIAN SINGER 3** steps forward.)*

*(**KHAN** and his **WIFE** enter stage right, pantomiming talking to one another. They stop center stage and continue to pantomime.)*

*(A **BIRD** appears stage left above the BLACK CURTAIN.)*

*(**KHAN** and his **WIFE** continue to pantomime talking as they exit stage left as the **BIRD** drops down behind the BLACK CURTAIN.)*

*(**RUSSIAN SINGERS 1** and **2** step up to join **RUSSIAN SINGER 3**. They sing another verse.)*

DIALOGUE	NARRATIVE
	(RUSSIAN SINGERS 2 and 3 step back.)

RUSSIAN SINGER 1

As a ferret, Volga raced about the armory tearing apart bowstrings and chopping the wood arrows in two with his sharp teeth. When the guards heard the noise, the ferret was long gone. And then they heard their horses scream the scream of death. When they reached the stables, they saw the shadow of a wolf on the wall and their dead horses on the ground. In an instant, the shadow disappeared and the screech of a falcon cut the clouds above. When the guards looked up, there was a falcon flying north towards Russia. The Golden Horde stood without horses or weapons.

*(A **FERRET** appears above the BLACK CURTAIN. It will duck down behind the curtain and then the curtain will bellow in and out from behind as if something behind it was fighting.)*

*(A **FALCON** rises above the BLACK CURTAIN and flies out stage right.)*

*(**RUSSIAN SINGER 1** steps back and **RUSSIAN SINGER 2** steps forward.)*

RUSSIAN SINGER 2

Not satisfied with leaving the Khan's fortress in chaos, Volga returned to Kiev and moved his troops south marching them to the Tartar fortress. But no one saw Volga and his soldiers coming. The clanging armor or tromping of marching boots did not break the night air. Were the sentries suspicious enough to know what to look for, they might have sounded the alarm upon seeing the thousands of ants creeping single file underneath the iron gates.

RUSSIAN SINGER 3

Come morning, the ants had dispersed throughout the fortress. And when the first rays of the sunrise burst into the center of the fortress, Volga sprang out of nowhere wielding his sword in the air. Suddenly, all the ants rose to become Volga's Russian army. Taken by surprise, the Tartars were no match for Volga's troops. In no time the Russian army defeated the Golden Horde and sent the Khan and his wife scurrying back to China. With cunning and resourcefulness, Volga, the wizard of Kiev, saved his Russian homeland.

*(**RUSSIAN SINGER 2** steps back and **RUSSIAN SINGER 3** steps forward.)*

*(**VOLGA** springs up from under the BLACK CURTAIN and stands center stage. On cue, he swings his SWORD in the air and **VOLGA'S SOLDIERS** roll out from under the BLACK CURTAIN.)*

*(**KHAN** and his **WIFE** scurry across the stage from left to right. **VOLGA'S SOLDIERS** chase after them and a exit stage right.)*

THREE RUSSIAN SINGERS

*Facing danger, Russia looked inward
And found a hero to fight the Golden Horde.
Wizard Volga used his great magic
And crushed a fierce foe,
The mighty Golden Horde.*

*(**VOLGA** stands regally at center stage.)*

*(The **THREE RUSSIAN SINGERS** bow when finished with their song.)*

*LIGHTING EFFECTS
Lights dim to off.

**END OF GILDED HORNS AGAINST
THE FRAY**

A Magical School
PAGE 1 (Developing a Setting Where the Story Takes Place)

J.K. Rowling's HARRY POTTER AND THE SORCERER'S STONE lends a perfect example and inspiration for this Project in developing the setting for a story.

Students will be asked to create a school of magic or enchantment like Hogwarts. It's recommended each student read HARRY POTTER AND THE SORCERER'S STONE to pick up more ideas in completing their school. When their school is ready, they'll use it in completing Project 2 of this **SECTION** dealing with story elements.

READING DESIRED BUT NOT REQUIRED

PREPARATION AND RESOURCES NEEDED: Have students read HARRY POTTER AND THE SORCERER'S STONE. Copy the 2 pages of this Project for each student.

Student Assignment: Read HARRY POTTER AND THE SORCERER'S STONE and then create your own school of magic and enchantment. Use the ideas given in the Chart below, or use your own in filling out the form provided on the next page.

This Chart suggests a few magical beings who would have their own school. It also gives three basic elements for a school; who it's for; it's purpose, and some classes it would have. It's hoped this chart is just a "starting" place. The rest is up to your imagination.

SCHOOL FOR	SOME THINGS THAT ARE TAUGHT	CLASSES
SORCERERS AND SORCERESS' (Harry Potter's Hogwarts)	Wizardry and magic.	• Spells • Broomstick Flying • Using Your Wand
GENIES	Studying the "three wishes" rule and getting around it. How to cram into a bottle or lamp and then blow up to gigantic proportions.	• Wish Granting • Majestic Posing • Gold Earring Cleaning
FAIRIES	Creating flowers and trees, controlling the weather, and sculpting clouds.	• Painting Flowers • Teaching Spiders to Spin the Proper Spider Web • Wing Styling
CHRISTMAS ELVES	Skills and craft expertise learned for Christmas elves and the special touches that make a good toy maker.	• Trucks and Dolls • The Perfect Ornament • How to Keep Your Shoes Curled Up
CANDY AND CAKES ELVES	What candy to make. How to make and package it. Who to give the confections to.	• Making a Good Candy Cane • The Magic of Putting the Cream in the Puff • *(Special Field Trip to Chocolate Island)*
DWARVES	Changing Coal into Diamonds and other ores into gold, silver, and copper.	• Coal—Not Just for Heating • Compounds and Dirt • Diamond Colors
MAGICAL BEASTS TRAINING	Who trains the beasts? What beasts are there and learning their temperaments. Keeping and caring for the beasts.	• Beast Identification • Proper Beast Nutrition • Beast Grooming

A Magical School (Developing a Setting) PAGE 2

SCHOOL FOR

NAME OF SCHOOL

WHERE IS SCHOOL? BUILDING(S)

HOW DO NEW STUDENTS GET TO THE CAMPUS?

NAME OF HOUSES WHERE STUDENTS STAY

NAME OF HEADMASTER (MISTRESS) AND TEACHERS

CLASSES TAUGHT

SCHOOL SUPPLIES NEEDED

ARE THERE UNIFORMS? WHAT KIND?

WHERE DO STUDENTS EAT? WHAT DO THEY EAT?

SCHOOL SPORTS & EXTRA CURRICULAR ACTIVITIES

WHAT DO STUDENTS DO FOR FUN?

DRAW SCHOOL MASCOT

DRAW SCHOOL LOGO AND WRITE SCHOOL MOTTO

A Magical School in Story
PAGE 1 (Advancing Story Elements)

This Project concentrates on story development.

After students have read J.K. Rowling's HARRY POTTER AND THE SORCERER'S STONE and after completing Project 1 of this **SECTION**, have them write an original story about a magical or enchanted school.

PREPARATION AND RESOURCES NEEDED: Have students read HARRY POTTER AND THE SORCERER'S STONE. Copy the 2 pages of this Project for each student.

READING DESIRED BUT NOT REQUIRED

*Student Assignment: Read HARRY POTTER AND THE SORCERER'S STONE and complete Project 1 of this **SECTION**. Then fill out the Suggestion Form and use the Outline to help you write your own story.*

A MAGICAL SCHOOL

TITLE OF STORY—The title of a story or book is very important. It should give the future reader an idea of what the story is about. It should also be an intriguing title to entice someone to read your story.

TITLE OF STORY

CHARACTERS OF STORY—Decide who your main character will be. He or she should be likable, but might have some quirks (like we all do) and weaknesses to make them human. Is he or she frightened to go to a new school, or shy, or have something he or she needs to overcome? A main character should grow or gain their self-assigned goal like wanting to be more outgoing or working to get outstanding grades for the year. Also write of their strength or something the character is really good at. You can use this strength when facing and overcoming the predicament or challenge he or she faces in the story.

NAME OF MAIN CHARACTER

MAIN CHARACTER'S PHYSICAL FEATURES (LOOKS)

MAIN CHARACTER'S QUIRKS, STRENGTHS, AND WEAKNESSES

SECONDARY CHARACTERS—Decide who your secondary characters or "buddy characters" will be. They should have common interests with the main character, but different enough to offer other ideas (of how to get out of the awaiting predicament). Physical differences help distinguish these characters from your main one.

NAME OF SECONDARY CHARACTER

SECONDARY CHARACTER'S PHYSICAL FEATURES

COMMON INTERESTS SHARED WITH MAIN CHARACTER

THE ANTAGONIST—Decide who your antagonists (the bad guy) will be. Creating the bad guy goes with figuring out what predicament or tasks the main and secondary characters will face. The bad guy will always try to keep your main character (or hero or heroine) from achieving their goal.

NAME OF ANTAGONIST

WHAT MAKES HIM OR HER THE BAD GUY?

A Magical School in Story (Advancing Story Elements) PAGE 2

THE PREDICAMENT—Besides attending school, the main character must face a predicament. This can be a dangerous thing that's come into the school or a big school test over a subject he or she isn't comfortable with, or engaging in a school sport. Whatever the predicament, the main character should call on and involve his or her friends (secondary characters) so they can all help in achieving the goal. The bad guy should come into play here as well, trying to stop the main character from achieving his or her goal. How the main character wins or achieves the goal over the predicament should also come here.

_____

_____

_____

_____

_____

IDENTIFY THE PREDICAMENT AND HOW ITS OVERCOME

WRAPPING UP THE STORY—Conclude your story by telling what the main character has learned. You can do this by having others notice how the character has changed, or how brave he or she was, or by earning an award. Show how he or she has triumphed in the end.

_____

_____

HOW DOES THE MAIN CHARACTER GROW?

An outline for your story is below. You may wish to go another way, but it's here to help you stay on course towards a good story. Each numbered item should be at least one paragraph in length. (MC = Main Character).

OUTLINE

A. *Introduction of Main Character (MC)*
   1. Tell about the MC. Is he or she special in some way? Is there a power the MC has but doesn't know about?
   2. Tell where the MC lives. Does he or she live in an unusual place?
   3. Tell how the MC receives the invitation or acceptance to the special school.

B. *Getting to the New School*
   1. Tell where the MC needs to go or where the special school is.
   2. Tell what mode of transport the MC uses to get there. Bus? Airplane? Comet?
   3. Is it an easy trip or does the MC run into problems?

C. *Arriving at School*
   1. Is the MC greeted at school? By whom? Is the school a friendly or scary place?
   2. MC goes to the assigned house. He or she meets friends (secondary characters).
   3. MC and friends talk about themselves and about the school before they go to sleep.

D. *Attending the First Day of School*
   1. Attending the first class. What's it about? Who's the teacher? Are there any unique supplies they're given to work with?

   2. MC meets his or her antagonist (bad guy or thorn in the side) in class.
   3. The antagonist confronts the MC after class. How does the MC handle the confrontation and how do the friends respond?

E. *The Predicament Comes Into Play*
   1. Identify the predicament, challenge, or problem the MC must overcome or win.
   2. The MC figures out what to do to "fix" the predicament.
   3. Will the friends by involved in this plan?

F. *Facing the Predicament*
   1. Tell how the MC comes up against the predicament (or situation).
   2. What is the difficulty the MC experiences to overcome the predicament, solve the problem, or win the match?
   3. What happens to the predicament? Does it disappear or go away defeated. Will it return to face the MC another day?

G. *Victorious and Happy*
   1. The MC realizes he or she has conquered their weakness.
   2. The MC recognizes his or her friends for helping them through the predicament and self-problem.
   3. Feeling good, the MC is ready for another day and challenge.

The Arthurian Legend
Overview in Brief

Pinpointing where the Arthurian Legend begins (or with whom) proves difficult. Finding where the legend begins in literature is easier. The following tries to satisfy each issue.

ARTHUR AS LEGEND
Was He a Real Person or Not?

Many a theory, essay, and daresay college thesis address the actual existence of King Arthur. Though many a possibility presents itself, a concrete source has yet to surface. Arthur "the man" is most likely a combination of several historical figures such as:

Lucius Artorrius Castus, A Roman Leader (2nd Century)

Ambrosius Aurelianus—Another Romano-British war leader against the Anglo-Saxons. (2nd Century)

Riothamus—King of the Brettones (5th Century)

Owain Ddantgwyn ap Yrthr, King of Rhôs. (6th Century)

Artur Mac Aidan, a war leader of the Scots. (6th Century)

If nothing more, the colorful names of these figures is enough to promote legend. However, Arthur as legend and its creation looks like a predominantly Dark Ages invention negating the first entry.

THE LEGEND

Recognized by many titles with the *Arthurian Cycle*, *Matter of Britain*, and *Arthurian Romances* as the most prevalent, the Arthurian legend has "picked-up" many a story tidbit from this poem or that telling along the way. But the crux of the story comes from Sir Thomas Malory's LE MORTE DARTHUR *(See Page 149 of **WINGS OF FANCY** for more on Malory's LE MORTE DARTHUR.)*

Breaking Arthur's story down to a couple of paragraphs for purposes here seems ambitious and arrogant, yet here it is:

Born from an unholy union between King Uther and Queen Igraine, the magician Merlin takes Arthur to Sir Ector to raise. As an adolescent, Arthur pulls the famed sword from the stone making him King of Britain. He spends a good deal of this young adulthood defending his crown from would-be claimants. He marries Guinevere who eventually commits adultery with Sir Lancelot. This egregious crime throws Arthur's idealistic Camelot and Round Table into chaos. A final battle pits Arthur against the chief rabble-rouser and insurgent leader Mordred (who just happens to be Arthur's son). Arthur kills Mordred , but falls mortally wounded in the fight. He's taken to the island of Avalon where Morgan Le Fey heals his injuries.

During these events, a good many fairies and enchanters wander in and out. The search for the Holly Grail also takes place and other unforgettable characters like Sir Perceval and Galahad come into play.

The Arthurian Legend
Overview in Brief *(continued)*

MILESTONE, CLASSIC, AND INFLUENTIAL LITERATURE WORKS CONCERNING THE ARTHURIAN LEGEND

The three "definitive" texts that all else stems and strays from are:

Geoffrey Monmouth's HISTORIA REGUM BRITANNIAE (History of the Kings of Britain) (1136)
A translation of Welch heroes into Latin. Here, Monmouth's account ties Arthur's birthright to King Uther and how he became mortally wounded in a battle against Mordred.

Thomas Malory's LE MORTE DARTHUR (1485)
The Arthurian Legend as story known and accepted today draws from Malory's telling. Including Merlin, the Lady of the Lake, Morgan Le Fey, Mordred, Guinevere, Lancelot, the Round Table, Camelot, Excalibur, and the Quest for the Holy Grail.

T.H. White's THE ONCE AND FUTURE KING (1958)
The ultimate modern text of the Arthurian Legend combines three of White's previous novels and relies heavily on Malory's Arthurian concept conspicuously omitting the Holy Grail sequence.

Although the three literary pieces above define the Arthurian Legend, other works from Malory to White and beyond continue to make up the legend as a whole with some of the more noted being:

THE RED BOOK OF HERGEST (1400)
Welsh manuscripts of prose and poetry. It includes the MABINOGION (The WHITE BOOK OF RHYDDERCH) and other tales and histories. Geoffrey of Monmouth's HISTORIA REGUM BRITANNIAE and a series of Triads also complete this collection.

Wace, the Norman Monk's ROMAN DE BRUT (1155)
Literary history of England covering the stories of King Arthur.

Chrétien de Troyes' LE CHEVALIER DE LA CHARRETE (The Knight of the Cart) or LANCELOT (1177)
French poem with numerous escapades. Camelot and Lancelot's love affair with Queen Guinevere occurs here for the first time.

The world seemed content accepting Malory's LE MORTE DARTHUR as the consummate Arthurian tale until the 19th Century when several Victorian poets like Lord Alfred Tennyson and William Morris wrote verse on various segments. In the 20th Century, famed Howard Pyle illustrated several books involving the King Arthur Legend. Equally famous illustrators took paint to canvas in illustrating Arthur like Aubrey Beardsly's TALES OF KING ARTHUR, 1905, and THE ROMANCE OF KING ARTHUR AND HIS KNIGHTS OF THE ROUND TABLE (1917) illustrated by Arthur Rackham.

Other novels written in the 20th Century and early 21st Century revolving around King Arthur and the many stories surrounding are too numerous to mention. Suffced to say, the interest in the Arthurian Legend and what Mike Ashley (expert in the history and development of **Fantasy Genre**) calls "[A] quasihistorical British king or war-leader whose mythical adventures have formed the basis for the largest single subcategory of fantastic literature" lives and thrives.

Merlin—The Tall, Yet Sinking Tower

Based on an Arthurian Legend
Original Script by Joan Garner

—BACKGROUND INFORMATION
(genre classification and other data deemed useful)

Undoubtedly the most famous of wizards, Merlin the Magician's roots gnarl deep into the Arthurian legend. Yet the story of Merlin begins before Arthur, and it's suggested Merlin founded the legend itself.

Merlin contributes mightily to the magic, enchantment, and supernatural slant of the saga. If Arthur is the might and right, Merlin is the mastermind behind it all. And where several historic figures make the composite known as Arthur, so is Merlin an amalgamation of people and supposed events—most notably Myrddin the Wild, a Welch bard who turned into a mad hermit.

Merlin ventures in and out of the many Arthurian stories, and it seems events either go right because he's there dispensing wisdom and magic, or wrong because he's not. Like many characters of the legend, Merlin projects a bevy of diversified personalities from an amused and wily wizard to a cantankerous curmudgeon to a wise adviser and to something of an absentminded professor.

And as noted in David Days', THE SEARCH FOR KING ARTHUR, Merlin the Magician continues to materialize in more current narratives. For example, Merlin serves as the model for J.R.R. Tolkien's Gandalf in THE LORD OF THE RINGS, and George Lukas' Obi-wan Konobe in the movie STAR WARS.

Merlin's wizardly powers change from telling to telling, but his greatest abilities include prophesying, time travel, and spellbinding. In that regard, the intrigue that surrounds Merlin the Magician should endure throughout the ages.

— SYNOPSIS OF STORY

(6th Century England) This story highlights Merlin in his youth. One of the first accountings tells of Merlin's encounter with King Vortigan whose first intention is to kill the apprentice magician. (Vortigan is trying to build a castle supporting a tall tower he believes will protect him when enemies come calling. But, no matter how many times the king builds his tower, it keeps sinking in the ground and falling down. To fortify the tower, his Soothsayer suggests mixing the building mortar with the blood of one born of a human mother, but without an earthly father.) This would be Merlin. However, being something of a prophet and thus knowing what's going on and what will happen, Merlin uses this knowledge to convenience the king to spare his life. This early story establishes Merlin's mystical aura.

Merlin—The Tall, Yet Sinking Tower
STAGING SUGGESTIONS AND HELPFUL HINTS

—GLOSSARY
(terms possibly unfamiliar to reader)

ABUTMENTS—An architectural structure that supports the weight and pressure of an arch.

ALLEGIANCE—Loyalty or the obligation to a sovereign (king, queen, royalty).

LACKEY—A servant and follower.

PERCEPTION—Insight. Recognizing a situation.

PREPOSTEROUS—Not possible. Beyond reason.

WANING—A gradual decrease in amount or degree such as enthusiasm or support for something.

— CHARACTER DESCRIPTIONS

MASTER ARCHITECT: (Male) A competent and confident professional though frightened of his fate knowing what has happened to his predecessors.

KING VORTIGAN: (Male) A selfish and domineering king focused only on his wants and wishes. Droll and sarcastic in personality.

SOOTHSAYER: (Male) No more a soothsayer than the rest of us, this fellow does his best to convince everyone he knows his craft.

WELT: (Male) A common peasant of common sense and humble deed—maybe a little scraggly.

NIMUE: (Female) Merlin's future love is a prisoner here; beautiful in face and gentle in spirit.

REDMOND: (Male) A brave and honorable knight.

MERLIN: A quiet presence, **MERLIN** knows he's superior to all, but always extends an effort not to be especially arrogant.

— PRESENTATION SUGGESTIONS
(6th Century English Clothing and Items)

COSTUMES
MASTER ARCHITECT—Square cap. Worn tunic with fancy belt. Tights or stockings.

KING VORTIGAN—Crown. Armor and cape.

SOOTHSAYER—Coif cap. Long cloak with hood over long tunic and tights or stockings.

WELT—Short tunic with rope belt. Tights.

NIMUE—Veil. Long bliaut of any color. Tights.

REDMOND—Helmet and long mail tunic. Tights.

MERLIN—A long, ragged cloak decorated with shredded strips of cloth. Short tunic with fancy belt. Tights or stockings.

PROPS
SMALL TABLE—standing in front of the **MASTER ARCHITECT**.

PARCHMENT PAPERS AND SCROLL—Parchment-like papers with castle blueprints drawn on them.

SOUND EFFECTS
Hammer and saws banging about behind the audience. Clanging items in a box. When the tower supposedly falls, roll the box with the objects across the floor behind the audience.

STAGING
Movement of these **PLAYERS** isn't vital, but keeping **MERLIN** offstage until his entrance will help build his mysterious aura.

___

STAGING

STAGE RIGHT   **STAGE LEFT**

RIGHT WALL   REDMOND   ARCHITECT   VORTIGAN   MERLIN   SOOTHSAYER   NIMUE   WELT   *LEFT WALL*

Merlin—The Tall, Yet Sinking Tower
SCRIPT

SETTING
An open field in England. 6th Century.

(KING VORTIGAN and the MASTER ARCHITECT stand behind a small TABLE. SCROLLS lie on the TABLE. The MASTER ARCHITECT holds open a SCROLL while KING VORTIGAN looks on. The SOOTH-SAYER, WELT and NIMUE stand off to the side and listen.)

* SOUND EFFECTS
Construction noises up and behind the audience. Noises start loudly and then lessen when the dialogue begins.

(The MASTER ARCHITECT points to the SCROLL.)

MASTER ARCHITECT
I have had prime timbers set in the corners of the foundation here and here.

KING VORTIGAN
And this will hold the tower this time?

MASTER ARCHITECT
It should, Your Majesty.

VORTIGAN
Mm… The Master Architect before you assured me the abutments would hold and that tower fell. And the Master Architect before him assured me the stone cast foundation would hold and *that* tower fell. My faith in Master Architects is waning.

MASTER ARCHITECT *(Pointing outward.)*
But you can see for yourself, Sire, the tower is the highest it's ever been. The timbers have succeeded where the other building ideas have not.

VORTIGAN
They had better succeed. I'm beginning to lose my patience with Master Architects.

WELT *(Aside to NIMUE.)*
"Beginning to lose his patience." As if King Vortigan had any patience.

SOOTHSAYER
Hold your tongue, Welt. Hold your tongue or lose it should King Vortigan hear you.

WELT
I'm a nothing, Soothsayer. What I say or do won't stop the sun from rising or the oceans from ebbing.

SOOTHSAYER
True enough. On the other hand, I *am* the king's soothsayer. If this Master Architect should fail like the others, Vortigan will come to me for answers.

WELT
And if you haven't any, it will be *your* head.

SOOTHSAYER
I haven't kept away from the chopping block all these years by being stupid, Welt. Expecting this very thing, I've placed a plan into action. You'll see in due time.

NIMUE
I don't see how anyone can keep their head around that tyrant. You—me—anyone.

SOOTHSAYER
Nimue, King Vortigan holds you hostage to keep your father's loyalty. He fears Lord Ardente will turn and join Prince Uther like so many others have. More and more are marching behind Prince Uther against Vortigan. Why do you think he's trying to build the tallest tower on the highest rocky hill in the country? He wants to protect himself from his enemies.

NIMUE
They're building a castle for a coward.

SOOTHSAYER
Yes, but he *is* the king and has the power and military to enforce his will. Although Vortigan demands your father's allegiance, Nimue, he has no obligation towards you. Pawns are easily eliminated, so I recommend you stay in the shadows. Should you come to the king's attention again, who knows what he'll do to you.

VORTIGAN *(Stilling reviewing the SCROLLS.)*
I see what you've done here. Still, what makes you believe your approach will work when the others have failed?

MASTER ARCHITECT
Your Majesty, with the utmost respect, I can merely look at the previously tried and advise alternatives.

VORTIGAN
Then advise alternatives….

MASTER ARCHITECT
I've seen what hasn't worked. All the methods used should have built you a perfectly fine castle tower. I don't know why the foundations didn't work before. If these special timbers fail, I'm at a loss.

VORTIGAN
If they fail, you'll be at a loss all right—the loss of your head.

* SOUND EFFECTS
A tremendous crashing of things in the distance.

VORTIGAN (*Looking out and smoldering.*)
How many times? How many times before someone gets it right? Soothsayer!

SOOTHSAYER
Yes, Your Majesty?

VORTIGAN
What's going on here? Why does the tower keep toppling over?

SOOTHSAYER
Your Majesty, as your soothsayer I haven't the power to tell you why things happen, just the power to tell you what things *will* happen.

VORTIGAN
Then what good are you to me? I think maybe your head should come off, too. I'm so mad—I must severe somebody's head!

SOOTHSAYER (*Trying to save his neck.*)
However, I think I might know why the tower keeps falling. It's the matter of the mortar.

VORTIGAN
Mortar? It's the same mortar I've used to build my other castles.

SOOTHSAYER
Yes, Your Majesty. But in this particular case—since you're not having much luck with it here—might I suggest a stronger if not unusual mixture.

WELT (*Aside to* **NIMUE**.)
Ah, here he goes. That head of his will be off his shoulders shortly. Listen to this….

SOOTHSAYER
I hear-tell that a mixture of lime, sand, water and blood is the strongest mortar anyone can make.

VORTIGAN
Blood? Whose blood?

SOOTHSAYER
It must be the blood of a man born not of an earthly father.

VORTIGAN
Not an earthly father? What nonsense.

MASTER ARCHITECT
Utterly preposterous.

SOOTHSAYER
This knowledge is part of my craft, Your Majesty. You asked me how to build a tower that wouldn't fall down and I offered my suggestion.

VORTIGAN
Say we were willing to try this special mortar of yours. Where do we find such a person?

SOOTHSAYER
Sensing you might be keen to my proposal, I took the liberty of sending Redmond to fetch a particular youth. They should be here any….

    (**REDMOND** *enters from stage left with* **MERLIN**. *They cross center stage.*)

REDMOND
Soothsayer, here is the lad as you requested.

VORTIGAN
And who is this young man?

MERLIN
My name is Merlin. How may I serve you?

VORTIGAN
You may serve me by donating your blood—all of it, actually.

MERLIN (*Staying calm.*)
I see. Although I'm prepared to give my king my all—which is obviously the case here—I believe I can serve His Majesty better should he deem it charitable to keep me alive.

VORTIGAN
How can you serve me?

MERLIN
Redmond has explained you're having problems building your castle on the rocky butte over there.

    (**MERLIN** *points out over the audience.*)

 (2006 © Joan Garner) **WINGS OF FANCY**: Using Readers Theatre to Study Fantasy Genre

VORTIGAN
As you can plainly see by all the broken stone scattered about.

MERLIN
And I assume many have suggested how to build your tower, but no one has said why it keeps falling down.

VORTIGAN
How did you know that?

MERLIN
I'm known by some as a prophet.

REDMOND
He also claims to be a child, though he looks older.

MERLIN
I live backwards and forwards. I can move from one time to another. I measure my age differently than you, and I can look whatever age I wish at whatever time I desire.

NIMUE
You're a wizard.

MERLIN
Among other things, lovely lady.

VORTIGAN *(Studying MERLIN.)*
Your mother was human?

MERLIN
Yes, Your Majesty.

SOOTHSAYER
—And his father was a demon living between the moon and the earth?

MERLIN
Correct, sir.

VORTIGAN
Mm—must be rather unpleasant.

MERLIN
To be honest, it hasn't posed that much of a problem until now.

MASTER ARCHITECT
Son, you said you know why the tower continues to fall. Tell us why.

MERLIN
You constructed a sturdy enough castle, Master Architect. The trouble is the ground under it.

REDMOND
But it's built on solid rock.

MERLIN
Rock, yes. Solid, no. Below is a vast cavern hosting a deep pool. Drain the pool and you'll find two hollow stones that rumble within the pool.

VORTIGAN
So the earth shakes and the tower comes down.

MASTER ARCHITECT
Preposterous.

MERLIN
You asked.

VORTIGAN *(To the MASTER ARCHITECT.)*
Where's *your* explanation, Architect? *(To MERLIN.)* Why should I believe you, boy?

MERLIN
Why would I lie?

VORTIGAN
Oh, I don't know—to save your neck? Rest assured, if I'm not convinced of your word, I'll slit your throat soon enough.

NIMUE
How free you are with threatening to harm everyone not in your favor.

VORTIGAN
You say another word, and it's back into the shackles for you, Nimue.

NIMUE
I'm not afraid of you. You're just keeping me to make sure my father does your bidding.

VORTIGAN
I'm king. What do you expect?

NIMUE
I expect a king to serve his people.

VORTIGAN
I fear your schooling misguided, precious Nimue. I expect my people to serve *me*. This is the primary principle of being a ruling monarch and one I hold close to my heart.

SOOTHSAYER
Enough of this. We're running out of time. Redmond, cut off the boy's head now.

REDMOND
Your Majesty?

VORTIGAN
No one commands beheading but me, soothsayer.

MERLIN
There's more you should know, King Vortigan. Inside the hollow stones are two dragons; one red and one white. The stones will soon burst apart and the dragons will emerge and immediately do battle.

REDMOND
King Vortigan, your heraldic crest is the white dragon. And Prince Uther's crest is the red dragon.

VORTIGAN
Does this fight of these dragons have anything to do with me and Uther?

MERLIN
His Majesty is a most perceptive man.

VORTIGAN
And who wins this battle, prophet?

MERLIN
The white dragon will finally get his tall tower, but I fear he'll perish in it.

VORTIGAN *(Thinking.)*
Mm... Well, I plan to prove you wrong.

MERLIN
Yes, Your Majesty. Please do.

SOOTHSAYER
Ridiculous. Redmond, kill this false prophet now!

REDMOND
Your Majesty, must I follow the orders of this pathetic soothsayer? After all, I'm a knight not a lackey.

VORTIGAN *(Hesitating.)*
Forget about the boy for now. I'm going to attack Uther before he attacks me—a surprise attack. *(To MERLIN.)* What do you think of that? How can your prophecy come true after that?

REDMOND
An excellent idea, Your Majesty.

VORTIGAN
Of course it's an excellent idea. I thought of it. We'll catch Uther at his own game—and the rest of my enemies. I'll kill them all before they kill me, and then there will be no need to build a tall tower for protection.

(VORTIGAN exits stage left with REDMOND and the MASTER ARCHITECT.)

WELT
You're a mighty brave fellow telling the king something like that.

NIMUE *(To MERLIN.)*
Is it true? Will Prince Uther kill King Vortigan?

MERLIN
There's nothing to fear, dear lady. King Vortigan will never return to this place.

WELT
Just how powerful a wizard are you, Merlin?

MERLIN
I still have much to learn. I hope in time I can use these powers of mine to help those around me.

NIMUE
I think you're going to be a great wizard, Merlin.

MERLIN
You humble me, dear lady.

SOOTHSAYER
What utter rubbish. He's no more a wizard than I am.

MERLIN
Sir, you impress me by admitting your own failings.

SOOTHSAYER
Be forewarned. I'm going to reveal you for the impostor you are.

(The SOOTHSAYER storms out stage left.)

WELT
You're threatening his job, you know.

NIMUE
Well, I for one look forward to seeing Merlin master his craft. I think I'll keep a keen eye on you with your permission.

MERLIN
With such a beautiful eye gazing my way, how can I not fulfill my destiny?

WELT
I'll remember your name, Merlin, for I believe Nimue is right. I have a feeling you'll be the most powerful wizard of all-time. People will write stories and sing of your deeds and magic through all eternity.

MERLIN
Then I'll strive to be worthy of all that is to come.

(MERLIN, NIMUE, and WELT exit stage right.)

END OF MERLIN—THE TALL, YET SINKING TOWER

(2006 © Joan Garner) **WINGS OF FANCY**: Using Readers Theatre to Study Fantasy Genre

Arthur—The Sword in the Rock

Based on an Arthurian Legend
Original Script by Joan Garner

—BACKGROUND INFORMATION
(genre classification and other data deemed useful)

One of the most endearing Arthurian legends, THE SWORD IN THE STONE has as many renditions as any other. To start, the stone's location comes into question. It's placed from deep in the forest, to a distant countryside, to a town square. Then there's the sword. It's just a sword in most stories, but some lay claim it's the famous sword Excalibur. Most versions have the magician/wizard Merlin driving the sword into the stone, while the sword becomes stuck there by diverse means in other interpretations. That Arthur is the only one able to pull the sword out of the stone seems the single constant in all stories. Here, his reason for taking the sword also varies.

For the few unfamiliar with the legend, a brief summary follows:

In guiding the future of young Arthur and Great Britain, the all-powerful wizard Merlin applies his magic and forces a sword into a large stone boulder; afterwards he proclaims that whoever pulls the sword from the stone is pure of heart and the true king of England.

Naturally the greedy and power-lust hearts try for years to dislodge the sword, but even the strongest man in the kingdom can't budge the metal from its imposed prison.

Arthur, ward of Sir Ector and squire to Sir Ector's son Kay travel to participate in a tournament. The overall winner at the end of the scheduled events becomes king of England. Only, right before a jousting round, Arthur discovers he left Kay's sword back in the tavern or camp. Rushing back to get it, Arthur sees a sword sticking out of a stone.

Thinking it will save time to just take that sword, Arthur tugs on it until the sword comes out. Spectators watching the boy perform this heroic feat immediately hail Arthur as the new and rightful king of England.

Besides it being a crafty way to place Arthur on the throne, THE SWORD AND THE STONE story provides another link of the Arthurian legend to its medieval time and events. Drawing the sword from the stone acts as a metaphor for the practice of metallurgy (removing metal from ore).

Medieval wizards like Merlin were originally alchemists practicing metallurgy and alchemy (chemical philosophy of turning other metals into gold). Though never achieving this lofty intent, by producing the potions and compounds to get there, an association with mysticism and conjuring soon surrounded the alchemist who eventually evolved into the magical wizard.

Arthur—The Sword in the Rock
STAGING SUGGESTIONS AND HELPFUL HINTS

— SYNOPSIS OF STORY

(13th Century England) Rupert, a cracker-jack troubadour of his day, takes center stage to entertain his audience. Beginning his song, he tells of the legend of Arthur and the Sword in the Rock. But he's interrupted by a woman joining him onstage. Ethel explains she's a scout for PSCTEPCW, The Proper Squad Championing Truth, Ethics, and the Politically Correct Way. Pish-Posh for short. Ethel takes issue with Rupert's song and some of its possible untruths and politically incorrect jargon. He argues with her, but she remains to hear all of his song to see if any more of the material might fall within the "no-no" guidelines of the Pish-Posh organization.

— CHARACTER DESCRIPTIONS

RUPERT: (Male—Female Optional) A professional entertainer, flashy in a Hollywood way. He loves to perform.

ETHEL: (Female—Male Optional) A "right brain" gal with a no-nonsense approach and limited flexibility.

— PRESENTATION SUGGESTIONS
(13th Century European Clothing and Items)

COSTUMES
RUPERT—Padded jupon or simple tunic. Tights. Pointed, cloth shoes, Large, floppy hat (beret).

ETHEL—Short sleeved dress over linen chemise, or blouse of long, puffy sleeves and long skirt. Slippers. Hair pulled back under veil. Veil draped over the head and flowing down the back.

PROPS
MANDOLIN—Realizing a mandolin might be hard to find, taping a plastic bowl to the back of a guitar, ukulele, or banjo may create an amusing effect.

STENO PAD and PENCIL—Found in desk drawers, or local stationery stores.

BOOKLET—Take a small, flat book and wrap a jacket around making it a generic title.

STAGING
Entrances and exits in this sketch should be easy enough to do whether performing the sketch or just reading it.

STAGING

STAGE RIGHT   **STAGE LEFT**

RIGHT
WALL   *LEFT*
■   RUPERT   ETHEL   *WALL*
                                                                                   ■

Arthur—The Sword in the Rock
SCRIPT

SETTING
England. 13th Century. The TOWN SQUARE of a small village in the English countryside. The stage is bare.

> *(**RUPERT** stands center stage with MANDOLIN.)*

RUPERT
Good evening ladies and gentlemen. Thank you for coming. I'm Rupert the Troubadour. We have a terrific program planned for you tonight, so sit back and relax and get ready for some great music.

> *(**RUPERT** begins to strum—not the correct cords—but he strums.)*

RUPERT (Continued.)
Oh, there once was a lad named Arthur
Who lived a long time ago.
He hadn't much might and wasn't too bright
To come in out of the snow.

Now Arthur's the boy of our story,
A story with some awe and shock,
Of magic and spells and heroes and swells,
The tale of The Sword in the Rock.

So Arthur—

> *(Enter **ETHEL** from stage left with STENO PAD, PENCIL, and BOOKLET.)*

ETHEL
Wait just one minute.

RUPERT
What are you doing? I'm in the middle of my act here.

ETHEL
I'm Ethel, forward scout for the PSCTEPCW.

RUPERT
The what?

ETHEL
PSCTEPCW, The Proper Squad Championing Truth, Ethics, and the Politically Correct Way. Pish-Posh for short.

RUPERT
You've got to be kidding.

ETHEL
I'm here to see that your song is accurate and inoffensive in every way.

RUPERT
What's wrong with my song?

ETHEL
Well, for one, it's The Sword in the *Stone* not The Sword in the Rock.

RUPERT
It's a fantasy story. Accuracy isn't a big deal.

ETHEL
Accuracy is a very big deal. Doesn't your audience here deserve the best? Also, the *not very bright* part is hurtful.

RUPERT
Hurtful to who—whom?—whoever.

ETHEL
Arthur.

RUPERT
Well, seeing how the guy has been gone for some time now, and seeing how he probably didn't exist in the first place, I don't think I'm hurting his feelings. May I continue my song now?

ETHEL
Don't let me stop you.

RUPERT
Right... *(He strums.)*

So Arthur was raised by his father,
Sir Ector the bold and the brave.
But his brother was not, a real little sot
Who treated him more like a slave.

ETHEL
All right. All right. What's a sot?

RUPERT
You don't know what a sot is? How can you object to it, if you don't know what it is?

ETHEL
It's a naughty word, isn't it?

RUPERT
Nooo. A sot is a drunkard.

ETHEL
So you're calling Arthur's brother a drunkard. Do you know for sure he was a drunkard?

RUPERT
Nooo. I called him a sot because it rhymes with not. It fits in the song, that's all.

ETHEL
Well, it will have to come out.

RUPERT
Look lady, this is *my* song and if I want to make Sir Kay a sot, he's going to be a sot.

ETHEL
I suppose it could have been worse. Go on.

RUPERT *(Sarcastically.)*
Oh, thank you ever so much. *(He strums.)*

Now the Britons had become despondent,
A king to rule they did seek.
Some had tried, some had died
Yet England was still up the creek.

Anything wrong with that?

ETHEL
No. That was all right. It's pretty dumb, but within the Pish-Posh guidelines here.

RUPERT *(He watches ETHEL suspiciously and strums.)*
So one day they held a big tourney
To see who was bravest of all.
The one so renowned would get the gold crown
Joining the land for us all.

Anything wrong with that one?

ETHEL
No. Other than you using *all* twice. That really isn't rhyming, you know.

RUPERT
I really don't care, you know. *(He strums.)*

So onto this field of valor
Stepped Arthur with brother and dad.
Sir Kay so devised to win the great prize
In armor true he was so clad.

> *(**RUPERT** stops and looks at **ETHEL**.)*

ETHEL
What?

RUPERT
You're frowning.

ETHEL
Well, there's nothing offensive in that verse. But I noticed you use the word "so" a lot.

RUPERT
So? *(Grumbling.)* No one appreciates the agony of the artistic process. *(Strums.)*

When it was time for the jousting
Kay needed his shield and his sword.
But Arthur forgot, the sword he had not,
And all he could say is "My Lord!"

ETHEL
Okay. Here we go. You're impugning a religious icon. That's definitely a no-no.

RUPERT
Oh, for Pete's sake. *Oh, Lord* is perfectly acceptable. Show me in that guideline book where *Oh, Lord* isn't acceptable.

ETHEL *(Frantically flipping through the book.)*
All right already. You can go on.

RUPERT *(Strums.)*
Arthur rushed back to the tavern
Where he and his dad had a room.
But his way had been blocked,
the door had been locked,
Poor Arthur now knew he was doomed.

Yet on his way back he so noticed
A curious sight by the dock.
A shiny bright plate rising up from the slate
The now famous Sword in the ROCK!

Ha, ha!

ETHEL
It's still The Sword in the *Stone*, you ninny.

RUPERT
Ho, ho. Name-calling. I'm sure that's a no-no in that book.

ETHEL
I apologize. Is there anymore to this song?

RUPERT
I have a terrific wrap-up. *(He strums.)*

When Arthur ran up to that big sword,
He grabbed on the hilt to so pull.
But the sword didn't budge, it didn't so nudge
That sword was just intractable.

ETHEL
You're really pushing the envelope here, Rupert. And it's still a stone.

RUPERT *(Angry.)*
I haven't gotten to that part, Ethel. *(He strums.)*

Yet, Arthur was really determined
To get that swell sword for Sir Kay
With one more good yank, the sword did go clank
It slid out from that stubborn clay.

> *(**RUPERT** stops for **ETHEL'S** input.)*

ETHEL
Actually, that wasn't too bad.

RUPERT *(Again, sarcastically.)*
Gee, thanks. *(He strums.)*

When Arthur had looked all about him,
A big crowd had gathered around.
Though some kind of sneered,
most loudly cheered
Saying Arthur was king to the crown.

Arthur so stood stunned and silent
He didn't know quite how to feel.
Till his dad took due note,
on the sword it was wrote
The words that made all want to reel.

On the side of the sword there was etched fine
A prophecy all witnessed on.
For whoever pulled the sword from the rock
Would be rightful king of all Briton!

> *(**RUPERT** ends his song with a multitude*
> *of quick strums on the MANDOLIN. He*
> *then bows.)*

RUPERT *(Continued.)*
So what do you think of that?

ETHEL
On the edge. Very on the edge. I'll have to take this matter back to Pish-Posh and confer.

RUPERT
You do that. Meanwhile, I have six more gigs to be at before the end of the week. So if you don't mind, I'll be moving on.

ETHEL
It's still the Sword in the Stone.

> *(They begin to exit stage right.)*

RUPERT
I could care less.

ETHEL
Actually, I think it's "I couldn't care less."

RUPERT
A lot you know.

ETHEL
Knowledge is power.

RUPERT
You're a real pain, you know that?

> *(**RUPERT** and **ETHEL** exit stage right.)*

END OF ARTHUR—THE SWORD IN THE ROCK

Morgan Le Fey—The Questing Beast

Based on an Arthurian Legend
Original Script by Joan Garner

—BACKGROUND INFORMATION
(genre classification and other data deemed useful)

Mention the name Morgan Le Fey and most develop an unpleasant taste in their mouth. Turns out, Morgan's nastiness in legend and infamy is a carefully mastered reinterpretation and purposeful "trashing" of an Arthurian icon.

Originally, Morgan (Morgen) appears in Geoffrey Monmouth's LIFE OF MERLIN as one of nine sisters who rule Avalon, the island King Arthur sails towards to die. Morgan, a healer, saves Arthur from death enabling him to live until he inevitably disappears into legend.

Sir Thomas Malory's LE MORTE D'ARTHUR credits Morgause, Morgan's sister and King Arthur's half sister for sleeping with Arthur and producing Mordred, the incestuous heir that would lead to Camelot's downfall. Through the ages it's Morgan, not Morgause saddled with this dastardly deed, so why should I correct the misconception? The following sketch pulls its plot from MORGAN LE FEY AND THE QUESTING BEAST, not Morgause.

Changing Morgan Le Fey from kindly enchantress to evil sorceress began with the Cistercian monks' PROSE LANCELOT (or the VULGATE CYCLE). Written in the 13th Century, the monks retooled PROSE LANCELOT and other Arthurian Romances into religious allegories to emphasize spiritual concerns over earthly desires. Believing healing and prophetic powers of women blasphemous and condemning matters of the flesh (also blamed on women), the monks took nearly all women in Arthurian legend and made them bad. (Or at least made it disastrous to associate with women.) Morgan Le Fey received the brunt of this demonizing. When the monks were through with the beautiful enchantress with magical healing powers, Morgan turned into a demonically possessed, incestuous adulteress finagling to thwart the "saintly" Arthur at every turn.

Having endured years of abuse, a more human and compassionate Morgan Le Fey has

resurfaced recently in stories like Marion Zimmer Bradley's MISTS OF AVALON (1982), and Grace Chetwin's children's books ONE ALL HALLOWS' EVE and OUR OF THE DARK WORLD (1984 and 1985).

— SYNOPSIS OF STORY

(6th Century England) In her cavern like home, evil sorceress Morgan Le Fey brews a spell to set King Arthur dreaming. In this telling, she sends the Questing Beast into Arthur's dream to set straight certain facts. One, that she's his half-sister, and two, that Arthur is the product of King Uther's unclean lust for Morgan's mother, Igraine. With two yes men (yes fairies?) looking on, the Questing Beast slithers over Arthur while he sleeps. When Arthur awakes and asks Merlin to explain the dream, it forces Merlin to tell the truth about the king's real father and mother.

Morgan Le Fey—The Questing Beast
STAGING SUGGESTIONS AND HELPFUL HINTS

—GLOSSARY
(terms possibly unfamiliar to the reader)

BLASÉ—Uninteresting. Without flare or splash.

BASILISK(S)—A dragon with lethal breath and glance.

HYDRA(S)—A many headed monster.

— CHARACTER DESCRIPTIONS

MORGAN LE FEY: (Female) Graceful and cunning in her evilness.

MAGWITCH: (Female) A flighty, brownnoser of a fairy.

APOCARESS: (Female) Cynical and sarcastic. Bored with it all.

ARTHUR: (Male) A good, young king, but a bit childlike and too trusting.

MERLIN: (Male) Middle-aged in this telling.

QUESTING BEAST: Can be nothing but a **PLAYER** wrapped in black (plastic bags?). Attach a monster head or mask to the **PLAYER** if desired. Costume should be freeing enough enabling the **PLAYER** to crawl in and over **ARTHUR**.

MERLIN: An older Merlin, wise and protective.

— PRESENTATION SUGGESTIONS
(6th Century English Clothing and Items)

COSTUMES
MORGAN LE FEY—Long, elegant gown with long, flowing sleeves. Slippers. Loose-fitting hood or jeweled headband. Long, flowing hair.

MAGWITCH and **APOCARESS**—Light silk or chemise, loose-fitting blouse and short skirt or shorts. Bare feet. Loose, uncombed hair. Small transparent wings (If you have them).

ARTHUR—Chain mail tunic with leather belt around waist. Long cloak flowing down back. Tights. Leather boots, half-calf high. Gold crown or headband. Semi-long hair.

MERLIN—Robe with long flowing sleeves. Tights and cloth shoes. Long hair and beard.

PROPS
TABLE and CHAIR—Small and wooden. Throw a cloth over them if otherwise.

BOWL—Flat shaped of wood.

LEAVES and HERBS—Dried.

STAGE
Because there are two playing areas, a bare stage might be best. Add structures suggesting **MORGAN'S** room if you want.

STAGING
The slime left on **ARTHUR** needn't be real, merely suggested through pantomime.

STAGING

STAGE RIGHT   **STAGE LEFT**

Morgan Le Fey—The Questing Beast
SCRIPT

SETTING
The time of King Arthur. A small TABLE with BOWL sits stage RIGHT. A CHAIR sits further down—stage right.

*(**MORGAN LE FEY** stands over the TABLE and BOWL. LEAVES and HERBS sit about. She'll crumple and sprinkle these into the BOWL. **MAGWITCH** stands next to **MORGAN** while **APOCARESS** sits lazily in the CHAIR.)*

MAGWITCH
It's a special brew you stir this day, Morganna.

MORGAN LE FEY
My powers usually extend far beyond mere potions, Magwitch. I can place a yearning spell on a damsel across the seas or down a knight from his horse with a glance of my eye.

APOCARESS
And yet, with all that magic you wield, you choose to spend it on avenging your plight in life.

MORGAN LE FEY
Apocaress, I always deserved more than I got, and it's always the fault of one man.

MAGWITCH
Arthur.

MORGAN LE FEY *(Sarcastically.)*
Good King Arthur. He's good because he doesn't know anything. Who he really is. Who I really am.

APOCARESS
Ignorance is bliss.

MAGWITCH
Are you going to tell him, Morganna? Are you going to tell him who you really are?

APOCARESS
Tell him? How blasé is that?

MORGAN LE FEY
Apocaress is right. Why simply tell Arthur I'm his sister. He wouldn't believe me anyway. It will take a good deal of convincing and from someone he trusts.

APOCARESS
Which certainly isn't you.

MORGAN LE FEY
You can keep quiet, you cynical little fairy.

MAGWITCH
Are you going to use magic to convince Arthur you're his sister?

MORGAN LE FEY
Not only that, I'll plant a seed of things to come into his thoughts.

MAGWITCH
Wonderful things?

APOCARESS
Hideous things if I know the great Morgan Le Fey.

MORGAN LE FEY
Why waste a perfectly good potion on just one thing when you can get two out of it?

*(**MORGAN** sprinkles HERBS into the BOWL.)*

MAGWITCH
How are you going to do it, Morganna?

MORGAN LE FEY
It will be a day like today. Arthur will be alone.

*(Enter **KING ARTHUR** from stage left.)*

MORGAN LE FEY *(Continued.)*
He'll tire and want to sleep.

*(**MORGAN** waves her hands over the BOWL. **ARTHUR** lies down to sleep. **MORGAN** and **MAGWITCH** look over and watch **ARTHUR**. **APOCARESS** will also look over from time to time.)*

MORGAN LE FEY *(Continued.)*
And when he's deeply asleep, he'll dream a nightmare of a dream with monsters and dragons, basilisks and griffons. All these creatures will writhe and bite at one another in a pool of slime.

*(**ARTHUR** begins to squirm in his sleep.)*

APOCARESS
And knowing you, these beasts will pull people down into this slimy pool and eat them.

MORGAN LE FEY
They will.

MAGWITCH
Can there be harpies and hydras? Maybe sphinxes?

MORGAN LE FEY
All creatures of scales, fins, and wings.

APOCARESS
What an awful, bubbling, churning cesspool of angry, savage, killing beasts. How wonderfully evil.

MORGAN LE FEY
And out of this ugly, miserable cesspool will spring the most monstrous serpent of all. One of iron scales and oozing slime. Its nostrils will snort poisonous flame and noxious smoke.

*(From stage left comes a large, black worm/ snake. the **QUESTING BEAST** moves over **ARTHUR** who struggles more in his sleep.)*

MAGWITCH *(Watching.)*
Is it going to eat Arthur?

MORGAN LE FEY
Eat him? I couldn't kill my own brother. No, the beast will bring forth the truth.

*(The **QUESTING BEAST** moves off **ARTHUR** and exits stage left.)*

APOCARESS *(Watching.)*
Your potion did that?

MORGAN LE FEY
It did.

APOCARESS
I'm impressed. Truly. If I ever have someone I'd like a big disgusting slug to crawl over, I'll come to you.

MAGWITCH
So what happens now?

MORGAN LE FEY
Arthur awakes.

*(**ARTHUR** awakes abruptly and sits up.)*

ARTHUR
Oh—Oh, what a frightful dream. It nearly stopped my heart.

*(**ARTHUR** feels his chest, then pulls away a slimy hand. He stands wondering what the slime is over his clothing.)*

ARTHUR *(Continued.)*
What is this?

*(Enter **MERLIN** from stage left. **MORGAN** and the others watch.)*

ARTHUR *(Glancing over.)*
Merlin. I'm glad you're here. I just had the most horrid dream.

MERLIN
Dreams can be very telling, Arthur.

ARTHUR *(Wiping his chest with a hand.)*
I'm not sure it was a dream. Look what has lain upon me?

*(**ARTHUR** lifts his hand to his nose and sniffs. His head jerks back. It's an unpleasant smell. He stands to let **MERLIN** smell.)*

MERLIN
Slimy and the smell of sulfur. Arthur, the Questing Beast visited you.

ARTHUR
The Questing Beast? I've never heard of it.

MERLIN
Once there was a princess who wanted to have a baby with her own brother.

ARTHUR
That isn't right.

APOCARESS
I think I see what you're after here, Morgan.

MORGAN
Shush, I'm trying to listen.

MERLIN
Yes, Arthur. And the prince would not agree to such an unholy practice. So in a fit of vengeance, the princess set her hunting hounds on the prince. The hounds tore him apart. For her punishment, the Questing Beast came from her sin and the blood of the prince.

ARTHUR
But what does that mean for me, Merlin?

MAGWITCH
Yes, what does that mean for Arthur?

MORGAN
Will you please be quiet?

MERLIN
Morganna.

ARTHUR
Morganna? Morgan Le Fey sent this Questing Beast? Why?

MERLIN
She wants you to know a secret I've kept from you since your birth. It was a horrendous deed I'm afraid I took part in.

MORGAN LE FEY (*Happy.*)
Yes. Had to force your hand, didn't I, Merlin? Now you have to tell Arthur what happened.

MERLIN
Long ago there were many wars and battles as similar to all battles and wars through the ages— someone wanting what someone else has. In this case it was King Uther wanting Queen Igraine who belonged to another. Uther insisted I help him satisfy his lust. With my magic I tricked Igraine into believing Uther was her husband. A child came from the unholy union. You, Arthur.

ARTHUR
Me? My father was King Uther?

MERLIN
There's more. Queen Igraine had a daughter.

ARTHUR
I have a sister?

MERLIN
You do.

ARTHUR
Who?

MERLIN
The one who sent the Questing Beast.

ARTHUR
Morgan Le Fey?

MORGAN LE FEY (*Stomping in victory.*)
There! There it is. Finally, Arthur knows who I am. I'm your sister, Arthur. Your sister. What are you going to do now?

MERLIN
Thinking of it, I'm certain Morgan sent the Questing Beast for force me to tell you of your true past and of her relation to you.

ARTHUR
What do I do, Merlin?

MERLIN
That will be up to you, Arthur. But whatever you decide—to accept Morgan Le Fey as your sister or not—be very careful.

ARTHUR
Yes. Indeed.

(*ARTHUR* and *MERLIN* exit stage left.)

MAGWITCH
What do you suppose Arthur will do?

APOCARESS
He'll never take you in as his sister, you know that.

MAGWITCH
It might help if you stopped using your magic to play dirty tricks on Arthur.

APOCARESS
You're after Arthur's crown. That's what this is all about. You want his regal power.

MORGAN LE FEY
Enough with the questions. What I want is what I want.

APOCARESS
But it won't be for goodness and benevolence. This I know.

MORGAN LE FEY
Arthur has never been a smart man. He leads with his heart. With my conjuring, I can do whatever I want and whatever I wish. And now that he knows I'm his sister, he'll hesitate in stopping me from doing whatever I'm inclined to do. My conjuring the Questing Beast was just the beginning. What comes after this will be more magnificent than Merlin can even concoct. You just wait and see.

(*MORGAN* exits stage right.)

MAGWITCH
Grand good or grand evil?

APOCARESS
Hard to tell. One thing I do know, we two fairies best stay on the good side of Morgan Le Fey.

(*APOCARESS* and *MAGWITCH* exit stage right.)

**END OF MORGAN LE FEY—
THE QUESTING BEAST**

Lady of the Lake—Brandishing Excalibur

Based on an Arthurian Legend
Original Script by Joan Garner

—BACKGROUND INFORMATION
(genre classification and other data deemed useful)

Finding the Lady of the Lake one of the more intriguing characters in the Arthurian Legend, including her in this compilation was a must. Deriving a way of placing the ethereal creature (who lives under water) in a sketch proved a difficult challenge.

The Lady of the Lake occupies so many Arthurian tales because she's a composite of several characters copped from other stories and parables. Born in a magical kingdom beneath an enchanted lake—both water fay and enchantress—the Lady of the Lake is perhaps best known for giving Arthur the sword Excalibur. Accredited to raising Lancelot du Lac (of the lake) and protecting King Arthur from his half-sister's (Morgan Le Fey) diabolical conjuring and spell bindings, the Lady's actions seem mostly benevolent. That she later traps Merlin in a tower of air after learning all Merlin taught her remains a mystery. But I wouldn't put it past those pesky Cistercian monks creating this unexplained wicked turn.

The Battle of Camlann—The Legend of King Arthur comes full circle with the Battle of Camlann. Without Merlin's guidance, Arthur's Camelot slips into disarray. Though not entirely his doing, and through a series of missteps from most around him, Arthur's son Mordred flings the kingdom into chaos. It's now up to Arthur to right all the wrong and end it (and Mordred). In a fierce battle between the armies, all succumb to the sword except Sir Bedevere. The result of a vicious fight, Mordred falls dead and Arthur lays mortally wounded. Arthur then asks Bedevere to return Excalibur to the Lady of the Lake before preparing to sail to the island of Avalon to die.

Supposedly this ends the Arthurian legend, but authors and storytellers have cleverly devised different ways of keeping the king and legend alive. The most notable story has Morgan Le Fey (yes, the evil pain in Arthur's side) healing the king's wounds once he arrives at Avalon. Why she would do this after creating havoc around the king for years is another perplexing oxymoron of this complex story.

— SYNOPSIS OF STORY

(6th Century England) Sir Bedevere helps a mortally wounded King Arthur to the edge of a lake where Arthur commands him to throw Excalibur back into the waters. Though reluctant to do so, Bedevere leaves to do as his king commands. While waiting, Arthur musters the spirit of Merlin to console his fading heart. They speak of how the Lady of the Lake gifted Excalibur to him and how she also helped Arthur through troubling times. In the end, the Lady of the Lake takes Arthur to Avalon to die.

Lady of the Lake—Brandishing Excalibur
STAGING SUGGESTIONS AND HELPFUL HINTS

—CHARACTER DESCRIPTION

SIR BEDEVERE: (Male) Fiercely loyal and brave. He would do anything for his king.

KING ARTHUR: (Male) Full of regret and sadness, he awaits his fate in solemn reflection.

MERLIN: (Male) Very old, yet wise and compassionate.

LADY OF THE LAKE: (Female) Mystical, but kindly and astute. Not of this world, she moves lightly and gracefully.

YOUNG ARTHUR: (Male) Innocent and feeling unworthy of praise and irreverence.

MAIDEN: (Female) With a definite mission, she scrambles when told to do what she knows will result in certain death for her.

— PRESENTATION SUGGESTIONS
(6th Century English Clothing and Items)

COSTUMES
BEDEVERE—Armor; a quilted coat/vest of metallic silver or gold metal cloth could serve as the knight's armor. A loose weave (gray) sweater possibly resembling chain mail underneath or a turtleneck shirt. Long pants. He should also wear a belt to hold his sword. If wearing boots such as hiking or weather boots, tuck pant legs into top of boots. Outfit should be dirted-up as he's coming from battle.

KING ARTHUR—Can be the same as **BEDEVERE'S**, but with cape down the back.

MERLIN—Robe with long flowing sleeves. Tights and cloth shoes. Very old with long white hair and beard.

LADY OF THE LAKE—Light blouse and skirt with cloak where all can wave in the breeze when walking. Powdered skin and face. Glitter on skin and face. Bare feet. Long, flowing hair. Like water.

YOUNG ARTHUR—Chain mail tunic with leather belt around waist. Long cloak flowing down back. Tights. Leather boots, half-calf high. Gold crown or headband. Semi-long hair.

MAIDEN—Simple blouse and long skirt or long chemise dress. Slippers. Hair pulled back to flow down the back.

PROPS
EXCALIBUR—Sword, preferably a "real" one as it *is* Excalibur.

JEWELED CAPE—Square cloth of velvet with jewels attached.

LIGHTING EFFECTS
Spotlight left area where **ARTHUR** sits. Dim when action at right takes place.

STAGE
LAKE/SHORE OUTLINE—On the floor, place a rope helter-skelter across the stage to represent the SHORELINE. Lay blue paper on the one side to represent the LAKE. The blue paper will help the setting, but isn't necessary.

STUMP—A log stump would work nicely— something for **ARTHUR** to sit on.

STAGING
Because **ARTHUR** is only reminiscing and because **MERLIN** isn't really there, **ARTHUR** should never look at **MERLIN**.

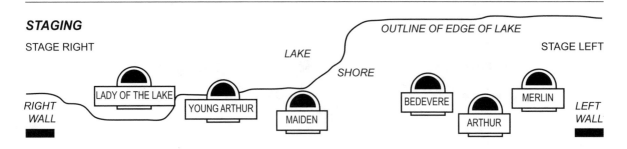

STAGING

STAGE RIGHT

LAKE

OUTLINE OF EDGE OF LAKE

STAGE LEFT

SHORE

RIGHT WALL

LADY OF THE LAKE

YOUNG ARTHUR

MAIDEN

BEDEVERE

MERLIN

ARTHUR

LEFT WALL

Lady of the Lake—Brandishing Excalibur
SCRIPT

SETTING
England. The time of King Arthur. The edge of a LAKE in the mist of a late misty day.

*(**SIR BEDEVERE** helps a wounded **KING ARTHUR** in from stage left. He sits **ARTHUR** down on a STUMP, stage left. **ARTHUR** struggles to stay alive.)*

SIR BEDEVERE
We're here in the clearing by the lake, just as you requested, Your Majesty.

KING ARTHUR
At such a time as this, I believe Arthur shall suffice over Your Majesty, Bedevere.

SIR BEDEVERE
You are my king, Your Majesty—now and forever.

KING ARTHUR
Is the day lost?

SIR BEDEVERE
All is lost, my king. You and I are the only ones still standing after this battle.

KING ARTHUR
All my knights?

SIR BEDEVERE
I'm sorry.

KING ARTHUR
It's all over, then.

SIR BEDEVERE
Truly not, sire.

KING ARTHUR
I killed Mordred and Mordred killed me. My blood and the blood of my blood stain this battlefield. It's the end of Camelot and the Round Table. There is but one task left to do.

SIR BEDEVERE
What would that be, Your Majesty?

*(**ARTHUR** takes his SWORD and holds it out for **BEDEVERE** to take.)*

KING ARTHUR
Excalibur. You must return this worthy sword to the lake.

SIR BEDEVERE
Sire?

KING ARTHUR
My faithful sword Excalibur. I need you to throw it back into the lake.

*(**BEDEVERE** takes the SWORD with reservation.)*

SIR BEDEVERE
I don't understand. You want me to take the most magnificent sword ever forged and throw it into the waters?

KING ARTHUR
A sword not forged of this Earth, Bedevere. Do as I say.

SIR BEDEVERE
Yes, Your Majesty

*(**BEDEVERE** exits via the SHORE, stage right.)*

KING ARTHUR
Merlin, my dear friend, where have you been for so long? How I need your counsel now. I feel the life leaving my body. How I wish you could console me as you have in the past.

*(Enter **MERLIN** from stage left.)*

MERLIN
I'm here, Arthur—in spirit if nothing else.

KING ARTHUR
Merlin, how I have missed you. I need your kind words, friend. I have fully ruined the dream.

MERLIN
It was more than a dream, Arthur. To ruin a dream is not to try to make it so.

KING ARTHUR
But I have erred so many times in so many ways.

MERLIN
You are merely human, Arthur. You must expect mistakes and misjudgments.

KING ARTHUR
You gave me so much.

MERLIN
And you have had to face many troubles and sorrows—the last having to kill your own son.

KING ARTHUR
Mordred was no more my son than Morgan Le Fey my sister.

MERLIN
But when all else is lost, there is always family.

KING ARTHUR
Guinevere? Where is my queen now? Lost to all this nonsense. No, you have been my family more than anyone else, Merlin. Do you remember when we first came to the edge of this lake?

MERLIN
I remember it very well. This is where you secured Excalibur.

KING ARTHUR (*Remembering.*)
Excalibur.

*LIGHTING EFFECTS
Lighting dims over **ARTHUR** and **MERLIN**.

*(Enter from stage left **YOUNG ARTHUR** who crosses to the edge of the **LAKE**. **MERLIN** and **ARTHUR** watch him. **MERLIN** will respond to **YOUNG ARTHUR**, but **YOUNG ARTHUR** will not look over and acknowledge **MERLIN**.)*

YOUNG ARTHUR
Why have you brought me here, Merlin?

MERLIN
A new king is in need of a new weapon to help him rule his kingdom. Stand before the lake and prepare to receive a wondrous gift.

YOUNG ARTHUR
But I see neither boat nor bird on the lake. Where is this gift?

MERLIN
Patience, Arthur.

YOUNG ARTHUR
Wait. There's a rippling in the middle of the lake.

MERLIN
What else do you see?

YOUNG ARTHUR
A blade. A blade is rising from the water's surface. It's a sword, Merlin. It's a magnificent sword... My stars, a woman is coming out of the lake. A beautiful woman dressed in white is walking on the top of the water. She's coming this way with the sword... Merlin, what do I do?

MERLIN
Stay your ground, Arthur. There's nothing to fear.

*(Enter from stage right—on the LAKE—the **LADY OF THE LAKE** carrying EXCALIBUR.)*

LADY OF THE LAKE
Arthur, I am called the Lady of the Lake. I come to give you Excalibur as deserving a great king.

YOUNG ARTHUR
Beautiful lady, I am no great king. I'm still uneasy being king.

LADY OF THE LAKE
Then take Excalibur to secure your crown. It's blade cannot break. It can cut through steel and stone, and whoever carries it will not see defeat.

YOUNG ARTHUR (*Taking EXCALIBUR.*)
I shall cherish and care for it for the rest of my days. Thank you.

LADY OF THE LAKE
Stay humble, Arthur, and be wise brandishing Excalibur, the sword of kings from the beginning of time.

*(**YOUNG ARTHUR** bows and exits stage right along the SHORE. The **LADY OF THE LAKE** exits on the LAKE stage right.)*

*LIGHTING EFFECTS
Lighting comes up over **ARTHUR** and **MERLIN**.

KING ARTHUR
But I wasn't wise brandishing Excalibur.

MERLIN
You became a great king with Excalibur by your side. No one will deny you that, Arthur.

*(**BEDEVERE** enters from stage right along the SHORE. He carries EXCALIBUR. He doesn't acknowledge **MERLIN**.)*

KING ARTHUR
Sir Bedevere, why do you still have Excalibur?

SIR BEDEVERE
I couldn't do it. Throwing away Excalibur would be like throwing away my king.

KING ARTHUR
My time is over, Bedevere, as is Camelot. Do as I say. As your king, I command you to return Excalibur to the lake.

*(A reluctant **BEDEVERE** bows and exits stage right along the SHORE.)*

MERLIN
Your knight believes more in you than the power of Excalibur.

KING ARTHUR
He'll believe in the power of Excalibur if he does what I say.

MERLIN
All the mystical powers that served this world will soon be gone. The days of Merlin and magic are ending. I'm honored to be a part of your story, Arthur.

KING ARTHUR
There wouldn't be a story without you, Merlin.

MERLIN
As long as men need heroes to put courage into their hearts, there will always be stories like yours, Arthur. And your story will be one of the greatest of all time.

*(**MERLIN** exits stage left. **ARTHUR** continues to talk, not noticing **MERLIN** is gone.)*

KING ARTHUR
I hardly think that. So many things went astray.

*(**BEDEVERE** enters along the SHORE from stage right. He is without EXCALIBUR.)*

SIR BEDEVERE
Sire, who are you speaking to?

KING ARTHUR *(Looking around.)*
Merlin. Merlin was here... Maybe he was here... Did you throw the sword into the lake?

SIR BEDEVERE
Yes, Your Majesty.

KING ARTHUR
And, what did you see?

SIR BEDEVERE
An astonishment, my king. I fear you won't believe what I saw.

KING ARTHUR
I daresay I will, Bedevere. What did you see?

SIR BEDEVERE
Just as Excalibur was to breach the top of the waters, a hand came from underneath and grasped it. And as quickly, the hand pulled the sword down under and the waters.

KING ARTHUR
Then you did as I commanded.

SIR BEDEVERE
Sire, who took Excalibur?

KING ARTHUR
The Lady of the Lake, Bedevere. The Lady was the one who gifted Excalibur to me many years past. Bedevere, please go find Merlin for me. I'm not finished with him just yet.

SIR BEDEVERE
Yes, Your Majesty.

*(**BEDEVERE** exits stage left. Momentarily, the **LADY OF THE LAKE** enters on the LAKE from stage right. She carries EXCALIBUR.)*

LADY OF THE LAKE
Arthur?

KING ARTHUR *(Looking over fondly.)*
Lady. I'm afraid you couldn't protect me this time.

LADY OF THE LAKE *(Stepping to **ARTHUR**.)*
No, not this time.

KING ARTHUR
Do you remember the jeweled cape? I was holding court in Camelot one winter's morning.

LADY OF THE LAKE
And, I was standing by your side holding Excalibur like I am now.

*(A **MAIDEN** enters from the SHORE, stage right. She carries a JEWELED CAPE.)*

MAIDEN
King Arthur, my mistress, Morgan Le Fey, wishes you take this beautiful cape as a token of the love and loyalty for her brother, the king.

LADY OF THE LAKE
Be wary, my king. How many times have I had to counter Morgan and her attempts to bewitch and cast evil over Camelot?

KING ARTHUR
Maiden, I'll accept my sister's token of love.

MAIDEN
Thank you. But my mistress instructed me to use my own hands to wrap the warmth of this cape over the king.

LADY OF THE LAKE
Arthur, how many times has the sweet words of your sister turned to venom against you? Be careful in accepting this gift that is so contrary to Morgan Le Fey's past conduct.

KING ARTHUR
So true, Lady. Maiden of my sister, I want you to place the cape over your shoulders first.

MAIDEN *(Flustered.)*
But this fine cape belongs to a king. I am but a humble servant. It wouldn't be proper.

LADY OF THE LAKE
Do as the king commands, Maiden.

MAIDEN
I fear a harsh response from my mistress should she find out I did such a thing.

KING ARTHUR
You have the king's permission. Surely your mistress won't mind you wearing the cape with the king's permission.

*(Not wanting to, the **MAIDEN** puts the CAPE on, screams and stumbles offstage, right.)*

KING ARTHUR *(Continued.)*
The poor girl died right there on the spot. Morgan poisoned the cape meant for me. Morgan has tried to get the better of me all my life. First it was Merlin who protected me and then you.

LADY OF THE LAKE
Yes. You have had to face many a perilous time.

KING ARTHUR
Lady of the Lake, what is my fate now?

LADY OF THE LAKE
Avalon across the waters where your tortured spirit may rest in peace, for you have endured many spears of battle and betrayal. Let me heal your mortal wounds and mend your broken heart.

KING ARTHUR
I am so very tired, Lady—so very tired.

LADY OF THE LAKE
All things end, Arthur. Come with me on my black barge. I'll take you to Avalon where all stories of noble intent end.

*(The **LADY OF THE LAKE** helps **ARTHUR** stand. She gives him EXCALIBUR to told against his chest and they exit along the SHORE stage right. **BEDEVERE** enters stage left to watch the two exit.)*

SIR BEDEVERE
It's the end of the greatest of all legends. The end of Camelot and King Arthur.

*(**BEDEVERE** exits stage left. Lights dim.)*

**END OF LADY OF THE LAKE—
BRANDISHING EXCALIBUR**

The Arthurian Icons

PAGE 1 (A Lesson in of Specific Character Development in Playwrighting)

This Project involves writing in theatrical play form.

Students will be directed to read and use one of the brief biographies of the more familiar characters of the Arthurian legend and then create a monologue for him or her. Guidelines on developing a character and creating a monologue are provided in this Project.

PREPARATION AND RESOURCES NEEDED: Copy the 6 pages of this Project for each student.

Student Assignment: This Project has you writing a dramatic monologue. The first part gives definitions and instructions on how to write a monologue. The second part details Arthurian Icons to use in writing your monologue.

NOTEWORTHY ARTHURIAN CHARACTERS

CHARACTER DEVELOPMENT

Obviously characters in a story or book are important (especially the main ones). Since they'll probably be with you from the first to the last page, a well-defined character is very important.

Developing a well-rounded character for a play is even more important. Because a play depends on the word and the visual to get its story across, it's good to identify main characters quickly.

Perhaps you've already studied the subject, and if not there are hundreds of books on character development. And although most of these sources are excellent in grasping character development, they can often be long and trying as they dig deeper than you probably want to go. So here are just a few things to think about in creating your character.

In considering your main character, think of other characters in stories you liked. And then think why you liked them. Chances are the person wasn't very different from you or someone you wish to be like. This is your first direction in two parts.

1. Your main character should be likable or at least have some redeeming (saving) qualities. This means your character should be a person people can get behind and cheer for. If your character struggles onward no matter what's thrown at him or her, this is an admirable quality the reader can appreciate. Without this,

where's the interest to continue with the story? Your character may not be "likable" at first, but his or her purpose or goal can be a noble one prompting the reader to see if the character carries out this goal.

2. The main character should have flaws or quirks. Nothing endears a person to another (fictional or real) than seeing they have similar weaknesses or fears. Seeing your main character overcoming their weaknesses or pressing through their fears gives hope to the reader that they can also overcome their own flaws. Using your character's strengths to help him or her achieve their goals is admirable, so use a person's strengths as well.

In developing a strong character include and repeat behavior. A character may nervously play with her hair when confronted with a sticky situation. Or, give him a saying or expression he uses a lot. This helps identify your character and distinguish him or her from the others roaming through a story.

Of course it's easier to introduce these simple things gradually during your epic story, but is more difficult to do during a play. Applying these tips to your monologue may be nearly impossible, but it can be done.

WRITING A MONOLOGUE
(The Dos and Don'ts)

A monologue is a long speech delivered by one performer. This can happen with a play or act independently of a play. Actors love and hate

---

The Arthurian Icons (Character Development) PAGE 2

monologues at the same time. They love how they'll be the center of attention for awhile yet hate having to memorize all those lines. This is something to consider when seeing a long monologue within a play. Another consideration is monologues can quickly become tedious and slow down the play—a mistake all playwrights try to avoid.

Fortunately for our purposes here, the monologue you will write is an expository Exercise. In other words, your character will explain their life and where they fit into the Arthurian Legend, so some description will be necessary. This doesn't mean it has to be boring! If you have read other readers theatre scripts (which I'm hoping and counting on), you have probably noticed anyone coming in the scene breaks into a little speech telling who they are. For example, let's take the famous scene between Alexander Graham Bell (the fellow who invented the telephone) and his assistant Mr. Watson when Bell accidentally hurts himself and discovers his telephone invention works at the same time. The following would be a typical readers theatre approach to the scene. (It's debated whether this actually happened. If not, it still makes for a good story.)

BELL AND WATSON

(BELL sits at a cluttered desk.)

BELL: Hi, I'm Alexander Graham Bell.
    (Reaching for his journal.)
I'm trying to invent the telephone here...
    (Bell hits a bottle with his journal spilling acid on his arm.)
Whoops, I just spilled acid on my arm. Gee, it hurts. Perhaps I should get my trusty assistant Watson in here to help me clean the acid off.
    (Calling out.)
Mr. Watson —come here—I want to see you!

(Enter WATSON.)

WATSON: Hi, I'm Mr. Watson, Alexander Graham Bell's trusty assistant. Did you want to see me, Mr. Bell?

BELL: I sure did. I just spilled acid on my arm and now fear it's eating away my skin. Can you help me?

WATSON: Why, yes I can.

BELL: Wait, Mr. Watson. How did you know I wanted you? You were away in the next room.

WATSON: I don't know. I must have heard you through the telephone.

BELL: You did? That means my telephone invention works. Zounds!

The End of BELL AND WATSON

Admittedly the scene was purposely exaggerated and "hokeyfied." In trying to identify the characters to the audience, it isn't effective writing (especially for some scenes) to pull the character from the scene to explain themselves to the audience. Although often used in some plays where a character plays in and tells the story, it doesn't work if it isn't your plan to have the character be the narrator. It doesn't mean you can't get all the information needed into your scene. Read the changed scene and see how better it flows with more interesting action.

BELL AND WATSON

(BELL sits at a cluttered desk talking out loud.)

BELL: I've been working on this invention for so long and still... Sound moving through wires—it should work. What am I doing wrong?
    (He reaches for his journal and hits a bottle with it. It spills acid on his arm as he quickly tries to mop it up.)
Drat, it's getting all over... No, it's burning through my clothing and skin. I need something... Mr. Watson—come here—I want to see you!

(WATSON enters.)

WATSON: What is it, Mr. Bell?

The Arthurian Icons (Character Development) PAGE 3

BELL: I was reaching for my journal and knocked over....

WATSON: The acid. It got on your skin.

BELL: Where is the....

(WATSON reaches into a drawer.)

WATSON: The solvent is right here. We'll need to apply it to the burns and then wash it all off and put a bandage on it.

(WATSON pours the solvent on BELL'S arm.)

BELL: That feels better already. I feel like such a klutz. It's a good thing you're my assistant and know where everything is, Watson. I'm glad you were in the next room and could hear me calling.

WATSON: But Mr. Bell, I didn't hear you from the next room. I realize it now, I heard you from the receiver box hooked up to your telephone.

BELL: Seriously?

WATSON: You did it, Mr. Bell. You actually did it! Soon everyone will talk on Alexander Graham Bell's telephone!

The End of BELL AND WATSON

Granted, it's still a little hokey, but more interesting to read and see, don't you think?

So how do you make your monologue interesting if the character must tell their history? You do the same as the changed BELL AND WATSON scene. Place your character at a "defining" point of their life, or at the end of a major happening, or at the end of their life.

Instead of having Lancelot stand and say:

LANCELOT: I'm Sir Lancelot, the greatest of all Knights of the Round Table. But I fell in love with Queen Guinevere and pretty much ruined Camelot.

Have Lancelot rush in, fleeing from Camelot. He stops to catch his breath. He looks back in agony and explains what happened—that he let his heart rule over his head—and how he left after the discovery of his (treasonous) love for Queen Guinevere. Have him anguish over leaving Guinevere alone to face punishment for their forbidden love. Let him also think out loud that now he needs to form an army and go save Guinevere from certain death.

Instead of having Sir Galahad stand and say:

GALAHAD: I'm Sir Galahad, son of Lancelot and the purest knight of all. I was the one who pulled the magical sword from the marble floating in Camelot and am the one who found the Holy Grail.

Have Galahad standing in the hallway about to go into the Knights of the Round Table to receive the honor of the Siege Perilous (the seat at the Round Table reserved for the Grail Knight). He might review his life to this point wondering if he's worthy of the title and admiration. Not only will this tell his story, but it shows his great humility—a strong character quality explained earlier in the Character Development section.

A SAMPLE MONOLOGUE

The following monologue sample (on page 164) uses all the suggestions offered above. Not that you have to pattern your monologue after this one, but it might help with your own. Also, Guinevere isn't the only Arthurian Icon you may wish to write about. Three others are identified here for your consideration.

The Arthurian Icons (Character Development) PAGE 4

QUEEN GUINEVERE, A LIFE OF REGRET

*(**QUEEN GUINEVERE** stands in front a window, looking forlornly.)*

It looks so peaceful out this window. If only my spirit were at peace. So many things have ended in tragedy. I've hurt so many innocent people. What do I do now? It's all over... Where did it all begin? When did it all go wrong?

*(**QUEEN GUINEVERE** turns into the room, looking nowhere particular as she speaks.)*

Arthur. Poor Arthur. He's such a good man—such a good king. He tries so. But it was an arranged marriage—purely political. When we married, you must have known I didn't love you as I should. We both tried, but how can a marriage survive without true love? And then came Lancelot. Beautiful, magnificent Lancelot. We didn't expect to fall in love, but our passion was too strong to ignore. We resisted each other for so long, and when we said good-bye... We were saying good-bye forever when the knights broke in on us. Lancelot, we were so close to making it right again.

Then came the day Arthur sentenced me to death by burning at the stake. He had to, it was the law. My dear Arthur, how your heart broke having to give that sentence to me—your queen—your Guinevere. You were the one hurt most of all and yet you were the only one with enough love in your heart to forgive me and Lancelot. Then Lancelot had to rescue me from the fire and now I'm here in this nunnery—lost, regretful, and so very sad. I'm so sorry. I chose my heart over duty. I have loved, but not loved well. What do I do for the rest of my life but pay penitence for my weaknesses? What a fool I've been. I'm Queen Guinevere, I should know better... It's over.

*(**QUEEN GUINEVERE** turns back to look out the window.)*

End of QUEEN GUINEVERE, A LIFE OF REGRET

QUEEN GUINEVERE

In early writings, Guinevere is a minor figure in the Arthurian Legend. But in more recent times she has gained in popularity and turned into a major character. Still, there isn't much about her. And what is there can be very different depending on who's telling the story. Simply, Guinevere marries King Arthur and becomes Queen Guinevere of Camelot. Afterwards, she falls in love with Lancelot du Lac. Since she's a queen and married to Arthur, her love for Lancelot marks her a traitor against Arthur and Camelot. Having no choice, Arthur sentences his queen to death by burning at the stake. But Lancelot rescues Guinevere before she dies by fire.

The Arthur, Guinevere, Lancelot story is one of the most familiar Arthurian stories today, but even this love triangle seems an invention of medieval writers. Guinevere's life before and after Lancelot tells many tales. One accounting says Guinevere was the daughter of Leodegrance of Cameliard. Another says Guinevere is really three queens names Gwenhwyfar. Some accounting say Guinevere worked with Arthur's son Mordred to overthrow Camelot. Another says she fled to a nunnery and lived there until she dies.

Whatever the case, Guinevere remains beautiful, loving, and regal.

The Arthurian Icons (Character Development) PAGE 5

LANCELOT DU LAC

Noted as the greatest of King Arthur's Knights, the Lady of the Lake raised Lancelot du Lac. Lancelot leads in two Arthurian stories; his love for Queen Guinevere and the resulting downfall of Camelot, and his travels afterwards. Where he was a bit pompous and impressed with his greatness and purity as a young man, he became and died a hermit.

The love between Lancelot and Guinevere begins at different times depending on the story. One story tells of his first assignment as a knight in Camelot was to bring Guinevere to court to wed Arthur. The two fell in love while making their way to Camelot.

Another version has Lancelot coming to court after Arthur and Guinevere wed. After successfully completing many a quest, Lancelot became a full Knight of the Round Table and close friend to Arthur.

Lancelot's Quests as a Round Table Knight
• He rescues Guinevere after Meliagaunce kidnapped her.
• He conquers the dark custom of the castle Dolorous Gard.
• He helps Arthur put down a rebellion of Prince Galehaut.
• He saves Elaine of Corbenic from an enchantment.
• He goes with son Galahad seeking the Holy Grail.

When Mordred (Arthur's son) reveals Lancelot and Guinevere's love, Lancelot flees Arthur's Court, but returns to save Guinevere when he hears the queen faces burning at the stake. He fights Arthur, but then returns to help Arthur defeat Mordred who plans to seize Arthur's throne. But Lancelot was too late. Mordred and Arthur mortally wound each other. Devastated, Lancelot visits Guinevere one last time, and then becomes a mad hermit living out his days.

ELAINE OF ASTOLAT

Like Guinevere, Elaine's story differs from telling to telling. Some combine Elaine of Carbonek with Elaine of Astolat. Perhaps this was to give Elaine more of a story. Whatever the case, she plays a part in the life of Lancelot, and because of her dramatic death, deserves mentioning here.

Elaine's father Bernard organizes a jousting tournament which Lancelot attends. Elaine is immediately smitten with Lancelot, but he doesn't return her admiration. She asks Lancelot to wear her colors during the tournament, but Lancelot refuses. Instead, he uses the shield of Elaine's brother to disguise who he is. Although Lancelot wins his joust, he's badly wounded, and Elaine nurses him back to health. Still, Lancelot cannot return Elaine's love and leaves her.

Eleven days later, Elaine dies of heartbreak. Before her death, she tells her attendants to place her in a small boat and float her down the river to Camelot. King Arthur's court finds and gives Elaine a burial worthy a queen.

The Arthurian Icons (Character Development) PAGE 6

SIR GALAHAD

According to one story, Elaine of Corbenic (after he saves her from a tub of scalding water) by Sir Lancelot, immediately falls in love with him. Because he doesn't return the affection, Elaine uses magic and tricks Lancelot into thinking she's Guinevere. Because he's in love with Guinevere, Lancelot obviously pays more attention to Elaine. This is how Galahad was born—or so the story goes.

Once grown and schooled in chivalry and all required in being a knight, Galahad goes to Camelot to find Lancelot. He's accepted by the other Knights of the Round Table because of his sincerity and noble heart. Placed around the Round Table are seats for each knight. And each knight has his name written on the back in gold. But one chair remained vacant— the Siege Perilous or Seat of Danger. There is no name on the back of the Seat Perilous because wizard Merlin placed a spell on the chair that would be certain death for anyone unworthy. When Galahad enters the hall with the old hermit Naciens, the letters on the back of the Siege Perilous form to say: *Sir Galahad, the High Prince*. All now know Galahad is worthy to find the Holy Grail.

King Arthur then takes Galahad down to the river. There sat a large red stone with a bejeweled sword lodged in it. Engraved on the blade of the sword are the words: *For the Best Knight in the World.* Galahad sees the sword as being his and easily pulls it out of the red stone. (A variation of this story has Galahad pulling the sword out of a slab of marble floating over Camelot.)

Galahad's great quest for the Holy Grail has him traveling to the barren land of King Pelles with Knights Perceval and Bors. The Holy Grail comes to him and he drinks from the vessel. Galahad then approaches King Pelles and heals the king's open wound that has been in his side for years. With the king's health restored, life would soon come back to the land.

A grateful Pelles let's Galahad take the Holy Grail to the city of Sarras where the Knights build a temple to house the Grail. There Galahad stays and becomes King and prayed before the Holy Grail every day. One day a great beam of light shines on Galahad and when it leaves, Galahad falls dead. The Grail had reveals such wonders to him; he doesn't want to live anymore. With Galahad's death, his lance and the Grail vanish from the world.

 (2006 © Joan Garner) **WINGS OF FANCY**: Using Readers Theatre to Study Fantasy Genre

Interpreting and Changing the Legend
PAGE 1 (A Lesson in Identifying Differences in Telling the Same Story)

This Project shows how legends continually change and evolve.

(Regrettably two excellent Arthurian movie tellings are not here because of content, THE MISTS OF AVALON (2001) told from Morgan Le Fey's point of view, and EXCALIBUR (1981), one of the most complete tellings of the legend.)

PREPARATION AND RESOURCES NEEDED: Watch the four films used in this Project and decide which two, three, or all four you want to use. Then have your students watch the films you have selected. Copy the first or all pages of this Project for each student and have them read it before watching these films. Then conduct a classroom discussion about the treatment of the Arthurian Legend in these films using the Guide provided in this Project. Providing this Guide to your students for the discussion is at your discretion.

VIEWING REQUIRED

Student Assignment: *Starting from the time of Arthur to the present, the Arthurian Legend (a sketchy telling to begin with) couldn't help but change through time. Even in modern times, interpretation of the story and characters within the legend varies dramatically. Limiting the span of time to a little over fifty years and using motion pictures as the visual tool, this Project looks at the changing Arthurian Legend. Read the article on Finding Your Critical Eye below and then apply it when watching two of the four films referenced in this Project. While watching these films, think about the questions posed below.*

FINDING YOUR CRITICAL EYE

Chances are you're already using your critical eye without knowing it. Your likes and dislikes closely work with your critical eye. Looking at a painting, reading a book, or watching a movie or television show because you like it begins the process. Obviously, this is your personal likes. But the *why* you like that TV show begins to show your critical eye. Knowing what makes a good performance or a masterpiece applies your critical eye. Realizing there's a different color than usual to the look of a movie is using your critical eye. Have you ever been so involved in a television show you notice something is wrong? Did that actor knock on the door wearing a green shirt then comes through the it wearing a read shirt? That's using your critical eye. Appreciating all the details placed within a stage set is using your critical eye. Recognizing a powerful drama over a so-so screenplay applies your critical eye. Simply, paying attention is using your critical eye. Study, discussion, and most importantly, observation will help you develop a cultured critical eye.

THE FILMS USED IN THIS PROJECT
The four films selected for this Exercise expertly demonstrate different interpretations of the same story. Each has King Arthur in it, but they are very different from movie to movie.

CAMELOT—a major motion picture made in the 1960s based on a big Broadway Musical.

MERLIN—a miniseries of more recent times.

FIRST KNIGHT—a big Hollywood movie.

A CONNECTICUT YANKEE IN KING ARTHUR'S COURT—an old movie musical that's amusing and a little corny.

Use the brief descriptions of each movie to assist in finding the differences in these stories, or watch them solely using *your* critical eye.

When watching these movies take note of two aspects to the production: the story and its likenesses and differences to the basic Arthurian Legend, and the production values used in making the movie.

Look for the following items in watching these movies. Not only will you find differences in the movies, but in telling the same story.

- Overall mood of the story

- Overall "look" of the movie

- Treatment of the three main characters—Arthur, Guinevere, and Lancelot.

- The primary character in this telling—the telling of this story is from whose point of view?

- Realistic treatment of costumes and sets for the times of King Arthur.

- The noted differences in the approach of the movie relating with the period produced.

- Special moments you'll remember best in the story and movie.

- Which movie do you like best and why?

Interpreting the Legend (Differences in the Same Story) PAGE 2

Camelot

WARNER BROTHERS (1967) Rated G
DIRECTOR: Joshua Logan
STARRING: Richard Harris, Vanessa Redgrave,
Franco Nero

This story uses Arthur's point of view. In the opening scene, King Arthur escapes to the forest outside his castle of Camelot to wait for Guinevere, his bride. An arranged marriage, the two have never met, and he's wondering if this marriage will be a good one. As he waits for the night to end, he hides from Guinevere who's fleeing from her entourage. He discovers she's experiencing the same apprehensions about the marriage as he is. Arthur reveals himself, but not as the king. The two speak and Arthur tells how nice it is to live in Camelot. Arthur give Guinevere an "out" from marrying him when she finds out he's the king, But she's attracted to Arthur's boy like charms and decides to go ahead with the marriage.

After an elaborate wedding, scenes follow showing Camelot with their new queen and Arthur forming his idea for the Round Table.

Sending word throughout the land that Arthur is looking for valorous knights to sit at his Round Table, Lancelot hears the decree and arrives in England wanting to be a knight to the king. Lancelot meets Arthur on a road near Camelot and, not knowing he's Arthur, challenges him to a duel on horseback. Lancelot wins not only the duel, but Arthur's admiration for his knightly skills and strength which Lancelot credits to his pure soul. Arthur introduces Lancelot to Guinevere who's less than impressed with Lancelot's lack of humility.

Wanting to teach Lancelot a lesson in modesty, Guinevere arranges for three of Camelot's best knights to fight Lancelot during a jousting festival. Lancelot handily takes on and does away with each knight until he fatally injures the last. Naturally upset with having caused another knight's death, Lancelot uses his "purity" of spirit to bring the knight back to life.

Guinevere falls in love with Lancelot and he with her, and Arthur knows his idyllic Camelot is over.

Lancelot and Guinevere meet in secret to share their love while Arthur turns a "blind-eye" to their trysts. Meanwhile, Mordred, Arthur's son shows up to make trouble.

Mordred talks Arthur into going hunting for the night. He knows if Lancelot and Guinevere find out Arthur is away, they won't be able to stay away from one another.

In the forest, Arthur calls out for his mentor Merlin who has been away for many years. He remembers fondly the days when he was a boy and how Merlin taught him many valuable things he now uses as king. But he realizes his absence is a mistake, and hurries back to the castle to keep Lancelot and Guinevere apart.

Unfortunately, King Arthur is too late as Mordred and several knights find Lancelot and Guinevere in an embrace. The knights hold Guinevere, but Lancelot escapes and flees the castle.

Now Arthur must use his new laws of justice against his queen. And since the law for unfaithfulness is death, Arthur has no choice but to sentence Guinevere to death by burning at the stake.

With all ready for the execution at dawn, Lancelot charges in with other knights loyal to him and rescues Guinevere. This sets the course of the story where Arthur must now wage a "retribution" war against Lancelot. He'd rather not, but his people would have it no other way, so at the end Arthur prepares for battle. Weary and sad, Arthur's spirits rise when a boy wanders into camp wanting to be a knight of King Arthur's famous Round Table. Arthur knights the young boy and sends him on a mission to spread the story of Camelot far and wide.

PAGE 3 (Differences in the Same Story) **Interpreting the Legend**

FINDINGS OF THE CRITICAL EYE

• Overall mood of the story:
Here the overall mood is solemn. Although there are several humorous moments, its main story concentrates on the love triangle between Arthur, Guinevere and Lancelot—a scenario that cannot end happily.

• Overall "look" of the movie:
The movie has a theatrical and glitzy look.

• Treatment of the three main characters—Arthur, Guinevere, and Lancelot:

Arthur is around thirty years old. He's boyish and holds onto his hopes and dreams even through difficult times. He's handsome.

Guinevere is in her midtwenties. She's more practical than Arthur, but abandons her good sense and queenly responsibilities to be with Lancelot. She's beautiful.

Lancelot is in his late twenties. He's honest in thought and deed until he falls in love with Guinevere. He's guilt-ridden with this love yet can't stay away. He's very handsome.

• Realistic treatment of costumes and sets for the times of King Arthur
Costumes and set design appear far from realistic for that time and age. Although some outside scenes are on location, other outside scenes play inside a movie studio. For instance, the first scene with Arthur is in the forest is a studio set.

• The noted differences in the approach of the movie relating with the period produced:
It's a much newer Camelot than existed in that day. Costumes especially look as if they're worn for the first time. Of course breaking into song takes this rendition away from the story, but it keeps the love triangle in tact and, if it stands alone, is a powerful telling.

• Special moments you'll remember:
Arthur jousting with Lancelot is an amusing scene and Arthur seeing Guinevere for the last time is especially poignant.

HALLMARK ENTERTAINMENT (1998) Rated PG
DIRECTOR: Steve Barron
STARRING: Sam Neill, Helena Bonham Carter, Isabella Rosellini

As the title suggests, this story concentrates on Merlin the Magician and great wizard of the Arthurian Legend. Because of this, only sequences involving Arthur, Guinevere, and Lancelot need mentioning.

After uniting the kingdoms on England, Arthur begins to build the castle of Camelot. He's to marry Lord Leo's daughter, Guinevere (an arranged marriage). Arthur plans to set out and find the Holy Grail. Merlin needs to find someone to defend Camelot from the fairy queen Mab while Arthur's gone. He takes Lancelot to Camelot where he meets

Guinevere. Before Arthur leaves, he hosts a joust seeking a champion to defend Camelot and Guinevere's honor. Lancelot handily takes care of all the knights, but also suffers injuries in the process.

Arthur leaves to find the Grail and the years roll on while Queen Mab grooms Arthur's son Mordred for trouble.

Merlin shadows Guinevere hoping to keep Lancelot from her, but knows he cannot keep the two from one another. Merlin warns Guinevere he can't protect her if she decides to follow her heart to Lancelot.

Interpreting the Legend (Differences in the Same Story) PAGE 4

Queen Mab shows Lancelot's unfaithfulness to his wife the Lady Elaine who dies of a broken heart.

Arthur returns to Camelot (without the Grail) to find Mordred there "protecting" his father's interests. He tells Arthur of Guinevere and Lancelot's betrayal. Mordred talks of treason and Arthur, upholding the law, tries and convicts Guinevere to the stake. Before she's burned, Merlin brings rain to quench the fire. Then Lancelot arrives to carry her away.

FINDINGS OF THE CRITICAL EYE

• Overall mood of the story:
Because it's a miniseries, characters and story have time to develop further creating a more satisfying telling.

• Overall "look" of the movie:
Although there are fairies and magic spewing all over, the look of this movie is more realistic than the others.

• Treatment of the three main characters—
  Arthur, Guinevere, and Lancelot:

Arthur is in his early twenties and goes to his early forties. He's not bright and makes many mistakes. He's handsome.

Guinevere is in her early twenties and goes to her thirties. She hasn't much of a character

in this telling. She resists Lancelot for a long time, but finally gives in to her attraction. She's beautiful.

Lancelot is about six to ten years older than the other two. He's good with a sword, but doesn't get much of anything else right. He's very handsome.

• Realistic treatment of costumes and sets for the times of King Arthur
But for the costumes and sets of the fairies and Lady of the Lake, their treatment in this movie is more realistic and representative of the period than in the other movies. The armor is of leather and chain mail, and gowns are of more natural cloths. Merlin's cloak is a bit overdone with feathers, but he is a wizard. Most scenes show realistic settings excepting the enchanted spots.

• The noted differences in the approach of the movie relating with the period produced:
Movies of more recent years like using ragged clothing and "shambled" sets. This production is no different.

• Special moments you'll remember:
Merlin's final battle with Mab is very good, but the man mountain is humorous in its flakiness. Martin Short's character Frik is most memorable.

FIRST KNIGHT

COLUMBIA PICTURES (1995) Rated PG-13
DIRECTOR: Jerry Zucker
STARRING: Sean Connery, Richard Gere, Julia Ormond

Told from Lancelot's point of view, the story begins with Lancelot as a vagabond wandering the countryside earning a meager wage by challenging the locals in swordsmanship.

In another part of the country (Leonesse), Lady Guinevere's people show up on her doorstep after Prince Malagant burns their village. This convinces Guinevere to accept King Arthur's

PAGE 5 (Differences in the Same Story) **Interpreting the Legend**

marriage proposal wanting his protection from Malagant.

On her way to Camelot, Malagant's men attack Guinevere's entourage. Guinevere jumps from her coach to escape and hides in the bushes. Here Lancelot finds her and helps her evade the deadly clutches of one of Malagant's men.

Finally in Camelot, Guinevere and Arthur meet and talk about old times. To celebrate their pending marriage, there is a festival. Lancelot shows up and makes his way through an obstacle game called the Gauntlet. As a reward, Guinevere promises a kiss to anyone making their way through the machine. But Lancelot declines the gift.

Later that night, Malagant's men kidnap Guinevere and Lancelot must go to rescue her once again. Afterwards, as a thank you, Arthur offers Lancelot a seat on the Round Table. So Lancelot becomes a knight and then all must go to Leonesse to stop Malagant's invasion and destruction.

There, Lancelot and Guinevere admit to their attraction, but agree not to act on it. Lancelot says good-bye with a kiss that Arthur walks in on. Angry and hurt, Arthur puts Guinevere and Lancelot on trial for treason. During the outdoor trial, Malagant and his men show up again. A battle ensues. Arthur suffers mortal wounds and Lancelot kills Malagant.

At the end, Lancelot and Guinevere place Arthur on a floating funeral pyre and cast him out on the water. An archer shoots a flaming arrow onto the pyre and it alights in flame. All raise a sword to King Arthur.

FINDINGS OF THE CRITICAL EYE

• Overall mood of the story:
This movie's "out-there" story of King Arthur, Guinevere, and Lancelot dramatically shows the difference in the same story. Miscast and misdirected, the story diverts dramatically from the legend keeping only the character's names. The mood is dark and trudging with little to no light moments.

• Overall "look" of the movie:
The castle of Camelot looks like an avenue down Disney World—completely out of time and setting. The people of Camelot wear mostly coordinated blue and tan—something that would never happen in Arthur's time.

• Treatment of the three main characters— Arthur, Guinevere, and Lancelot:

Arthur is in his sixties. He's noble and royal, but also quick to judge and places his feelings over what's best for his people. He's handsome (for an older man).

Guinevere is in her midtwenties. She's a bit scattered, but hasn't much time to show a character since Lancelot is always there saving her. She's beautiful.

Lancelot is in his forties. He's a misfit not knowing what he wants. He's very handsome.

• Realistic treatment of costumes and sets for the times of King Arthur
Costumes and set design appear far from realistic for that time and age. The outrageous knight armor looks as if it wouldn't stop a charging hornet (a little shield attached to the shoulder?).

• The noted differences in the approach of the movie relating with the period produced:
There seems a concentrated effort in the art design and direction of this movie. However, the intent for this effort isn't certain. Taken purely as an adventure movie it has its merits, but as a telling of the Arthurian Legend it misses the mark on many levels.

• Special moments you'll remember:
The oubliette is interesting. Where Malagant puts a captured Guinevere isn't a true oubliette, but it's interesting.

Interpreting the Legend (Differences in the Same Story) PAGE 6

A Connecticut Yankee In King Arthur's Court

UNIVERSAL (1949) Rated G
DIRECTOR: Tay Garnett
STARRING: Bing Crosby,
Rhonda Fleming,
William Bendix

An outsider's point of view tells this lighthearted tale. Hank Martin (a blacksmith from 1912 U.S.A.) is hit on the head and wakes up in 528 England. This movie takes its plot from the Mark Twain's book and adds music. Hank's modern clothing automatically makes him a monster to capture which Sir Sagramor le Desirous does. "Saggy" takes Hank to King Arthur's court where Hank spots and instantly becomes enamored with Lady Alisande La Carteloise, Arthur's niece. It's decreed Hank burn at the stake for being a monster until he creates instant fire with his modern spyglass lens (he just happens to have with him). Now afraid of the new wizard, Arthur gives Hank whatever he wishes (a small blacksmith's shop). He courts Alisande, fights Lancelot (Alisande's betrothed) in a joust, and shows Arthur how he's ignoring the tough plight of his subjects.

Trying to avoid Merlin's scheme to kill Hank, he's hit on the head again and wakes up back in the 20th Century.

FINDINGS OF THE CRITICAL EYE

• Overall mood of the story:
Like Hank who winks at Alisande a lot, this movie's mood is a playful wink of the eye.

• Overall "look" of the movie:
Hollywoodfied—colorful, pleasant, but far from accurate.

• Treatment of the three main characters: Arthur, Guinevere, and Lancelot

Arthur is old and absentminded. He's a weary old man tired of most everything. He's wrinkled with a scraggly beard.

Guinevere isn't in this telling.

Lancelot is in his fifties. He's large and overbearing. He's pleasant looking.

• Realistic treatment of costumes and sets for the times of King Arthur
With a small effort to get close to the period, there's too much gold armor, metallic glitter, and gold lame to have anyone believe it's a real Camelot. The sets are just that—sets.

• The noted differences in the approach of the movie relating with the period produced:
The songs are nice, but hardly move the story forward. It feels like they're put in just for Crosby to sing.

• Special moments you'll remember:
Alisande's innocence is both charming and unbelieving at the same time.

Which movie did you like best and why?

This is a personal question. But perhaps viewing these movies with more of your critical eye has helped you form an appreciation of one over another. Here's "The Good, the Bad, and the Ugly," about them:

CAMELOT: An excellent story and production— if only the major characters could actually sing.

MERLIN: An interesting look at Merlin, but because it's all about the wizard, the other characters (even Arthur) seem shortchanged.

FIRST KNIGHT: Some actors should stay in their current decade and not try period pieces. Richard Gere is one of these.

A CONNECTICUT YANKEE IN KING ARTHUR'S COURT: Nice and entertaining, but needed more—not sure *what* more, but more.

Timeslips and Accursed Wanderers
Overview in Brief

TIMESLIPS

Timeslips equate to events in which the extension or loss of time plays a key part in the story. Displacements of time, timeslips can pluck a person from a specific time line or plop them back at a different spot. A timeslip often connects an ancestor with a descendent or brings together (and then separates) lovers who would otherwise never meet because of their predicated time lines.

Timeslips may offer characters the opportunity to reassess their life (and failure of it), and to do it over again. However, the "righting the wrong" motif cannot happen without applying the timeslip.

The Difference Between Timeslips and Time Travel—
Again, here are two *Fantastic Elements* where the differences blur. Timeslips typically involve one character moving through long periods of time (forward or backward) and where moving to another time usually has a personal purpose. Whereas time travel generally moves to a specific time with the character knowing where and wanting to go there commonly for research and reference intent. Sometimes the character defies paradox wanting to change history to benefit their life coming along the progressive time line. *(See Page 181 of WINGS OF FANCY for more information regarding timeslips and time travel.)*

ACCURSED WANDERERS

Explaining the accursed wanderer *Fantastic Element* takes us down a darker and uncomfortable path of fantasy. Almost always dealing with death, accursed wanderers are taboo-breaking archetypes dealing with Quibbles to get away with wrongdoing. (Quibbles in fantasy are pacts as in a pact with the devil or contracts with other magical beings where fate, curses, and destiny figure in.)

Accursed wanderers also includes characters caught in pathetic situations like obsessed seekers. (Obviously obsessed seekers spend a goodly amount of the story seeking a special object or self-truth. Several obstacles normally hinder this search and the journey may seem excruciatingly long or never ending.) At times hidden monarchs fall under accursed wanderers. They're generally youngsters not knowing his or her identity or destiny. This plot device allows vengeance and wish-fulfillment to slip in. A subcategory of hidden monarchs could be the reluctant monarch who stumbles through the story denying his right, but eventually accepting his obligations and duties. Perhaps the best example of a hidden or reluctant monarch is King Aragon in J.R.R. Tolkien's THE LORD OF THE RINGS.

Timeslips and Accursed Wanderers
Overview in Brief *(continued)*

MILESTONE, CLASSIC, AND INFLUENTIAL LITERATURE WORKS CONCERNING TIMESLIPS

Washington Irving's RIP VAN WINKLE (1819)
Around the time of the Revolutionary War in the New York Catskill Mountains, Rip leaves his house and falls asleep under a shade tree only to wake up 20 years later. He finds that his wife has died and friends are no longer around. He also gets into trouble hailing King George when everyone just fought a war for their freedom from Britain.

Mark Twain's A CONNECTICUT YANKEE IN KING ARTHUR'S COURT (1889)
The lead character, a 19th Century fellow from Connecticut awakes and unexplainably finds himself in the day of King Arthur. He uses his knowledge of the 20th Century and its technology to make his way through old English traditions, morals, and laws. (This story is explored further in Project 2, **SECTION 5**: Interpreting and Changing the Legend.)

J.M. Barrie's MARY ROSE (1924).
In this play a mother, who in searching for her lost child, becomes a ghost and visits him when he's much older.

Virginia Woolf's ORLANDO (1928)
A young man from Elizabethan times decides not to grow old. He passes through centuries remaining the same age until one day he awakes in more recent times as a woman.

MILESTONE, CLASSIC, AND INFLUENTIAL LITERATURE WORKS CONCERNING ACCURSED WANDERERS

Samuel Taylor Coleridge's THE RIME OF THE ANCIENT MARINER (1798)
An old seafarer tells of his misery when his ship becomes stuck in a great ice barrier, their resulting experiences with mystical and magical entities, and eventual death of the crew. The crew rise as spirits and the ship sails back home. A Pilot rescues the seafarer right before the unfortunate ship breaks apart and sinks. (This poem is explored further in Project 2 of this **SECTION**: THE RIME OF THE ANCIENT MARINER.)

Edward Fitzball's THE FLYING DUTCHMAN (1826)
A stage play where a Dutch sea captain goes ashore every hundred years to find a bride willing to share his wandering fate. (See Page 193 of **WINGS OF FANCY** for the Script adapted from a DUTCHMAN tale.)

As mentioned, *Accursed Wanderers* often depict the darker side of human want and what a person will do or sacrifice to satisfy this want. In the end, the *Accursed Wanderer* discovers the price too high. Sometimes he or she can get out of the predicament— sometimes not.

                (2006 © Joan Garner) **WINGS OF FANCY**: Using Readers Theatre to Study Fantasy Genre

Mystics in the Mist

Original Script by Joan Garner

—BACKGROUND INFORMATION
(genre classification and other data deemed useful)

As explained and separated in this **SECTION** Overview, timeslips and time travel varies thus: Timeslips deal with expansive amounts of time usually moving forward where the character or characters seems not to age or are unaware of time passing. Time travel is passing from time and place usually through machine or other device. Timeslips move forward or backwards, time travel bounces around.

The study of timeslips continues in the next sketch, INTO THE FORBIDDEN CITY.

This sketch incorporates a different result concerning timeslips. Here, those entrapped in a recurring timeslip have ominous magical abilities. As said, they're also trapped in reliving a specific sequence over and over. Although not used as often as long periods of time passing, recurrence of an event or day has also proved a successful plot ploy with the more current movie GROUNDHOG DAY (1993) coming immediately to mind. Also, the male character in this sketch presents a questionable disposition which merely highlights the flexibility timeslips provide.

Shamanism—Besides dealing with Old California and the vaquero (Spanish cowboy), this sketch includes a story involving an American Indian Shaman or medicine man (woman). These people were an invaluable member of every tribe acting as healer, contact to the spirit world, and "go-between" from the human to the animal world (an important Native American source in life and story). Shamans also appear in African and Asian cultures, but with different duties and abilities. Though possessed of certain supernatural talents, rituals and ceremonies comprise most of the shaman's activities.

— SYNOPSIS OF STORY

(1860 in California, U.S.A.) Arcadia shows her friend around their new ranch in Old California. When a work hand joins them at an outer corral, stories begin on why the ranch sold at such a low price, and about an occurrence every night at sunset. Caught in time, a band of marauders come riding from the sunset only to disappear in their dust once nearing the ranch. It's explained a mystic Native American woman placed the marauders in a timeslip or time warp to prevent them from invading the ranch. The girls watch to see if the mystics in the mist ride up at sunset with possibly disastrous results.

—GLOSSARY
(terms possibly unfamiliar to the reader)

ARROYO—A dry gully or gulch, or stream.

RANCH—A ranch or ranch owner.

VAQUERO—A Spanish cowboy.

WRANGLER—One who works with and tends horses.

Mystics in the Mist
STAGING SUGGESTIONS AND HELPFUL HINTS

— CHARACTER DESCRIPTIONS

ARCADIA: (Female) A bit spoiled, a bit of a snob, but friendly and outgoing.

CARA: (Female) Adventuresome and full of life.

HILDAGO: (Male) Mysterious and charismatic.

— PRESENTATION SUGGESTIONS
(1860's Old California Clothing and Items)

COSTUMES
ARCADIA—Riding outfit of colorful blouse, riding skirt (hemmed up middle for straddle riding), short embroidered jacket. Boots. Hat. Long, loose flowing hair.

CARA—Blouse. Short jacket. Full skirt. Boots. Long hair pulled back.

HILDAGO—Bib front shirt. Jeans. Large bandanna. Caparro (tight fitting leg chaps) with jinglebobs and leather strips down sides. Leather belts. Boots. Sombrerro. Semi-long hair with mustache.

LIGHTING EFFECTS
Lights to dim. From stage right, a floodlight with red gel in front. Wave cloth in front of light to suggest a dust storm.

SOUND EFFECTS
Recording of horses galloping and people "whooping" and yelling. Or, have crew backstage "whoop" and holler and make the sound of horse hoofs galloping.

STAGE
SHED—Side of shed. Best looking old and weatherworn.

CORRAL—Weatherworn railings and posts stacked to suggest a corral.

STAGING

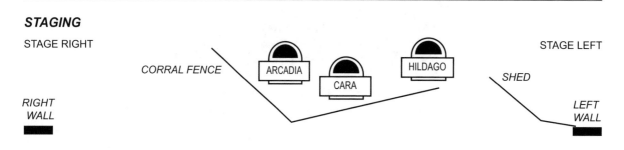

Mystics in the Mist
SCRIPT

SETTING
Old California. 1860. The FENCE of a CORRAL and HORSE SHED stands stage left.

(ARCADIA and CARA enter from stage left and rest their arms on the CORRAL FENCE.)

ARCADIA
And this is the far west corral.
(Pointing.)
Papa says our ranch goes all the way down to the arroyo.

CARA
That's nearly to the horizon, Arcadia.

ARCADIA
I know. Isn't it a splendid estate, Cara? Ordinarily our family wouldn't be able to afford such a grand ranch, but the selling price was way below its value.

CARA
I wonder why.

ARCADIA
We don't know. Papa thought the water reserve had dried up or the winds coming across the prairie too strong. But when talking to the other landowners in the valley, all seemed in order.

CARA
Then there must be another reason.

(Enter HILDAGO from stage left.)

HILDAGO
There is another reason.

ARCADIA *(Looking back.)*
Hildago? Have you been listening to us?

HILDAGO
Forgive me, señorita. Your father wanted me to look at the new pinto back in the stall. I couldn't help overhear the two of you.

ARCADIA
Cara, this is Hildago, our wrangler.

CARA
Hildago, do you know why this ranch sold for such a low price?

HILDAGO
For one, this place has been abandoned for over eight years. It will take a lot more money to get it back to the way it was.

CARA
And for another?

ARCADIA
Hildago tells this silly story. It couldn't possibly be true, but *he* believes it.

CARA
Believes what?

ARCADIA
Don't encourage him, Cara.

CARA
Well, I'm always ready to hear a good story. What is the harm in hearing the vaquero?

ARCADIA
All right. But if you believe any word of it, you're no longer my best friend.

CARA
Oh, Arcadia, for goodness sakes. Go ahead, Hildago. Tell me the story

HILDAGO
Well, many years ago—before the war with the Americans—missionaries built great missions along the coast of California and settled the land. Many of the land barons in Mexico came here and staked out large ranches.

CARA
What is it that's so mysterious about this place?

ARCADIA
Don Pedro owned the ranch to the west of here and wanted this property, but Don Bautista wouldn't sell. So Don Pedro began gathering a band of marauders to attack this place.

HILDAGO
When word got back to Don Bautista, he sent for an old Indian woman who lived in the rocks with the rattlesnakes. They say she possessed magical powers, and he called on her for help.

ARCADIA
Don Bautista didn't want anyone hurt, but he didn't want Don Pedro to just take the ranch from him either. So he asked if the Indian woman could do something to stop the marauders.

HILDAGO
The old woman, a mystic of her people, came out to this corral and waited for dusk. She figured the marauders would come from the west and at dusk where it would be hard to see them in front of the setting sun.

CARA
What did she do?

ARCADIA
We don't know. The story gets a little vague at that point.

HILDAGO
Don Bautista and his men waited right here in this corral and when the sun was nearing the horizon, they could see a red dust storm stirring in the distance.

HILDAGO
Don Bautista's men could hear the marauders approaching as they yelped and shot their guns. Everyone here was getting nervous as they got nearer.

ARCADIA
The cloud dust was very thick, but you could see the heads of the men and horses above the cloud. There were so many—too many for the Don Bautista's men to fight off.

HILDAGO
Some began to panic as the red cloud of dust and mist drew ever closer. But just then the old Indian woman strolled out to meet the marauders. And it looked like right when the horsemen were to run over the woman, she raised her arms and the men and dust simply disappeared in thin air.

ARCADIA
Then she turned and walked back to the cliffs where she lived with the rattlesnakes.

HILDAGO
No one knows what the Indian woman did to the marauders. Some think she sent them to another place or time. Others think she put them in a cycle that goes on and on.

ARCADIA
Hildago thinks the marauders are stuck in time and every sunset you can see them galloping towards our ranch only to disappear as the sun goes down.

CARA
Seriously? You mean if we wait a few minutes, we will be able to see them in the mist of the sunset?

ARCADIA
See? I told you not to believe this silly story.

CARA
Oh, Arcadia. What harm would it do if we waited to see what happened?

ARCADIA
Papa wouldn't like it.

HILDAGO
And there are terrible things that could happen.

CARA
Terrible things? As in?

HILDAGO
If you get too close, and lock eyes with one of the phantom marauders, you could go blind. If you get too close and start coughing from the red dust, you'll die of consumption. And if you get too close where one of the marauders can lasso and pull you in the mist, he'll drag you behind the horses forever.

CARA
Well, it sounds like the trick is not to get too close. Hildago, have you seen these ghost riders?

HILDAGO
Many times.

CARA
Then we have to stay.

ARCADIA
Cara, you're awful.

CARA
Arcadia, aren't you curious to see the phantom men stuck in time? If anything, I feel sorry for them.

ARCADIA
For pity sake why?

CARA
Just think of it—stuck there on their horses to ride night after night after night. Now *that* would be terrible. In fact, that would be really interesting....

ARCADIA
What would be?

CARA
If one of them could lasso us into the dust cloud, I wonder if we could lasso one of them out of it? Wouldn't it be fascinating to hear what he had to say?

ARCADIA
How utterly ridiculous.

CARA
What do you think, Hildago? Are you a good enough wrangler to rope in one of these men?

ARCADIA
It's too dangerous.

CARA
Who believes the story now, Arcadia? How about it, Hildago? Would you try for me?

ARCADIA
You can see what she's doing, can't you, Hildago? She's goading you into doing what she wants.

HILDAGO
I know. But it would relieve a great curiosity to know what happens after they disappear.

CARA
Bravo, Hildago. Bravo.

ARCADIA
Hildago, you can't.

HILDAGO
I left my horse grazing off to the side there.

CARA
You better get him and ride out before you miss the sunset.

    *(**HILDAGO** smiles and exits stage right.)*

ARCADIA
Shame on you, Cara.

CARA
Arcadia, why are you getting so upset if it's just a story? *(Hollering out.)* Ride, Hildago, ride!

***LIGHTING EFFECTS**
Normal lighting dims and a red, flickering light comes from stage right.

CARA *(Continued.)*
Hey, look—there at the horizon. Here it comes. Where's Hildago? I can't see him.

ARCADIA
That isn't it. It's just the light of the sunset.

***SOUND EFFECTS**
Horse hoofs. Men shouting. Guns firing off.

CARA
You hear that? Even if you can't see it, can't you hear it? It's true. Look at that, Arcadia.

ARCADIA
They're riding right for us!

CARA
I can hardly believe it.

***SOUND EFFECTS**
Sounds of before becoming louder.

    *(Frightened, **ARCADIA** slouches against the CORRAL FENCE and covers her eyes.)*

ARCADIA
Make it go away!

CARA
I see Hildago. He's going for one of the men at the edge of the gang.

ARCADIA
They're too close!

***SOUND EFFECTS**
Sounds of before fade off to nothing.

***LIGHTING EFFECTS**
The red light dims. Lighting of stage is also dim.

ARCADIA *(Continued.)*
Is it over? It sounded just horrible.

    *(**ARCADIA** rises and looks out with **CARA**.)*

ARCADIA *(Continued.)*
Well, what happened? Did Hildago get that man?

CARA
Hildago rode up close to a handsome vaquero wearing a green bandanna under his sombrerro.

ARCADIA
They got close enough you could see that?

CARA *(Acting strangely.)*
I saw Hildago whirling his lasso above the vaquero. The vaquero looked up just as the rope dropped around him, and then in another instant he looked right at me. After that everything was gone.

ARCADIA *(Stretching to look.)*
Everything? Even Hildago and the vaquero?

CARA
Everything.

ARCADIA
Oh, no. You don't suppose Hildago slipped into the Indian woman's time enchantment, do you?

CARA
I couldn't say. I didn't see it.

ARCADIA
Well, Cara, what *did* you see?

CARA
Nothing.

> *(**ARCADIA** looks at **CARA** closely and becomes concerned.)*

ARCADIA
Oh, Cara, you didn't.

CARA
I can't see, Arcadia. Anything. I looked into that vaquero's eyes and he looked into mine and now I can't see.

ARCADIA
It's nothing, I'm sure. There was so much dust kicking up; I bet you just got dust in your eyes. Or maybe you were staring into the sun too long. That's it. You know how you can't see anything for a few moments after you stare into the sun.

> *(**CARA** feels for and takes **ARCADIA'S** arm.)*

CARA
I'm frightened, Arcadia. Help me.

ARCADIA
It will be all right, Cara. I'll take you back to the hacienda and Mamma will put some medicine in your eyes.

CARA
That Indian woman—that mystic who came out of the mist—does she still live with the rattlesnakes? Do you think she's still there?

ARCADIA
I don't know. It was a long time ago and she was already old.

CARA
If we can't find her, I'm doomed. I'm blind for the rest of my life, Arcadia.

ARCADIA
Don't talk like that. Everything's going to be fine. Come on. We need to get back to the hacienda.

> *(**ARCADIA** leads **CARA** out stage left.)*

END OF MYSTICS IN THE MIST

Into the Forbidden City

Original Script by Joan Garner

—BACKGROUND INFORMATION
(genre classification and other data deemed useful)

Time variation has proven a major *Fantastic Element*. Time travel, timeslips, or merely time advancing years or hundreds of years within one story establishes a true fantasy tale even when including other components. Although time may rapidly advance in timeslip stories, often the characters do not age like in Virginia Woolf's ORLANDO (1928).

Washington Irving's RIP VAN WINKLE (1819) is another story where time advances dramatically. And, although the main character does age; it's not to the extent where natural progression results in death.

Sleep is one of the most frequently applied plot setups used for timeslips/time travel stories. When the character awakes, he or she has somehow traveled to another era and often another locale—past or future. The actuality of these events then becomes speculative; was the person only dreaming these things?

This little story also has time advancing several years with little change to the main characters. But unlike the above plot device where time changes during sleep, here the lack of sleep serves for plot development.

— SYNOPSIS OF STORY

(Long Ago in China) Pang-Pang has little success getting into the Forbidden City because of his peasant status. An old man outside the gates has an idea of how the young man could get inside, but it's an unusual way. The old man can turn Pang-Pang into a cricket and he can pass under the guard's feet. The only catch, if he wants to become human again, he must get a princess to let him sleep on her pillow the entire night. The problem with that is—as a cricket—Pang-Pang rubs his legs together making a chirping sound keeping the princess' up all night. Irritated with this, they kick Pang-Pang off the pillow before the sun rises.

—GLOSSARY
(terms possibly unfamiliar to the reader)

FORBIDDEN CITY—A walled in city in China comprised of palaces where emperors lived.

— CHARACTER DESCRIPTIONS

GUARDS 1 AND 2: (Male) Big and bully like.

OLD MAN: (Male) Wise and a bit mysterious.

PANG-PANG: (Male) A nice young man with modern ideals. Frustrated, but determined.

PRINCESS LUTANG: (Female) Dainty and modest. Sincere and compassionate.

PRINCESS FLAUN: (Female) Dainty and modest. Sincere and compassionate.

PRINCESS POLEE: (Female) Dainty and modest. Sincere and compassionate.

NOLING: (Female) A nice young woman with modern ideals. Frustrated, but determined.

Into the Forbidden City
STAGING SUGGESTIONS AND HELPFUL HINTS

— PRESENTATION SUGGESTIONS
(Old China Clothing and Items)

COSTUMES
GUARDS 1 & 2—Plain Chinese, high collared every day jacket. Plain pants. Small box caps. No shoes. Short hair.

OLD MAN—Large, simple Chinese robe with wide sleeves.

PANG-PANG—Chinese everyday dress of shan (jacket) and pants. No shoes. As a cricket, antenna headband. Short hair or hair with small, single braid down back.

PRINCESSES—Mandarin robes with wide long sleeves. Bold embroidered patterns on robes. Neutral colored tights. Slippers. Hair lifted and pinned on the back of the head.

NOLING—Chinese everyday blouse and pants (to just below the knee). No shoes. Antenna headband.

PROPS
TABLE or BASKET—A small wooden table or large basket. Something for the **OLD MAN** to sit on (legs crossed) to lift him off the ground.

STAGE
GATE—Partition painted to look like gates.

COURTYARD—Partition painted to look like a decorated wall inside a Chinese palace.

PILLOW PEDESTAL—A large pillow on top of a pedestal or some object to lift the pillow high off the ground.

STAGING
When **PANG-PANG** turns into a cricket, he'll immediately fall to his knees and put on his antenna headband. Afterwards, he'll walk on his knees back and forth from the **OLD MAN** and to the COURTYARD. **NOLING** also walks on her knees. The PILLOW PEDESTAL should be high enough so **PANG-PANG** and the **PRINCESSES** can merely bend over and place their heads on the pillow when sleeping.

STAGING

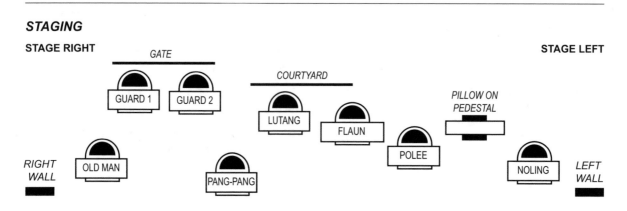

STAGE RIGHT   STAGE LEFT

Into the Forbidden City
SCRIPT

SETTING
Old China. At stage right is a STREET outside the FORBIDDEN CITY. An **OLD MAN** sits on top of a WOODEN TABLE or LARGE BASKET. A GATE (partition) sits to the right of the **OLD MAN**. A COURTYARD (another partition) inside the CITY sits just to the right (down a little) from the GATE. A TALL PEDESTAL or any object with an elegant ROUND PILLOW on top sits stage left.

> *(GUARDS 1 & 2 manhandle PANG-PANG from behind the GATE and throw him to the ground next to the OLD MAN.)*

GUARDS 1 & 2
And stay out!

> *(GUARDS 1 & 2 cross back to the GATE and stand in front of it as sentinels.)*

OLD MAN *(Looking at PANG-PANG. Calmly.)*
Problem?

> *(PANG-PANG stands and dusts off.)*

PANG-PANG
Ohhh, I keep trying to get through that gate and the guards keep throwing me out.

OLD MAN
Which is why they're called gate guards.

PANG-PANG
There must be a way of getting past them.

OLD MAN
They don't want anyone in there. This is why it's called the Forbidden City. And for peasants like us, entrance is impossible.

PANG-PANG
It isn't fair.

OLD MAN
Young man, fair and peasant will never exist on the same plain.

PANG-PANG
I guess—whatever it is you said.

> *(PANG-PANG begins to tiptoe across the stage. The GUARDS look at each other, step down and grab PANG-PANG by the shoulders, and throw him back to the ground in front of the OLD MAN.)*

GUARD 1
You're trying our patience.

GUARD 2
The next time you try to get past this gate, we'll toss you in the stockade. Got that?

PANG-PANG
Yeah, I got it.

> *(The GUARDS cross back to the GATE.)*

OLD MAN
It must be an important reason.

PANG-PANG *(Standing again.)*
Reason for what?

OLD MAN
For you wanting to get inside the Forbidden City.

PANG-PANG
Oh, it's a stupid idea, really.

OLD MAN
There are no stupid idea, only those not willing to act on them.

PANG-PANG
I'm trying to act, but I keep getting kicked out.

OLD MAN
It's possible I could help you enter the Forbidden City if I knew why you wanted to get in.

PANG-PANG
My big brother was a miner. He discovered a rich gold mine and gained favor with the emperor who awarded him with the biggest house in the village. When a great flood came near the village, my second brother saved many people and gained favor with the emperor who awarded him with the second biggest house in the village. Everyone's very proud of my brothers. I'm the third brother— a nobody.

OLD MAN
A nobody is only a somebody waiting to emerge.

PANG-PANG
I thought if I could meet a royal princess and have her fall in love with me—

OLD MAN
—Then *you* would be in the Emperor's favor.

PANG-PANG
Not very good, huh? But I can't even get in to try.

OLD MAN
I know how you can get in. If you were a cricket, you could hop past the guards.

PANG-PANG
A cricket? Right.

OLD MAN
I have some powers. I could turn you into a cricket.

PANG-PANG
Okay. Let's just say you can turn me into a cricket—which is pretty unbelievable—how do I get a princess to fall in love with me if I'm a cricket?

OLD MAN
I didn't say the plan wasn't foolproof.

PANG-PANG
All right. If you can, turn me into a cricket.

*(The **OLD MAN** waves his hand and **PANG-PANG** turns into a cricket. **PANG-PANG** looks down feeling his arms and stomach.)*

PANG-PANG *(Continued.)*
Hey, I'm a cricket!

OLD MAN
Such a bright boy.

PANG-PANG
So I'm going to try it.

*(**PANG-PANG** tiptoes past the **GUARDS** who do not notice him. Pleased, **PANG-PANG** crosses back still unnoticed. He then walks past once again thumbing his nose at the **GUARDS**—still unnoticed. **PRINCESS LUTANG** enters from stage left.)*

PANG-PANG
Hi, there. Are you a princess of the royal court?

PRINCESS LUTANG
A talking cricket. How amazing. Yes, I'm a princess.

PANG-PANG
My name is Pang-Pang. Do you think you could fall in love with me?

PRINCESS LUTANG
Fall in love with you? I think I'd rather step on you.

PANG-PANG
No, no, no. You can't do that. Stepping on a cricket is bad luck, you know.

PRINCESS LUTANG
No, I didn't know that.

PANG-PANG
It's true. Falling in love with a cricket is very good luck—and you'd be in for a big surprise at the end.

PRINCESS LUTANG
Oh, I like surprises. But I'd have to get to know you first, and it's bedtime, so I guess not.

PANG-PANG
This isn't working like I thought it would. Could you wait here a minute, please?

PRINCESS LUTANG
As long as you said "please," I suppose I could.

*(**PANG-PANG** crosses back to the **OLD MAN**. **PRINCESS LUTANG** exits stage left.)*

PANG-PANG *(To the **OLD MAN**.)*
This isn't working. I need to turn back into a human once I'm inside the Forbidden City or a princess will never fall in love with me.

OLD MAN
There is a way. A princess must allow you to sleep on her pillow the whole night. If she does, you will turn back into a young man.

PANG-PANG
Well, that doesn't sound too hard.
(He turns to look stage left.)
Hey, I specifically asked that princess to wait.

OLD MAN
She did for a long time, but as a cricket time passes much faster. One hundred years have passed since you saw her last. You couldn't have expected her to wait for you for a hundred years.

PANG-PANG
What else are you not telling me about this special little favor you did for me?

OLD MAN
No, I think you know it all now.

PANG-PANG
If a hundred years have passed, why haven't the guards changed?

OLD MAN
Guards are guards. They all look the same.

PANG-PANG
That's true. I guess I need to meet another princess.

    (2006 © Joan Garner) **WINGS OF FANCY**: Using Readers Theatre to Study Fantasy Genre

*(When **PANG-PANG** crosses, he pops **GUARD 1** on the foot. **PRINCESS FLAUN** enters from stage left.)*

GUARD 1 *(To **GUARD 2**.)*
Hey, what did you do that for?

GUARD 2
Do what?

PANG-PANG *(To **PRINCESS FLAUN**.)*
Hello. Are you a princess of the royal court?

PRINCESS FLAUN
A talking cricket. That's good luck, isn't it?

PANG-PANG
Why, yes it is. How did you know that?

PRINCESS FAUN
Someone told me about it a long time ago.

PANG-PANG
Do you know what would bring you more luck? Let me sleep on your pillow tonight.

PRINCESS FLAUN
How strange. But all right. Come this way.

*(**PRINCESS FLAUN** leads **PANG-PANG** to the **PILLOW PEDESTAL**. The two rest their heads on the pillow.)*

PRINCESS FLAUN *(Continued.)*
Good night, cricket.

PANG-PANG
Good night, princess.

*(**PRINCESS FLAUN** and **PANG-PANG** close their eyes. After a moment, **PANG-PANG** turns and rubs his legs together.)*

PANG-PANG *(Continued.)*
Ree-deet. Ree-deet.

PRINCESS FLAUN *(Waking.)*
What was that?

PANG-PANG
What was what?

PRINCESS FLAUN
Never mind. Good night.

(The two go back to sleep.)

PANG-PANG *(Rubbing his legs together.)*
Ree-deet. Ree-deet.

PRINCESS FLAUN *(Waking.)*
It's you!

PANG-PANG
Is not.

PRINCESS FLAUN
How do you expect me to sleep if you make that racket?

PANG-PANG
I didn't—you—I just... Excuse me, please.

*(**PANG-PANG** crosses back to the **OLD MAN**. **PRINCESS FLAUN** exits stage left.)*

PANG-PANG *(Continued.)*
Old man, I have a gripe with you. What's with the rubbing the legs together and the ree-deet?

OLD MAN
You're a cricket. Crickets rub their legs together, especially at night.

PANG-PANG
How am I expected to get a princess to let me sleep on her pillow all night if I keep her awake ree-deeting?

OLD MAN
I never said this would be easy.

PANG-PANG
But you—oh, forget it... I suppose another hundred years have passed away.

OLD MAN
It has.

PANG-PANG
So all the people I wanted to impress with gaining the emperor's favor are long gone now.

OLD MAN
And that which you thought was so important is not.

PANG-PANG
All I want is to be myself again. But I guess that will never happen. This really stinks.

*(**PANG-PANG** crosses back in front of the **GUARDS** and pops **GUARD 2** on the foot. **PRINCESS POLEE** enters from stage left.)*

GUARD 2
Ow! Why did you do that?

GUARD 1
Do what?

GUARD 2
Don't do it again.

GUARD 1
What are you talking about?

GUARD 2
You know good and well what I'm talking about.

(The GUARDS tussle and exit stage right.)

PANG-PANG
Hello, are you a princess of the royal court?

PRINCESS POLEE
A talking cricket. My, my.

PANG-PANG
That's right. So will you let me sleep on your pillow?

PRINCESS POLEE
I've heard about you, talking cricket. Why would I let you—

PANG-PANG
—Thought so. Thanks anyway.

PRINCESS POLEE
Well, I *am* a princess. We princesses need our beauty sleep, you would keep me awake.

PANG-PANG
Yes, yes. I got it. You better leave so another hundred years can pass.

PRINCESS POLEE
I don't understand.

PANG-PANG
I'm sorry. It's not your fault. I'm just a little upset.

PRINCESS POLEE
Don't be upset. After all, how many crickets can talk?

PANG-PANG
Yes, I'm a very fortunate cricket.

PRINCESS POLEE
Well, good-bye.

(PRINCESS POLEE exits stage left. PANG-PANG turns to look at the OLD MAN.)

PANG-PANG
Hey, if hundreds of years keep passing by, why are *you* still here?

OLD MAN
I have some power—

PANG-PANG
I don't want to hear about your powers anymore.

(NOLING, also a cricket, enters from stage left.)

NOLING
Another talking cricket. How wonderful. I'm Noling.

PANG-PANG
Hello. I'm Pang-Pang. Are you really a cricket or a human like me changed into a cricket?

NOLING
I don't remember. It's been so long.

PANG-PANG
Me too... Would you like to go for a cup of tea?

NOLING
I'd love to. I must say you're a very attractive cricket as crickets go.

PANG-PANG
And you're a most lovely cricket. I'm so happy to know you.

NOLING
And I'm so happy to have finally met someone I can talk with and maybe sleep on a pillow with— the whole night through. How wonderful that would be.

PANG-PANG
You're so right. This is great.
(To the OLD MAN.)
I have a feeling you had this planned all along.

OLD MAN
If you look beyond the obvious, you will miss the true treasure.

PANG-PANG
I tried to gain importance as a man and couldn't, but as a cricket it looks like I've found a reason to be—just me. She likes me as I am.
(To NOLING.)
You know, Confucius say, "He who meets sweetness will know sweetness."

(PANG-PANG and NOLING exit stage right.)

OLD MAN *(To the audience.)*
I never said that. That doesn't make sense at all. Confucius say, "It may take a long time to find what your heart desires, but never stop searching or happiness will never come your way." I hope it doesn't take a hundred years for you to find true happiness.

(The OLD MAN exits stage right.)

END OF INTO THE FORBIDDEN CITY

The White Knight
His Next Move

From THROUGH THE LOOKING-GLASS: AND WHAT ALICE FOUND THERE by Lewis Carroll
Script adaptation by Joan Garner

—BACKGROUND INFORMATION
(genre classification and other data deemed useful)

Admittedly, placing Carroll's White Knight in the *Timeslips and Accursed Wanderer* **SECTION** is a stretch. Nevertheless, he's here for a specific reason (explained later).

Critique on critique identifies the White Knight and his antics as a metaphor for law, the principles of orderliness, and the fall of man. It's said Carroll's entire world(s) of Alice are but platforms to satirize prominent members of society and for social comment. This may be, but all this theory and analysis puzzles this author since both books: ALICE'S ADVENTURES IN WONDERLAND and THROUGH THE LOOKING GLASS: AND WHAT ALICE FOUND THERE were originally simple sketches written by Carroll to amuse the children of the Reverend Liddell during a boating trip.

Interpretations aside, Lewis Carroll was a master in creating logical nonsense. Apparently so much so, it's said brilliant illustrator John Tenniel refused to illustrate "The Wasp in a Wig" chapter from the original manuscript of THROUGH THE LOOKING-GLASS: AND WHAT ALICE FOUND THERE believing it too ridiculous (or so the story goes). Subsequently, they dropped the chapter.

Essays abound with the whys and wherefores of the story lines and characters, but within all the words and all the studies, two nouns ring true throughout: nonsense and chaos. This explains placing the White Knight in the *Timeslips and Accursed Wanderers* **SECTION**.

However, the White Knight is not an antihero or antisocial figure which typically defines accursed wanderers. Yet, in not knowing where he's going and not admitting his behavior abnormal, he falls within an expanded accursed wanderer classification. Therefore, it's decreed *clueless* is hereby and officially from this point forward (for this author's purposes at least) another order of accursed wanderer.

The White Knight is also a sad character. Labeled a comical buffoon, no matter how much he misses his mark, he's there rescuing Alice and adhering to the credo of knightly honor. And, for any character to be part of Lewis Carroll's imbecilic assemblage is a humiliation in itself. For the White Knight to remain likable in the middle of a mostly obnoxious and unpleasant ensemble is nothing short of remarkable. Even Alice isn't especially endearing because of her toleration or dense recognition of the ridiculous.

LEWIS CARROLL (Charles Lutwidge Dodgson) (1832–1898). United Kingdom.
Regarded as a mathematician and teacher, his other interests were photography, art, religion, medicine, and science.
Other literary works of Carroll's include THE HUNTING OF THE SNARK (1876), a classical nonsense epic, and EUCILD AND HIS MODERN RIVALS (1882), a humorous work dealing with mathematics. SYLVIE AND BRUNO (1889) published towards the end of his and life.

The White Knight
STAGING SUGGESTIONS AND HELPFUL HINTS

— SYNOPSIS OF STORY

This script follows the rescue of Alice by the White Knight (Chapter 8: It's My Own Invention). While continuing with the book's basic theme of classic nonsense, the White Knight isn't the dolt in this telling. He's more of an amalgamation of the White Knight and Humpty Dumpty (Humpty Dumpty being the more intelligent of the two in the LOOKING-GLASS story—go figure). Although still maintaining his bumbling nature, the White Knight demonstrates a certain expository flare in this version which deals more with the play on words and their meaning.

Most illustrations show the **WHITE KNIGHT** as rather old. However, there is no mention of his age in the book. Perhaps John Tenniel (the original illustrator) and others thought of Pellinore of King Arthur lore when they sat down to sketch this character as this is who most drawings remind this author of. Who is to know?

—GLOSSARY
(terms possibly unfamiliar to reader)

ADIEU—Goodbye.

CONCENTRATE—To direct one's thoughts. To focus on a specific idea or concern.

IMPERTINENT—Not showing a proper respect.

— CHARACTER DESCRIPTIONS

ALICE: (Female) A young girl with an unquenchable curiosity.

RED KNIGHT: (Male) A knightly knight of valor and duty.

WHITE KNIGHT: (Male) An absentminded professor.

—PRESENTATION SUGGESTIONS
(19th Century English Clothing and Items and Medieval Knight's Armor)

COSTUMES
ALICE—Dress with puffy short sleeves and full, knee length skirt. Full apron over dress.

RED KNIGHT—Red, long sleeved sweatshirt and red sweatpants. Red poncho (square piece of cloth with hole for head in the middle). A herald symbol appliquéed on poncho. Cloth sash over poncho that cardboard sword can slip into.

WHITE KNIGHT— White, long sleeved sweatshirt and white sweatpants. White poncho (square piece of cloth with hole for head in the middle). A herald symbol appliquéed on poncho. Cloth sash over poncho that cardboard sword can slip into.

PROPS
HORSES—Office chairs (with a cutout horse head—hobby horse—attached to back of chair that's now the front of the horse.)

SWORDS—Made of wood or purchased plastic swords.

TIN BOX—Like a tin Spam can.

SOUND EFFECTS
Use plastic cups rhythmically beating on a table for the horses hoofs coming in and out. Use a muted clip-clop as the **WHITE KNIGHT** escorts **ALICE** to the end of the wood.

SPECIAL NOTE
KNIGHTS can come in and out on wheeled office chairs. If they turn the chair (with no arms) around and straddle the seat, it will look like they are riding in. Also, the falling off the chairs (horses) won't be as injurious if they are on chairs of a normal "sitting" height. Another way of having the **KNIGHTS** fall down would be to place a chair behind them. When they are to fall, they plop down on the chair.

STAGING

STAGE RIGHT   **STAGE LEFT**

RIGHT   *LEFT*
WALL   *WALL*

The White Knight
SCRIPT

SETTING
On the Chessboard in Wonderland.

*(**ALICE** rushes in from the left to center stage. She calls out to downstage, right.*

ALICE
Wait! What of the Lion and the Unicorn? What of—Oh, dear. Do you suppose I have been dreaming of them as well? Perhaps I have been dreaming it all. Oh, I do hope this is my dream and not the Red King's. After all, it's much easier to wake from your own dream than someone else's.

*(Enter the **RED KNIGHT** charging in on his HORSE from stage right. He swings his sword in the air.)*

RED KNIGHT *(Blustering.)*
Ahoy! Ahoy, there! Check!

*(**ALICE** turns towards the noise and takes a step or two away with a gasp when she sees the **RED KNIGHT** approaching. He abruptly stops at her side and proceeds to fall off his HORSE. **ALICE** helps him to stand.)*

ALICE
Heavens, are you all right?

*(The **RED KNIGHT** quickly scrambles to his feet, climbs back on his HORSE, poses majestically, and points his sword at **ALICE**.)*

RED KNIGHT
You are my prisoner.

*(When **ALICE** does not react as he thinks she should, he continues.)*

RED KNIGHT *(Continued.)*
Didn't you hear me? I said you are my prisoner.

*(The **RED KNIGHT** loses his balance and falls off his HORSE once more.)*

ALICE *(Helping him up again.)*
I daresay you won't be holding anyone prisoner if you can't keep upright.

RED KNIGHT
And I say again, you are my—

*(At that moment, the **WHITE KNIGHT** comes charging in on his HORSE from stage left. He swings his sword in the air.)*

WHITE KNIGHT *(Blustering.)*
Ahoy! Ahoy, there! Check!

*(**ALICE** now turns towards the new noise and takes a step or two away with another gasp when seeing the **WHITE KNIGHT** approach. He abruptly stops at her side and—like the **RED KNIGHT**—falls off his HORSE. The **RED KNIGHT** scoffs at the **WHITE KNIGHT**, but then falls off his HORSE a third time. Now both **KNIGHTS** scramble up and back onto their HORSES to pose majestically while watching each other out of the corner of their eye. Meanwhile, **ALICE** takes a step forward placing herself between the two looks at one, then the other as if viewing a tennis match.)*

RED KNIGHT *(Calmly.)*
She's my prisoner, you know.

WHITE KNIGHT
Do tell. Well, I have come to rescue her, you know.

RIGHT KNIGHT
That being the case, I suppose we must fight for her.

WHITE KNIGHT
We must.

RED KNIGHT *(Drawing his sword up.)*
To the death?

WHITE KNIGHT *(Drawing his sword up.)*
Or worse.

ALICE
Mercy!

*(**ALICE** quickly steps aside, stage right to get out of the way. The **KNIGHTS** begin banging their SWORDS together in battle. After a second or two of this, the **KNIGHTS** once again lose their balance and fall off their HORSES at the same time. They slowly rise—winded and panting to catch their breath.)*

RED KNIGHT
Right then. Are we finished here?

WHITE KNIGHT
I believe we are.

(The knights shake hands.)

RED KNIGHT
Smashing. Ever so smashing.

(The RED KNIGHT remounts his HORSE.)

RED KNIGHT *(Continued.)*
Adieu, then.

WHITE KNIGHT
Adieu, then.

(The RED KNIGHT rides offstage right. The WHITE KNIGHT watches the RED KNIGHT leave, then turns to ALICE.)

WHITE KNIGHT *(Continued.)*
It was a glorious victory, was it not?

ALICE
Yes—if you say so. But I thought you had agreed to fight to the death.

WHITE KNIGHT
We did and we did.

ALICE
I must confess your idea of fighting to the death is much different from mine.

WHITE KNIGHT
Is it now? What is your idea of fighting to the death, exactly?

ALICE
Well, you do battle until someone dies.

WHITE KNIGHT
You do? How horrid. You wanted one of use to die?

ALICE
Certainly not. What I want is to be Queen.

WHITE KNIGHT
Do you, now? Well then, so you shall—just as soon as you go down that hill and cross over the little brook. If you like, I will see you to the end of the wood. Then I must go back. It will be the end of my move.

ALICE
That would be very nice of you.

(The WHITE KNIGHT holds out a little TIN BOX attached around his neck.)

WHITE KNIGHT
I see you have been admiring my little box. It's my own invention, you know. It's to keep clothes and sandwiches in.

ALICE
But it hasn't a lid. How can you keep anything in it without a lid to close shut?

WHITE KNIGHT *(Going back to his HORSE.)*
If you think that way, I suspect you'll be questioning my other invention.

ALICE
And what is that?

WHITE KNIGHT *(Pointing to HORSE'S backside.)*
It's a mousetrap, and it works magnificently, thank you very much.

ALICE
Sir Knight, I have no doubt it works quite well. Have you caught many a mouse on the back of you horse?

WHITE KNIGHT
No, but I could. Here is one of my best inventions.
(He points to his HORSES hoofs.)
See the anklets on my horse's feet? How about that!

ALICE
Most impressive, but what are they for?

WHITE KNIGHT
Why, to guard against shark bites, naturally.

ALICE
I see. And are there many sharks swimming down this road?

WHITE KNIGHT *(A bit miffed.)*
My dear, no one likes an impertinent child. Now help me on to my horse and we'll travel to the end of the wood.

(ALICE helps him onto the HORSE and then stands to his side. As they both face outward, the WHITE KNIGHT will gently sway back and forth as if on a slow walking HORSE.)

WHITE KNIGHT
What are you thinking?

ALICE
Oh, nothing.

(2006 © Joan Garner) **WINGS OF FANCY:** Using Readers Theatre to Study Fantasy Genre

WHITE KNIGHT
You can't think of nothing. What an absurd concept—nothing. You can't have nothing.

ALICE
What do you mean, you can't have nothing? Nothing is used all the time.

WHITE KNIGHT
It may be used in a moronic society, but it's still an absurdity. If it's used, how can it be nothing? For example, in mathematics one times nothing is nothing. Ten times nothing is nothing. One hundred times one hundred times ten times nothing is still nothing. Now isn't that just about the most awful waste of someone's time there ever was? If you speak the word nothing, then it becomes a spoken thing and a thing cannot be a nothing. If it's written down, then it is a word on something, and something cannot be a nothing.

ALICE
So if we are to apply your logic, isn't everything also an absurdity? I mean everything is a something to be sure, but you can't have everything either, can you?

WHITE KNIGHT
How clever. Yes, you have a point. But everything is a something, not a nothing.

*(Suddenly the **WHITE KNIGHT** loses his balance and falls off his HORSE yet again. And again, **ALICE** helps him to his feet.)*

ALICE
I'm afraid you haven't had much practice riding.

WHITE KNIGHT *(Remounting his HORSE.)*
What makes you say that?

ALICE
Because people don't fall so often when they've practiced staying on.

WHITE KNIGHT
I've had plenty of practice—plenty of practice.

ALICE
Yes, of course. It might be that you fall so often because you're not concentrating on riding, but on something else like your inventions.

WHITE KNIGHT
Right. I have many—more than many, you know. Brilliant inventions. Now the cleverest thing of the sort that I ever did was to invent a new pudding during the next course.

ALICE
Indeed. And how did it taste?

WHITE KNIGHT
I couldn't say. It was never cooked.

ALICE
But if it was never cooked, then it was never invented, wouldn't you agree? And if this is so, then it couldn't very well be your cleverest invention, could it?

WHITE KNIGHT
How brave you are—calling me on my inventions. Quite a risky move on your part.

ALICE
Sorry, I didn't mean to be.

WHITE KNIGHT
Now your next move is to go down that hill and over the little brook. And then you will be Queen.

ALICE
How wonderful. Will you come with me? I have come to enjoy your company very much. Please come with me.

WHITE KNIGHT
Thank you, my dear, but no. It isn't my move and it's in the wrong direction at that.

ALICE
What direction will you go in now?

WHITE KNIGHT
I can only go two up and one to the left... or two up and one to the right; or two back and one to the left; or two back and one to the right, or two left and one up; or two left and one down; or two right and one down; or two right and one up.

ALICE
Then I should think you have several choices at hand.

WHITE KNIGHT *(A bit sarcastically.)*
All right, missy. On your way, now.

ALICE
I shall stay here for awhile and see you off—just in case you should fall again.

WHITE KNIGHT
What makes you think I will fall?

ALICE
Well... Thank you, Sir Knight, for seeing me to the end of the wood.

WHITE KNIGHT
My pleasure, dear. Adieu.

> (The **WHITE KNIGHT** exists stage left.)

ALICE *(Waving good-bye.)*
Adieu. All the best.

> (**ALICE** *turns back to face outward.*)

ALICE *(Continued.)*
Now it is my move. At last, to be Queen. If this is a dream, I do hope I don't awake now—not when I'm so close... Down the hill and over the little brook. Isn't it most wondrous how one simple move can change you entire life? All right then. I step forward as Queen Alice!

> (**ALICE** *exits offstage right.*)

END OF THE WHITE KNIGHT

(2006 © Joan Garner) **WINGS OF FANCY:** Using Readers Theatre to Study Fantasy Genre

The Flying Dutchman

Based on the Legend
Original Script by Joan Garner

—BACKGROUND INFORMATION
(genre classification and other data deemed useful)

Two misconceptions about the FLYING DUTCHMAN come to life when gathering information for this sequence. One: the Flying Dutchman can refer to the Captain of the doomed ship, or the ship. Two: The well-known opera is much different from the legend.

The story often falls within the folklore category with its ghosts and time variance components, yet it could also be a legend as it's based on a real person and event. THE FLYING DUTCHMAN fits this category in **WINGS OF FANCY** for it's both an accursed wanderer and timeslip story.

The folklore tale identifies the Flying Dutchman as a ghost ship doomed to wander forever on the seas. When approached by other vessels, the crew tries to pass letters and messages to their families (who have long since passed on).

The legend recognizes 17th Century Dutch Captain Bernard Fokke as the source of the story. Fokke's ability to sail his ship quickly from Holland to Java and back produced reactions of marvel and envy. Because he was so astute at this feat, some thought he made a deal with the devil. This would make him the perfect commander of a doomed ghost ship.

Still, others claim the WANDERING JEW story in Christian literature as the Dutchman's point of origin.

Although many versions of the tale exist, its basic plot has the Captain of the ship defying nature and God by sailing the ship straight into a fierce storm. Though those on board plead with him to turn around and find a safer route, the belligerent Captain refuses to see reason and continues to sail against the storm and forever until Judgment Day.

Wagner's FLYING DUTCHMAN—
This article should mention the opera, THE FLYING DUTCHMAN by Richard Wagner with book by

Heinrich Heine. Wagner's version has Captain Daland seeking a safe port from stormy weather. A ghostly vessel breaks against Daland's vessel and becomes stuck to it by grappling irons. Daland meets a figure from the ghost ship who confesses he's cursed to sail the seas forever without rest. However, every seven years the man (with his ship) comes to shore to find a wife. Finding love or marrying releases the curse. The ghost bribes Daland with great treasure for his unmarried daughter's hand. Daland agrees and both ships set sail for home.

Daland's daughter Senta dreams of the Dutchman and when Daland brings the ghostly stranger to his house, he and Senta feel an immediate attraction. However, Senta's intended foils any relationship and the stranger retreats to his ghost ship in despair. When Senta hears the stranger has returned to his ship, she plunges into the waters trying to follow him. Senta's "faithful unto death" saves the Dutchman from the curse and the two soar up to heaven.

WILHELM RICHARD WAGNER (1813–1883)
Germany. Influential composer known for his groundbreaking symphonic-operas (or "music dramas"). His best known opera is the four-opera cycle THE RING OF THE NIBELUNG, a powerful and dramatic work.

— SYNOPSIS OF STORY

(17th Century On the Open Seas)
Passengers aboard a ship fear for their lives as a fierce storm worsens. Having already pleaded with the ship's Captain, they implore the First Officer to intervene. Although it means mutiny, the First Officer commands the ship to turn around out of the storm. This draws the drunken Captain out of his cabin. During a physical fight, the Captain throws the First Officer overboard and orders the ship to turn back into the storm. However, a specter of the First Officer reappears to condemn the Captain and save the passengers.

The Flying Dutchman
STAGING SUGGESTIONS AND HELPFUL HINTS

—GLOSSARY
(terms possibly unfamiliar to the reader)

BOW—The front section of a ship.

SEA WITCH—A witch with magical powers living under the sea.

— CHARACTER DESCRIPTIONS

SHIPMAN WILHELM: (Male) Likable. Uneducated. Small comic relief in story.

SEEVE VOLKER: (Male) Upper class gentleman greatly concerned for the safety of his wife and friends.

KESS VOLKER: (Female) Demure and feminine. Wishing she were home in front of a fire.

LIEF BORG: (Male) Like **SEEVE**, but a little more forceful.

DARKUS BORG: (Female) Adventuresome, but sensible and not a risk-taker.

FIRST OFFICER PARQUETT: (Male) Brave and heroic. Later as a specter, direct and vengeful.

CAPTAIN SHANKS: (Male) Bullheaded. Misuses the little power he has. Drunk and overbearing.

— PRESENTATION SUGGESTIONS

COSTUMES
SHIPMAN WILHELM—Snug vest with long sleeves and no collar buttoned down the front. Tight fitting breeches. Tights and shoes. Bandanna over head. Short hair.

SEEVE VOLKER and **LIEF BORG**—Long doublet with large Puritan collar. Loose breeches. Tights and shoes. Pilgrim hat. Short hair.

KESS VOLKER and **DARKUS BORG**—Long dress with Puffy sleeves over puffy sleeved chemise. Lace cap. Tights and slippers. Hair tucked under cap.

FIRST OFFICER PARQUETT— Buffcoat with falling band (collar). Loose, full breeches. Wide top boots. Short, curly hair. **PARQUETT'S GHOST**—Heavily sprinkle baby powder over him.

CAPTAIN SHANKS—Cock beaver hat with feather and fringe. Short doublet. Loose, full breeches. Wide top boots. Long wig. Mustache.

LIGHTING EFFECTS
Lights need to dim. Lightning. (If capable, have a low constant light in the general playing area, then quickly flip light switch on and off for lightning.

SOUND EFFECTS
Recording of strong wind blowing if needed. Noise of fans may satisfy this effect.

SPECIAL EFFECTS
Place one or two box fans offstage, left. Regulate speed on cue given in script.

STAGE
SHIP'S WHEEL—You may have to build this special object. Attach a cutout wheel to a post. Turning of the wheel isn't necessary. Pantomiming holding ship's wheel will also work.

SHIP'S RAILING—A single or double span rope across two posts.

STAGING
Obviously with fans on offstage, **PLAYERS** need to speak loudly. Shouting at time will help indicate the strong storm.

STAGING

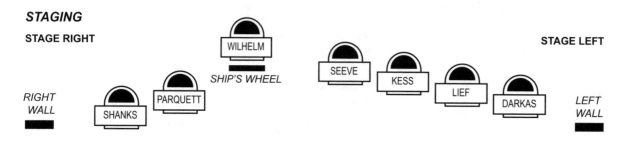

STAGE RIGHT   STAGE LEFT

The Flying Dutchman
SCRIPT

SETTING
At Sea. 17th Century. A large SHIP'S WHEEL stands center stage right. A SHIP'S RAILING stands downstage left.

> *(SHIPMAN WILHELM holds hard to the SHIP'S WHEEL. Passengers SEEVE and KESS VOLKER hold tight to the SHIP'S RAILING.)*

* LIGHTING EFFECTS
Occasional lightning. Otherwise dim lighting.

*SOUND EFFECTS
Wind and thunder.

*SPECIAL EFFECTS
Wind coming from stage left.

KESS VOLKER
Oh, please, blessed Lord, save us from this storm!

SEEVE VOLKER
Darling, we would fair better below deck.

KESS VOLKER
It's flooding below deck. I'd rather be here.

SEEVE VOLKER
But this wind... We could blow overboard.

SHIPMAN WILHELM
This is nothing yet, peoples. Wait until the rain begins. It can sleet across the bow and pelt you with stinging pops.

SEEVE VOLKER *(Looking over to WILHELM.)*
Sir, the Captain needs to turn this ship around before it's too late.

> *(LIEF and DARKUS BORG enter from stage right and cross to the SHIP'S RAILING.)*

LIEF BORG
He won't do it. He's down in his cabin drinking and cursing a blue streak. But he won't turn the ship out of the bad weather. He wants to sail around the Cape of Good Hope storm or no storm.

DARKUS BORG
This is madness.

SEEVE VOLKER
There must be someone on this lousy ship with common sense enough to see we're headed for disaster. Someone we could plead to.

KESS VOLKER
I'm getting so tired and weak, Seeve. I don't think I can hold on much longer.

> *(Enter from stage right FIRST OFFICER PARQUETT. LIEF and SEEVE cross to meet him.)*

LIEF BORG
Mr. Parquett, please—if we continue to go against this storm, the ship will begin to break apart.

FIRST OFFICER PARQUETT
I know, Mr. Borg, but I have my orders.

SEEVE VOLKER
Hang the orders. Hang the Captain. We're all going to drown because of that drunk.

SHIPMAN WILHELM
Mr. Parquett, those green clouds ahead are hurricane clouds—the sea witch herself is coming down to greet us in all her fury. We must move to the soft side of her if we want to make it through.

LIEF BORG
Mr. Wilhelm, what happens if we stay on course?

SHIPMAN WILHELM
Well, sir, I'd say be prepared to swim for you life, I'd say.

SEEVE VOLKER
Mr. Parquett, your Captain's drunk and irresponsible. We have women onboard, man. You must do something.

FIRST OFFICER PARQUETT
Mr. Volker, I have my orders. To go against them would mean mutiny.

LIEF BORG
And to stay with them would mean death.

FIRST OFFICER PARQUETT
I am a First Officer of His Majesty's Royal Navy. I cannot disobey a Captain's orders no matter what.

LIEF BORG

You're jeopardizing everyone on this ship obeying those orders, Mr. Parquett.

FIRST OFFICER PARQUETT

But mutiny, Mr. Volker.

LIEF BORG

But death, Mr. Parquett.

*LIGHTING EFFECTS

Lightning.

*SOUND EFFECTS

A crack of thunder.

> (*KESS* and *DARKUS* scream and hold tighter to the *SHIP'S RAILING.*)

SEEVE VOLKER

Mr. Parquett, you're our only hope.

> (*PARQUETT* looks around, struggling with what to do.)

FIRST OFFICER PARQUETT

Mr. Wilhelm, turn this ship around.

SHIPMAN WILHELM

Yes, sir.

KESS VOLKER

Bless you, sir.

> (*LIEF* and *SEEVE* rejoin the women at the *SHIP'S RAILING* while *WILHELM* turns the *SHIP'S WHEEL* several turns.)

*SPECIAL EFFECTS

The winds lessen.

DARKUS BORG

We would have perished for sure, Mr. Parquett. Thank you.

FIRST OFFICER PARQUETT

There will be the devil to pay, Mrs. Borg. I don't know which will be worse, facing the storm or facing Captain Shanks.

> (*CAPTAIN SHANKS* enters from stage right.)

CAPTAIN SHANKS

The worst will be facing me, you ungrateful louse. Wilhelm, did Parquett here tell you to turn this ship?

SHIPMAN WILHELM

Yes, sir. And I was mighty glad to do it.

SEEVE VOLKER

Captain Shanks, we asked Mr. Parquett to turn the ship around. To keep it on your course would have meant certain peril and death.

CAPTAIN SHANKS

Taking orders from the passengers now, Mr. Parquett? What a pitiful disappointment you turned out to be. Mr. Wilhelm, against the wind once more.

SHIPMAN WILHELM

Sorry, Captain, but I—and I think it safe to say the rest of the crew—stand behind Mr. Parquett on this one.

CAPTAIN SHANKS

Mutiny is it? Parquett, this is your fault!

FIRST OFFICER PARQUETT

No, Captain Shanks. This is *your* fault for commanding a ship in a drunken stupor.

CAPTAIN SHANKS

My drinking has nothing to do with my running this ship. I know what I'm doing.

FIRST OFFICER PARQUETT (*Becoming angry.*)

Listen to me, you drunken Dutchman. You're gambling with the lives of everyone on board just to prove yourself right. I went to you time and time again asking you take the safer route around the Cape, but you'd have none of it. And now we're here in the middle of damaging gales with the rest of your crew precariously manning the sails atop, and you still can't see the danger past your stubbornness.

> (A furious *SHANKS* lunges for *PARQUETT* and grabs him by the neck. They struggle to the left where *LIEF* and *SEEVE* try to intercede and stop the fight. All but *WILHELM* exit stage left.)

*SOUND EFFECTS

The sound of wind stops.

*LIGHTING EFFECTS

Lighting up to full.

> (Dead silence. *WILHELM* looks left trying to see what happened. *SHANKS* stumbles back in from stage left. He's in a daze and out of breath. After a moment, *SEEVE*, *KESS*, *LIEF*, and *DARKUS* enter from stage left. They're stunned.)

(2006 © Joan Garner) **WINGS OF FANCY**: Using Readers Theatre to Study Fantasy Genre

SHIPMAN WILHELM
What is it? What happened here? Where's Mr. Parquett.

CAPTAIN SHANKS *(Mumbling.)*
No one takes over my ship—no one.

DARKUS BORG *(To* **SHANKS***.)*
Murderer!

CAPTAIN SHANKS
He was a mutineer. I was well within my rights to take back this ship in any manner I felt necessary.

KESS VOLKER
You didn't have to throw him overboard like that.

SHIPMAN WILHELM
Mr. Parquett?

SEEVE VOLKER
We tried to get to him. I saw him bob up on top of the water once, and then a wave came over him. We couldn't see him anywhere after that.

CAPTAIN SHANKS
I was well within my rights as Captain of this ship, I was.

LIEF BORG
We'll see when we tell the authorities what happened just now.

CAPTAIN SHANKS
You'll say nothing. Now go below and keep quiet if you know what's good for you.

SEEVE VOLKER
We're paying passengers on this vessel. You can't order us around.

CAPTAIN SHANKS
I'm the Captain and this is my world. I can do whatever I want.

> *(Enter* **PARQUETT'S SPECTER** *from stage left looking ghostlike.)*

PARQUETT'S SPECTER
As always, you're a very belligerent man, Captain Shanks.

> *(All swing around to see* **PARQUETT'S SPECTER***.* **KESS** *and* **DARKUS** *gasp surprised.)*

DARKUS BORG
Mr. Parquett? How did you ever manage to get back on board?

KESS VOLKER
We saw you go under a wave way out in the distance. We didn't think you could make it back or we would have come for you.

PARQUETT'S SPECTER
I have some unfinished business here before I meet my maker, Mrs. Volker.

DARKUS BORG
Your maker? Are you dead, Mr. Parquett?

PARQUETT'S SPECTER
In a way, Mrs. Borg. Only in a way.

KESS VOLKER
Mr. Parquett, are you a ghost?

CAPTAIN SHANKS
Mr. Wilhelm, chain this man below. We'll deal with him when we get to port.

PARQUETT'S SPECTER
You are the one to deal with here, you wretched Dutchman. You have condemned yourself and your crew, Captain Shanks. You have condemned them all with your defiance, incompetence, and murderous ways.

CAPTAIN SHANKS
Murderous? What are you talking about?

PARQUETT'S SPECTER
You broke my neck and then tossed me overboard. How could anyone survive that?

CAPTAIN SHANKS
But you're right here before my eyes.

PARQUETT'S SPECTER
I have returned into a specter to haunt you through eternity, you pathetic Dutchman. I condemn this ship to wander the seas forever looking for a safe port to dock in. But you'll never find it, nor will other vessels on the waters bid you to board. Yours is a cursed ship and none will take mercy upon your sorry lot.

CAPTAIN SHANKS
Nonsense. What nonsense you speak. Who's the drunk now?

PARQUETT'S SPECTER
Yours will be a ghost ship with its sails torn and rotting and its masts creaking against the wind. Your crew will turn to meager skeletons and laugh at you from above.

SEEVE VOLKER
Mr. Parquett—Specter Parquett, what of we passengers? We're innocent in this. Must we share the same fate?

CAPTAIN SHANKS
Pleading with a phantom, Volker? Parquett was your best friend doing as you begged. Well, who's your best friend now? I may be a stubborn mule, but I'm flesh and bone, not a wisp of nothing.

KESS VOLKER
Mr. Parquett, we're so sorry about this. If we hadn't insisted you do something to save us, you might still be alive.

PARQUETT'S SPECTER
Take the longboat and set your sails due east. You will come to land in two days.

DARKUS BORG
But what of the storm?

PARQUETT'S SPECTER
Foul weather will not follow you. When you land, stay on the beach and build a signal fire. Another vessel passing by will pick you up within the week.

LIEF BORG
This being in a longboat is very risky. To trust the word of a—

PARQUETT'S SPECTER
—Specter? Trust my word or trust the word of a mad Dutchman. It's your choice... Mr. Wilhelm.

SHIPMAN WILHELM
Yes, sir, Mr. Parquett, sir. Mr. Specter, sir.

PARQUETT'S SPECTER
I suspect you'll want to go with the civilians in the longboat?

> (**WILHELM** releases the SHIP'S WHEEL and scurries over to join the passengers.)

SHIPMAN WILHELM
Yes, sir. Very much so, sir. Thank you, sir.

CAPTAIN SHANKS
Get back to that wheel, Wilhelm.

SHIPMAN WILHELM
If it's all the same to you, Captain Shanks, you can stuff it, sir.

SEEVE VOLKER
We'll look to your sailing knowledge to get us to land safely, Mr. Wilhelm.

SHIPMAN WILHELM
I'll do my best, Mr. Volker.

> (**KESS VOLKER** crosses to **PARQUETT'S SPECTER**.)

KESS VOLKER
Thank you, Mr. Parquett. You're still saving our lives. That must count for something in the hereafter.

PARQUETT'S SPECTER
You best be going now before the storm rears again.

> (**WILHELM**, the **VOLKERS** and **BORGS** exit stage left while **SHANKS** crosses and takes the SHIP'S WHEEL.)

CAPTAIN SHANKS
Think I'm taken in by this ghostly business, do you? Well, I'll just point the ship in the same direction as the longboat and save us.

PARQUETT'S SPECTER
You just took hold of a wheel you'll be steering for a very long time, Dutchman.

CAPTAIN SHANKS
I don't believe in you, you hear me? I'm still master of this vessel.

PARQUETT'S SPECTER (Grinning.)
You'll think that for a decade or two. Then it will become all too real that you're at the helm of a phantom ship. No one will ever come to save you now. Others may pass by and see you listing in the water, but they'll quickly sail away not wanting your curse on their heads. The flying Dutchman forever doomed to sail the high seas.

> (**PARQUETT'S SPECTER** smiles and exits stage left.)

*LIGHTING EFFECTS
Lights dim and lightning streaks from stage right.

*SPECIAL EFFECTS
The winds picks up again.

*SOUND EFFECTS
Thunder and strong wind.

> (**SHANKS**, in shadow, steers the SHIP'S WHEEL. He'll hold this pose for a moment and then all becomes silent.)

LIGHTING EFFECTS
Lighting out.

END OF THE FLYING DUTCHMAN

(2006 © Joan Garner) **WINGS OF FANCY**: Using Readers Theatre to Study Fantasy Genre

Knights of the Doleful Countenance
PAGE 1 (A Lesson in Extending the Character Beyond the Story)

This Project reviews two doleful knights in **Fantasy Genre** and gives students the opportunity to expand the character's story and history.

PREPARATION AND RESOURCES NEEDED: Read the chapters referenced in this Project. Whether you have your students do tone or both assignments, copy the 3 or 4 pages for each student. Then have your students read the summary of the Doleful Knights and complete the assignment for either Don Quixote or Alice's White Knight.

READING DESIRED BUT NOT REQUIRED

*Student Assignment: Some stories leave the reader with more questions than answers. **Fantasy Genre** often leaves the reader with more questions. Where did that beast come from? What else can Tolkien's Elves do? This Project looks at one of the most intriguing figures in Fantasy Genre: The Sad Knights. Paraphrasing the quote from Cervantes' Sancho Panza in describing Don Quixote, "he's like a knight of the doleful (woeful) countenance—one pitied—one you feel for." Also, these knights have their own stories, but it's easy to imagine what each might do beyond their story line. Your assignment (explained further on the following assignment sheets) will be to continue their story.*

TWO DOLEFUL KNIGHTS

The WHITE KNIGHT and DON QUIXOTE

*So many knights in **Fantasy Genre** and fairy tales are the "knights in shining armor" types facing great challenges and odds. They kill dragons and become the heroes in horrific battles. Yet some knights experience hardships and difficult quests that nearly ruin them. And then there are the knights who just can't get it right. This Project and Exercise highlights two knights of the latter kind: The White Knight in Lewis Carroll's THROUGH THE LOOKING GLASS AND WHAT ALICE FOUND THERE and Don Quixote, the wanna' be knight in Miguel de Cervantes' DON QUIXOTE.*

If Alice's White Knight wasn't purposely patterned after Don Quixote in spirit, it seems illustrators drawing him certainly had the Don in mind. Not only are both similar in appearance, they're forever

THE WHITE KNIGHT WITH ALICE

DON QUIXOTE IN A TOWN SQUARE

bumbling, humbling, keep trudging away characters. At times you can't help feel they should be wearing clown outfits instead of suits of armor, yet you anger when they're treated like clowns and not the pure-of-heart knights they are. It's interesting how the reader easily sees the errors of their ways, but the White Knight and Don Quixote never do. They believe their actions normal if not noble. And for this reason, we can safely say they're both in the league of Knights of the Doleful Countenance, a phrase Don Quixote's squire dubs his master because of his pitying behavior. Now for some, DON QUIXOTE may not fall into **Fantasy Genre**, but it's recognized as a *Taproot Text* (writings including the fantastic) which slides nicely into fantasy and works well for this Project.

Doleful Knights (Extending the Character) PAGE 2

The White Knight

The White Knight in THROUGH THE LOOKING GLASS AND WHAT ALICE FOUND THERE is a perfect "sad" knight. The *quixotic*[1] White Knight is charming and ridiculous, or ridiculously charming. He charges in to rescue Alice and proceeds to fall off his horse with great regularity. He also talks about his wonderful inventions (which are worthless). And hard as it is to believe, the White Knight's behavior seems so foolish; it shows Alice at her sensible best (which is a feat in this story). It's said the White Knight represent government with his constant fumbling and falling down. He insists this strange behavior is normal, but what he thinks is important isn't.

The White Knight proves a contradiction in many ways. He's a successful knight, but a failure in life. He's a joy to read about, but also effects sadness because you know no matter how hard her tries, he'll never get off the chessboard. But throughout his tumbles and mishaps, there's a dignity about him.

[1]*Quixotic* is a term and word taken from the behavior of Don Quixote (below) meaning caught up in the romance of noble deeds and chivalry. It also mean quirky, humorous, and impulsive without much thought of practicality.

Don Quixote

Señor Quixana lives in a village in La Mancha, Spain. Nearly 50, he's thin and gaunt. He becomes enraptured with his books about knights and chivalry and, in going mad, decides to become a knight-errant. Donning an old rusty suit of armor, he picks up shield and lance, and on his scraggly horse sallies forth to do good as Knight Don Quixote de la Mancha. Of course most of the people he meets thinks he's daft and absurd. Even Sancho Panza, the man who becomes his squire and traveling companion believes the Don insane, yet stays with him believing riches will come his way (eventually). Don Quixote travels the Spanish countryside sighting inns and other buildings as enchanted castles; believing mere peasant girls are beautiful princesses; and fighting windmills thinking they are horrible giants. His adventures never live up to the chivalrous heroics he dreams of. In fact, Don Quixote mostly gets into trouble and suffers physical harm and humiliation. At the end of the story, back home, Don Quixote burns his books on knight-errantry and develops a fever thought brought on by depression. In a final defeat, Don Quixote dies with those around him still captivated by his folly.

Illustrations used in this Project are by Renowned 19th Century Illustrator John Tenniel for drawings from THROUGH THE LOOKING GLASS AND WHAT ALICE FOUND THERE.

Illustrations used in this Exercise are by Renowned 19th Century Illustrator Gustave Doré for drawings from DON QUIXOTE.

PAGE 3 (Extending the Character) **Doleful Knights**

CONTINUING THE STORY

Student Assignment: *After having read the short summary of the White Knight in this Project and Chapter 11 of THROUGH THE LOOKING GLASS AND WHAT ALICE FOUND THERE, now is your chance to write another chapter for the humorous knight. Use the Guidelines below to help write a new chapter for the "doleful" knight. Be it funny or ridiculous, help the White Knight continue his story.*

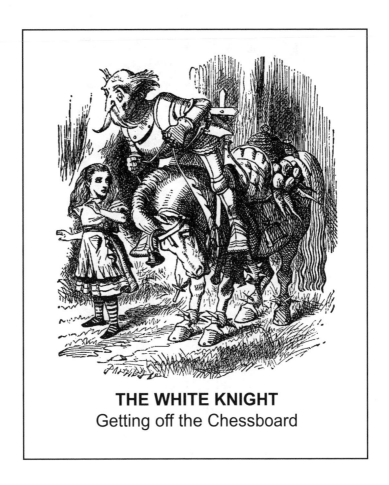

THE WHITE KNIGHT
Getting off the Chessboard

Where does the White Knight go after leaving the chessboard?

Will the White Knight meet Alice again? Does he rescue Alice from another predicament? Does he get the better of Alice this time instead of Alice getting the better of him?

Will he invent another outrageous item? Will it be a worthy or worthless invention? Does he get rich off this invention?

Will he be able to move more freely than the steps of a knight chess piece?

Will he learn how to stay on his horse?

Will he meet other characters on the chessboard? What happens then?

Will he help put Humpty-Dumpty back together again, or maybe just take Humpty-Dumpty's brain for another invention?

Does he find someone to love?

Does he retire and if so where?

Will he go on a knightly crusade to rescue the rest of the chess pieces off the chessboard?

Doleful Knights (Extending the Character) PAGE 4

CHANGING THE STORY

Student Assignment: *After having read the short summary of Don Quixote in this Project and a selected chapter in the book, now is your chance to write a different chapter for the woeful knight. Use the Guidelines below to select and rewrite a chapter in the book, or use a chapter of your choice. Be it funny or tragic, help Don Quixote change his story.*

DON QUIXOTE
The Unknown Chapter

PART I, Chapter 4. Instead of mule drivers beating up Don Quixote, have Don Q. get the better of them.

PART I, Chapter 8. Instead of Don Quixote fighting windmills, have Don Q. fight (and win) _____.

PART I, Chapter 15. Instead of Don Quixote battling muleteers (and losing), have him fight _____.

PART I, Chapter 46. Instead of those "who know best" caging Don Quixote to get him home, have Don Q. cage them and send them off to an exotic land.

PART II, Chapter 22. Instead of lowering Don Quixote into the Cave of Montesinos where he experiences a dream about life, have him go into a _____ and dream about _____.

PART II, Chapter 58. Instead of having Don Quixote and Sancho Panza run over by bulls, have them caught in rampaging _____s.

PART II, Chapter 74. Instead of Don Quixote dieing, have him regain his health and go on another adventure through Spain.

The Rime of the Ancient Mariner
PAGE 1 (A Lesson in Enhancing Interpretive Skills)

Although usually saved for higher grades, why not introduce students to "Rime" now?

Ease interpreting verse by breaking the class into seven sections (for each part of the poem). The poem and an interpretation are included in this Project. The interpretation may be passed to each group as a guide, or may be used for content integrity comparison. *Though admittedly, since it's the author's own interpretation, its integrity may come into question.* Groups may then interpret each verse within the section, or create their own rhyming verse concerning the Part's content.

PREPARATION AND RESOURCES NEEDED: Read the poem and an interpretation. Copy the 12 pages of this Project for each student.

Student Assignment: Read the Part of RIME OF THE ANCIENT MARINER assigned to you by your instructor. Then with your group, rewrite the section with your own modern interpretation of the verses.

THE RIME OF THE ANCIENT MARINER BY SAMUEL TAYLOR COLERIDGE

Part the First

It is an ancient Mariner,
And he stoppeth one of three.
"By thy long grey beard and
        glittering eye,
Now wherefore stopp'st
        thou me?   *Verse 1*

"The Bridegroom's doors are
        opened wide,
And I am next of kin;
The guests are met, the feast is set:
May'st hear the merry din."   *Verse 2*

He holds him with his skinny hand,
"There was a ship," quoth he.
"Hold off! unhand me, grey-
        beard loon!"
Eftsoons his hand dropt he.   *Verse 3*

He holds him with his glittering eye --
The Wedding-Guest stood still,
And listens like a three years child:
The Mariner hath his will.   *Verse 4*

The Wedding-Guest sat on a stone:
He cannot chuse but hear;
And thus spake on that ancient man,
The bright-eyed Mariner.   *Verse 5*

The ship was cheered, the
        harbour cleared,
Merrily did we drop
Below the kirk, below the hill,
Below the light-house top.   *Verse 6*

The Sun came up upon the left,
Out of the sea came he!
And he shone bright, and on the right
Went down into the sea.   *Verse 7*

Higher and higher every day,
Till over the mast at noon --
The Wedding-Guest here beat
        his breast,
For he heard the loud bassoon.   *Verse 8*

The bride hath paced into the hall,
Red as a rose is she;
Nodding their heads before her goes
The merry minstrelsy.   *Verse 9*

The Wedding-Guest he beat
        his breast,
Yet he cannot chuse but hear;
And thus spake on that ancient man,
The bright-eyed Mariner.   *Verse 10*

And now the Storm-Blast came,
        and he
Was tyrannous and strong:
He struck with his o'ertaking wings,
And chased south along.   *Verse 11*

With sloping masts and dipping prow,
As who pursued with yell and blow
Still treads the shadow of his foe
And forward bends his head,
The ship drove fast, loud roared
        the blast,
And southward aye we fled.   *Verse 12*

And now there came both mist
        and snow,
And it grew wondrous cold:
And ice, mast-high, came floating by,
As green as emerald.   *Verse 13*

And through the drifts the snowy clifts
Did send a dismal sheen:
Nor shapes of men nor beasts we ken-
The ice was all between.   *Verse 14*

The ice was here, the ice was there,
The ice was all around:
It cracked and growled, and roared
        and howled,
Like noises in a swound!   *Verse 15*

At length did cross an Albatross:
Thorough the fog it came;
As if it had been a Christian soul,
We hailed it in God's name.   *Verse 16*

It ate the food it ne'er had eat,
And round and round it flew.
The ice did split with a thunder-fit;
The helmsman steered
        us through!   *Verse 17*

And a good south wind sprung
        up behind;
The Albatross did follow,
And every day, for food or play,
Came to the mariners' hollo!   *Verse 18*

In mist or cloud, on mast or shroud,
It perched for vespers nine;
Whiles all the night, through fog-
        smoke white,
Glimmered the white
        Moon-shine.   *Verse 19*

"God save thee, ancient Mariner!
From the fiends, that plague thee
thus! --
Why look'st thou so?" -- With my
cross-bow
I shot the Albatross.   *Verse 20*

Part the Second

The Sun now rose upon the right:
Out of the sea came he,
Still hid in mist, and on the left
Went down into the sea.   *Verse 21*

And the good south wind still
        blew behind
But no sweet bird did follow,
Nor any day for food or play
Came to the mariners' hollo!   *Verse 22*

And I had done an hellish thing,
And it would work 'em woe:
For all averred, I had killed the bird
That made the breeze to blow.
Ah wretch! said they, the bird to slay
That made the breeze
        to blow!   *Verse 23*

The Rime of the Ancient Mariner (Enhancing Interpretive Skills) PAGE 2

Nor dim nor red, like God's own head,
The glorious Sun uprist:
Then all averred, I had killed the bird
That brought the fog and mist.
'Twas right, said they, such birds
        to slay,
That bring the fog and mist.   *Verse 24*

The fair breeze blew, the white
        foam flew,
The furrow followed free:
We were the first that ever burst
Into that silent sea.   *Verse 25*

Down dropt the breeze, the sails
        dropt down,
'Twas sad as sad could be;
And we did speak only to break
The silence of the sea!   *Verse 26*

All in a hot and copper sky,
The bloody Sun, at noon,
Right up above the mast did stand,
No bigger than the Moon.   *Verse 27*

Day after day, day after day,
We stuck, nor breath nor motion;
As idle as a painted ship
Upon a painted ocean.   *Verse 28*

Water, water, every where,
And all the boards did shrink;
Water, water, every where,
Nor any drop to drink.   *Verse 29*

The very deep did rot: O Christ!
That ever this should be!
Yea, slimy things did crawl with legs
Upon the slimy sea.   *Verse 30*

About, about, in reel and rout
The death-fires danced at night;
The water, like a witch's oils,
Burnt green, and blue
        and white.   *Verse 31*

And some in dreams assured were
Of the spirit that plagued us so:
Nine fathom deep he had followed us
From the land of mist
        and snow.   *Verse 32*

And every tongue, through utter
        drought,
Was withered at the root;
We could not speak, no more than if
We had been choked
        with soot.   *Verse 33*

Ah! well a-day! what evil looks
Had I from old and young!
Instead of the cross, the Albatross
About my neck was hung.   *Verse 34*

Part the Third
There passed a weary time.
        Each throat
Was parched, and glazed each eye.
A weary time! a weary time!
How glazed each weary eye,
When looking westward, I beheld
A something in the sky.   *Verse 35*

At first it seemed a little speck,
And then it seemed a mist:
It moved and moved, and took at last
A certain shape, I wist.   *Verse 36*

A speck, a mist, a shape, I wist!
And still it neared and neared:
As if it dodged a water-sprite,
It plunged and tacked
        and veered.   *Verse 37*

With throats unslaked, with black
        lips baked,
We could not laugh nor wail;
Through utter drought all dumb
        we stood!
I bit my arm, I sucked the blood,
And cried, A sail! a sail!   *Verse 37*

With throats unslaked, with black
        lips baked,
Agape they heard me call:
Gramercy! they for joy did grin,
And all at once their breath drew in,
As they were drinking all.   *Verse 39*

See! see! (I cried) she tacks no more!
Hither to work us weal;
Without a breeze, without a tide,
She steadies with
        upright keel!   *Verse 40*

The western wave was all a-flame
The day was well nigh done!
Almost upon the western wave
Rested the broad bright Sun;
When that strange shape drove
        suddenly
Betwixt us and the Sun.   *Verse 41*

And straight the Sun was flecked
        with bars,
(Heaven's Mother send us grace!)
As if through a dungeon-grate
        he peered,
With broad and burning face.   *Verse 42*

Alas! (thought I, and my heart
        beat loud)
How fast she nears and nears!
Are those her sails that glance in
        the Sun,
Like restless gossameres!   *Verse 43*

Are those her ribs through which
        the Sun
Did peer, as through a grate?
And is that Woman all her crew?
Is that a death? and are there two?
Is death that woman's mate?   *Verse 44*

Her lips were red, her looks were free,
Her locks were yellow as gold:
Her skin was as white as leprosy,
The Night-Mare Life-in-Death was she,
Who thicks man's blood with cold.   *Verse 45*

The naked hulk alongside came,
And the twain were casting dice;
"The game is done! I've won! I've won!"
Quoth she, and whistles
        thrice.   *Verse 46*

The Sun's rim dips; the stars rush out:
At one stride comes the dark;
With far-heard whisper, o'er the sea.
Off shot the spectre-bark.   *Verse 47*

We listened and looked sideways up!
Fear at my heart, as at a cup,
My life-blood seemed to sip!   *Verse 48*

The stars were dim, and thick the night,
The steersman's face by his lamp
        gleamed white;
From the sails the dew did drip --
Till clombe above the eastern bar
The horned Moon, with one bright star
Within the nether tip.   *Verse 49*

One after one, by the star-dogged
        Moon
Too quick for groan or sigh,
Each turned his face with a
        ghastly pang,
And cursed me with his eye.   *Verse 50*

Four times fifty living men,
(And I heard nor sigh nor groan)
With heavy thump, a lifeless lump,
They dropped down one
        by one.   *Verse 51*

The souls did from their bodies fly, --
They fled to bliss or woe!
And every soul, it passed me by,
Like the whizz of my
        Cross-Bow!   *Verse 52*

Part the Fourth
"I fear thee, ancient Mariner!
I fear thy skinny hand!
And thou art long, and lank, and brown,
As is the ribbed sea-sand.   *Verse 53*

PAGE 3 (Enhancing Interpretive Skills) **The Rime of the Ancient Mariner**

"I fear thee and thy glittering eye,
And thy skinny hand, so brown." --
Fear not, fear not, thou Wedding-
    Guest!
This body dropt not down.   *Verse 54*

Alone, alone, all, all alone,
Alone on a wide wide sea!
And never a saint took pity on
My soul in agony.   *Verse 55*

The many men, so beautiful!
And they all dead did lie:
And a thousand thousand slimy things
Lived on; and so did I.   *Verse 56*

I looked upon the rotting sea,
And drew my eyes away;
I looked upon the rotting deck,
And there the dead men lay.   *Verse 57*

I looked to Heaven, and tried to pray:
But or ever a prayer had gusht,
A wicked whisper came, and made
my heart as dry as dust.   *Verse 58*

I closed my lids, and kept them close,
And the balls like pulses beat;
For the sky and the sea, and the sea
    and the sky
Lay like a load on my weary eye,
And the dead were at
    my feet.   *Verse 59*

The cold sweat melted from their limbs,
Nor rot nor reek did they:
The look with which they looked on me
Had never passed away.   *Verse 60*

An orphan's curse would drag to Hell
A spirit from on high;
But oh! more horrible than that
Is a curse in a dead man's eye!
Seven days, seven nights, I saw
    that curse,
And yet I could not die.   *Verse 61*

The moving Moon went up the sky,
And no where did abide:
Softly she was going up,
And a star or two beside.   *Verse 62*

Her beams bemocked the sultry main,
Like April hoar-frost spread;
But where the ship's huge
    shadow lay,
The charmed water burnt alway
A still and awful red.   *Verse 63*

Beyond the shadow of the ship,
I watched the water-snakes:
They moved in tracks of shining white,

And when they reared, the elfish light
Fell off in hoary flakes.   *Verse 64*

Within the shadow of the ship
I watched their rich attire:
Blue, glossy green, and velvet black,
They coiled and swam; and every track
Was a flash of golden fire.   *Verse 65*

O happy living things! no tongue
Their beauty might declare:
A spring of love gushed from my heart,
And I blessed them unaware:
Sure my kind saint took pity on me,
And I blessed them unaware.   *Verse 66*

The self same moment I could pray;
And from my neck so free
The Albatross fell off, and sank
Like lead into the sea.   *Verse 67*

Part the Fifth
Oh sleep! it is a gentle thing,
Beloved from pole to pole!
To Mary Queen the praise be given!
She sent the gentle sleep from Heaven,
That slid into my soul.   *Verse 68*

The silly buckets on the deck,
That had so long remained,
I dreamt that they were filled with dew;
And when I awoke, it rained.   *Verse 69*

My lips were wet, my throat was cold,
My garments all were dank;
Sure I had drunken in my dreams,
And still my body drank.   *Verse 70*

I moved, and could not feel my limbs:
I was so light -- almost
I thought that I had died in sleep,
And was a blessed ghost.   *Verse 71*

And soon I heard a roaring wind:
It did not come anear;
But with its sound it shook the sails,
That were so thin and sere.   *Verse 72*

The upper air burst into life!
And a hundred fire-flags sheen,
To and fro they were hurried about!
And to and fro, and in and out,
The wan stars danced
    between.   *Verse 73*

And the coming wind did roar
    more loud,
And the sails did sigh like sedge;
And the rain poured down from one
    black cloud;
The Moon was at its edge.   *Verse 74*

The thick black cloud was cleft,
    and still
The Moon was at its side:
Like waters shot from some high crag,
The lightning fell with never a jag,
A river steep and wide.   *Verse 75*

The loud wind never reached the ship,
Yet now the ship moved on!
Beneath the lightning and the Moon
The dead men gave a groan.   *Verse 76*

They groaned, they stirred, they
    all uprose,
Nor spake, nor moved their eyes;
It had been strange, even in a dream,
To have seen those dead
    men rise.   *Verse 77*

The helmsman steered, the ship
    moved on;
Yet never a breeze up blew;
The mariners all 'gan work the ropes,
Were they were wont to do:
They raised their limbs like lifeless
    tools --
We were a ghastly crew.   *Verse 78*

The body of my brother's son,
Stood by me, knee to knee:
The body and I pulled at one rope,
But he said nought to me.   *Verse 79*

"I fear thee, ancient Mariner!"
Be calm, thou Wedding-Guest!
'Twas not those souls that fled in pain,
Which to their corses came again,
But a troop of spirits blest: *Verse 80*

For when it dawned -- they dropped
    their arms,
And clustered round the mast;
Sweet sounds rose slowly through
    their mouths,
And from their bodies passed.   *Verse 81*

Around, around, flew each sweet
    sound,
Then darted to the Sun;
Slowly the sounds came back again,
Now mixed, now one by one.   *Verse 82*

Sometimes a-dropping from the sky
I heard the sky-lark sing;
Sometimes all little birds that are,
How they seemed to fill the sea and air
With their sweet jargoning!   *Verse 83*

And now 'twas like all instruments,
Now like a lonely flute;
And now it is an angel's song,
That makes the Heavens
    be mute.   *Verse 84*

The Rime of the Ancient Mariner (Enhancing Interpretive Skills) PAGE 4

It ceased; yet still the sails made on
A pleasant noise till noon,
A noise like of a hidden brook
In the leafy month of June,
That to the sleeping woods all night
Singeth a quiet tune. *Verse 85*

Till noon we quietly sailed on,
Yet never a breeze did breathe:
Slowly and smoothly went the ship,
Moved onward from beneath. *Verse 86*

Under the keel nine fathom deep,
From the land of mist and snow,
The spirit slid: and it was he
That made the ship to go.
The sails at noon left off their tune,
And the ship stood still also. *Verse 87*

The Sun, right up above the mast,
Had fixed her to the ocean:
But in a minute she 'gan stir,
With a short uneasy motion --
Backwards and forwards half
        her length
With a short uneasy motion. *Verse 88*

Then like a pawing horse let go,
She made a sudden bound:
It flung the blood into my head,
And I fell down in a swound. *Verse 89*

How long in that same fit I lay,
I have not to declare;
But ere my living life returned,
I heard and in my soul discerned
Two Voices in the air. *Verse 90*

"Is it he?" quoth one, "Is this the man?
By him who died on cross,
With his cruel bow he laid full low,
The harmless Albatross. *Verse 91*

"The spirit who bideth by himself
In the land of mist and snow,
He loved the bird that loved the man
Who shot him with his bow." *Verse 92*

The other was a softer voice,
As soft as honey-dew:
Quoth he, "The man hath penance
        done,
And penance more will do." *Verse 93*

Part the Sixth
First Voice.
But tell me, tell me! speak again,
Thy soft response renewing --
What makes that ship drive on
        so fast?
What is the Ocean doing? *Verse 94*

Second Voice.
Still as a slave before his lord,
The Ocean hath no blast;
His great bright eye most silently
Up to the Moon is cast -- *Verse 95*

If he may know which way to go;
For she guides him smooth or grim
See, brother, see! how graciously
She looketh down on him. *Verse 96*

First Voice.
But why drives on that ship so fast,
Without or wave or wind? *Verse 97*

Second Voice.
The air is cut away before,
And closes from behind. *Verse 98*

Fly, brother, fly! more high, more high
Or we shall be belated:
For slow and slow that ship will go,
When the Mariner's trance
        is abated. *Verse 99*

I woke, and we were sailing on
As in a gentle weather:
'Twas night, calm night, the Moon
        was high;
The dead men stood
        together. *Verse 100*

All stood together on the deck,
For a charnel-dungeon fitter:
All fixed on me their stony eyes,
That in the Moon did glitter. *Verse 101*

The pang, the curse, with which
        they died,
Had never passed away:
I could not draw my eyes from theirs,
Nor turn them up to pray. *Verse 102*

And now this spell was snapt:
        once more
I viewed the ocean green.
And looked far forth, yet little saw
Of what had else been
        seen -- *Verse 103*

Like one that on a lonesome road
Doth walk in fear and dread,
And having once turned round
        walks on,
And turns no more his head;
Because he knows, a frightful fiend
Doth close behind him tread. *Verse 104*

But soon there breathed a wind on me,
Nor sound nor motion made:
Its path was not upon the sea,
In ripple or in shade. *Verse 105*

It raised my hair, it fanned my cheek
Like a meadow-gale of spring --
It mingled strangely with my fears,
Yet it felt like a welcoming. *Verse 106*

Swiftly, swiftly flew the ship,
Yet she sailed softly too:
Sweetly, sweetly blew the breeze --
On me alone it blew. *Verse 107*

Oh! dream of joy! is this indeed
The light-house top I see?
Is this the hill? is this the kirk?
Is this mine own countree! *Verse 108*

We drifted o'er the harbour-bar,
And I with sobs did pray --
O let me be awake, my God!
Or let me sleep alway. *Verse 109*

The harbour-bay was clear as glass,
So smoothly it was strewn!
And on the bay the moonlight lay,
And the shadow of the moon. *Verse 110*

The rock shone bright, the kirk no less,
That stands above the rock:
The moonlight steeped in silentness
The steady weathercock. *Verse 111*

And the bay was white with silent
        light,
Till rising from the same,
Full many shapes, that shadows were,
In crimson colours came. *Verse 112*

A little distance from the prow
Those crimson shadows were:
I turned my eyes upon the deck --
Oh, Christ! what saw I there! *Verse 113*

Each corse lay flat, lifeless and flat,
And by the holy rood!
A man all light, a seraph-man,
On every corse there stood. *Verse 114*

This seraph band, each waved
        his hand:
It was a heavenly sight!
They stood as signals to the land,
Each one a lovely light: *Verse 115*

This seraph-band, each waved
        his hand,
No voice did they impart --
No voice; but oh! the silence sank
Like music on my heart. *Verse 116*

But soon I heard the dash of oars;
I heard the Pilot's cheer;
My head was turned perforce away,
Verse 117

PAGE 5 (Enhancing Interpretive Skills) **The Rime of the Ancient Mariner**

And I saw a boat appear.

The Pilot, and the Pilot's boy,
I heard them coming fast:
Dear Lord in Heaven! it was a joy
The dead men could
    not blast.   *Verse 118*

I saw a third -- I heard his voice:
It is the Hermit good!
He singeth loud his godly hymns
That he makes in the wood.
He'll shrieve my soul, he'll wash away
The Albatross's blood.   *Verse 119*

Part the Seventh
This Hermit good lives in that wood
Which slopes down to the sea.
How loudly his sweet voice he rears!
He loves to talk with marineres
That come from a far
    countree.   *Verse 120*

He kneels at morn and noon and eve --
He hath a cushion plump:
It is the moss that wholly hides
The rotted old oak-stump.   *Verse 121*

The skiff-boat neared: I heard
    them talk,
"Why this is strange, I trow!
Where are those lights so many
    and fair,
That signal made but now?"   *Verse 122*

"Strange, by my faith!" the Hermit said --
"And they answered not our cheer!
The planks looked warped! and see
    those sails,
How thin they are and sere!
I never saw aught like to them,
Unless perchance it were.   *Verse 123*

"Brown skeletons of leaves that lag
My forest-brook along;
When the ivy-tod is heavy with snow,
And the owlet whoops to the wolf
    below,
That eats the she-wolf's
    young."   *Verse 124*

"Dear Lord! it hath a fiendish look --
(The Pilot made reply)
I am a-feared" -- "Push on, push on!"
Said the Hermit cheerily.   *Verse 125*

The boat came closer to the ship,
But I nor spake nor stirred;
The boat came close beneath the ship,
And straight a sound
    was heard.   *Verse 126*

Under the water it rumbled on,
Still louder and more dread:
It reached the ship, it split the bay;
The ship went down
    like lead.   *Verse 127*

Stunned by that loud and dreadful
    sound,
Which sky and ocean smote,
Like one that hath been seven days
    drowned
My body lay afloat;
But swift as dreams, myself I found
Within the Pilot's boat.   *Verse 128*

Upon the whirl, where sank the ship,
The boat spun round and round;
And all was still, save that the hill
Was telling of the sound.   *Verse 129*

I moved my lips -- the Pilot shrieked
And fell down in a fit;
The holy Hermit raised his eyes,
And prayed where he did sit. *Verse 130*

I took the oars: the Pilot's boy,
Who now doth crazy go,
Laughed loud and long, and all
    the while
His eyes went to and fro.
"Ha! ha!" quoth he, "full plain I see,
The Devil knows how to row." *Verse 131*

And now, all in my own countree,
I stood on the firm land!
The Hermit stepped forth from
    the boat,
And scarcely he could stand.   *Verse 132*

"O shrieve me, shrieve me, holy man!"
The Hermit crossed his brow.
"Say quick," quoth he, "I bid thee say --
What manner of man
    art thou?"   *Verse 133*

Forthwith this frame of mine
    was wrenched
With a woeful agony,
Which forced me to begin my tale;
And then it left me free.   *Verse 134*

Since then, at an uncertain hour,
That agony returns;
And till my ghastly tale is told,
This heart within me burns.   *Verse 135*

I pass, like night, from land to land;
I have strange power of speech;
That moment that his face I see,
I know the man that must hear me:
To him my tale I teach.   *Verse 136*

What loud uproar bursts from that door!
The wedding-guests are there:
But in the garden-bower the bride
And bride-maids singing are:
And hark the little vesper bell,
Which biddeth me to prayer!   *Verse 137*

O Wedding-Guest! this soul hath been
Alone on a wide wide sea:
So lonely 'twas, that God himself
Scarce seemed there to be.   *Verse 138*

O sweeter than the marriage-feast,
'Tis sweeter far to me,
To walk together to the kirk
With a goodly company! --   *Verse 139*

To walk together to the kirk,
And all together pray,
While each to his great Father bends,
Old men, and babes, and loving friends,
And youths and maidens gay! *Verse 140*

Farewell, farewell! but this I tell
To thee, thou Wedding-Guest!
He prayeth well, who loveth well
Both man and bird and beast.   *Verse 141*

He prayeth best, who loveth best
All things both great and small;
For the dear God who loveth us
He made and loveth all.   *Verse 142*

The Mariner, whose eye is bright,
Whose beard with age is hoar,
Is gone: and now the Wedding-Guest
Turned from the
    bridegroom's door.   *Verse 143*

He went like one that hath been
    stunned,
And is of sense forlorn:
A sadder and a wiser man,
He rose the morrow morn.   *Verse 144*

THE END

(Before beginning the project, it might be interesting to ask, "Why did the Ancient Mariner kill the Albatross?" This question has been asked since the poem was written. Many theories have been offered, but no one knows for sure... Perhaps it's supposed to be that way.)

The Rime of the Ancient Mariner (Enhancing Interpretive Skills) PAGE 6

Interpretation

THE RIME OF THE ANCIENT MARINER BY SAMUEL TAYLOR COLERIDGE

Part the First

1 of 3 men is stopped by an Ancient Mariner who has a long gray beard and a glittering in the eye. The man (Wedding Guest) asks why the Mariner stopped him.
Verse 1

The Wedding Guest explains he and his friends are expected at his relative's wedding. Can't the Mariner hear the party (nearby)?
Verse 2

But the Mariner keeps the Wedding Guest from joining the festivities as he begins to explain about a ship. The Wedding Guest is impatient with the Mariner and tells him to unhand him.
Verse 3

But the Mariner holds the Wedding Guest spellbound by his intent stare, and the Wedding Guest decides to hear the Mariner's story.
Verse 4

The Wedding Guest sits down to listen and the Mariner begins his story.
Verse 5

(The Mariner begins:) The ship's crew were excited to get started, and made ready to set sail.
Verse 6

The ship sets out to sea with good weather.
Verse 7

The Wedding Guest listens to the Mariner until he hears the bridal music.
Verse 8

The wedding ceremony begins as the bride enters into the hall. All watch, happy to see the bride pass by.
Verse 9

The Wedding Guest feels he should attend the ceremony, but the Mariner doesn't let him go.
Verse 10

(The Mariner continues with his story.) A violent storm grips the seas and the turns the ship towards the south pole.
Verse 11

The ship is tossed up and down win the waves. Trying to get out of the storm, the ship turns further south.
Verse 12

They sail so far south, they meet snow storms. It becomes frightfully cold as they move the vessel between floating pieces of ice.
Verse 13

The ship drifts into a land of ice where no living thing exists.
Verse 14

The ice is now everywhere making great howling, cracking, and roaring (grinding) noises.
Verse 15

Strangely, an Albatross (bird) lands on the ship. The ship's crew happily welcomes the sight of another creature thinking it a good omen.
Verse 16

The crew feeds the bird who then takes off. The crew decides to follow the bird.
Verse 17

A south wind helps steer the ship back northwards and the Albatross flies alongside the ship.
Verse 18

The ship makes it way through fog during its trek back north.
Verse 19

The Ancient Mariner shoots the Albatross with an arrow.
Verse 20

Part the Second

The sun rises up, but is still hidden in the mist until it sits again into the sea.
Verse 21

The ship still has the aid of the south wind blowing behind it. But the "good luck" bird hasn't returned for food or fun.
Verse 22

The Mariner realizes he did a foolish thing in killing the bird that the ship's crew believes brought them the good southerly wind moving the ship northward.
Verse 23

But since the sun has come out, the ship's crew changes their mind and thinks maybe the bird brought the mist and fog that took the ship into the frozen south pole. So now, it's a good thing that the Mariner shot and killed the Albatross.
Verse 24

A goodly wind continues and the sails catch it taking the ship northward (into the Pacific Ocean).
Verse 25

But the wind stops and the sails sag. All becomes sad and calm, and the crew speaks to one another only to break the silence that's all around.
Verse 26

Without the wind, the hot sun—no bigger than the moon in the sky—beats down above the mast at noontime.
Verse 27

Days go by as the ship drifts on a still ocean surface.
Verse 28

The ocean stretches out on all sides of the ship and the crew runs out of drinking water.
Verse 29

PAGE 7 (Enhancing Interpretive Skills) **The Rime of the Ancient Mariner**

The men (or just the Mariner) begin to hallucinate seeing creatures coming up and over the sea's surface. *Verse 30*

The hallucinations of these creatures continues as they dance around the ship. *Verse 31*

And now the Albatross reappears (as a dream) having followed the ship back from the frozen waters. *Verse 32*

But the crew— so parched from not having drinking water they can't speak—blame the Mariner once again for killing the bird. *Verse 33*

The crew look on the Mariner in contempt and then hang the dead bird's carcass around the Mariner's neck. *Verse 34*

Part the Third
But the days continue to pass and the crew begins to become weak from not having water. The Mariner sees something far off in the horizon. *Verse 35*

The small, far-of speck is difficult to make out. It looks like just a (cloud bank) of mist until it get closer and the Mariner can distinguish a shape he was hoping to see. *Verse 36*

The shape nears as if sailing through the waves. (But how can that be?) *Verse 37*

With his throat so dry, the Mariner can't holler that a ship approaches. So he bites down on his arm and sucks the blood to moisten his throat. He's then able to shout out, "A sail! A sail!" *Verse 38*

Still unable to speak, the crew grins and looks hopefully at the approaching ship. *Verse 39*

"See!" cries the Mariner watching the ship draw near. But then all realize this ship is sailing towards them without any wind. *Verse 40*

As the sun sets, the ship they hope will save them sails between them and the setting sun. *Verse 41*

Now they see the ship clearly. It's a skeleton ship. *Verse 42*

Now the Mariner's heart beats strongly because a "ghost ship" draws near. *Verse 43*

They see the broken and rotting ship with only two aboard. Once is a ghost of a woman and the woman's mate is Death. *Verse 44*

The woman ghost has red lips and golden hair with pale-pale skin. She is life wrapped in death and make's a man's blood run cold with fright. *Verse 45*

As the skeleton ship comes alongside the Mariner's ship, they see the woman ghost playing a game of dice with Death. When the game is over, she cries out, "I've won! I've won!" (She wins the Ancient Mariner.) *Verse 46*

The sun sets and stars come out as it becomes dark. A whisper across the sea can be heard. *Verse 47*

As the ship's crew listen, the Mariner feels his "life's blood" slipping away. *Verse 48*

The crew member at the ship's wheel gleams white from the lamp light while the quarter moon comes out with one bright star shining at its lower tip. *Verse 49*

The crew now turns to the Mariner looking at him with hatred. *Verse 50*

The crew begins to drop dead with a sigh or groan. Their bodies drop down with a heavy thump. *Verse 51*

And after their death, each man's soul rises and passes by the Ancient Mariner to go to heaven or hell. *Verse 52*

Part the Fourth
The Wedding Guest is now frightened of the Ancient Mariner. He thinks a spirit or ghost is talking to him. *Verse 53*

The Wedding Guest says he's afraid of the Mariner, but the Mariner assures him he wasn't one of the crew that dropped dead. *Verse 54*

(The Mariner goes on with his story.) The Mariner is now all alone on the ship because a saint (angel?) hasn't come down to take his soul. *Verse 55*

The rest of the crew dies and goes to an afterlife, but the Mariner remains on board while the slimy sea creatures return. *Verse 56*

He looks on the sea of creatures and then on the deck of dead men. *Verse 57*

The Mariner tries to pray for mercy (and death), but hears an evil whisper that death isn't for him. *Verse 58*

The Rime of the Ancient Mariner (Enhancing Interpretive Skills) PAGE 8

The Mariner closes his eyes trying to keep from seeing the awful sea creatures and dead men all about him. *Verse 59*

Sweat (life) left men's bodies, though they had yet to smell of rot. Still, their eyes looked on at the Mariner. *Verse 60*

The Mariner's curse continues. He lives for seven days watching the dead men's eyes. Yet he doesn't die. *Verse 61*

The moon rises in the sky with a couple of stars around it. *Verse 62*

The moon shines on the ship creating a shadow on the red ocean's calm surface. *Verse 63*

By the light of the moon, he sees water snakes swimming in the ocean. *Verse 64*

In the shadow of the ship, the green and black snakes swim by leaving a golden fire in their wake. *Verse 65*

The Mariner appreciates the water snakes for what they are (living creatures). He's thankful they are there. *Verse 66*

Lifting him from loneliness, the Mariner prays. At that moment, the dead Albatross hanging around his neck falls off and sinks into the sea. *Verse 67*

Part the Fifth
To spite all that has happened, The Mariner is very tired and able to sleep. *Verse 68*

It begins to rain and refill the water barrels on deck. *Verse 69*

The rain wets the Mariner's lips and soaks his clothing. He thinks he's dreaming (about the rain). *Verse 70*

His body feels so light, he surely must have died in his sleep and is now a ghost. *Verse 71*

Winds comes up to fill the sails. *Verse 72*

Lightning fills the sky like a hundred fire-flags. Stars continue to shine. *Verse 73*

The rain pours from a dark cloud, but the moon can still be seen at the cloud's edge. *Verse 74*

With the moon still shining at the edge of the black cloud, there is more lightning. *Verse 75*

Although the bigger storm stays at a distance, enough wind comes up to move the ship. *Verse 76*

The dead men now rise up. Though there is no life in their eyes, they still move. *Verse 77*

The (dead) helmsman begins to steer the boat that is now moving though there isn't any wind to propel it. The (dead) crew begin to work the ropes. *Verse 78*

The Mariner's dead nephew stands by the Mariner's side helping him pull a rope. But the nephew stops when the Mariner tells him he's not to help. *Verse 79*

Again, the Wedding Guest says he's frightened (of what is obviously the Ancient Mariner's ghost). But the Mariner explains all was done by angels. *Verse 80*

At dawn, the dead men drop lifeless again. All are clustered around the ship's mast. Sweet sounds come from their bodies (the sound of peace). *Verse 81*

The sound of peacefulness surrounds the ship. *Verse 82*

The Mariner hears birds. *Verse 83*

The singing of birds turns into the songs of angels. *Verse 84*

The sweet song of angels continues. It's like listening to a babbling brook in the summer. *Verse 85*

The ship continues to sail smoothly though there still isn't any wind. It's as if it's being moved from underneath. *Verse 86*

The spirit from the south pole is moving the ship. But then the ship is once again motionless. *Verse 87*

The sun is high in the sky as the ship sways. *Verse 88*

There is sudden movement of the ship that awakens the Mariner from his sleep. *Verse 89*

The Mariner isn't sure how long he has been asleep (or dead), but life returns to him and he hears voices. *Verse 90*

One voice asks the other if they're looking at the man who killed the Albatross. *Verse 91*

The spirit of the south pole loved the Albatross who loved the Mariner who shot him down. *Verse 92*

The other voice (a gentle spirit) tell the south pole spirit that the Mariner has done some penance, but must do more. *Verse 93*

PAGE 9 (Enhancing Interpretive Skills) **The Rime of the Ancient Mariner**

Part the Sixth

The first voice asks what the ocean is doing to make the ship move so fast?
Verse 94

The second voice replies it isn't the ocean, but the moon.
Verse 95

The moon is overpowering the ship and making it move.
Verse 96

Again, the first voice asks why is the ship going so fast?
Verse 97

The second voice replies the air closes in behind it.
Verse 98

The ship will slow down once again when the Mariner wakes from the trance he was placed under.
Verse 99

The Mariner awakes to find the ship sailing in pleasant weather, but still must do penance as the dead ship's crew haunts him again.
Verse 100

Under the moon, all the crew stand on deck staring at the Mariner.
Verse 101

The curse of the crew still haunts the Mariner. He can't turn away from then even to pray.
Verse 102

The spell he was under staring at the dead ends and he's able to look on to the green sea. Still, he sees nothing else.
Verse 103

Like walking down a lonely road and sensing something, you turn around yet there's nothing there.
Verse 104

A wind comes over the Mariner though it couldn't be heard, nor does it make a path on the sea or ripple the sails.
Verse 105

The welcoming wind lifts the Mariner's hair and crosses his cheek.
Verse 106

The ship sails on swiftly and smoothly. A sweet breeze blows.
Verse 107

The Mariner thinks he sees his country land with the light house, hill, and kirk (church).
Verse 108

The Mariner prays that what he's seeing is real, let him be awake. But if it's just a dream, let him keep sleeping.
Verse 109

The harbor is clear and its waters clear as glass that the reflection of the moon is seen on it.
Verse 110

The moon also shines on the rocks and the kirk. All around is steeped in silence.
Verse 111

Spirits leave the dead crew.
Verse 112

The Mariner sees the spirits rise, then looks back on the deck.
Verse 113

Each corpse falls flat and lifeless again, and from each rises from the body a spirit of light.
Verse 114

Each spirit waves signaling to anyone on land.
Verse 115

Not speaking, they wave forgiveness of the Ancient Mariner.
Verse 116

The Mariner then hears the oars of a boat slapping in the water. He also hears the boat's "Pilot" cry out.
Verse 117

A man and boy in a boat row towards the Mariner.
Verse 118

He then hears the Hermit's (a holy man) voice. The Mariner hopes the Hermit can help wash away his sin of killing the Albatross.
Verse 119

Part the Seven

The Hermit lives in the wood and likes talking to sailors from foreign lands.
Verse 120

The Hermit kneels to pray every morning, noon, and evening on the moss next to an old oak stump.
Verse 121

But the boat approaches and the Mariner hears the men talking about the signal light that caught their eyes. But where is the signal light now?
Verse 122

The Hermit cries in wonder on seeing the tattered ship with its warped planks and ripped sails.
Verse 123

The Hermit says the ship is like the brown skeleton leaves along the brook where he lives.
Verse 124

The Pilot is afraid of how the ship looks and wants to turn back, but the Hermit encourages him to keep rowing to the ship.
Verse 125

The boat nears the ship, but the Mariner doesn't call out or motion for them. Suddenly a fearful sound rings out.
Verse 126

A rumble comes from under the water growing louder until it hits the ship and splits it in two. The ship quickly sinks.
Verse 127

The Mariner finds himself floating on the water and then in the Pilot's boat.
Verse 128

The Rime of the Ancient Mariner (Enhancing Interpretive Skills) PAGE 10

A part of the ship is seen spinning round and round in the whirlpool created by its sinking.
Verse 129

When the Mariner tries to speak, the Pilot of the boat falls to his knees in fright praying to be saved.
Verse 130

The Mariner takes the oars from the boy. The boy is also frightened and exclaims that the Mariner (the Devil) knows how to row!
Verse 131

The Mariner rows the boat to shore and finally stands on firm land, though when the Hermit gets out of the boat, he has trouble steadying himself.
Verse 132

The Mariner asks the Hermit to "shrieve" (forgive him). The Hermit asks the Mariner what he wants forgiveness from.
Verse 133

The Mariner tells the Hermit his tale of woe and agony, setting his guilt free after the telling.
Verse 134

Ever since, when the agony of his plight returns to pain his heart, the Mariner must tell his tale to ease his guilt.
Verse 135

He now travels from land to land telling his story. The Mariner knows by looking in a man's face if he should teach him the Mariner's story.
Verse 136

Now the doors of the wedding burst open and the wedding guests spill out. The bride and bridesmaids sing.
Verse 137

The Mariner tells the Wedding Guest how along he was at sea—so alone God wasn't even there.
Verse 138

For the Mariner, it's sweeter than marriage to walk in the wood with a friend.
Verse 139

To have everyone walk to the kirk and pray including young and old.
Verse 140

The Mariner tells the Wedding Guest good-bye urging him to love all things of God—man, animal, and bird.
Verse 141

Love all things great or small because not only did God make man, but everything else of heaven and earth.
Verse 142

The Mariner then leaves the Wedding Guest. But the Wedding Guest turns away from the wedding.
Verse 143

Stunned by the Ancient Mariner's story, the sadder but wiser Wedding Guest goes home to sleep and rise again in the morning.
Verse 144

THE END

(2006 © Joan Garner) **WINGS OF FANCY:** Using Readers Theatre to Study Fantasy Genre

Otherworlds and Fantasylands
Overview in Brief

One of the most magnificent *Fantastic Elements* in **Fantasy Genre** deals with otherworlds and fantasylands. If the story is too big for this world to hold, simply create one that will.

Often indistinguishable, slight differences between otherworlds and fantasylands are so noted:

OTHERWORLDS

Otherworlds also mean *autonomous impossible* or a world ruled by whim and impulsiveness. Otherworlds usually have a connection to or method of getting from the real world to the other like a wardrobe in THE LION, THE WITCH, AND THE WARDROBE, or a farmhouse like in THE WONDERFUL WIZARD OF OZ.

Otherworlds usually coexist with (a floating island) or within (a subterranean habitat under the ocean) the real world. Also, the (usually human) hero or heroine travels back and forth from the real world to *Otherworlds* like Dorothy in THE WONDERFUL WIZARD OF OZ or Gulliver in GULLIVER'S TRAVELS.

FANTASYLANDS

Where otherworlds may serve as the background for the fantastic story, fantasylands serve as primary narration. Fantasylands may be wide in scope encompassing continents and oceans or as small as an island or meadow. Enchanted areas may crop up in a fantasyland landscapes and nearly always have ominous places where the antagonist (bad and evil guy) lives.

Taking their cue from J.R.R. Tolkien's THE LORD OF THE RINGS, most following fantasy stories include maps showing the geographical makeup of the land. Though of undisputed assistance in forming the fantasyland in ones mind, it's argued maps and drawings act as substitutes for describing the land in the narrative. The other argument counters how the story is just too big to include a fantasyland description and maps and drawings act as quick guides.

*(See Page 215 of **WINGS OF FANCY** for more on otherworlds and fantasylands.)*

Fantasy Genre
Overview in Brief *(continued)*

**MILESTONE, CLASSIC, AND INFLUENTIAL
LITERATURE WORKS CONCERNING
OTHERWORLDS AND FANTASYLANDS**

Jonathan Swift's GULLIVER'S TRAVELS
(1726)
*A satire on human nature takes Gulliver to
different worlds and societies. First with tiny
people, then with giants, onward to a floating
island and finally to a world with intelligent
horses, Gulliver travels and reports his findings.
(See Page 235 of **WINGS OF FANCY** for the
Script adapted from this novel.)*

J.M. Barrie's PETER PAN (1911)
*Barrie adapted his play into a book with
Wendy, John, and Michael following Peter
Pan and Tinker Bell to the fantasy island
Neverland where the lost boys live as well as
mermaids, Indians, and pirates. (See Project 2
of **SECTION** 1 for more on this story.)*

Robert E. Howard's THE PHOENIX ON THE
SWORD (1932)
*First novel introducing Conan the Barbarian
and his exploits through an ancient and
mystical world.*

David Eddings' THE BELGARIAD (Series)
(1982-1984)
*Orphaned farm boy Garion with his guardian
Polgara and sorcerer Belgarath experience
many journeys through 5 books.*

Raymond Feist's THE RIFTWAR SAGAS
(1982-1985).
*Another series of 3 books about war between
two worlds connected by a dimensional gap.*

In the Land of Ashaun

Original Script by Joan Garner

—BACKGROUND INFORMATION
(genre classification and other data deemed useful)

Otherworlds and fantasylands provide a perfect setting for the different and unusual—especially with life forms. Animals and humans take on exotic shapes and manners, often melding together to create a whole new species like the gentle Hobbits in J.R.R. Tolkien's THE LORD OF THE RINGS, or monstrous Morlocks in H.G. Wells' THE TIME MACHINE. The difference in these two "subspecies" is as vast as imagination itself.

Utopias of all kinds fall within this *Otherworld and Fantasyland* **SECTION**. (Utopia—A perfect place within its accepted social, political, and moral structure.) In general those within their utopia possess better sense and display a greater tolerance of all things than mere mortal man and woman. Seemingly knowing much more than we—like the secret of the universe—these superhumans nearly always wish to keep the common man out or their founded paradise (no doubt believing the common man's influence disruptive and destructive). Only when forced to deal with man's usually blundering intrusion, do they address the "problem" with a degree of insight and patience like the people of James Hilton's Shangri-La in LOST HORIZON.

However, fantasylands can be far from ideal. Because the most basic plot device in any story be it fantasy or otherwise is conflict, otherworlds and fantasylands also contain "bad" countries, cities, and people. The hero of the story must face some form of natural or unnatural adversity.

— SYNOPSIS OF STORY

(13th Century Japan and Present Day) High in the Japanese mountains where the snow falls all year, a beautiful valley exists where the Ashauns live. Unlike the smaller Japanese people of that time, Ashaun's are quite tall and thinly with a cool blue tinge to their skin and long white hair that matches the snow. They're also intelligent, strong, and have great vision of outward events and the inward soul.

One day the Wise Seer tells all the sun has lost its way and will soon journey towards Earth and melt their precious land. To save their ice palaces and frosty land, the Ashaun's equip a gigantic phoenix with a special machine, then fly the bird up into the clouds in order to fling the sun back to its correct course.

In the Land of Ashaun
STAGING SUGGESTIONS AND HELPFUL HINTS

— CHARACTER DESCRIPTIONS

AKURI: (Male) A confident young man, excitable and energetic.

NUMORI: (Female) Skeptical, but ready to believe once evidence comes to light.

OTSU and **MENJI:** (Males) Good men.

SHIGA and **YORITO:** (Females) Good women.

KENKO: (Male) Like a wise and caring grandfather.

SAGATO: (Male) Ready to see the science in everything, he appreciates ideas and solutions.

BALKI: (Male) A true hero willing to put his life on the line to save his people.

— PRESENTATION SUGGESTIONS
(13th Century and Present Day Clothing and Items)

COSTUMES
AKURI—Heavy parka. Hiking pants. Tall snow boots. Small stocking hat. Ski goggles. Gloves. Short hair.

NUMORI—Same as **AKURI**, but of feminine cut and color.

ASHAUN MEN—White haori (silk coat of knee-length) over a white kimono with wide, white sash. White quilted cloth boots. Long hair.

ASHAUN WOMEN—Quilted white kimono with wide, white satin sash. White quilted cloth boots. White hair (wig) pinned up.

BALKI—White quilted thigh-length tunic with wide cuffs. White, long quilted pants. White quilted cloth boots. Long hair.

PROPS
LANTERN or FLASHLIGHT—Modern equipment.

CRATES—Of wood, looking very old and beat up.

SCROLLS—Old looking and made of silk with Japanese symbols on them.

GEARS—Metal gears and springs from machines.

BASKET—Large, loose weave "floppy" baskets.

LIGHTING EFFECTS
Capabilities to dim normal lighting and spotlight CAVE area would help set it apart from the rest of the stage.

STAGE
CAVE—A structure needs to set the cave area apart from the rest of the playing area. Partitions painted to look like cave walls will greatly help the blocking mentioned for **AKURI** and **NUMORI**.

STAGING
If a simple reading, separate **AKURI** and **NUMORI** from the rest of the people of Ashaun.

STAGING

STAGE RIGHT   **STAGE LEFT**

CAVE

RIGHT WALL — NUMORI — AKURI — TABLE

KENKO — SAGATO — BALKI

OTSU — YORITO — MENJI — SHIGA — LEFT WALL

(2006 © Joan Garner) **WINGS OF FANCY**: Using Readers Theatre to Study Fantasy Genre

In the Land of Ashaun
SCRIPT

SETTING

Japan. 13th Century (and current). An old CAVE stands far downstage right. WOODEN CRATES and a TABLE stand about. The rest of the stage is vacant.

*LIGHTING EFFECTS

Dim lighting. A spotlight shines on the CAVE.

> (*AKURI* enters from stage right into the CAVE area. He carries a LANTERN or large FLASHLIGHT.)

AKURI

This has to be it. Numori, this is it!

> (Right behind **AKURI**, **NUMORI** also comes into the CAVE. She's brushing off her coat.)

NUMORI

I've never been so cold in my life.

AKURI

It must be around here. This *has* to be the cave.

NUMORI

It's only the hundredth cave we've been in, Akuri. What makes you think this is the one?

AKURI

It just has to be the one. We're running out of places to look.

> (**AKURI** exits back out stage right.)

NUMORI

We're trying to find a myth. Talk about crazy. Akuri, this is nothing more than an old mining cave.

AKURI (*From offstage.*)

A mining cave with old manuscripts?

NUMORI

What are you talking about?

> (**AKURI** comes back in the CAVE with an OLD WOODEN BOX of SCROLLS.)

AKURI

Scrolls. Really *old* scrolls. The Wise Seer Scrolls of Ashaun detailing how they saved planet Earth.

NUMORI

You found the Wise Seer's Scrolls just around the corner in an old crate. Come on.

AKURI (*Rummaging through the CRATE.*)

It sure looks like it.

NUMORI

Akuri, there's no way this crate has the scrolls you're looking for. Wouldn't they be buried in a secret hiding place or something?

AKURI

And this isn't a secret hiding place? How long have we been looking for this cave?

NUMORI

They've been telling this story for thousands of years, Akuri. It's just a legend. It couldn't have really happened.

AKURI

Numori, if you don't believe in the story, why are you here?

NUMORI

You're my boyfriend. I go where you go. But Akuri, if these scrolls say they are the Ashaun Scrolls, it must be a hoax.

AKURI

Hah. Look at this. It's the Wise Seer's signature. We did it, Numori! We found it!

> (**AKURI** points to a place on a SCROLL. **NUMORI** looks where he's pointing.)

NUMORI

What does it say?

AKURI

"I believe the events of the coming days worthy of placing ink to paper. I am Kenko, advisor to the people of Ashaun."

NUMORI

It looks really old.

AKURI

Well, it would be, wouldn't it?
(He reads from the SCROLL.)
"First, I will tell you of my beloved land of Ashaun. We are a simple people living high in the mountains of Japan."

> (As **AKURI** reads the SCROLL, the people of Ashaun enter from stage left, greet others by bowing, mingle, and pantomime talking.)

AKURI *(Continued. Reading.)*
"Large glaciers stand on all sides of this land isolating us from the rest of the world. We live happily in our frozen city. All of our buildings are made of ice. We grow food in flat clay trays where fires underneath burn day and night to keep the soil warm. In appearance, Ashaun people are very tall and our hair is long and white. We are a cultured people whose interest are invention, literature, and music. We are a gentle people meaning no harm to anyone."

NUMORI
Yes, but what about saving the Earth?

AKURI *(Reading the SCROLL.)*
"On this day I have asked everyone to meet me in the ice palace to discuss a most pressing matter..."

*LIGHTING EFFECTS
The spotlight fades over the CAVE. Full lighting comes up over the rest of the playing area.

OTSU
Menji, are you here, too?

MENJI
Everyone is here, Otsu. The Wise Seer has summoned us all to the ice palace.

SHIGA
It must be very important for the Wise Seer to call everyone in Ashaun to this meeting.

OTSU
Ah, here he comes with Sagato.

(KENKO and SAGATO enter from stage left.)

KENKO
Thank you for coming. As most of you know, this is Sagato, our most revered scientist. I'm afraid he has rather ominous news. I'll let him explain.

SAGATO
Thank you, wise Kenko. People of Ashaun, I must alert you to an occurrence I've been observing for some time now. I'm convinced the sun has changed it's course. From the beginning of time, the size of the sun has stayed the same from sunrise to sunset. But in the past months, I have noticed an increase in its size.

SHIGA
What does that mean, Sagato?

SAGATO
It means the sun is headed for Earth at an alarming rate. I fear in one month's time the sun will be close enough to our land to start melting all our buildings to nothing. Our special world as we know it will be no more.

YORITO
Are we all going to die? What can we do?

KENKO
Sagato tells me the only way to save our land is to move the sun back onto its normal path.

MENJI
Move the sun? How can that be done?

KENKO
Has anyone an idea of how this can be done?

YORITO
But Wise Seer, we are a simple people. How can the few of us save the Earth? It can't be done.

BALKI
We need to rope the sun and fling it back onto its proper course. But to rope the sun—even from the highest mountain peak—won't be high enough.

SHIGA
Balki's idea may work. It would have to be a very long rope, and we would have to be up in the sky to toss it.

SAGATO
Higher than the sky. Beyond the clouds.

OTSU
How do we do that?

BALKI
Cree, the giant phoenix bird nesting in the Western glacier—I'm sure Cree could fly beyond the clouds.

MENJI
The bird would need training, and it would have to be a special rope not to burn up once around the sun.

SHIGA
And how do we lasso the rope around the sun?

SAGATO
Perhaps a machine could be made to sling the rope far enough. Someone would need to turn it on at the right time. The machine and man would have to ride on the back of Cree.

KENKO
Can this be done?

SAGATO
It might be possible.

MENJI

So let me understand this idea. One—we need to make a very long rope. Two—we need to invent a machine to shoot the rope towards the sun. Three—we would have to train the wild giant phoenix to fly into the stars. And finally—one of us must be willing to fly with this bird and turn the machine on... No. There's no way this idea would be successful.

YORITO

Do you have a better idea, Menji?

BALKI

I'll do it. I'll train the giant phoenix and go with him beyond the clouds.

KENKO

Your bravery is commendable, Balki. Friends, I say we try to do this. Some part of the idea may not work, but we need to try. We'll divide into three groups. Sagato will lead the first group in inventing the rope machine. Menji, you know of many earthly elements. Your group needs to develop a rope that won't burn. And Balki, take your group the Western glacier and into Cree's giant nest.

(The people of Ashaun begin to split up and pantomime talking as they walk offstage left.)

*LIGHTING EFFECTS

The lights in the general area dim and the spotlight comes back up on the CAVE.

NUMORI

Amazing. It goes along just like the stories say with Balki the hero.

AKURI

It happened, Numori. It actually happened.

NUMORI

Do you know what this means, Akuri? It means you have discovered one of the greatest finds ever. You can prove how the land of Ashaun saved the planet Earth.

AKURI

We have discovered, Numori. How *we* have discovered this great find.

NUMORI

Thank you, Akuri.

(AKURI and NUMORI share an endearing smile before NUMORI continues reading the SCROLL. As NUMORI reads, SAGATO and YORITO cross the stage from left to right with GEARS and SCROLLS of blueprints.)

NUMORI *(Continued.)*

"For weeks everyone worked night and day on their assigned projects. Sagato and his group collected all the gears and springs they could find to build the unique rope tossing machine."

(MENJI and SHIGA cross the stage left to right.)

NUMORI *(Continued.)*

"Menji first sat with his people and discussed all the elements of the world and what could be combined to make a rope flexible enough to loop around the sun yet strong enough not to burn. And Balki took his volunteers to the Western glacier to meet with the giant phoenix Cree."—That must have been interesting."

(As AKURI speaks, BALKI and OTSU trek across the stage from left to right with large BASKETS strapped to their backs.)

AKURI *(Chuckles. He reads.)*

"Otsu believed that the best way to tame a wild bird was with food. So he and the others brought baskets of food for Cree. Defensive at first, the giant phoenix smelled the good food and was soon eating from the friendly arms of the men. The men even slept with the bird at night to gain its trust. Within a few days they began training the bird to fly at their command."

NUMORI

Good plan. Feed the bird. The Seer continues to say, "Each week we would meet in the ice palace to see how everyone was coming along with their projects. And each week our confidence in the plan grew. Finally— towards the end of one month's time—the rope had been coiled over and over from the bottom of our valley to the top of the Western glacier. The rope projecting machine was mounted to Cree, and Balki climbed on its back with instructions given him by Sagato on how to work the machine. All the people of Ashaun climbed the Western glacier to cheer Balki off on this most important mission. We're hopeful, but know the risk our brave Balki is taking."

LIGHTING EFFECTS

The spotlight fades over the CAVE. Full lighting comes up over the rest of the playing area.

(The people of Ashaun enter from stage left and right to mingle. All look to the sky.)

SAGATO

Although he's near the clouds now and we can hardly see the giant phoenix, I still see the long rope hanging down from it.

YORITO
It looks like the tail of a kite. Menji and his team did an excellent job of making that rope so long.

KENKO
Everyone worked hard, Menji. It's up to Balki now.

SAGATO
It won't be long until Balki will need to turn the settings on the machine. I put a timing device on it to alert Balki to the exact time he needs to activate the rope machine.

OTSU
Can we hear it from here, Sagato?

SAGATO
I made the bell pretty loud, Otsu. But I think Balki is up too high for us to hear it.

SHIGA
Then all we can do is wait for Balki to return.

SAGATO
Yes, I'm afraid so.

(All become silent. Pause.)

MENJI *(Pointing upward.)*
There he is. I see him!

OTSU
The rope is gone. Do you think he did it?

(SAGATO pulls out a little LOOKING DEVICE from a pocket and uses it to look upward.)

SAGATO
The sun appears to be in a different spot. Yes, I think Balki did it.

(All cheer and wave happily. After a moment, BALKI enters from stage right. The people of Ashaun cheer loudly.)

KENKO
Did you do it, son?

BALKI
I think so. It all went as Sagato planned. Everything worked just as he wanted it to. Cree took me beyond the clouds, the bell rang, I set the gages and wheels on the machine and hit the button.

MENJI
Did the machine project our rope to the sun?

BALKI
Yes, Menji. I wish you could have seen it. The rope went up and up with a swoosh and wrapped around the sun. And it didn't burn up, Menji. What a magnificent rope.

(People of Ashaun congratulate themselves.)

BALKI *(Continued.)*
Then I grabbed the rope and pulled the loop tight around the sun and then—with all my might—I swung the sun to the eastern sky like Sagato instructed. By that time, Cree was all too eager to return to Ashaun, so we turned around and came streaking back to Earth. He's happily back in his nest now for a well deserved rest.

YORITO
You are a true hero, Balki.

BALKI
We're all heroes, Yorito. Everyone worked on this and triumphed. I'm honored to be part such a wonderful people. Thank you—everyone!

*(The people of Ashaun huddle around **BALKI** as all exit stage left.)*

*LIGHTING EFFECTS
The lights in the general area dim and the spotlight comes back up on the CAVE.

NUMORI
It really happened. To discover such a find, you're going to be famous, Akuri.

AKURI
I don't know, Numori. These are a humble people. If the world knows Ashaun really existed, people from far and wide will converge on this mountain looking for artifacts and souvenirs. Maybe we should let our ancestors rest in peace.

NUMORI
Are you sure, Akuri? No one will know that you discovered the greatest archeological find of all.

AKURI
I'll know, Numori. I'll know. Let's put this box back and let the stories remain stories.

NUMORI
Well, if you think best, Akuri. Yes, maybe it's for the best.

*(**AKURI** and **NUMORI** smile at one another as **AKURI** picks up the OLD WOODEN CRATE. The two then exit stage right.)*

LIGHTING EFFECTS
All lighting off.

END OF IN THE LAND OF ASHAUN

(2006 © Joan Garner) **WINGS OF FANCY**: Using Readers Theatre to Study Fantasy Genre

Monkey Island

Original Script by Joan Garner

—BACKGROUND INFORMATION
(genre classification and other data deemed useful)

It's feared a little of Lewis Carroll's ALICE IN WONDERLAND'S nonsense has slipped into this sketch. Dealing with monkeys, how could it not? MONKEY ISLAND easily fits into the *Fantastic Beasts and Talking Animals* **SECTION**, but it's here because only monkeys inhabit the island. Not that this makes it terribly extraordinary, but the monkeys talk. Since the island serves as the background for these fanciful creatures, it acts as an otherworld. Placing MONKEY ISLAND in this **SECTION** also demonstrates how most fantasy stories load up with several *Fantastic Elements*. (Rationale aside, four sketches already reside in the *Fantastic Beast and Talking Animals* **SECTION**. This one had to go somewhere.)

As explained in *Otherworlds and Fantasylands Overview in Brief*, the difference between the two wobbles from slight to nil. However, this author wishes to insert yet another supposition here with clearer if not wholly accurate descriptions.

Fantasylands—Where the setting can be as fanciful and uncommon as its characters. Where the land becomes an important plot ingredient extensively described, used throughout the story, and where fantastic geographical spots function as obstacle or aid in the central character's goal. Again, J.R.R. Tolkien's THE LORD OF THE RINGS landscape serves as a perfect example of this definition.

Otherworlds—A place familiar enough not to distract from the plot, but "someplace else" where inhabitants or events fall within *Fantastic Element* guidelines. Often landing in an otherworld involves a "fantastic" method traveled, or a mistake or blunder of some kind. But again, once there, an otherworld landscape isn't strange or exotic enough to become another character of the story. James Gurney's DINOTOPIA island bodes well as an example of this definition.

— SYNOPSIS OF STORY

(15th Century India) Princess Burendi of Southern India travels to Monkey Island in search of food for her starving people. In the throws of famine for several years, other options have come and gone, and now their only hope lies in the island's bountiful fruits and plants. The only problem is with the monkeys living on Monkey Island. Wanting the princess and her entourage to go away, they toss nutshells and squirt fruit juice from lemons and limes at her party. But the monkeys prove nothing more than an annoyance. However, their supposed nonsense makes a good deal of sense in some respects, and the people and monkeys come together in the end to help the situation in Southern India.

Monkey Island
STAGING SUGGESTIONS AND HELPFUL HINTS

— CHARACTER DESCRIPTIONS

PRINCESS BURENDI: (Female) Prideful but ever mindful of her duties as princess and obligations to serve her people.

MINISTER NAJAB: (Male) Kindly and diplomatic. Willing to listen to all sides of a situation before pressing an opinion.

SHIPMASTER PUNTA: (Male) A "take charge" fellow, he's easily annoyed with the monkeys and decides to proceed with the mission on his own.

SHIP MAN BOKI: (Male) A follower yet capable and smart.

MONKEYS TUFUTTI, JIB-JIB, LUB-LUB, and **WICKI-WEE:** (Male or Female) Bouncy and ready to laugh at the drop of a banana. Prepared to engage in great battles as long as no one is hurt.

KING COCO: (Male) Like a peacock in walk and manner.

QUEEN EUCALYPTUS: (Female) A true diva, she also struts and gestures grandly to emphasize her status and importance.

— PRESENTATION SUGGESTIONS
(15th Century Indian Clothing and Items)

COSTUMES
PRINCESS BURENDI—Colorful satin sari. Jeweled headband. Sandals. Hair long and flowing.

MINISTER NAJAB—Plain colored sherwani coat with pants. Cloth shoes. Fez. Short hair.

SHIPMASTER PUNTA—Colorful waist length kurta with dhoti (bellowed loincloth or breeches). Boots. Short hair.

SHIP MAN BOKI—Plain kurta (shirt) and jodphurs (trousers). Bare feet. Short hair.

MONKEYS—Brown or black turtleneck sweaters and tights. Use a long sash or wrap a piece of rope around the waist and let it hang down the back for a tail. Bushy hair.

KING COCO—Like the monkeys with added items of a large felt hat with feathers and a leaf vest. Also bushy hair.

QUEEN EUCALYPTUS—Like the monkeys with added items of fur collar and sleeves, and fur tutu. Long, bushy hair and heavy makeup with long, false eyelashes, rosy cheeks, and red lipstick.

PROPS
NUTSHELLS and FRUIT—The genuine article.

POUCHES—Like waist wallets, perhaps.

LEMONS and LIMES—Take the plastic lemon and lime shaped bottles of juice, wash out, and add water to squirt.

STAGE
ROYAL BARGE—A rope on two posts. A sign indicating "Royal Barge" could be an amusing addition.

BEACH—Though not necessary, some form of outline separating the beach from the sea is desirable.

PALM LEAVES—Hanging from stage left will help identify the beginning of the jungle.

STAGING
Discourage **PLAYERS** from behaving like monkeys. The sketch will be funnier if they act more human.

STAGING

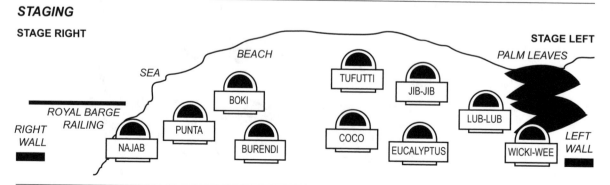

Monkey Island
SCRIPT

SETTING
India. 15th Century. Stage right holds the front of the ROYAL BARGE with RAILING. The BEACH of Monkey Island begins center stage and continues stage left. PALM LEAVES hang over stage left.

(PRINCESS BURENDI, MINISTER NAJAB, and SHIPMASTER PUNTA stand stage left behind the RAILING.)

SHIPMASTER PUNTA
We're coming up on Monkey Island, your highness. Are you sure you want to do this?

PRINCESS BURENDI
Not at all, Shipmaster. I'd rather be doing anything else than landing on Monkey Island. But my people suffer from the great famine. We need the bountiful fruits and plants here.

SHIPMASTER PUNTA
Yes, but all who have come here return quite mad. Isn't it irresponsible for the ruler of her kingdom to attempt something that could render her insane?

MINISTER NAJAB
Shipmaster Punta, as Princess Burendi's Minister, I've tried to talk her out of this dangerous mission. She's most insistent.

PRINCESS BURENDI
How can I ask anyone to subject themselves to something I would not allow myself to face? That would be cowardly and not the behavior of a sovereign.

(SHIP MAN BOKI enters from stage right.)

SHIP MAN BOKI
Land ho, Shipmaster. Anchor down. Ready to disembark.

SHIPMASTER PUNTA
Very good, Boki. With your permission, Princess.

(PUNTA gestures for BURENDI to disembark. BURENDI and NAJAB cross to center stage on the beach. PUNTA and BOKI follow.)

MINISTER NAJAB
So here we are, the infamous Monkey Island.

PRINCESS BURENDI
Why it seems peaceful and quiet.

SHIP MAN BOKI
Prepare yourself for anything, Princess.

PRINCESS BURENDI
Such drama. Surely it isn't that bad.

(Small items come flying in from stage left and hit the group.)

PRINCESS BURENDI *(Continued.)*
Ow... What was that?

MINISTER NAJAB
Perhaps an insect, highness.

(Now many little PELLET LIKE THINGS fly in hitting the group.)

SHIPMASTER PUNTA
What the? I think we're being attacked, your highness.

PRINCESS BURENDI
With these things? They don't really hurt, they're just annoying.

(MONKEYS TUFUTTI and JIB-JIB enter from stage left. They have POUCHES tied around their hips containing NUTSHELLS.)

MONKEY TUFUTTI *(With hands on hips.)*
Annoying? Annoying? How dare you say our frontal attack is annoying.

(TUFUTTI and JIB-JIB toss more NUT-SHELLS at the group.)

MINISTER NAJAB
Will you stop that? What are these things anyway?

JIB-JIB
Nutshells.

(TUFUTTI and JIB-JIB toss more NUT-SHELLS at the group.)

SHIPMASTER PUNTA
Nutshells? What good is throwing nutshells? That doesn't hurt.

TUFUTTI
Why would we want to hurt anyone? How human is that?

(TUFUTTI and JIB-JIB laugh outrageously.)

MINISTER NAJAB
Don't you mean how *inhuman* is that?

MONKEY TUFUTTI
Most certainly not. Only humans set out to hurt others on purpose.

MONKEY JIB-JIB
We only want to see you go away.

MONKEY TUFUTTI
Yes. Go away.

(*TUFUTTI* and *JIB-JIB* toss more NUTSHELLS at the group.)

PRINCESS BURENDI
Please. Please. We only want your help.

MONKEY JIB-JIB
Only want *our* help? How ridiculous is that? What human ever wants help from a monkey? We're wild animals, you know. The only thing you humans know to do with wild animals is move them, cage them, or kill them.

MONKEY TUFUTTI
One moment, please.

(*TUFUTTI* and *JIB-JIB* exit stage left.)

SHIP MAN BOKI
What was that all about?

MINISTER NAJAB
I'm sure I don't know. We've been warned to be prepared for anything on this island.

(*Squirts of WATER come in from stage left.*)

PRINCESS BURENDI (*Feeling her arms.*)
What is—am I bleeding?

MINISTER NAJAB
No, it looks like just water. That's harmless enough.

PRINCESS BURENDI (*Laughing a little.*)
They certainly have a different idea of warfare.

(*MONKEYS LUB-LUB* and *WICKI-WEE* enter from stage left with LEMONS and LIMES in their hands.)

MONKEY LUB-LUB (*Squirt.*)
Be gone you pesky humans.

MONKEY WICKI-WEE (*Squirt.*)
Be gone. Vanish.

SHIPMASTER PUNTA
Don't tell us—you're the second offensive.

MONKEY LUB-LUB (*Squirt.*)
Well, we're certainly not the first offensive. Do we look like we're adept at throwing nutshells?

(*The MONKEYS laugh outrageously.*)

MONKEY WICKI-WEE (*Squirt.*)
People are so silly.

SHIP MAN BOKI
Is there going to be a third offensive? Will you be throwing leaves at us this time?

MONKEY LUB-LUB (*Squirt.*)
Why aren't you going away? You need to go away right now or else.

SHIPMASTER PUNTA
Or else what?

MONKEY LUB-LUB (*Squirt.*)
Or else you won't go away. Are you people dense?

PRINCESS BURENDI
Is there someone of authority we could talk with?

(*Enter MONKEYS TUFUTTI* and *JIB-JIB* from stage left.*)

MONKEY WICKI-WEE
Someone of authority? We're monkeys!

(*The MONKEYS laugh outrageously.*)

PRINCESS BURENDI
Come along, gentlemen. Maybe we can find what we're looking for by ourselves.

(*The MONKEYS abruptly stop laughing.*)

MONKEY JIB-JIB (*Tossing NUTSHELLS.*)
Can't do that.

MONKEY TUFUTTI (*Tossing NUTSHELLS.*)
You haven't permission.

MINISTER NABJAB
Who gives permission?

MONKEY LUB-LUB
The king and queen of Monkey Island, naturally.

SHIPMASTER PUNTA
If you have a king and queen, wouldn't they be the authority we need to speak with?

MONKEY TUFUTTI
You're trying to make sense. Now we *know* you're human.

(*The MONKEYS laugh outrageously.*)

PRINCESS BURENDI (*Aside to NAJAB.*)
Talk about annoying.

(*Enter from stage left KING COCO and QUEEN EUCALYPTUS.*)

KING COCO
What's with all the merriment?

MONKEY JIB-JIB
More humans have invaded our island, Your Majesty.

PRINCESS BURENDI
I'd hardly call it *invading*.

KING COCO
Are you here?

PRINCESS BURENDI
Of course we're here.

KING COCO
Then you're invading. Jib-Jib was right.

MINISTER NAJAB
Are you the king of this island?

KING COCO
I'm certainly not the queen.

(*The MONKEYS laugh outrageously.*)

PRINCESS BURENDI
Then you must be the queen.

QUEEN EUCALYPTUS
Then I must be. This one isn't so stupid.

KING COCO
Must be one of those authority figures humans are so fond of.

PRINCESS BURENDI
Yes, I'm just like you.

KING COCO
Oh, you're nothing like me. How absurd.

(*The MONKEYS laugh outrageously.*)

PRINCESS BURENDI (*A little irritated.*)
Will you please stop laughing!

QUEEN EUCALYPTUS
How dare you raise you voice to a queen. Who are you anyway?

PRINCESS BURENDI
I'm Princess Burendi of Southern India. Our people are suffering and we've come to Monkey Island to take food back to them.

QUEEN EUCALYPTUS
What food?

SHIPMASTER PUNTA
Your food.

MINISTER NAJAB
Any food you have to spare.

KING COCO
What makes you think we have spare food? We eat our food, there's none to spare.

MINISTER NAJAB
We're told there is fruit and plant life plentiful on this island.

QUEEN EUCALYPTUS
Who told you that?

MONKEY LUB-LUB
I didn't.

MONKEY WICKI-WEE
Me neither.

PRINCESS BURENDI
Please, would you consider helping us?

QUEEN EUCALYPTUS
Our help? How ridiculous. What human ever wants help from a monkey?

MONKEY JIB-JIB
That's what I said.

PRINCESS BURENDI
Please, Your Majesty... May I have your name?

QUEEN EUCALYPTUS
You can't have my name, it belongs to me.

PRINCESS BURENDI
May I speak it, then?

KING COCO
I'm King Coco. This is Queen Eucalyptus—Tufutti, Lub-Lub, Jib-Jib, and Wicki-wee. Did you get all that? I bet not which is why names are of little importance.

SHIPMASTER PUNTA
If names are of little importance, why do you have them?

KING COCO
Who are you?

SHIPMASTER PUNTA
Punta, Shipmaster.

KING COCO
I didn't ask what you were, just who you were. Humans are always so concerned with what they do.

WICKI-WEE *(Squirt.)*
Or don't.

MONKEY LUB-LUB *(Squirt.)*
I'm Lub-Lub, the squirter. Isn't that important? There's nothing more important than being a squirter?

MINISTER NAJAB
Isn't a king more important than a squirter?

MONKEY WICKI-WEE *(Squirt.)*
A king? What does a king do?

PRINCESS BURENDI
King Coco, we'd like to requisition some food with your permission.

MONKEY JIB-JIB *(Tossing NUTSHELLS.)*
You people have a one-track mind.

SHIPMASTER PUNTA
We really don't need your permission. We can just take what we need.

QUEEN EUCALYPTUS
Now that is as human as you can get.

SHIPMASTER PUNTA
I've had enough of this. Let's go get what we need.

> *(PUNTA and BOKI exit stage left.)*

MONKEY JIB-JIB
Where are they going?

MINISTER NAJAB
To get food.

MONKEY LUB-LUB *(Squirt.)*
Without asking? How rude.

PRINCESS BURENDI
We've been asking. We've been asking since we got here. Are all of you nuts?

> *(The **MONKEYS** laugh outrageously until **PUNTA** and **BOKI** enter from stage left carrying FRUIT.)*

SHIPMASTER PUNTA
There's plenty of food on this island. We no more than stepped into the jungle and found this just lying on the ground. We'll load the ship and come back for more.

KING COCO
You stupid people. You just can't take what you want.

QUEEN EUCALYPTUS
If you want to feed your people you need to be smarter than that.

PRINCESS BURENDI
Seeds. We need seeds to grow our food.

QUEEN EUCALYPTUS
Yes, very wise—this is why you're the princess.

PRINCESS BURENDI
May we have some of your seeds?

KING COCO
Well, why didn't you ask for that in the first place? Give a monkey a fish and he eats for a day. Show a monkey how to fish and he eats forever. That's a wise saying from a very smart monkey.

MINISTER NAJAB
A *smart* monkey?

KING COCO
Who has food and who doesn't? Who are the silly ones here?

PRINCESS BURENDI
I'm beginning to wonder. May we please have some of you seeds?

QUEEN EUCALYPTUS
Well, of course you may. We're not heartless humans, you know. Come with us.

> *(**EUCALYPTUS** and **COCO** exit stage left with **BURENDI** and **NAJAB**.)*

MONKEY LUB-LUB
What idiots. Imagine thinking a king more important than a squirter.

MONKEY TUFUTTI
Or a shell tosser.

> *(The **MONKEYS** start to squirt WATER and toss NUTSHELLS at **PUNTA** and **BOKI** to their protest as all exit stage left.)*

END OF MONKEY ISLAND

The Surprising Adventures of Baron Munchausen
The First Trip to the Moon

Adapted from THE SURPRISING ADVENTURES OF BARON MUNCHAUSEN
Original Adaptation by Joan Garner

—BACKGROUND INFORMATION
*(genre classification and other
data deemed useful)*

The adventures of the Baron traditionally fall into the tall tale genre, but it's placed here under the *Otherworlds and Fantasylands* **SECTION** because of his visits to the moon and related descriptions of its fantastic world.

The residents on the Munchausen's moon are giants, able to remove their heads, and can eat by opening their sides and dumping food directly into their stomachs. The human like creatures come from trees of various sizes and foliage.

Features of the moon's environment—ecological and social—also place it into **Fantasy Genre** and specifically into the *Otherworlds and Fantasylands* **SECTION**. "...great land in the sky, like a shining island, round and bright..." "...we saw huge figures riding upon vultures of a prodigious size, each of them having three heads." And climate: "The stones of their grapes are exactly like hail; and ... when a storm or high wind in the moon shakes their vines, and breaks the grapes from the stalks, the stones fall down and form our hail showers."

The Book, THE SURPRISING ADVENTURES OF BARON MUNCHAUSEN begins with the man himself, German noble Karl Friedrich Hieronymus (Baron von Munchausen, 1720 –1797), who told several preposterous stories about his adventures while serving in the military.

Subsequently, the collected tales published in 1785 (English version) by Rudolf Erich Raspe. This collection was called BARON MUNCHAUSEN'S NARRATIVE OF HIS MARVELLOUS TRAVELS AND CAMPAIGNS IN RUSSIA, or THE SURPRISING ADVENTURES OF BARON MUNCHAUSEN.

(Obviously, brevity in titles was not Raspe's forte.) It might be important to note that several of the humorous episodes and exploits come from other stories. Apparently, though a boastful man, the Baron's stories did not include the texture and depth Raspe believed necessary to sell the book.

Since Raspe's translation, the stories have experienced many expansions and transformations with over 100 editions published.

RUDOLPH ERICH RASPE (1737–1794). Germany. Something of a rogue like the Baron, Raspe started out as a German professor and librarian who fled to England after selling precious gems and medals placed in his care. He fled again to Ireland after swindling his English employer. He began collecting tall tales and serialized several stories after which he then expanded them into BARON MUNCHAUSEN'S NARRATIVE OF HIS MARVELOUS TRAVELS AND CAMPAIGNS IN RUSSIA (1785). Other Baron adventures published late also brandish exceedingly long titles. A more recent edition uses the title noted here.

The Surprising Adventures of Baron Munchausen
STAGING SUGGESTIONS AND HELPFUL HINTS

— SYNOPSIS OF STORY

(18th Century Turkey and the Moon) An enslaved Baron Munchausen, his Turkish Guard, and a slave girl climb up to the moon on a bean stalk to fetch the Baron's hatchet (which accidentally ricocheted off a bear and flew up to the moon). There they meet Mooncat, a creature of the moon who tells of her world and tries to help the trio figure out how to get back to Earth.

— CHARACTER DESCRIPTIONS

BARON MUNCHAUSEN: (Male) Boastful and full of himself.

GISELLE: (Female) A regular person annoyed at being a slave.

THE TURK: (Male) Easily swayed. One ready for adventure.

MOONCAT: (Female) A docile creature of the moon. Smart and cooperative.

— PRESENTATION SUGGESTIONS
(18th Century Turkish and European Clothing and Items.)

COSTUMES
BARON MUNCHAUSEN—Blouse with large puffy sleeves rolled up. Long, Eighteenth Century waistcoat if possible. Long shorts cinched tight to the leg below the knees to represent breeches. Tights. Regular shoes with large buckle attached to top. Fancy tricorne hat and white wig would be great!

GISELLE—Loose blouse with large puffy sleeves rolled up. Long, Eighteenth Century waistcoat if possible. Long skirt. Bare feet.

THE TURK—No shirt. Open vest rounded at the bottom. Bloomer pants (sweatpants?). Bare feet.

MOONCAT—Metallic colored cloth wrapped over the body. Brown, tan, or black form-fitting blouse and tights. Socks for shoes pulled over bottom of pants. Makeup to create cat face preferred. Cat ears head band.

PROPS
HATCHET—for **BARON**.

TALL SPEAR—for **THE TURK**.

BEAN—Any form of dry bean.

SOUND EFFECTS
Students offstage can buzz like bees and roar like bears.

STAGE
WALLS—Sight barriers at stage left and right.

STAGING
When the HATCHET takes off up into the sky and when the bean stalk grows so rapidly, the BARON, THE TURK, and GISELLE need to look out and then up in unison. Rehearse this direction to accomplish the cue.

STAGING

STAGE RIGHT   **STAGE LEFT**

RIGHT WALL

LEFT WALL

The Surprising Adventures of Baron Munchausen
SCRIPT

SETTING
Turkey and the Moon. 18th Century. The PASTURE-LAND of the Sultan's palace. All is empty and quiet.

(BARON MUNCHAUSEN enters from stage right followed by GISELLE. THE TURK comes in behind them. THE TURK carries a tall SPEAR. The BARON has a smaller HATCHET attached to his belt)

* SOUND EFFECTS
The loud buzzing of bees.

BARON MUNCHAUSEN
I say, fellow, this business is becoming irksome. It's demeaning for one of my stature to be herding bees. I *am* a baron, you know.

THE TURK
Here, you are the sultan's prisoner and slave. That makes you nothing.

BARON MUNCHAUSEN
I am Baron Munchausen and Baron Munchausen I will always be no matter what the situation I find myself in.

THE TURK
You may be a baron and I may be a guard, but this big spear I hold in my hand gives me the power to make you do as I say.

BARON MUNCHAUSEN
Mm, brute force. That will work.

GISELLE
It works for me.

BARON MUNCHAUSEN
Sweet Giselle, how terrible for you to be the Sultan's slave. Why to treat a gentle woman like this—it simply isn't done.

GISELLE
It isn't done where you come from. It's done here.

THE TURK
Enough babbling. See to your work

BARON MUNCHAUSEN
Herding bees to the pasture of the sultan's palace every morning and then back to their hives at night is far from work. As a slave to the sultan you would think he'd find something more suited to my talents for me to do.

GISELLE
And what would that be?

BARON MUNCHAUSEN
Leading a great army in battle.

THE TURK
Do you think the sultan a stupid man? If he put you in charge of his army, you could turn it against him and run him through.

BARON MUNCHAUSEN
Sir, I am a man of honor. If the sultan were to place me in charge of his army, I would fight the sultan's enemies, not him.

THE TURK
Since this will never happen, there is little value talking about it. Now see to your work!

GISELLE *(Pointing offstage left and counting.)*
One thousand, three hundred and forty-three. One thousand, three hundred and forty-four... Oh, dear. One of the bees is missing.

THE TURK
See? All this talk has made you neglect your duties and now we have a missing bee.

BARON MUNCHAUSEN
My good man, I am never negligent. At times I may become distracted, but I'm never negligent.

* SOUND EFFECTS
Bears roaring loudly offstage, left.

GISELLE
Oh, no. Look! Two bears are fighting over there.

THE TURK *(Looking.)*
They're fighting over something.

GISELLE
The missing bee! They must be fighting over the bee to get its honey.

BARON MUNCHAUSEN *(Pulling his HATCHET.)*
No, they don't—not one of my bees.

(The BARON aims and tosses his HATCHET offstage left.)

* SOUND EFFECTS
Thump! Then a loud bear like growl.

*(The **BARON**, **THE TURK**, and **GISELLE** all start to look up and up and up. Pause.)*

THE TURK
That's the best ricochet I've ever seen.

GISELLE
Your hatchet just bounced off that bear's head and flew up in the sky.

THE TURK
And it's still going up. I didn't think you were that strong.

BARON MUNCHAUSEN
Never underestimate a baron.

GISELLE
It looks like it's headed straight for the moon.

BARON MUNCHAUSEN
Appears to be.

THE TURK
There. It landed on the moon.

BARON MUNCHAUSEN
Drat. I hate to lose that hatchet. The king of Gimagru gave it to me.

GISELLE
But there's no way we can get it back.

BARON MUNCHAUSEN *(Thinking.)*
Maybe not... Maybe so. Mr. Turkish Man, this country of Turkey—your Turkey beans grow very quickly, do they not?

THE TURK
Turkey beans grow faster than any other in the world.

BARON MUNCHAUSEN
Excellent. If we only had one, we could plant it and then climb the stalk up to the moon to retrieve my hatchet.

GISELLE *(Pulling a BEAN out of a pocket.)*
I have a bean. I was saving it to eat on a special occasion.

BARON MUNCHAUSEN
Would you mind terrible parting with it?

GISELLE *(Handing the BEAN to the **BARON**.)*
Not at all.

BARON MUNCHAUSEN
Thank you, sweet Giselle. We'll plant it over here in this rich soil.

*(The **BARON** exits stage right with the BEAN.)*

THE TURK
Stay where I can see you. You're not escaping from me.

*(The **BARON** steps back to **THE TURK** and **GISELLE**. Soon they're all looking up again at stage right like they did earlier on stage left.)*

GISELLE
Mercy, I've never seen anything grow so fast in my life.

BARON MUNCHAUSEN
If we start climbing it now, the stalk should be to the moon by the time we reach its end.

THE TURK
You can't climb to the moon. That would be escaping.

BARON MUNCHAUSEN
It isn't escaping if you come with us.

*(The **BARON** and **GISELLE** exit stage right.)*

THE TURK
Wait a minute!

*(**THE TURK** exits stage right. Momentarily, **MOONCAT** enters from stage left. She holds the HATCHET and rubs her head.)*

MOONCAT *(Annoyed.)*
Owwww! Who threw this hatchet?

*(The **BARON**, **THE TURK**, and **GISELLE** enter from stage right.)*

BARON MUNCHAUSEN *(Dusting off his hands.)*
I told you. That didn't take any time at all.

GISELLE
I'm exhausted.

*(The **BARON** looks up to see **MOONCAT**.)*

BARON MUNCHAUSEN
Hello. Are you a moonarian? Do you understand English or Turkish or German or French? I'm fluent in several languages, although I must confess Moonish is not one of them.

GISELLE
Baron, look. She has your hatchet.

MOONCAT *(To the **BARON**.)*
This is your hatchet?

BARON MUNCHAUSEN
She speaks English. How grand. May I have my hatchet back, please?

   *(**MOONCAT** slaps the **BARON** on the arm.)*

BARON MUNCHAUSEN *(Continued.)*
Ouch. What did you do that for?

MOONCAT
This hatchet hit me on the head. I was peacefully sleeping on some chopped straw over there when—clunk!

BARON MUNCHAUSEN
I apologize. Please know I wasn't aiming for you. The hatchet got away from me.

THE TURK
If you wouldn't mind giving the baron his hatchet back. We have to get back down to Earth before the sultan notices we're gone.

GISELLE
I think we should stay here and learn more about the moon.

BARON MUNCHAUSEN
An excellent idea, Giselle. We shouldn't squander an opportunity to learn a new culture. And if we can impress the sultan enough with our stories, maybe he'll set us free.

GISELLE
I like that plan.

BARON MUNCHAUSEN
So, moon person.

MOONCAT
Mooncat. I'm a mooncat.

GISELLE
Miss Mooncat, could you tell us some things about the moon we could take back with us?

MOONCAT
Well, we have creatures similar in look to you, but they're much larger.

BARON MUNCHAUSEN
You don't say.

MOONCAT
And they ride giant vultures.

GISELLE
Well, they would have to be giant vultures for the human giants to ride, wouldn't they?

MOONCAT
And the vultures have three heads.

BARON MUNCHAUSEN
Say, I'd like to see one of those.

MOONCAT
Our king is engaged in a war with the sun. He's using radishes as darts. Those wounded by the radishes die instantly.

THE TURK
Die by radishes?

MOONCAT
When our people grow old, they don't die but turn into air and dissolve like smoke. They have but one finger on each hand, and place their heads under their right arm.

GISELLE
How odd.

MOONCAT
Not at all. When they travel or about to face any violence, they can leave their heads at home. But if they wish to see something, they leave the body home and send the head.

GISELLE
Oh, yuck.

MOONCAT
They can take their eyes out whenever they want and can change them in and out—sometimes with green eyes—sometimes with yellow.

THE TURK
I've never heard of such a thing.

MOONCAT
Of course you haven't. This is the moon.

GISELLE
I don't know, Baron Munchausen. These stories may be too fantastic for the sultan to believe.

BARON MUNCHAUSEN
Nonsense. I've told many a fantastic tale to kings and queens around the world. These stories will work on the sultan, I guarantee it.

THE TURK
This is all well and good, but how do we get back to Earth?

BARON MUNCHAUSEN
We climb back down the bean stalk.

THE TURK
We could, but while you were talking with this cat, the sun has burned the bean stalk down.

GISELLE *(Looking out stage right.)*
It can't be! We can't stay up here for the rest of our lives. We don't belong here.

BARON MUNCHAUSEN
We'll get back to Earth, sweet Giselle. We can take the straw the Mooncat was sleeping on and make a rope of it.

MOONCAT
There isn't enough straw to make a rope long enough to reach the Earth.

BARON MUNCHAUSEN
When we get to the end of the rope, we'll cut off the section we've already climbed down and tie it to the bottom. And when we get to the end of the tied rope, we cut off the section we've just climbed and tie it to the bottom. We'll do this until we get back to Earth.

MOONCAT
Are you serious?

BARON MUNCHAUSEN
Quite serious. It's a good thing I found my hatchet to cut the rope with.

MOONCAT
You found your hatchet.

THE TURK
Then we should go.

BARON MUNCHAUSEN
Thank you, Mooncat. We greatly appreciate you stories. Good-bye.

GISELLE
Good-bye, Mooncat. It was nice to meet you.

    *(The **BARON**, **GISELLE**, and **THE TURK** exit stage right. **MOONCAT** watches after them.)*

MOONCAT
And they think my world is fantastic and strange. They're going to chop off the top part of the rope and tie it to the bottom to continue climbing down. How incredibly stupid. But then, I guess any world other than your own would seem strange.

    *(**MOONCAT** rubs her head again.)*

MOONCAT *(Continued.)*
Owwww!

    *(**MOONCAT** exits stage left.)*

END OF THE SURPRISING ADVENTURES OF BARON MUNCHAUSEN

Gulliver's Travels
I Shall Not Trouble the Reader with a Particular Account

Adapted from GULLIVER'S TRAVELS by Jonathan Swift
Original Adaptation by Joan Garner

—BACKGROUND INFORMATION
(genre classification and other data deemed useful)

Called brilliant, a masterpiece, and one of the most indisputable classics of the English language, GULLIVER'S TRAVELS had to be in this compilation. With many *Fantastic Elements* entwined in his travels (traveler's tales), the story belongs in **Fantasy Genre**.

Accolades aside and still enthralling with its wonderfully fanciful characters and locales, GULLIVER'S TRAVELS as literature flounders in its telling.

The subtitle of this sketch reveals a problem this author has with the book as story. *I Shall Not Trouble the Reader with a Particular Account* plays as contradiction because the story continually bogs down with too much detail. If this is an unrealized "tongue in cheek" offering by Swift, I stand corrected and apologize. But once introduction of Lilliputians takes place and their diminutive size revealed, paragraph upon paragraph describing this oddity afterwards isn't necessary for story progression. Perhaps being a playwright at heart, I find lengthy and meticulous description of peripheral sundries detracting and exhausting. And perhaps because it's nearly always referred to as children's fantasy (which it isn't), its appeal among juvenile readers also perplexes.

But all in all, GULLIVER'S TRAVELS with all its satire, parody, and social and political comment, shows an imagination (Swift's) unparalleled with any other writer with the possible exception of J.R.R. Tolkien.

JONATHAN SWIFT (1667–1745). England. Writer, satirist, essayist, and pamphleteer, Swift's early career was as secretary for Sir William Temple. Though of little use in his later author years, this job with Temple brought him to meet Charles Perrault, arguably one of if not the giant of fairy tale stories. Obviously influenced to write by this acquaintance, Swift went on writing many books, poems, prayers, and essays. However, his political activism gradually turned him misanthropic, and his fear of eventually becoming mentally diminished came to pass with aphasia (loss or impairment of the ability to produce or comprehend language because of brain damage). Unlike a good many authors, Swift died a rich man. He left most of his wealth to start a hospital for the mentally ill.

— SYNOPSIS OF STORY

(18th Century England) The head of the asylum asks Mary Gulliver to attend a session with her husband Lemuel. Since committed, Lemuel Gulliver insists the stories he relates of his travels are true though hard to believe. Claims of visiting tiny people and giants, floating islands and horses possessed of high intelligence have tested the loyalty of his wife and friends. Wanting out of the asylum, Lemuel nears recanting his stories if they would just release him. But his sincerity moves Mary who decides to take her husband home.

Gulliver's Travels
STAGING SUGGESTIONS AND HELPFUL HINTS

—GLOSSARY
(terms possibly unfamiliar to the reader)

TESTIMONIES—Declarations of events. A public declaration.

IRRELEVANT—Not about the matter at hand. Of no significance to the subject.

— CHARACTER DESCRIPTIONS

DR. GRAY: (Male) Logical and practical yet wise enough to be open to the unproven.

BRENDA WELCH: (Female) A bit too ambitious and pushy in wanting to make a good impression.

POINDEXTER: (Male) A layperson of little education, but hard worker and friendly.

MARY GULLIVER: (Female) Looking and feeling tired from the long ordeal with her husband. Still, she only wants what's best for him.

STANFORD TILTON: (Male) A good friend standing by **MARY** and **LEMUEL** though not believing in **GULLIVER'S** claims.

HORTENSE TILTON: (Female) Caring and loyal to friend and family.

LEMUEL GULLIVER: (Male) Always moving nervously since his travels and time spent in the asylum, but adamant about what he experienced—no matter how unbelievable.

— PRESENTATION SUGGESTIONS
(18th Century English Clothing and Items)

COSTUMES
DR. GRAY—Loose frilly shirt. Neutral colored frock coat. Long, 18th Century waistcoat if possible. Long shorts cinched tight to the leg below the knees to represent breeches. Tights. Regular shoes. Small, curled wig.

BRENDA WELCH—Simple boned chemise with plain stomacher. Long skirt with small bustle. Apron over all of outfit. Hose. 18th Century shoes. Hair pulled back into a bun.

POINDEXTER—White shirt. Simple ascot. Long frock coat buttoned up. Breeches. Tights. Shoes. Hair short or semi-long and uncombed.

MARY GULLIVER—Simple day dress with small bustle and laced stomacher. Hose and shoes. Hair tucked under butterfly cap.

STANFORD TILTON—Clothing of a richer person with coat, waistcoat, breeches, and boots.

HORTENSE TILTON—Clothing of a richer person with laced gown and underskirt, and lace stomacher. Hose and shoes. Hair nicely combed under a lace cap.

LEMUEL GULLIVER—Outfit closer to **POINDEXTER'S** than **STANFORD'S**.

PROPS
TABLE AND SMALL TABLE—Of the period.

LARGE CHAIRS—Of the period.

STAGE
WALL—Defining the back of the room desired but not necessary.

STAGING
If able, move LEMUEL around from MARY to the TILTON'S and back, wanting to touch them to stress his request, but staying at a distance. No doubt showing any signs of aggression could get him into trouble in the asylum, so he's learned to restrain his actions.

STAGING

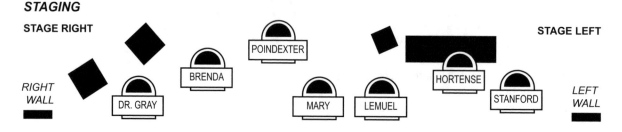

STAGE RIGHT | STAGE LEFT

RIGHT WALL — DR. GRAY — BRENDA — POINDEXTER — MARY — LEMUEL — HORTENSE — STANFORD — LEFT WALL

(2006 © Joan Garner) **WINGS OF FANCY**: Using Readers Theatre to Study Fantasy Genre

Gulliver's Travels
SCRIPT

SETTING
England. 18th Century. A meeting room at the DUTTON HILL ASYLUM. A TABLE with a small CHAIR stands stage left. Two larger CHAIRS stand stage right.

> *(DR. GRAY and BRENDA WELCH stand center stage.)*

BRENDA WELCH
This is likely to be an awkward encounter, Dr. Gray.

DR. GRAY
You'll face many an awkward encounter in an institution for the insane, Miss Welch.

BRENDA WELCH
Yes. May I say again how grateful I am you have allowed me to assist in this case? I know you've faced great opposition accepting a woman to study here.

DR. GRAY
It's difficult finding qualified students willing to work at Dutton Hill Asylum—male or female. I'm fortunate to have you by my side.

*SOUND EFFECTS
A door knocking at stage left.

> *(POINDEXTER enters from stage left.)*

POINDEXTER
Excuse me, Gov'nor. You wanted to know when Mrs. Gulliver arrived.

DR. GRAY
Yes, Poindexter. Please see her in.

POINDEXTER
Good enough, Gov'nor.

> *(POINDEXTER motions offstage left. MARY GULLIVER enters from stage left.)*

MARY GULLIVER
Dr. Gray, I came as soon as I got your message. Is there something wrong?

DR. GRAY
I'm sorry, Mrs. Gulliver. I didn't mean to alarm you. You're husband is fine—well, as fine as expected in a place like this. May I introduce my assistant, Brenda Welch.

BRENDA WELCH
Mrs. Gulliver, Dr. Welch and I are trying to compile a complete record of you husband's claimed travels that we may access his progress here.

MARY GULLIVER
But I don't understand. You already have a full account of Lemuel's explorations from his journals and public records.

*SOUND EFFECTS
Another knock of the door at stage left.

> *(POINDEXTER enters from stage left with STANFORD and HORTENSE TILTON.)*

POINDEXTER
Mr. and Mrs. Tilton, Gov'nor.

STANFORD TILTON
Mary, had we known you were coming, we would have offered you our carriage.

HORTENSE TILTON
How have you been, Mary? Is everything all right?

MARY GULLIVER
I'm not sure, Hortense. But it's comforting you and Stanford are here.

DR. GRAY
Please, everyone, allow me to explain. We have examined Lemuel Gulliver and haven't come to any firm conclusions other than his continual insistence that all the fantastic things he claims happened to him actually did.

MARY GULLIVER
Do you now think Lemuel is telling the truth?

STANFORD TILTON
The little people, the giants, and those yahoos?

HORTENSE TILTON
An island floating in the sky—you believe that?

BRENDA WELCH
No, Mrs. Tilton. We thought the testimonies of Mr. Gulliver's wife and close friends would help us—

MARY GULLIVER
Again, we've been all through this.

DR. GRAY
Yes, Mrs. Gulliver. I apologize for putting you through this trial again. But there is so much to this case and Lemuel has been so charmingly convincing in retelling his adventures, I often find myself pulled into his fantasies.

BRENDA WELCH
Dr. Gray and I have devised an exercise to prove or disprove Mr. Gulliver's claims. We have formulated a set of questions to ask. We would like the three of you to tell us if Mr. Gulliver's answers now differ from what he's told you in the past.

MARY GULLIVER
You're asking us to participate in an exposition designed to trip up my husband? That would be like betraying him. I can't do that. I'm beginning to think it a mistake committing Lemuel here.

(POINDEXTER enters from stage left with LEMUEL GULLIVER. POINDEXTER will then stand and listen off to the side.)

POINDEXTER
Here's the patient, Gov'nor.

LEMUEL GULLIVER *(Rushing to MARY.)*
Mary, you're here. And Stanford and Hortense. How good it is to see you. This is wonderful. Have you come to take me home? Do you believe me now?

MARY GULLIVER
Lemuel, you know that I've always wanted to believe you.

LEMUEL GULLIVER *(Disappointed.)*
So you're not here to liberate me. But you *are* here. Mary, I need ink and paper. They won't give me ink and paper and I'm afraid I'll forget what happened unless I write it down. I shall not trouble the reader with a particular account, but I need to write down the basics.

MARY GULLIVER
Lemuel, you *did* write everything down.

LEMUEL GULLIVER
Yes, dear. But I haven't any of that with me in here. What if they burn my accountings?

MARY GULLIVER
Who are *they*, Lemuel? You're reports have published. You can't erase what's been in the public eye.

LEMUEL GULLIVER
Yes, of course. It's this place. It does things to the mind. Please take me home, Mary. Stanford, Hortense, you know I'm not insane.

DR. GRAY
Lemuel, we'd like to ask you some questions.

LEMUEL GULLIVER
More questions? I've answered so many. Do I need to stop talking about the Lilliputians or Brobdingnag. I'll do it if you let me out of here.

BRENDA WELCH
The Lilliputians, Mr. Gulliver. How tall were they?

LEMUEL GULLIVER
Six inches.

BRENDA WELCH
And they captured you—a veritable giant.

LEMUEL GULLIVER
I was unconscious when I washed up on the beach after the shipwreck. They bound me up during that time.

BRENDA WELCH
And during that short time they made this huge wagon to transport you to their king?

LEMUEL GULLIVER
Emperor, not king. Excuse me, but who are you?

DR. GRAY
But you said the worst part of your travels was with the Yahoos.

LEMUEL GULLIVER
Yes—just before I came home. Despicable creatures, though they were more like humans than any of the others. What does that say about us, eh? The horses were very intelligent, and tolerant. Isn't intelligence simply tolerance of the rest of the lot?

DR. GRAY
Wouldn't you say it odd how in your travels you came upon these unique creatures, but not ordinary people like us?

LEMUEL GULLIVER
But I did. The—

HORTENSE TILTON
—The evil man with the flying island in the sky.

LEMUEL GULLIVER
Yes, Hortense—a remarkable piece of technology.

BRENDA WELCH
And how did you say this island flew?

LEMUEL GULLIVER
It's all on record. Mary, I'm so tired of all this.

MARY GULLIVER
I know, Lemuel.

LEMUEL GULLIVER
And you're tired of it as well. I know I've put my family through such tortures.

MARY GULLIVER
I only wanted what was best for you, Lemuel. But I don't know what that is anymore.

LEMUEL GULLIVER
Dr. Gray, what if I denied it all?

DR. GRAY
Denied what, Mr. Gulliver?

LEMUEL GULLIVER
All of it... I have always had a taste for adventure. Since my practice here was failing and there was a ship bound for... Where was it going? I don't remember. It's irrelevant to the story anyway. I became the ship's surgeon. During a fierce storm, the ship wrecked and I found myself on the shores of Lilliput where the little people lived.

HORTENSE TILTON
The ones six inches high.

LEMUEL GULLIVER
Yes, Hortense... At first the Lilliputians resented me for eating all their food, but then I proved to be a valuable asset for them in their war against the kingdom of Blefuscu. My size alone made me a mighty war machine.

STANFORD TILTON
And that was your first voyage.

LEMUEL GULLIVER
I told you about it when I arrived home... On my second voyage I came to Brobdingnag, a land of giants. Here I was an amusement to the people there—my slightness in size. I was fortunate their queen took a fancy to me, or I daresay someone would have had me for dinner. *Had* me. Yes.

HORTENSE TILTON
And your third voyage found you on a floating island.

LEMUEL GULLIVER
You remember, Hortense. Yes, the land of Laputa.

BRENDA WELCH
I don't believe it's wise to prompt the patient, Mrs. Tilton.

LEMUEL GULLIVER
But she isn't prompting, Miss—whoever you are. My friend in merely remembering what I have previously reported... The island boasted scholars and academics that researched inconsequential matters and seemed stupidly out of touch with concerns surrounding every day life.

STANFORD TILTON
And your final voyage landed you on the island with horses.

LEMUEL GULLIVER
The Houyhnhnms—magnificent creatures of brilliant and rational minds. They ruled the island with a population of Yahoos—those filthy, animal like humans. I enjoyed my stay with the Houyhnhnms learning their language and relaying my other voyages to them, but one day upon seeing my bared body, the horses took offense thinking I looked too much like a Yahoo. They banished me. Imagine that—animals banishing humans. Well, on reflection, I could hardly blame them. Look what humans have done to the animal kingdom since the beginning of time.

BRENDA WELCH
There you are. Mr. Gulliver's travels are nothing more than a self-analysis of his worth and the world about him.

(A slight pause as all reflect.)

MARY GULLIVER
I believe him.

LEMUEL GULLIVER
Mary?

MARY GULLIVER
I *do* believe you, Lemuel. Every word. Why couldn't I believe you before? You're my husband and I trust you.

LEMUEL GULLIVER
I can spend the rest of my days happily—in here if I must—as long as you believe me.

STANFORD TILTON
Hortense and I believe you, too, Lemuel.

MARY GULLIVER
Dr. Gray, I want to take my husband home.

BRENDA WELCH
That would be against procedure. Once a patient is committed—

STANFORD TILTON
—Dash procedure.

DR. GRAY
Mrs. Gulliver, you're the one who asked us to look at your husband. If you want to remove him from this institution, we can't stop you.

MARY GULLIVER
Maybe one day people will accept my husband's travels for the fantastic journey it was. But today Lemuel is going home to a normal house and a normal dinner in front of a warm fire.

LEMUEL GULLIVER
Right now having dinner in my own home is the most amazing adventure I care to experience. Thank you, Mary. Stanford and Hortense, would you like to join us? Please say yes.

HORTENSE TILTON
We would love to join you, Lemuel.

> (***MARY*** *and* ***LEMUEL GULLIVER****, and* ***STANFORD*** *and* ***HORTENSE TILTON*** *exit stage left.*)

BRENDA WELCH
Dr. Gray, I can't believe you let that man walk out of this asylum. I can't believe you let any of them leave. Obviously they're all delusional.

DR. GRAY
Yes, obviously. Or perhaps we're the odd ones here, Miss Welch. We're the ones not willing to believe Gulliver's travels.

> (***DR. GRAY*** *and* ***BRENDA WELCH*** *exit stage left.* ***POINDEXTER*** *follows them out.*)

END OF GULLIVER'S TRAVELS

Looking at Other Fantastic Elements
PAGE 1 (A Review of Other Fantastic Elements Not Included in this Book)

Although fairly complete, this book does not address all *Fantastic Elements*. This Project reviews a few of the more popular or intriguing *Fantastic Elements* related to otherworlds and fantasylands.

Meant as a simple class read and discussion, this Project winds down our study of **Fantasy Genre**.

PREPARATION AND RESOURCES NEEDED: Read the poem and an interpretation. Copy the 2 pages of this Project for each student.

Student Assignment: Read the following to further your knowledge of Fantastic Elements in **Fantasy Genre**.

OTHER FANTASTIC ELEMENTS

LOST RACES

Lost races involve lost, forgotten, and hidden civilizations. These races live beneath the sea, underground, in unknown mountain valleys, or any other hidden place. The island hidden from the rest of the world by a cloud bank in the 1930's movie KING KONG (and now the more recent remake) gives us a perfect example of a hidden place and civilization.

Lost races stories grew in popularity during the 19th Century. Springing from traveler's tales and fantastic voyages, these stories entail groups of explorers or travelers searching for or stumbling upon an unknown world not previously discovered and mapped. Sometimes characters search for a fantastic land that's become a part of legend and lore with a slim thread of fact behind it like Atlantis. Lost races may want to stay hidden like James Hilton's Shangri-la in LOST HORIZON.

After mapping the world in its entirety at the end of the 19th Century, lost races and lands required greater creative thought. Interest in lost races heightened with the introduction of serial novels in the 1930s. Still, nowadays, lost races and lands need to be well-hidden.

Sub Fantastic Element:
Traveler's Tales
Closely linked to quests, traveler's tales concern travels of discovery. Not engaged as much with inner discovery like a quest, traveler's tales are journeys to a land or special place. A traveler's tale deals as much with the getting there as it does finding the land or item.

Sub Fantastic Element:
Fantastic Voyages
Closely related to traveler's tales, fantastic voyages began in ancient mythology. Jason and the Argonauts looking for the Golden Fleece and Sinbad the Sailor of Arabian fantasy have become two classic fantastic voyage tales. (Jason and Sinbad are also semi-accursed wanderers where it seems like they'll never reach their goal and destination.)

LOST LANDS

Ultimately, lost lands concern land and civilizations lost (wiped-out) by disasters of one form or another. Atlantis also falls into this category. The city of El Dorado (a city in the Americas built of gold) is an example of a lost land. Whether these places exist doesn't matter. The quest to find them in fiction or reality continues.

A curious note to the lost lands *Fantastic Element*—if the land never existed, how is it lost? Then again, in **Fantasy Genre** anything's possible.

IMAGINARY LANDS

Like other *Fantastic Elements*, imaginary lands (and universes) serve as the author's setting for their fantasy story. Less important than the story, imaginary lands fall into Science Fiction Subgenre more than the other land and world *Fantastic Elements*. Atlantis is such a land.

Looking at Other Fantastic Elements (A Review) PAGE 2

Broken in categories, imaginary lands chart like this:

Lands of the deep past
A story taking place in a land before ancient history. Usually taking place on Earth, this land may be prehistoric or have a highly advanced civilization yet still supposedly existing before recorded history. Atlantis is such a land.

Lands of the far future
The opposite of above, these lands exist in a time after our own. Clark Ashton Smith invented the far future land of Zothique for his stories.

Lands overlooked by history
Closely related to lost races, these lands for one reason or another are not recorded in history. They can be lands of the past that are no more, or lands that exist now, but no one knows about. These lands are often stumbled upon by explorers like H. Rider Haggard's Allan Quartermain in KING SOLOMN'S MINES.

Lands of secondary worlds
Lands and civilizations similar to that on Earth yet never recognized as on Earth—possibly somewhere else. Of course, the ultimate land of this kind is J.R.R. Tolkien's Middle Earth in THE LORD OF THE RINGS Trilogy.

Lands of the mind
Lands identified as being only in a person's mind. Alice's wonderland poses like a dreamland in her mind. (Alice from Lewis Carroll's ALICE IN WONDERLAND).

Sub Fantastic Element:
Polder
Here's a fascinating "land" that has great potential for future stories by adding a special fantasy twist to its definition.

Polder (actual definition): A low-lying track of land drained and reclaimed of water. Building dykes around it keep the land dry.

Polder (fantasy definition): A land where its residents live safely from the calamity that occurs all around them. Imagine living in a town that has an invisible bubble over it. This bubble protects the town from what happens to the rest of the world (war, floods, fires, a comet crashing to Earth, and so on). There may be "portals" that people go through to get in and out of the town, but the bubble repels everything else. Or perhaps the *Polder* is not effected by time. The town lives as it has for hundreds of years while progress continues around it. This idea is close to the *Fantastic Element* used in the musical play and movie BRIGADOON (1954) where the village goes to sleep for the night and wakes up one hundred years later. Think of the story possibilities using a *Polder*?

BONUS FANTASTIC ELEMENT

This study of **Fantasy Genre** *and Fantastic Elements would be incomplete without mentioning immortality, a plot device taking its characters beyond the boundaries of human life. With some space left in this Project, a description of Immortality follows:*

Whether appropriate or not, immortality as a *Fantastic Element* often appears in **Fantasy Genre**. Immortality means never dying or not dying of natural causes. Gods and demons—often immortal themselves—may gift or curse humans with everlasting life. Although immortality generally falls under the Supernatural Subgenre, it also aligns with other *Fantastic Elements* such as accursed wanderers and timeslips. And immortality may travel a more spiritual path to an afterlife. Immortality may be granted, but without the stipulation of never aging as in H.Rider Haggard's SHE. Several immortality tales concern pacts with evil and warns "be careful what you wish for, you could get it." A character wishing for and receiving immortality may live to regret it—for a very long time!

The True Power of The Lord of the Rings
PAGE 1 (A Look at J.R.R. Tolkien and His Works)

This final Project looks at J.R.R. Tolkien and his most notable work, THE LORD OF THE RINGS.

Focusing primarily on the first book, THE FELLOWSHIP OF THE RINGS, Tolkien's RING TRILOGY is also addressed. Though reading FELLOWSHIP isn't necessary for this Project, it's recommended to better understand Tolkien's significant contribution to **Fantasy Genre.**

READING DESIRED BUT NOT REQUIRED

PREPARATION AND RESOURCES NEEDED: Copy the 4 pages of this Project for each student.

Student Assignment: Read the following with your classmates to acquire a better understanding of the importance of J.R.R. Tolkien and THE LORD OF THE RINGS Trilogy.

*So why devote an entire Project to one person and his works? Because he's noted as the 20th Century's single most important author of fantasy and his LORD OF THE RINGS TRILOGY hailed as the most influential fantasy novel **ever written**. "Most important" and "most influential" merits review. So let's start with J.R.R. Tolkien and then continue with a look at how THE LORD OF THE RINGS has influenced other writings and cinematic pieces.*

J.R.R. TOLKIEN

J.R.R. TOLKIEN

(John Ronald Reuel Tolkien) was born January 3, 1892 in South Africa to English parents. Tolkien is German meaning foolhardy. And though later with his fantasy writings some would say the name fit Tolkien well, others would argue he was far from foolhardy.

At age three, Tolkien's mother took him and his younger brother to England for an extended visit which turned out to be permanent when his father died of a brain hemorrhage in South Africa. The family settled in Birmingham with his mother's parents where she tutored her boys. Young Tolkien liked drawing landscapes of the rich English countryside, a talent later used in his writings.

Orphaned at age twelve when his mother died of diabetes (1904), he went to live with Father Francis Xavier Morgan.

Tolkien's realm into the unbelievable began in real life when at sixteen Tolkien met and fell in love with Edith Mary Bratt (three years his senior). Father Francis forbade him any association with her until he was at least twenty-one.

On his twenty-first birthday, Tolkien asked Edith to marry him, and although already engaged (she thinking Tolkien had forgotten about her), Edith broke her engagement and married Tolkien.

Graduating from the University of Oxford with a first-class degree in English language in 1915, he joined the British Army and served as a second lieutenant during World War I. He developed a "trench fever" in France, and returned to England. While recuperating from this fever, he began writing his first work called THE BOOK OF THE LOST TALES.

After World War I, he worked on the Oxford English Dictionary then became a full professor of Anglo-Saxon at Pembroke College.

During his time at Pembroke, Tolkien wrote THE HOBBIT and the first two volumes of THE LORD OF THE RINGS. Through the following years, these novels received praise and criticism in equal parts.

Edith Tolkien died at the age of 82 on November 29, 1971. Tolkien died 21 months later, September 2, 1973, at the age of 81.

The Lord of the Rings (Looking at a Special Fantasy) PAGE 2

POSSIBLE INFLUENCES FOR TOLKIEN IN WRITING THE LORD OF THE RINGS

It's curious to note (and why this Project started off with J.R.R. Tolkien's biography) what caused Tolkien's interest in writing fantasy—especially such elaborate fantasies as THE HOBBIT and THE LORD OF THE RINGS TRILOGY. It isn't as if there was one special moment in his life that awakened a need to write fantasy, but there may be a few happenings contributing to the path Tolkien followed.

In the years before writing the two important fantasy books, Tolkien's life helped form his writing. As a schoolboy, his fondness for language grew when, with his cousins, he made-up languages like "Animalic."

While studying at Oxford, Tolkien formed a friendship with C. S. Lewis (of THE CHRONICLES OF NARNIA—another important and wonderful fantasy piece). They discussed myths, languages, and storytelling. And when Tolkien became a father, he honed his storytelling skills for his children. Using these skills he began gathering stories around 1917 which later became THE SILMARILLION (edited and published posthumously by his son Christopher R. Tolkien in 1977).

> **THE SILMARILLION** is a complex work displaying Tolkien's interests in ancient, medieval and modern themes from the Finnish Kalevala, the Hebrew Bible, Norse sagas, Greek Mythology, Celtic Mythology, and World War I. This is where Middle-earth began.

As a youth, Tolkien loved to wander the rich English countryside giving him thought for the Shire. Visiting other impressive areas such as the Swiss Alpine mountains inspired how other geographical areas in his books would look. His joy for drawing and painting through his childhood would later carry over to his illustrating THE HOBBIT (dust jacket), and other points of interest like a landscape of Rivendell.

His studies of Philology during his higher education would fill Tolkien with a wonder for language and his desire to create his own. It's said the foundation for THE LORD OF THE RINGS wasn't the story as much as it proved a place where Tolkien could create another language.

> **Philology** The study of ancient texts and languages. More broadly, it's the study of grammar, history, and interpretation of authors within a specific language.
>
> J.R.R. Tolkien was a noted philologist of his day.

Many a theory exists on how Tolkien began his worlds of THE HOBBIT, and THE LORD OF THE RINGS. But, perhaps the most believable reason is the one Tolkien gives:

One summer's day in the 1930s, Tolkien sat in his study marking school papers. Years later he recalled: "One of the candidates had mercifully left one of the pages with no writing on it (which is the best thing that can possibly happen to an examiner), and I wrote on it: 'In a hole in the ground there lived a hobbit.' Names always generate a story in my mind. Eventually I thought I'd better find out what hobbits were like. But that's only the beginning."

> **Inklings** With C.S. Lewis, Charles Williams and other friends, Tolkien formed an informal literary group called The Inklings whose interest in story-telling promoted discussion and suggestions of one another's work.

Books and critiques abound with why Tolkien wrote THE LORD OF THE RINGS. It's safe to say some of these theories are correct while most are only guesses by assumption. Whatever the reason, the literary world can only be thankful that on that summer's day long ago, bored with the drudgery of his duties, J.R.R. Tolkien wrote on a blank page, "In a hole in the ground there lived a hobbit."

PAGE 3 (Looking at a Special Fantasy) **The Lord of the Rings**

THE LORD OF THE RINGS

SUMMARY AND THE LORD OF THE RINGS CONTRIBUTIONS

Summary Hobbit Frodo Baggins comes into possession of a magic ring, the Ring of Power, the instrument of evil Sauron's power. Sauron has been searching since the end of the Second Age (previous Age in Middle-earth).

Escaping many an enemy sent by Sauron to steal the Ring from Frodo, he takes it to a high council attended by other inhabitants of Middle-earth. It's decided the only way to save Middle-earth is to destroy the Ring by tossing the Ring back into the volcano of Mount Doom at Mordor where it was originally forged.

A "Fellowship of the Ring" forms with 4 Hobbits (including Frodo), 1 Wizard, 2 Humans, 1 Elf, and 1 Dwarf to aid Frodo with this task. However, at the end of the first book, the Fellowship falls to 7. The dwarf, elf, and one human set out to rescue two Hobbits while friend Samwise Gamgee stays with Frodo to continue their way to Mordor on their own.

Legendarium A book or series of books of collected legends. J.R.R. Tolkien used Legendarium to describe his mythical Middle-earth. Meant as a fiction of ancient Earth's history, "Middle-earth Mythology" also defines Tolkien's Legendarium.

Middle-earth A part of Earth's own past, Middle-earth isn't as much a setting as a time. Estimating the end of the Third Age to about 6,000 years before this time, the book is in part northwest of the Endor continent, or the land relating to modern-day Europe.

"Ages" divides Middle-earth with THE LORD OF THE RINGS happening around the end of the Third Age.

Taking this approach, Tolkien creates a new and intriguing world. Setting his story in another time, it doesn't suggest Middle-earth is another world, but could be.

Language As mentioned previously, THE LORD OF THE RINGS purpose (or excuse) may have been for Tolkien to create a new language. Indeed, the Elfan speech or "elf-tongue" is another language altogether, though conjured from many old languages Tolkien obviously studied and taught in Academia. Though confusing at times (especially in the text—it's easier to understand with the subtitles placed in movie representations), the language invented and inserted into the story gives it an ancient and "Otherworld" flavor.

WRITINGS AND OTHER PROJECTS INSPIRED BY J.R.R. TOLKIEN AND THE LORD OF THE RINGS

Illustrators Taking their cue from the stories, the following have illustrated THE LORD OF THE RINGS.

John Howe (*Fantasy Artist. He created some of the Concept Art for Peter Jackson's Film Trilogy. See next page.*)

Alan Lee (*Fantasy Artist. He also created some of the Concept Art for Peter Jackson's Film Trilogy. See below.*)

Ted Nasmith (*Tolkien books illustrator.*)

The Lord of the Rings (Looking at a Special Fantasy) PAGE 4

The Brothers Hildebrant *(Fantasy illustrator.)*

Queen Margaret II of Denmark *(Tolkien remarked how the queen's illustrations were similar to his own.)*

Film and Animation Tolkien was open to having his RINGS adapted into a movie. Though there were many attempts (most far from successful), it's regrettable he died before Peter Jackson finished his RINGS TRILOGY— by far the best cinematic representation created to date.

The First Attempts Though holding the rights to THE LORD OF THE RINGS for ten years, the Walt Disney Company failed to get a film made of the story.

Director Stanley Kubrick dallied with the idea of filming RINGS thinking it too daunting a task.

In the mid 1970s, director John Boorman considered a live action picture of RINGS, but declared it too expensive to do.

Rankin-Bass studios produced the first film adaptation of THE HOBBIT, an animated feature for television. Shortly after, Saul Zaentz picked up where Rankin-Bass left off by producing an animated adaptation of THE FELLOWSHIP OF THE RING and part of THE TWO TOWERS in 1978.

THE LORD OF THE RINGS PART 1 directed by Ralph Bakshi used an animation method called rotoscoping—tracing over footage of live actors.

Later, Rankin-Bass returned to make THE RETURN OF THE KING (largely considered a big flop).

THE LORD OF THE RINGS TRILOGY
In properly telling the story, Peter Jackson made three movies (2001-2003), for each book in the TRILOGY, with each clocking in at around three hours. Using state-of-the-art computer imagery and fantastic location shooting in New Zealand, Jackson created a Middle-earth worthy of Tolkien's massive work.

Ground-breaking visual effects enhanced the telling with the digitally incorporated Gollum becoming almost magical. The scale of the production alone—three films shot and edited over a period of little more than three years—is unprecedented.

Most RINGS fans embraced Jackson's vision, though some criticized its tone which is decidedly different from Tolkien's version feeling Mr. Jackson took the enchanted story and turned it into an action-adventure film. Still, the TRILOGY has garnered many awards and has become one of the highest grossing film efforts ever.

Yet none of the above would be possible without the creation of Hobbits, Middle Earth, and the "Rings." This is but four pages looking at J.R.R. Tolkien and THE LORD OF THE RINGS.
Pull up Tolkien's name or book(s) on the internet and notice the millions of sites mentioning this fantasy. This alone shows the importance of the man and his works.

A PARTING THOUGHT—Could Russian Tsar Ivan the Terrible's Oprichniks (his private army who dressed all in black and road black horses while terrorizing the countryside) have inspired Tolkien's Nazgûls on Horseback? Could the design of Peter Jackson's Black Riders come from illustrator Frank Frazetta's Death Dealer painting?